WINGS of HISTORY

the Air Museums of Europe

Louis Divone

Judene Divone

oHp

Oakton Hills Publications

Oakton, Virginia

Library of Congress Cataloging-in-Publication Data

Divone, Louis, 1934—
  Wings of history.

  Bibliography: p.
  Includes index.
  1. Aeronautical Museums—Europe.
  2. Aeronautics—Europe—History.
    I. Divone, Judene. II. Title.

TL506.E85D58 1989   069'.962913'00254 88-5158

  ISBN 0-939047-21-7

Published by Oakton Hills Publications,
  P.O. Box 557, Oakton, Virginia, 22124.

Printed in the United States of America
First Edition 10 9 8 7 6 5 4 3 2 1

Design and Production: Oakton Hills Publications.
Editing and proofreading: Suzanne Halverson, Judith
Curtiss.
Translations: Robert E. Hall, Carl Aspliden, Dan
Ancona, Radboud Hack and Helene Sumoska.
Photographic processing: Ernie Newhouse & Associates.
Computer Typesetting: Drye's Graphics
Printed by: WPi, We Print Inc., Fairfax, Va.

Cover: Sopwith Tabloid and Avro Vulcan, Bomber
Command Museum.

Photographic Credits: All photographs are by the
authors except the following which are copyright by,
and through the courtesy of:
The Shuttleworth Trust: page 50.
Fleet Air Arm Museum: pages 64, 69.
Royal Scottish Museum: pages 72-78.
Finnish Aviation Museum Society: pages 154-158.
Centro Documentazione Umberto Nobile: pages
    169-176, 181.
Royal Swedish Aero Club: pages 199-201 upper.
Royal Swedish Air Force: page 201 lower.
Muzeul Militar Central: pages 221-223.
Smithsonian National Air and Space Museum: pages
    219, 220, 224-228.

Preface

The telephone rang just as we were finishing dinner. The speaker for the following night's meeting of our local antique airplane club had cancelled at the last minute. Could we fill in with our collection of European air museum slides accumulated over the years from various and sundry overseas trips? As we hung up, the appalling nature of what we had just volunteered for sunk home. The hundreds of slides were still in those little yellow boxes in which they come back from the photo store, all good intentions to sort and organize long forgotten. As midnight passed and the coffee pot overheated, we dumped the slides into cassettes, hopefully right side up, and decided to wing it from there.

Applause is not a good indicator of a speech; normal inhibitions in most audiences precludes standing bravos or the throwing of vegetables in all but extreme cases. One clue was that a visitor to the meeting (it was free) asked if we could give the talk to his club the following month. We did and the same thing happened again. Before long we had a travelling road show. Perhaps not surprisingly, many Americans quite familiar with our aviation history had little knowledge, but considerable curiosity, about the contemporaneous events and aircraft in Europe.

It was from that convoluted beginning, and after several more years of research, correspondence, and additional visits, that this book evolved. It presents the history and the stories behind many European aircraft, some famous and others little known, and of their flights and the pilots and personalities behind them. It is not a definitive history of European aviation; that would take volumes. Rather it tries to tell the story in terms of the airplanes and artifacts that still exist; aircraft that one can still observe and touch and sometimes even see and hear once again in the air. The ravages of time, the impact of wars, and the mundane problems of cost have led to some randomness in what aircraft have been preserved. One could, in fact, cry for the loss of some truly historic aircraft which did not survive or of which no examples of the type remain. There are also a surprisingly large number of aircraft, originally built in fair quantities, for which only a singular specimen remains.

This selectiveness is compounded by the fact that we have covered in detail only locales which we have had the opportunity to visit personally, for only in that way could we provide some feeling for the emotions involved with those old airplanes. If occasionally the tales appear to go off on tangents, it is because the aircraft and the events they were part of led us down those paths. By telling those tales, some familiar and some obscure, perhaps the sense of adventure, drama, coincidence and tragedy behind them will make those aircraft come alive. For in a sense, they are alive. Anyone who flies knows that.

That we give short shrift to helicopters and more modern aircraft and essentially none to spacecraft and missiles is strictly a reflection of the idiosyncrasies of the authors. We have also endeavored to describe something of the museums themselves, their location and character, for each museum, like an airplane or a friend, has its own individual character. While we attempted to include every aircraft in every museum in the appendixes, we regret that some newer collections in England and France, for reasons of time and space, could not be included, nor could all the gate guardians or individually owned antiques. Material on some East European museums is also relatively weak. Even with all of our correspondence and perseverance, the clock finally ran out; perhaps by the next edition.

Lastly, for those like ourselves whose total language capability consists of a marginal grasp of contemporary English, we have appendixed a small dictionary translating common aeronautical terms, aircraft given names, and manufacturer's names from a dozen European languages. It also includes shorthand metric conversions. With all that and the fact that signs for the more social needs, such as highways and rest-rooms, are almost universally pictorial, one should be able to get through most non-English-speaking museums with reasonable comprehension.

Be that all as it may, we have tried to put together a book that captures one part, in one area of the world, of man's quest for the sky as represented by the airplanes that he left behind. It is also to provide a reference source for those who wish to delve deeper or to see for themselves those fascinating machines. Some of the stories, certainly those of the more famous flights, you may have read of before. Others are more obscure and may come to you afresh. But regardless, those wonderful old airplanes still exist. So whether you are planning your next vacation overseas or are just curled up in an armchair looking for a good read until the weather turns VFR, and you love old airplanes, consider those in the air museums of Europe—and come along with us.

Table of Contents

Foreword

Evident to any that love the sky is that airplanes are not just machines, but are instead the outward manifestation of the hearts and souls of designers, builders, and pilots. Airplanes in museums are especially poignant subjects and it is rare to be able to convey the restless spirit of museum aircraft, which seem always to be tugging at the chocks, anxious to fly again as once they did.

Lou and Judy Divone are not only aviation experts, but humanists who provide a massive amount of information in an engaging style. Their tender, often amusing, portrayal of the air museums of Europe provides both the lay person and the buff a fascinating tour through aviation history and those grand museums.

Wings of History visits the two great flying collections: the Shuttleworth Trust at Old Warden Aerodrome in Great Britain and the Jean Salis Collection at la Ferté-Alais, south of Paris. Both are magnificent experiences, and if possible one should plan a European trip to take advantage of their flying days.

The survey of museums of Eastern Europe is especially valuable. The same sense of love for the wonderful hardware of flight pervades these museums. One suspects that many problems of the world could be settled readily if museum personnel from both sides of the Iron Curtain were brought together to sort things out.

Wings of History is an unusual combination of reference book and inspirational reading; it makes you want to get up and go visit. And, from my personal point of view, the Divone's motivation and personality came through in their gracious dedication ''To The Docents, Everywhere.'' Docents are often overlooked, yet it is the volunteer docent who keeps museums functioning during the constant battle of the budget; certainly they did while I was Director of the National Air and Space Museum. Docents who read *Wings of History* will know immediately that the Divone's labor of love was based on a genuine understanding of the purpose of museums of flight.

Walter J. Boyne
Alexandria, Virginia

Acknowledgements

We now know why authors put acknowledgements in the front of books. It is because without the help of scores of people, one would end up in the State Home for the Bewildered long before publication. Some who helped are close friends. Others we have never met but know only from their letters. And some special ones we did not know at the beginning, but we now consider as our friends.

For being willing to seriously critique the manuscript (at the risk of voodoo curses), we would particularly like to thank Jim and Linda Densmore, even if they claim "Triple-Five Alpha" has five knots on "Eighty-Charlie"; Bill Tinkler, whose Luscombe is far better looking than his '727; Dick Hadcock, a de Havilland man and a Grumman man; Kurt Klunder, for more than helping on this book; and Don Berliner, an aviation writer who knows his airplanes and air museums.

Bob Ogden and Gordon Riley provided the utmost in graciousness in allowing us to update our listings from their personal notes and data. Their books on British and European aviation collections are discussed in more detail in the Appendix and are required reading for a prospective museum visitor. Our thanks to Bob Mikesh at the Smithsonian's National Air and Space Museum and to the library staffs at NASM, the Federal Aviation Administration, NASA, and the Library of Congress.

But most of all, our appreciation must go to those overseas and at the museums without whose help this book would not have been possible. We can't possibly thank all of those that took time out from their work or who worked on their own time to check information, provide aircraft collection data, open museum doors at times they were closed, gather material, route messages and answer innumerable dumb questions. The assistance of Sid Smith, Cynthia Miller, Colonel John Fisher, Jasna Kunic and a host of others at U. S. Embassies overseas who smoothed our searches is gratefully acknowledged.

Our special thanks to Sven Hugosson, Secretary General of the Royal Swedish Aeroclub, an old friend in whose SAAB coupe we have travelled faster than in any Tiger Moth; Borge G. Hielm, Director, Finnish Aviation Museum, who hand-carried photographs across the Atlantic to us; P. Symes, General Manager of the Shuttleworth Collection for rushing us the latest pictures of the de Havilland Comet restoration and Mr.

Ceda Jamic, Director, Yugoslav Air Museum for opening up an unopened museum for us.

We must thank Major General Constantin Antip, Director, Central Military Museum, Bucharest; Toni Bernhard, Conservator, Museum der Schweizerischen Fliegertruppe; Colonel Ovidio Ferranti, Director, Museo Storico dell'Aeronautica Militaire; L. F. Lovell at the Fleet Air Arm Museum; Y. Lumbreras, Musee Aeronautique de Champagne; Slobodan Razumenic, JAT; Dr. Nikolaus, Director, Armeemuseum, Dresden; Laszlo Farkas, General Director, Mem Repuloges Szolgalat, Budapest; I. Veress, General Director, Kozlekedesi Museum, Budapest; Jacques Avril, Vice President, Reseau du Sport de L'Air; Hans J. Roth, Air Classic GmbH; Ing. Josef Smejkal, Director, and Ing. Brinek at the Technicke Muzeum V Brne; Ing. Antonov, Director, Naval Museum, Varna; M. Kalonkin, Director, Military History Museum, Sofia; Mr. G. Glerum, Conservator, Militaire Luchtvaart Museum, Soesterberg; Ms. B. Morton, Royal Scottish Museum: and Peter F. A. van de Noort, Aviodome.

We extend our very special gratitude to Mrs. Gertrude Nobile who lent us rare photographs of General Umberto Nobile's airship flights and provided information, insight and encouragement from the Centro Documentazioni Umberto Nobile at Vigna di Valle where she lovingly cares for the archives and collections from her husband's polar expeditions.

Lastly, we must most of all thank the docents, those unpaid, unsung volunteers without whom no air museum could function. They help restore aircraft, do paperwork and research, guide tours, and anything else around museums that needs doing, all for their love of aviation. We don't know their names; rarely does anyone. They spent hours taking us around, trying to explain in a second language, providing assistance and staying after hours, portraying to us the story of the airplanes in their museums and showing us their pride in the pioneers of flight in their country. We can only say thank you.

TO THE DOCENTS, EVERYWHERE

Introduction

It is nearly impossible, we would wager, for anyone truly alive to be near an airport and, should an airplane take off, not turn their head and watch. Only after it breaks ground and climbs off into the sky does attention return to the road ahead, the ticket counter, the girl next to you, or even the panel of one's own airplane. It is not due to the noise and commotion, although that certainly is what first alerts the mind. After a hundred thousand years of wonder at the flight of birds, man learned to imitate them—to fly. And consciously or unconsciously, it is still a wonder to him for it has only been within the span of one lifetime that man achieved that dream.

In that short span the airplane has developed from a primitive contraption into the technological marvels of today. Along the way men devoted their lives—and sometimes gave them—to build and to fly and to explore with those airplanes. The span of time has been so short that many of those machines that mark that incredible development still exist for us to examine and admire.

The first successful airplane, the first New York to Paris flight, the first breaking of the sound barrier and today's most numerous airliners and most ferocious fighter planes are all claimed by the United States. We Americans then tend to feel that the airplane somehow belongs solely to us. Far from it. For every Charles Lindbergh or Amelia Earhart or Jimmy Doolittle there was a Louis Blériot or an Amy Johnson or a Mario de Bernardi. For every Jack Northrop or Donald Douglas there was a Sidney Camm or an Anthony Fokker. And for every General Billy Mitchell there was a General Umberto Nobile. No, the history of aviation in Europe is as rich in stories of dedication, brilliance, courage, and of sometimes the other side of the coin, as it is in this hemisphere; some are just less familiar.

By our count there are somewhere over six thousand aircraft in museums and collections around the globe that mark the development of the airplane, not counting gate guardians and individually owned antiques. The largest number, approximating twenty-five hundred, is as expected in the U. S. and there are another thousand scattered around the other continents. But over three thousand are in Europe! The reason for such a large number is simply that Europe is comprised of thirty or so individual countries. Each has had its own air force, aviation industry, airlines and pioneers. Almost all European countries have also, unfortunately, had wars on or over their country's soil since the airplane came into being. Tragic as it may be, wars have been one of the predominant forces behind the development of aviation.

The history of aviation in Europe is told by the airplanes and artifacts that still hang in their air museums. An airplane, sitting still, can appear as merely an inanimate collection of wood and cloth or of aluminum and steel. But it is more. It represents the dreams and skill and brains of the men who designed and built it. At one time it was not inanimate. Each one once flew and a pilot coaxed and guided it. He sat within its confines, hands on the controls, feet on the pedals and rear end in the seat—and sweated. Whether he was about to take a new machine into a flight regime where man had never flown before, to attempt a new record for speed or distance to a place far away, to enter deadly combat with an unknown enemy he would never know, or just to take off on his first solo in a simple trainer, he sweated. He pushed the throttle home, bounced over a grass field or roared down a runway, lifted off and became airborne. He realized each time what man had dreamed of for eons. And he was alone when he did it, regardless of the size of the crew.

Some of the individual aircraft—and their pilots—achieved great things. Others depict one of a class of aircraft that achieved great things, although perhaps not by that particular example. Still others represent the more mundane training, cargo and passenger carrying airplanes that mark the slow but continuous progress from year to year. Yet each has its story to tell. Some of those stories are famous, the achievement so great. For others the particular stories are obscure, buried in a log book somewhere in the museum's basement library or long since put away when its pilot went home after some war ended—except in his memories. The stories behind those aircraft, now hanging silently in some museum, convert them from their inanimate and dusty bulk to the challengers of the skys that they were back in the days when they first flew. For each of them once flew. And in each of them, a pilot once sweated.

This book tries to tell the story of some of those aircraft. Or rather it is of the stories that those aircraft could tell.

1

There is an Old Saying

There is an old saying amongst European airline travellers that when you die, it doesn't matter whether you are going to heaven or to hell, you still have to change at Heathrow. That makes London a logical place to start searching for the origins from whence those airliners grew.

In the West End, not far from Hyde Park and a short walk south from that temple to explorers of times past, the Royal Geographical Society, is the temple to another type of explorer. It is the British Science Museum and the explorers it fetes are mostly those who explored with their minds and who conquered nature, not with maps, but with science and technology. But there is one hall in the museum which is a tribute to both forms of exploration. It contains the treasures of those who tried to push forward the frontiers of technology and the frontiers of the world at the same time. Some succeeded and some did not, for it is not a small task to ask. But with success or failure, each added a small notch to the stick on which we measure our progress and which some-one coming after can read and add his notch.

The Science Museum encompasses all of those brass and cast iron artifacts from the industrial revolution that laid the technological base for those who thought that they could imitate the birds. So take the lift (that's an elevator for those Americans who do not speak English) to the third floor. There the National Aeronautical Collection is devoted to those who did imitate the birds—and did them one better.

Two very old manned gliders, a Lilienthal and a Pilcher, greet you at the entrance. They were made by two of the first serious and rigorous experimenters into the problems of controlled flight. Both men probed the unknown just before the turn of the century and left a core of data that others could use. Both men were also killed during those experi-ments, part payment of the price that went into man's first attempts to conquer the sky. The Wright brothers used some of that data, partic-ularly Lilienthal's, one of the notches along the stick.

1

Beyond those frail craft, a huge, twin-engined biplane dominates the hall. It is the Vickers Vimy in which Alcock and Brown made the first nonstop crossing of the Atlantic Ocean. It was 1:45 on the afternoon of June 14, 1919, not long after the end of the First World War, that Captain John Alcock and Lieutenant Arthur Whitten-Brown lurched the 13,300-lb Vimy across Lester's field near St. Johns, Newfoundland, the two 350-hp Rolls-Royce Eagles barely managing to get the beast airborne. They had 1,890 miles of open ocean to cross in a machine with the streamlining of a shipping crate; the modified FB.27 Vimy would do 103 mph flat out.

Other than the freezing cold of the open cockpits, the first four hours were routine, but then things went to hell in a handbasket. First they encountered thick fog such that navigation became impossible. Next, the inboard exhaust pipe of the starboard engine split and they could only sit and sweat while little red-hot globs melted off. After a while, it started to rain so they could stop worrying about the little hot globs setting fire to the now sopping-wet wing fabric. All they had to worry about was staying right side up in the clouds, since the gyroscopic artificial horizon had not yet been invented. Alcock could do pretty well by feel until they encountered strong turbulence. Three times they ended up in an uncontrolled spiral dive. Each time, Alcock was able to right the Vimy in the last few hundred feet as the angry waves below became visible.

By now it was snowing, which made life in the open cockpit truly miserable. At about 4 A.M., that time in the early hours of the morning when life seems to be at its lowest ebb, ice began to form on the wings

From a beach in Newfoundland to an Irish bog: Alcock and Brown's 1919 Vickers Vimy.

2

and control surfaces. Worse, the engines began to lose power. With not much else to lose, Brown did the unthinkable. He climbed out of the cockpit onto the snow-covered fuselage. They had to be able to read the fuel flow gauges, brilliantly located on the upper wing struts, to adjust the engines properly. Clinging to the struts in the freezing wind, Brown hacked the ice off the gauges. Later writers exaggerated that he actually crawled out to the nacelles, but Brown's memoirs confirm that he was "only" atop the fuselage, as if that wasn't enough. During those pre-dawn hours, while Alcock grunted over the ice-stiffened controls, Brown accomplished his incredible "if it doesn't work, hit it harder" routine not once, but four times!

Then, as if to say enough is enough, the sun rose ahead of them, and with it came clearing skies and warming temperatures. They had flown across the North Atlantic in 16 hours and 28 minutes in a collection of struts and wires built just 15 years after the birth of flight. Landfall was just ahead, and while they were a bit south of course, land is land. Unfortunately, sometimes it isn't. The Irish bog looked like a good field from the air to the two tired and wretched men, but it wouldn't support the Vimy's weight. And so, slightly ignominiously the Vimy upended on its nose and cracked the fuselage longerons, a small price to pay. The longerons were repaired and the Vimy hangs today in the museum. If you lean forward from the center balcony you may get a bit nervous, it being twenty feet to the floor. But then you can almost touch the struts that Brown clung to a thousand feet or so above the North Atlantic while Alcock flew the Vimy into history.

A young Secretary of State named Winston Churchill gave Alcock and Brown, Lord Northcliffe's check for 10,000 pounds, the Daily Mail newspaper's prize for the first flight across the Atlantic. A few days later they were knighted by King George V at Buckingham Palace. The following December, the now Sir John Alcock was killed ferrying a new Vickers through fog up the Seine valley.

As an aside, if you are ever in the west of Ireland, you can visit the landing site of that first transatlantic flight. Take the N59 north from Galway through the moors and hills and just after the town of Clifden hunt for a pair of small signs. Don't bother looking around for shops or post cards as there is not much local interest. Remember Alcock and Brown were English not Irish. And besides, the thought of crashing through night and storm over the ocean in a flying pigeon coop when you could be in a warm pub having a few pints has never made a great deal of sense to the locals. But if you turn right at the sign and go up a short hill, there is a splendid overview of the moors and the coast and a simple, sleek monument to Alcock and Brown. Go back down and across the coast road and up the other dirt road that has the sign that says "Alcock and Brown Landing Site This Way." Not thirty feet further is another sign that says "Road Impassable to Motorcars;" Irish directions are perplexing. After a mile or so of scraping the oil pan on rocks, we decided that the rental-car company's "no drop-off charges" policy should not be taken too literally. Since all moors look the same, we convinced ourselves that we had indeed seen the Vimy's boggy landing site.

There is also a statue of Alcock and Brown at London's Heathrow Airport. One suspects that it was originally placed such that their images could stare up at the sky that they conquered. Their view is now a parking lot and a radar antenna, Heathrow having exploded into the chaotic zoo that it is. You can get a glimpse of their statue from the bus transiting between Terminal 2 and Terminal 3. Is it possible that Alcock and Brown's spirits realize that now some ten thousand people fly across the Atlantic to or from Heathrow each and every day?

Memorial to Alcock and Brown in the wide open spaces north of Clifden overlooking their landing site. County Galway, Ireland.

Memorial to Alcock and Brown in the wide open spaces of Heathrow Airport, London.

Back at the Science Museum, across from the Vimy and dwarfed by it, is another long-distance, record-setting aircraft, but one of quite a different stamp. It is a small single-engined biplane, a de Havilland D.H.60G Gipsy Moth named *Jason*. Amy Johnson was not a debutante or the wife of a wealthy publisher. She was a secretary earning a few pounds a week and her father ran a fishing trawler, but she loved the sky. Every penny she earned went to flying lessons at Stag Lane outside of London where de Havilland was building his machines. After getting her pilot's license, she still went out to the airfield before dawn and after work to become the first woman to earn an English aviation mechanic's licence. Where she wanted to fly, airplane mechanics would be few and far between.

Badgering any wealthy contact she could meet, she was only able to raise half of the 600 pounds needed for a well-used Gipsy Moth. She had lost her job by then due to lack of attention, but her father, regardless of what he thought about all this silliness, scraped up the other 300 pounds. She named the Moth *Jason* for the Argonaut that was the trademark of her father's fishing business. After several false starts she took off from Croydon Airport on May 5, 1930 to become the first woman, and the third person ever, to fly solo from London to Australia. Her longest previous flight had been 147 miles!

Amy's first legs to Vienna, Istanbul and Aleppo went reasonably well except for terrifying weather over the Taurus Mountains during the last portion. Enroute to Baghdad severe winds and turbulence made a precautionary landing in the desert the only alternative to a crash. Blocking the wheels with luggage and tools, Amy spent the next several hours riding out the blinding sandstorm. She spent them sitting on *Jason's* tail to keep it from blowing over in the gale and clutching a revolver in fear of the wild desert dogs whose howling she could hear over the noise of the wind. Getting airborne after the storm subsided, she made Baghdad and then Karachi and Allahabad. Each were stops with more problems and repairs, but Amy Johnson had set a London to India speed record. She was also living on but a few hours sleep a night.

Across the Bay of Bengal to Burma and in worsening weather, Amy couldn't find the airfield outside of Rangoon. In desperation, she put the Gipsy Moth down in the only open space she could find. Groggy with fatigue and in low visibility she overshot and rolled into a ditch, smashing part of a lower wing, the landing gear and the propeller. Fortuitously, the open space she had landed in was the soccer field belonging to a local engineering college. Students and faculty pitched in and made up replacement parts from native woods that looked more or less the same as the broken pieces. They also helped her mount a new propeller—she had carried a spare strapped to the outside of *Jason's* fuselage for just such an eventuality. A local seamstress patched and sewed the wing's fabric and a friendly pharmacist concocted some brew that resembled airplane dope enough to tighten the fabric. Amy continued down the Malay Peninsula to Singapore, on to Indonesia and across the Timor Sea in the precariously repaired *Jason.* On May 24, 1930, after nineteen and a half days alone in an open cockpit biplane that could do all of 90 mph, Amy Johnson touched down at Darwin, Australia.

The Gipsy Moth, and its slightly more advanced descendent, the Tiger Moth, trained tens of thousands of pilots including most of those who fought in the Battle of Britain. Other Moths—Gipsies, Tigers, Puss' and Hornets— would be flown by other pilots setting distance records all across Europe, Asia and the Far East. But none of the other Moths would represent the conquering of the sky, alone, by a woman, as would the stalwart *Jason.* It is so small alongside the Vickers Vimy.

Amy Johnson went on to fly more oceans and set more records, both alone and later with a husband, Jim Mollison, also a long-distance flyer. The marriage did not last long, and when war started, Amy Johnson joined the Air Transport Auxiliary as a ferry pilot. In 1941, she was forced to bail out over water when the Airspeed Oxford she was flying suffered mechanical failure in bad weather. A trawler spotted her parachute and was within feet of her when she went under. With all the great bodies of water that Amy Johnson had conquered, it was in the River Thames estuary that she went down.

Amy Johnson's stalwart de Havilland D.H.60G, Jason, *in which she flew solo from London to Australia in 19½ days in 1930.*

Nearby to *Jason* are two biplanes; one is original and the other a replica. The replica is a reproduction of the original Wright Flyer, but it was not always a replica that hung in that spot. The Wright brothers and Glenn Curtiss got into a patent dispute. The Wrights claimed that Curtiss was violating their patent on lateral control. Curtiss claimed that the Wright's patent only covered their wing-warping and not his independent ailerons. Curtiss, probably to muddy the waters, added that in any event Langley's *Aerodrome,* even though unsuccessful, predated the Wrights and negated their priority. The argument wasn't really valid, but the Smithsonian supported Curtiss in what was perhaps a bit of bureaucratic nepotism; Langley had been Secretary of the Smithsonian during his experiments. During all this squabbling, the Europeans merrily forged ahead, ignored patents and outpaced both the Wrights and Curtiss. The Wrights were bitter and donated their original Flyer to the British Science Museum rather than give it to the Smithsonian. It hung in the Science Museum for twenty years and, hidden later for safekeeping, survived the bombings of World War II. It wasn't until 1948 that that most famous and important of all airplanes arrived at the Smithsonian and a replica put in its place at the British Science Museum. In any endeavor with brilliant minds and high stakes, emotions run strong, and so it was a human, if not perhaps a very illustrious, episode in the history of aviation.

The other of the two old biplanes was built by Samuel Franklin Cody. Cody might well have been a distant relative of "Buffalo Bill" Cody. This Cody was also an American "cowboy" and habitually dressed in flambouyant western garb, even to a beard in the style of his namesake. Cody was a pioneer in kites and worked for the English military in setting up manned kite and balloon observation systems. He was also one of the most outspoken supporters of the potential military use of the airplane. On October 16, 1908, his powered biplane, while it did not provide any technical advance over the Wrights, made the first sustained powered flight in Britain. Coupled with Cody's flambouyance, his flights stimulated Britain's entry into aviation. Cody might have stimulated even more, except by 1913 he had joined those other pioneers killed in the quest for flight. Alliot Vernon Roe's Triplane hanging next to Cody's biplane, and the first English airplane designed and flown by an Englishman, was much more successful. So was A.V. Roe; he survived those early flights and named the company he formed by the acronym, Avro. Thirty years later Avro Lancasters would carry World War II into Germany and twenty years after that, Avro Vulcan jet bombers would patrol the British skys.

Nearby are several World War I vintage airplanes, a beautifully restored S.E.5a, an Avro 504K, and a Fokker E.III monoplane. The E.III was the airplane behind the so-called "Fokker Scourge" of 1915-16. Prior to that time, and after the first impromptu jousts with pistols, rifles, and occasional bricks, there were only two methods of applying firepower to an airplane. One could place a machine gun in the front, but that meant that the engine had to go in the rear. That approach led to the clumsy and generally unmaneuverable twin-boomed pusher gun buses, although effective enough at first. The other technique was to

A. V. Roe's 1909 Triplane, the first successful English-built, Englishman-flown airplane.

The S.E.5a, one of the most outstanding fighting scouts of World War I.

place a gunner and his gun behind the pilot. While this allowed for a conventional aircraft of reasonable performance (given the weight of the second crewman), the gunner could only fire sideways or upwards, essentially a defensive configuration.

In frustation at the existing techniques, French pilot Roland Garros, took the simple, if slightly maniacal approach of mounting the machine gun right on the cowl of his Morane–Saulnier and shooting through the propeller arc. He did condescend to sanity enough to have little steel plates mounted on the back of the propeller to deflect those bullets that hit the prop. Much to the skeptics' surprise, that aerial Russian roulette sort-of worked. Garros downed three enemy aircraft in three weeks before his abused machine quit while over the German lines. He was caught before he could burn the wreck. The Germans appreciated the idea, even if its implementation left a bit to be desired. Within weeks, Fokker's factory developed the first interrupter gear that timed the firing of the machine gun such that the bullets went between the blades, at least most of the time. The airplane as a gun platform, a weapon system, had been born. During the next few months, the Fokker E.IIIs nearly wiped out the Royal Flying Corp. The RFC replied by mounting a machine gun atop the upper wing of aircraft such as the early Sopwith Pups. That helped a bit, but the gun was hard to register and aim and out of reach when it jammed, a not infrequent occurrence.

Tit-for-tat, in early 1916 a Fokker E.III came down behind the English lines and the secret was out. The S.E.5a represents somewhat of a transition. It has one synchronized Vickers gun on the cowling, with a Lewis gun atop the upper wing; the Royal Aircraft Factory apparently didn't quite trust the interrupter gear on the Vickers. One improvement, however, is that the Lewis gun is on a curved rail. You could unlatch it and slide it back into reach to replace the 100-round drum or bang on it when it jammed. Pushing the Lewis gun back up against the airstream while flying the plane·with the other hand was not easy. There are stories, possibly apocryphal, of pilots hanging half out of the cockpit while upside down as they lost control during all those gyrations. Still, the S.E.5a was extremely successful, one of H.P. Folland's best designs, although he never got the reputation he deserved until he quit working for others and started his own airplane company twenty years later. The S.E.5a is probably our favorite World War I airplane, having been the most frequent subject of cover art on all those aviation pulp magazines of the 1930s. Garros, who had started it all, escaped from his German POW camp and flew combat throughout the rest of the war. He was killed in his SPAD on October 5, 1918, poignantly, only a month before the Armistice and peace.

As you proceed toward the end of the hall, you suddenly come across "It." "It" is an airplane that you have never seen before, but perhaps only read about or saw blurred pictures of in an old magazine. But it was an airplane which caught your imagination and whose memory stayed with you; an airplane which was just as important or with just as heroic or skilled a pilot as any more familiar American plane. Perhaps you built a stick and tissue model of it when you were a kid, but at this point the memory has all but faded. Then, there "It" is, unexpectedly appearing 'round a corner or from behind the wing of another ship. That first sudden appearance is one of the great pleasures in visiting European air museums.

We each have our own "It." For us it was the Supermarine S.6B sitting there at the end of the hall. It is incredibly beautiful, the work of an artist as much as an engineer. Memories come back: the Schneider Trophy competition through the years between the Italians and the English; the story of Lady Houston putting up the cash because the English government at the time was too penurious, the S.6B winning and retiring the Schneider Trophy in 1931 and a few weeks later setting the world air speed record of 407 mph—on floats yet!

It all started during the banquet following the 1912 James Gordon Bennett race when Jacques Schneider, scion of the French Schneider armaments company family, announced the donation of the trophy which bears his name. Schneider was an avid seaplane enthusiast and, although disabled from flying due to a bad crash, he wanted a race for seaplanes to surpass those for landplanes. The first race was held at Monaco in 1913 and was won by Maurice Prevost in a Deperdussin with its speed recorded at a blistering 45 mph. Actually, the Deperdussin

10

had flown the course at a more spectacular 61 mph, but Prevost had misunderstood the rules, landed short and taxied across the finish line. The French predilection for vociferous arguments sometimes overcomes common sense. In this case Prevost and the rules committee got into a 'Donnybrook.' Prevost finally threw up his hands, took off again and flew across the finish line to stop the clock, which explains the speed discrepancy. It didn't really matter since the only other aircraft to finish at all had violated the rules even worse. It was the only time that the French ever won the Schneider Trophy, and I expect they are still arguing over the rules.

In 1914 the Sopwith Tabloid raised the winning pace to 86 mph but as the 1920s went by, speeds exceeding 200 mph were achieved. By then, the Schneider seaplanes were not only fast, they were the fastest airplanes in the world. Since the closed-circuit races (actually time trials—the airplanes took off at 5-minute intervals and raced against the clock) were only 150 miles or so total, the aircraft could be quite specialized. They also didn't have to last very long.

There was a more important reason why most of the fastest airplanes in the world during the era between the Wars were seaplanes, even with all the weight and drag of the floats, and that had to do with the simple ability to get airborne. Flaps had not yet been perfected, and thus a landplane needed a larger wing to fly slow enough to get off and on a runway of any reasonable length. And that larger wing was a handicap at high speeds. Even more significant was that the practical controllable-pitch propeller was also off in the future. A landplane had to compromise on the pitch of the propeller in order to get off the ground without running into the bushes. The seaplane could use a propeller optimised for its top speed and suffer the loss in takeoff performance. The Schneider racers were beasts to fly, much less to take off and land. They could bounce along the waves for miles before getting off and they stalled at over 100 mph, which was higher than the top speed of most aircraft of the day. But once airborne they moved faster than anything else in the world. It was principally the controllable pitch propeller and the flap that spelt the death knell for the seaplane racer, and for similar reasons, those majestic long distance flying boats of the 1920s and 1930s.

In 1925 Supermarine's brilliant designer, young Reginald Mitchell, produced the revolutionary S.4 monoplane racer. It crashed just prior to that year's Schneider contest, but in 1927 its successor, the S.5, took the Schneider Trophy away from the Italians. The two S.5s placed first and second; actually they were the only two planes to finish at all. Speeds were now approaching 300 mph, but to beat the Italians again in 1929 something even more advanced would be clearly needed.

R. J. Mitchell sat down at Supermarine to design the S.6 while Sir Henry Royce of Rolls-Royce began work on a new engine. The Honorable Charles Rolls, the other half of Rolls-Royce, had been the first

The Supermarine S.6B, in 1931 the fastest airplane in the world—and the inspiration behind the Spitfire and the Merlin.

Englishman to fly the English Channel—he did it both ways—but he had been killed in 1910 when his Wright biplane came apart at Bournemouth. Sir Henry stayed on the ground building expensive motor cars as well as engines for other people's airplanes. And for the Schneider racers, Sir Henry came up with one of the most magnificent mechanical monstrocities of all time—the special 'R' racing engine. When funds finally became available, not much time was left for development. Testing of the new engine at the Rolls factory went on around the clock. Three 600-hp Rolls-Royce Kestrels were used for the testing: one to supply cooling air, one to exhaust the test bay and one to simulate the airflow. The three Kestrels and the 'R' running flat out in test rattled windows for miles around the plant. By late spring, the 'R' could produce 1,850 hp for over an hour before coming apart and that meant that flight tests could begin.

The race would be held at Calshot on the Solent close to Supermarine's Southampton plant. Flight Lieutenants H. R. D. Waghorn, R. L. R. Atcherley and D'Arcy Greig were the three principle pilots, although since only two S.6s were available, Greig would have to fly a leftover S.5. Preparation time was now extremely short. The 'R' engine required rebuilding after every couple of hours of running and there were only a few of the new engines available. So Rolls-Royce made a special body for one of their new Phantom motorcars. Instead of a luxurious interior, they fitted it with skids to ferry 'R' engines to and fro from Southampton on the coast to the factory at Derby in the Midlands. Speeding through the night, the Phantom would drop off one engine, pick up an overhauled replacement, and head back to Southampton. They would occasionally slow to 70 mph going through villages in the wee hours before dawn and the Phantom needed its brakes relined after every other round trip, but it kept the airplanes flying.

The S.6 also had its problems, not the least of which was control surface flutter, a phenomenon not well understood at that time. It took some deep work on Mitchell's part to stop the flutter by the proper surface balancing. Up to the week of the race, the S.6 was also plagued by cooling system leaks; the Schneider racers were almost flying radiators due to the need to reject several thousand horsepower worth of heat. Pilot D'Arcy Greig was having a similar problem with radiator leaks in his tiny Austin Seven and had been dumping a patent radiator anti-leak gunk into the car. In desperation, Supermarine technicians poured the stuff into the S.6 while Rolls-Royce engineers looked on in dismay. The gunk cut the leaks down to livable rates.

Race rules included a number of requirements that the airplanes had to accomplish prior to the race and the last minute problems became almost insurmountable. One of the requirements was for the airplanes to float at mooring for six hours. Half-way through, Atcherley's S.6 started to list; one float was leaking. The airplane would be disqualified if anyone touched it during the floatation trials—or for that matter, if it sank. Mitchell ran some calculations on the seepage rate and concluded that it might just make it. Some mechanics sat alongside in a rowboat hour after hour, watching the airplane sink inch by inch. It stayed afloat just long enough and the instant the time requirement was met, the mechanics grabbed the airplane and frantically pumped out the float.

Later in the evening, Waghorn's S.6 was getting last minute touches, including new sparkplugs when a mechanic let out some choice expletives. One of the plugs showed some bright metal particles, a sure sign of a scored cylinder. The rules precluded changing an engine after the preliminary trials, although replacing parts was allowed. Unfortunately, the 'R' engine had its massive cylinders cast in blocks of six and besides their weight, they would be at an angle. At the factory they always tilted the V-12 so a block could be lowered straight down; a cylinder block change couldn't be done in the airplane. Mitchell was trying to figure out if he could tilt the whole airplane over when someone remembered that a great contingent of Rolls-Royce mechanics had come down from Derby on their own to watch the race.

In the middle of the night, and with the help of local police, Mitchell's men shanghied Rolls-Royce mechanics from hotels and pubs all over

Southampton. Swarming over the Supermarine S.6 in various stages of dress and sobriety, the mechanics horsed the old block off and lowered the new one on by sheer muscle power and skill. Fortunately, there was one mechanic along who had long arms and was left-handed, the only physiology that would allow reaching one of the rear nuts with the engine in the airplane. As dawn came, mechanics lay collapsed all over the hanger floor, but the job was done. Mitchell, between the leaking float and feeding coffee to the mechanics all night, was about done himself. When pilot Waghorn arrived, he was given careful instructions on how to handle the engine controls during start and going to full power, which the engineers thought would preclude the cylinder scoring problem. Waghorn, however, was not told what had transpired during the night; he would have enough worries.

At the signal, Waghorn plowed, bounced and porpoised through the water, but safely became airborne. Between spray and haze, he lost his orientation for a moment and got confused by all the ships in the harbor. He finally spotted his first pylon, but had lost time for the confusion. From the ground, Waghorn was seen to be flying with precision and incredible speed, cornering the pylons in close, near vertical banks, but in the cockpit Waghorn's mind was in a clutter. Deafening noise, smoke, vibration, trying to navigate in the haze a few hundred feet up at over 300 mph and worried about his meandering start all added up to enormous emotional pressure. The knowledge that he had the fastest preliminary times of the British ships, but that soon the Italians would be on his tail didn't help. Lap after lap went by and finally the end seemed in sight. Then on the next to last pylon of the last lap, his engine began to misfire. Waghorn clenched his teeth, hoping the 'R' would run for just a few minutes more, but the fates are not always kind. As Waghorn rounded the final pylon with only the last straightaway remaining, the massive 'R' engine ground itself into scrap metal. Waghorn had to dead-stick the S.6 onto the water just a few miles short of the finish line.

The S.6 bobbed in the choppy water off Old Castle Point while Waghorn sat in the cockpit, distraught almost to the point of tears. He had lost the race and it was his fault. He hadn't handled the temperamental engine's controls right. He hadn't remembered those last-minute instructions correctly. He had ruined England's chances and now the Italians would win. He looked up with dispair—and saw three motorboats roaring up alongside loaded with yelling, cheering, waving engineers and mechanics. What Waghorn had done in all his confusion was to miscount the number of laps. He had completed the course on the prior leg and the ground crew had all thought he was doing an unauthorized victory lap when his engine failed. The fates were not unkind—just mischievous. Waghorn in the Supermarine S.6 had won the Schneider and set a new record at 328.63 mph. The Italian Macchi

The Schneider Trophy and the seaplane that won it for all time. The first airplane to exceed 400 mph—the 1931 Supermarine S.6B.

M.52R came in second and D'Arcy Greig in the outclassed Supermarine S.5 made third.

For 1931 the competition appeared to be even tougher. Mussolini was going to pull the stops to keep the British from winning three times in a row, which would retire the trophy. England was in the midst of a depression with millions out of work and, while many in the government wanted to support the race, it was politically impractical. It was then that Lady Lucy Houston, an eccentric, jingoistic, and particularly wealthy widow, gave 100,000 English pounds to the Royal Aero Club to have England in the 1931 race. Royce and Mitchell rolled up their sleeves again. The two remaining Supermarine S.6s were modified into S.6As and two new ones, the S.6Bs, were built. Engineers at Rolls-Royce muttered some incantations, pumped up the supercharger, fiddled with the innards and by April, the 'R' engine could produce 2,350 hp, albeit for only ten minutes at a time before the cylinder head bolts would launch off in various and sundry directions. By June they could get an hour's running time.

Mitchell at Supermarine was also playing magic games, delving into his aerodynamic bag of tricks and the S.6Bs were even slipperier than their earlier stablemates. That old tail flutter came back again, even worse this time. On its first test flight over 300 mph, the S.6B suddenly vibrated so badly that from the ground it turned into a blur. Mitchell had learned a lot about flutter and control surface balancing again cured the problem (at least to the degree that the sheet metal wasn't permanently deformed on each flight), although the pilots would land with quaking muscles.

Tragedy then struck when Lieutenant Jerry Brinton was killed during practice in one of the machines. The Schneider racers of this era were nearly uncontrollable on takeoff. One float would dunk almost completely underwater from engine torque alone. The takeoff was normally started over 90 degrees from the wind. With full right rudder, the plane would swing left under power as it got up on the step and by then, with luck, one was aimed roughly in the right direction. If the controls were handled just right, maybe the porpoising wouldn't get out of control. Brinton didn't and it did and he got killed. Tragedy and fatalities hit the French and Italian teams even worse such that neither could be ready in time for the race. The British team faced a difficult decision. If they agreed to delay for a year, there would likely not be another Lady Houston around with a spare 100,000 pounds, while to proceed alone would invite criticism for lack of sportsmanship.

There really was no choice. They had to go it alone, but they didn't pull any punches just because there was no competition and they risked ridicule if none of the machines could stay the course. They took that risk. On September 13, 1931, Flight Lieutenant John Boothman climbed into the Supermarine S.6B, S1595, and made history. Only two hundred feet off the deck, he firewalled the throttle and set a Schneider Cup record of 340.08 mph—and retired the Schneider Trophy for all time.

Meanwhile, a special sprint version of the 'R' engine had been built. It had been planned to go into the other S.6B for an all-out speed record attempt, but that machine had been pranged. So the engine in S1595 was switched for the sprint version and the S.6B was loaded up with everything—everything that is except gasoline. All the Schneider racers of this period used assorted exotic blends in their engines, but for the record attempt the back room boys had brewed up a noble concoction; a mix of benzole, methanol and acetone with not a drop of gasoline in it. With this high-class oven cleaner in its carburetor and a stepped-up supercharger, the 'R' could put out 2,800 hp, although the engine would melt after a few minutes. They backed things off to 2,650 hp, whence it would last the better part of a half hour and that would be enough. On September 29, 1931 Flight Lieutenant G. H. Stainforth set a world's absolute speed record of 407.50 mph with the S.6B; S1595 was the first airplane in the world to exceed 400 mph. The top speed of the Schneider racing planes had increased from Prevost's 45 mph by nearly tenfold in less than twenty years.

Supermarine S.6B, license number S1595, sits on some wooden blocks at the far end of the aviation hall of the British Science Museum behind a case that holds the Schneider Trophy, the trophy that it captured for all time. A prodigious fixed-pitch propeller on the Supermarine pulls a knife thin wing, and the two underslung floats are nearly as large as the silver and blue fuselage. Every spare inch of surface is covered by thin tubes needed to cool the Glycol and oil for that huge 'R' engine. Still, the S.6B is perfectly proportioned, although I had never realized how small it really was. The pilot must be sitting with his feet straddling the sump and his view, the narrow tunnel between the cylinder humps of that monstrous V-12. The sprint 'R' engine sits on the floor alongside the Supermarine. And it was their experience with the 'R' that led Rolls-Royce to the development of the Merlin—the immortal Merlin that powered Spitfires and Hurricanes and Lancasters and Mustangs and Mosquitoes and a dozen others into combat less than a decade later.

Go up into the little coffee shop on the mezzanine (get tea—don't try the awful coffee) and grab a table by the windows overlooking the hall. You can gaze down at the Supermarine S.6B and remember the old movie *Spitfire* with actor Leslie Howard playing designer R. J. Mitchell as Mitchell developed the Spitfire from his experiences with the Schneider Racers, all the while dying slowly from illness and overwork. Howard himself died shortly after making the movie when the actor's transport was shot down in that war that Mitchell saw coming. To your left hangs one of those Spitfires and you can see the image of the S.6B in its lines. You can also speculate on how things could have been very, very different except for the genius and dedication of just a few.

The Spitfire hanging above the S.6B is a Mark 1A which first flew on April 2, 1940 and bears the markings of No. 72 Squadron with which it flew until it made a forced landing in July of the same year. Next to it hangs a Hurricane I which flew in No. 615 County of Surrey Squadron ("Churchill's Own") during the Battle of Britain. It was damaged during an engagement on August 18, 1940, but Pilot Officer D. J. Looker managed to get it down more or less in one piece at Croydon Aerodrome.

As the clouds built up for that war, engineers and designers were pressing aviation technology forward. When Frank Whittle was a cadet at Cranwell in 1928, he had written an article on the theory of gas turbines and how they could be applied to aircraft. No one particularly believed him. He continued his career and became a Pilot Officer with the RAF, but he persevered with his invention. Part of the technology he needed came from the metallurgy and experience gained from that great big supercharger on that great big Rolls-Royce 'R' engine that had powered the Supermarine S.6B racer. The Gloster E28/39 with the markings W4041/G, hanging at the end of the hall, was the test bed for Whittle's engine. It was Britain's first jet airplane, and from whence

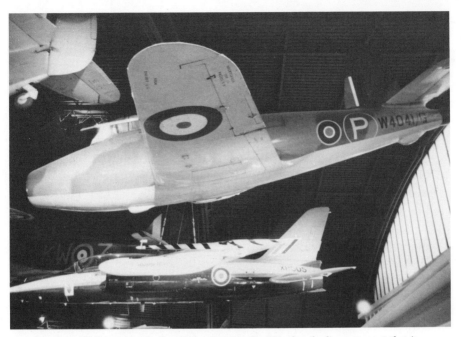

The first Allied jet aircraft, the Gloster E28/39; the '/G' after the license meant that it was to be kept under guard at all times.

all the other stovepipes have evolved. It first flew on May 15, 1941 piloted by Flight Lieutenant P. E. G. Sayer. His flight test report form, under the item labeled "Airscrew," blandly states "No airscrew fitted with this method of propulsion." The 'G' suffix on the plane's number indicates that an armed guard was to be placed on the aircraft at all times to preserve its secrets, although the fact that it had no propeller should have been reasonably obvious even from a fair distance. One of the pieces of lend-lease that went westbound was a Whittle engine. It was that Whittle engine which was used for the initial taxi tests of the Bell XP-59 and which started America on the road to the jet age.

The hall at the Science Museum is too small to hold the complete collection. A large number of rare aircraft are in storage at Wroughton, about halfway between London and Yeovilton. They range from a 1934 Boeing 247 airliner to the only Handley Page Gugnunc ever built. The latter was runner up to another biplane, the Curtiss Tanager, in the 1929 Guggenheim safe airplane design competition. The Gugnunc proved out Handley Page's automatic wing slot concept later used on planes as varied as Handley Page's own H.P.42 Hannibal biplane transport to the North American F-86 Sabrejet fighter twenty-five years later. The collection at Wroughton is normally closed to the public, but the museum has begun opening it on a few special weekends and hopefully that schedule will expand.

Head out from the Science Museum into the sun, or more likely the drizzle, for your next stop. As long as you are in central London, take one of those delightful double-decker buses, the No. 14, to Picadilly Circus and transfer to the No. 3 to take you across the Thames to the Imperial War Museum off the Lambeth Road. Their main aircraft exhibit is way off at Duxford (of which more in another episode), but there are a number of interesting airplanes on display at Lambeth. These include an old Royal Aircraft Factory B.E.2c and a Bristol Fighter from World War I and a Heinkel He 162 and a Focke-Wulf Fw 190A-8 from World War II, as well as the nose sections of a Lancaster and a Halifax. Of course, the museum itself is filled with the "thin red line" sort of stuff, and cannons, uniforms and tanks galore.

Here also, some of the aircraft are not just random examples of the type. The Sopwith Camel, for example, has a dramatic history. On August 11, 1918, Camel N6812, piloted by Lieutenant D. S. Culley shot down the German Zeppelin L.53—the fly attacking the elephant. The Supermarine Spitfire I, R6915, is also more than just a Spitfire. It probably has more operational time in actual combat than any other Spitfire in existence. It fought with No. 609 (West Riding) Squadron during the Battle of Britain and later with No. 602 (City of Glasgow) Squadron. It has ten enemy aircraft to its credit!

On August 11, 1918, this tiny Sopwith Camel N6812 shot down the Zeppelin L53 over the North Sea.

There is another saying, this time from the Bible. It goes something like "Seek and ye shall find." Those who flew those old airplanes—for speed, for distance, to fight a war, to explore distant lands—sought and found their dreams and left their aircraft behind for us.

A Supermarine Spitfire I appears to be strafing a Focke-Wulf Fw 190. This Spifire, R6915, shot down ten enemy aircraft.

The Heinkel He 162 Salamander was one of Hitler's last ditch jet fighters.

2

Per Ardua Ad Astra

From the 1860s through the turn of the century, Mill Hill, just north-west of what were then the boundaries of London, was a major center for the tranquil art of ballooning. Then in 1909 Claude Graham-White brought back a new-fangled flying machine, a Blériot, from the air meet at Rheims and established at nearby Hendon one of the first flying schools. Hendon rapidly became one of the major military airfields surrounding London. Throughout the 1930s Hendon was the locale for the great Air Pagents, the aviation equivalent of Ascot or Henley. Once famous as a major RAF base, Hendon has been overgrown by London's suburbs. It is no longer an active airfield, but the airplanes that once flew from there still remain, for Hendon is now the home of the Royal Air Force Museum.

Brave the Underground to Charing Cross or Leicester Square and transfer to the Edgeware branch of the Northern Line. Getting off at Hendon would appear logical, but if you do you will see a sign as you leave the station saying, "For RAF Hendon, use Colindale." Don't bother running back to the platform either, because your train will have already left. It is timed that way deliberately—English directions are even more perplexing than Irish ones—but the wait for the next train is short. Turn left at the Colindale station exit, don't get clobbered crossing the round-about, and you will see the RAF Hendon Museum on the right.

Plan on spending lots of time—and money. They have an excellent museum shop; just about every book and poster printed, racks of paintings and models as well, and some unusual souvenirs. Besides RAF mugs and ashtrays, we picked up a small plank of wood. On it is an enameled RAF crest and a brass plaque on which is engraved, "Part of the Oak Flooring of Bentley Priory, Headquarters Fighter Command, from where Air Chief Marshal Lord Dowding directed the Battle of Britain." A strange relic perhaps, but then not all aviation history was made in the air. I wonder if it was from that part of the floor where

A Blackburn Beverly transport patrols the parking lot at the RAF Museum, Hendon.

Air Vice-Marshals Keith Park and Trafford Leigh-Mallory stood and complained to Dowding about each other's tactics—and got roundly chewed out by Dowding for wasting his time. Never a patient or tactful man, Dowding had other worries. In particular, at that point in the Battle of Britain, Fighter Command had only a few hundred pilots left and was losing them faster than replacements could be trained. The battle was won—largely through Dowding's planning and tenacity and Park's tactics and leadership. Both would be put out to pasture in an outrageous injustice after the battle was over, while the more politically astute and maneuvering Leigh-Mallory would later take over Fighter Command. It is only a small plank of wood, but I do wish it could talk.

Before looking into the Battle of Britain, one should first go back a war. Take the stairs up to the left and you will catch the galleries in chronological order as well as having an overview of the aircraft on the main floor. The World War I gallery is particularly well set up, with re-creations of repair sheds, an armory, and training rooms. Looking down one can view the fine collection of World War I aircraft below, including a Blériot XI and XXVII, a Vickers F.B.5 Gunbus, and a Caudron G.3 among others. The Vickers Gunbus used the twin-boom arrangement to allow for a pusher engine and thus room for a machine gun in the nose; this was before machine guns synchronized to fire through the propeller arc were available. The Caudron also used the twin-boom arrangement but with a tractor engine, thus defeating the only possible excuse for that configuration; a decision which ranks with the Boulton-Paul Defiant's gun turret and the jet seaplane fighter as classic lapses of common sense in aircraft design.

Nowhere else in the world, besides Hendon, can you see four Sopwith machines side by side. The early Sopwith Pup is followed by the Triplane, the legendary Camel and the 1 1/2-Strutter. The reason for the unbelievable maneuverability of the Sopwith Camel becomes obvious once you look at one. What other airplane has the weights of the engine, pilot, machine guns and fuel tank all within three and a half feet of the center of gravity? The Sopwith 1 1/2-Strutter was officially and forgettably named the Two-Seater by the Royal Flying Corps and the even less memorable Type 9400 by the Royal Naval Air Service. It acquired and became universally known by its nickname because of the unusual arrangement of its wing struts. In addition to the cabane struts, the 1 1/2-Strutter has inboard struts but they attach to the fuselage longerons rather than the lower wing, so it's not really a two-bay machine a la the SPAD, nor a single bay as with the Camel. The 1 1/2-Strutter, with a synchronized Vickers firing forward and a Lewis gun on a Scarff mount in the rear cockpit became the progenitor of the two-seat fighter and reconnaissance aircraft designs for the next two decades. The Sopwiths are accompanied by a rare Belgian Hanriot HD-1 and two immortals: the S.E.5a and the Fokker D.VII, facing each other as they did sixty-five years ago.

Further along on the main floor are the between-the-wars era aircraft. No one built more beautiful biplanes toward the end of their golden age than did the British, excepting maybe the Curtiss folks with the P-6E Hawk. Clustered in the Sir Sidney Camm Memorial Hall are a Hawker Hind, a pair of Hawker Harts, and a Hawker Cygnet. It is a shame that no authentic single-seat Hawker Furys exist, for that was

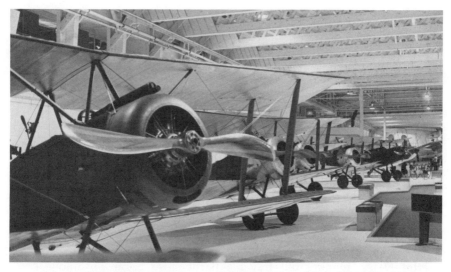

A lineup of Sopwith's: a 1 1/2-Strutter, Camel, Triplane, and Pup, followed by their competitors and their enemies.

A graceful Hawker Hart stands in front of her later brethren, the Sea Fury, the Typhoon and the experimental P.1127.

surely the most beautiful of the lot. But the Hind and Harts, even as two-seaters show that silver grace of the in-line engined biplane fighters of the 1930s. The Hind on view actually continued in service through World War II with the Royal Afghan Air Force; shades of the Khyber Pass. Camm Hall is actually a connecting structure tying together the original hangers of Nos. 600 and 604 Squadrons to form the museum building. Near to the Hawker exhibit is the hulk of a Gloster Gladiator biplane that was raised from a Norwegian lake, obsolete and a victim of the aborted rescue of that country invaded early in World War II.

Down the hall are the World War II machines starting with two more Hawkers, a Typhoon and a Tempest—mean looking aircraft; I'd hate to be on the road with one of them screaming down at me. The Typhoon used the enormous 2,200 hp Napier Sabre engine with its strange but effective sleeve valves. You can always spot a Napier-powered aircraft. The Sabre had 24 cylinders in an "H" shaped configuration; in appearance it was essentially two 12-cylinder, horizontally-opposed engines, one atop the other and geared together. This meant that the engine was very short for its displacement and the combined exhaust stacks from each bank lie right on the centerline. The performance of the Typhoon fell off disappointingly with altitude, but down low it became an unbeatable fighter-bomber and was about the only fighter that could intercept the Focke-Wulf Fw 190s. With four 20-mm Hispano cannons, Typhoons were removing 150 locomotives a month during the days just after D-day, making rail travel a particularly hazardous mode of transportation.

24

It is amazing how what may appear to be a minute change in the curvature of an airfoil can cause significant changes in an airplane's performance. The Typhoon encountered aileron reversal when it exceeded 500 mph in a dive and encountered transonic airflow phenomena. The Tempest originally was a Typhoon with a slightly thinner wing and airfoil that delayed the onset of that effect. Later, the Mark V was superseded by the Mark II which was powered by the Bristol Centaurus radial. That makes the Tempest a bit of a confusing airplane since it came in both in-line and radial flavors and, due to delays in development of the Centaurus engine, the numbering is chronologically backwards. Either way, the Tempest went like hell and its favorite sport was chasing the V-1 buzz-bombs. Clipping the wings and going to an advanced version of the Centaurus led to the Sea Fury. With a top speed of over 480 mph, it was one of the fastest propeller-driven fighters ever made, to the point where Sea Furies actually had several MiG-15 jets to their credit during the Korean War. It is also why unlimited-class racing pilots will sell their mothers to get their hands on one.

Several Spitfires are on display and a Beaufighter and a Mosquito are side by side further on. For some reason neither Germany nor the U.S. developed truly outstanding twin-engined heavy fighters, with the possible exception of the P-38 Lightning although even that is a bit light by comparison. With a crew of two or three, a Beaufighter weighed in at over 21,000 pounds, which for a fighter, made even the P-47 Thunderbolt look like a dwarf. The Northrop Black Widow would count in this class, except it arrived near the end of the war and was used

A lighning-fast de Havilland Mosquito fighter-bomber, its wooden structure holding twin Rolls-Royce Merlins and a raft of guns.

principally in the Pacific theatre against a then ineffective defense. Both the Beaufighter and the Mosquito fought toe to toe with the best Germany could put up and came out with spectacular records.

The Bristol Beaufighter was the first aircraft to effectively carry airborne radar. The British leaked stories of specially tested and selected pilots with uncanny night vision, such as "Cat's Eyes" Cunningham, so the Germans would not tumble to the radar. It took them a long time to figure out just why so many of their night bombers and reconnaissance aircraft were simply disappearing. With four 20-mm cannons in the nose and six wing-mounted .303-caliber machine guns, the Beaufighter had enormous firepower. The Japanese called it "Whispering Death" due to the relatively low-pitched whistling sound of the sleeve-valved Bristol Hercules radials.

The Bristol Beaufighter, however, must have one of the most convoluted genealogies of any aircraft. It is, in reality, a Bristol Beaufort torpedo bomber of the Fleet Air Arm with a smaller fuselage, more powerful engines, and all those guns in the nose. But the Beaufort is actually a significantly modified Bolingbroke bomber with a narrow fuselage half-containing the torpedo and using more powerful Taurus engines over the Mercurys, Pratt and Whitneys and Wright Cyclones that were fitted to various forms of the Bolingbroke. With even less changes, the Bolingbroke was really a Bristol Blenheim with various engine and cockpit layout changes, most versions of which were made in Canada as part of her contribution to the Commonwealth.

The Bristol Blenheim itself was one of the more modern light bombers at the start of the war and was not only used by the RAF, but

The heavily-gunned Bristol Beaufighter, with its sleeve-valved Bristol Hercules engine alongside, originally stemmed from a newspaperman's patriotism.

Blenheims were sold, sometimes along with license rights, to friendly countries such as Yugoslavia, Finland, Turkey and Greece. Blenheims fought in many of those early battles in France, Holland, Norway and North Africa in a valiant effort to slow down the Axis advance.

And just how did such an advanced light bomber *cum* fighter-bomber come about in the depression-ridden, politically pacifist, funds-short Britain of the mid 1930s? It came about because Lord Rothermere was one of those who foresaw the possible war with Germany. As then proprietor of the Daily Mail, that most aviation minded of newspapers, his strings of news sources were giving him information on how fast Germany was rearming and how obsolete Britain's aircraft were. His sources also told him that there were some designers up at Bristol with some ideas on how a modern aircraft could be built. So Lord Rothermere called in those designers to a meeting on March 29, 1934 and contracted with them, at his expense, to design and build a twin-engined airplane for his executives and for the fast express of news and photographs across Europe. What was understood at the meeting, but not stated in the contract, was that this fast mail plane could be easily converted into a light bomber. In a little over a year, officials were stunned when this privately developed thunderbolt, owned by a newspaper and named "Britain First," screamed across the RAF field at Martlesham at 300 mph—a speed over 50 mph faster than the top speed of the best RAF fighter then in service. The Daily Mail's headlines screamed just as loud and embarrassed politicians started voting for more funds for the RAF. Specifications were issued for all sorts of new aircraft, including one for a new light bomber. And so the singular "Britain First," the Bristol Type 142, was modified and became the Blenheim, which was modified and became the Bolingbroke, which was modified and became the Beaufort, which was modified and became the Beaufighter—surely one of the strangest of results from "the power of the press."

Not just landplanes, but some seaplanes are also based at the museum. Against the wall with its docking gear removed so it will clear the ceiling is the only existing Supermarine Stranraer biplane flying boat. The Stranraer is one of those collections of engines, struts and wires that sedately flew—and flew and flew—uniting the Empire throughout the mid 1930s. Another flying boat nearby is the unusual Dornier Wal, a sleek, tri-motored, sponsoned machine looking for all the world like a snake with wings. Of German origin, it served time with the Spanish Air Rescue Service before ending up at Hendon.

During the early 1980s, a major wing was added to the complex to house the Bomber Command Museum and many bombers previously in the original buildings were moved into this area. The oldest authentic aircraft on display is the de Havilland D.H.9A, named *Hyderabad.* Its career lasted less than ninety days—typical of many wartime aircraft—from August to October 1918 when it made a forced landing

This de Havilland D.H.9A light bomber's career lasted less than 90 days before it was shot down in 1918.

behind the German lines. It spent twenty years in the Berlin War Museum until it was carted off to Krakow, Poland for safekeeping after the Berlin Air Museum was hit by RAF bombs in 1943. Poland kept it until 1977 when it was exchanged for a Spitfire and the D.H.9A returned to its home at Hendon.

The Vickers Wellington was the mainstay of the British bombers at the onset of World War II. Affectionately known as "Wimpy" by its crews, it flew the bulk of Bomber Command's raids into Europe and Germany during the early part of the war. It was designed in the mid '30s during that time when aircraft structures were evolving from the old tubes and struts to the then unperfected monocoque stressed-skin. Barnes Wallis was another of those gifted British aircraft designers. He had been Chief Designer of the R 100 dirigible and was an expert in the spider web structure of the rigid airship. He designed the Wellington with a unique geodetic structure and you can see the shape of the diamond patterned members through the skin and windows. It was light weight and effective; Wellingtons were noted for returning from missions with flak damage all over them but with the pieces somehow managing to hold themselves together. It was a very flexible structure, however, and pilots who flew the Wellington claimed that when you made a turn it took several seconds for the tail to come around and follow the direction in which the nose was heading.

Wallis was also the "boffin" behind the "Dam Busters" adventure. Much of the electric power for the industrialized Ruhr Basin came from three heavily protected and massive hydro-electric dams; the Mohne, the Eder, and the Sorpe. Wallis devised a special cylindrical bomb to be mounted crosswise under an aircraft and spun for stability by belts from a motor. When dropped at low altitude, it would skip across the surface of the water and over the torpedo nets. When the bomb reached the dam, it would sink down against the surface of the dam, and with the weight of water behind it send a pressure shock strong enough to crack the concrete. Scale models were test flown on a modified Wellington; full scale would require a Lancaster.

For the device to work, it had to be dropped at an exact distance from the dam, while doing exactly 220 mph, and from an altitude of exactly 60 feet! Airspeed could be held with the benefit of extensive practice, much to the annoyance of the residents (and the monster) at Loch Ness where much of the practice was done. The range was obtained by sighting along a simple wooden triangle designed to line up with the towers on the dam when at the right distance. The altitude problem was the bear; exactly 60 feet over water at night in a narrow valley. With considerable ingenuity, it was solved by mounting two searchlights under the aircraft. They were tilted inwards at an angle such that the two spots merged when the airplane was at just the right altitude, the lower gunner calling off the height to the pilot.

On the night of May 15, 1943, nineteen specially modified Lancaster bombers led by Wing Commander Guy Gibson headed off by groups of three into one of the most incredible attacks of the war. One after the other, the Lancasters of 617 Squadron skimmed over the ground to evade detection, dropped down over the surface of the lakes and held rock steady while flak and tracers sprayed at them. The Mohne and the Eder were successfully breached (the Sorpe survived the only two hits that were made on it). Three hundred million tons of water flooded fifty miles downstream from the two dams; factories, coal mines, bridges

Of the over 10,000 Vickers Wellingtons that first carried the War to Germany in 1940, only one is left in the world.

and even a major airfield were under water. It was one of the most damaging raids of the war to the Reich's industrial might.

After the mission and while the crews were celebrating and drinking their success, Barnes Wallis went off into a corner by himself and cried. Nine of the nineteen Lancasters had not returned. His invention was a great success for the war effort, but Wallis, the ever bemused and distracted scientist, had not realized before the price that it would entail. Years later Wallis was given a grant from the government of 10,000 pounds for his wartime inventions; he donated it to a charity for RAF widows. Wing Commander Gibson received the Victoria Cross, and thirty-two DFCs, DFOs and other medals were awarded to participants in the raid. A year later, Gibson was lost when his damaged Mosquito crashed into a low hill in Holland; the Dutch buried him there.

The Wellington at the Bomber Command Museum was the one used in the filming of *The Dam Busters*, one of the best war movies ever made. Behind it is a Lancaster. None of the "Dam Buster" Lancasters exist, but many artifacts and photos from the raid are on exhibit. However this Lancaster also has a history. Flying with Nos. 83 and 467 Squadrons, it logged over 800 operational flying hours and flew 137 bombing missions. Not many aircraft have survived 137 combat missions. The Avro Lancaster also has to be the biggest tail dragger you've ever seen.

The special exhibit nearby displays the only Handley Page Halifax in existence. The Halifax was the second of the three main four-engined bombers that the British developed during World War II, (the Short

A Lancaster gets some last minute engine work done in preparation for the night's raid; the mission markers on its side belie Goering's quote.

Sterling was the first but none remain). Numbered TL-S, it flew its first and last operational sortie on April 27, 1942 as part of an attempt to sink the German battleship *Tirpitz,* lying at anchor in the heavily protected Foettenfjord near Trondheim, Norway; *S for Sugar* was hit by flak just as she dropped her four 1,000-pound mines, and her starboard outer engine burst into flames. With no chance of making it back to Scotland, the pilot made a successful belly landing on the ice of frozen Lake Hoklingen. Five of the crew made it safely by foot to neutral Sweden, while the flight engineer with a broken ankle ended up a POW. The Halifax dropped through the melting ice and sank. In 1973, *S for Sugar* was raised from the lake bottom and is now at Hendon displayed as she was after her one and only adventure in war.

Two of the three types of "V" bombers, the series of jet bombers that the British built in the 1950s, are on display in the hall. All are mean and sinister looking aircraft with the British practice of embedding engines in the wings rather than using external nacelles as we do. The Vickers Valiant is slightly smaller and lighter than the Avro Vulcan and has a cranked sweep to the wing's leading edge. The Vulcan is a delta-winged machine looking like a gigantic Douglas Skyray. Both of the bombers were capable of carrying nuclear weapons.

Off toward the exit of the main building are the early jet fighters and light bombers including the Meteor, Canberra and English Electric Lightning. The latter always seemed a strange name, rather more fitting to a maker of light bulbs than fighter aircraft. It was, however, the first British operational aircraft capable of Mach 2 speeds. The Hawker Hunter, on the other hand, looks like its namesake, a sleek, sexy, fast, jet fighter of the purest lines. Check what films and special exhibits are showing on the ground floor as sometimes there are gems. On one occasion they had recreated the whole episode of a downed pilot from the parachute landing to the escape through occupied territory. Outside again, cross the parking lot and have lunch and a pint of bitter at the restaurant there and rest the mind and feet before tackling the Battle of Britain Museum next door.

3

Their Finest Hour

The scene has been filmed a dozen times: an operations room is dominated by a map of the English Channel on what looks like an over-sized pool table. The players are WAAFs and the pool cues move placards representing the waves of oncoming German raiders and the British fighters clawing their way upwards to intercept the Heinkels and Dorniers approaching Dover. Around the first balcony, officers and ranks man batteries of phones coordinating the defense and sending orders to the surrounding airfields to scramble the interceptors.

It is one thing to watch the scene in a movie. It is another to stand where the second balcony for the observers would be and look down on what was, at the time, the center of the last defense of England against the armadas being thrown at her. The figures don't move, they're just dummies; the phones don't ring and the clock hands don't tick. They don't have to for the mind fills it all in.

Even though it is a reproduction, it brings emotions of what it must have been like to have been there. The room is a replica of the No. 11 Group Operations Room at Uxbridge where Air Vice-Marshal Keith Park directed the air defenses over the approaches to London and the south of England. Names like Biggin Hill, Hornchurch and Tangmere head the toteboard on the back wall where lights indicate the status of each fighter squadron. The scene is frozen in time at 1130 hours on 15 September 1940. That was at the peak of the German onslaught and when the outcome was still in doubt. It was also the time when Winston Churchill visited Uxbridge to see first hand how the defense of England was holding up. As he viewed the toteboard on the wall, he looked puzzled and asked about the status of Fighter Command's reserves. The reply was that there were no reserves! At that point every last flyable fighter in the south of England was engaged.

The locale is not Uxbridge, it is at the Battle of Britain Museum at Hendon and across from the RAF Museum; the two museums make

Fighter Command's No. 11 Group Operations Room at Uxbridge, frozen in time at 1130 hours on September 15, 1940 at the height of the Battle of Britain.

a good day trip for the airplane buff. When you enter the Battle of Britain Museum, go directly up the stairs to take in the slide show first. It does a good job of putting the whole battle in perspective. The show also brings home that the battle didn't comprise just the RAF fighters; it encompassed everything from the factories, the air raid wardens, fire brigades and anti-aircraft emplacements to the whole of the civilian population. In large part it also depended on the first integrated early warning system. Besides the control centers, observer corps and the acoustic locators near the coast, were the critical Chain Home stations, the first operational use of radar.

In 1932, Sir Robert Watson-Watt was investigating the problem of aircraft interference with high frequency radio signals. By taking advantage of what was otherwise considered a problem, radar was born. The

Germans also played with the idea in the late 1930s, but without much success. During the battle there were only a few desultory attacks on those weird looking radio towers on the coast, but they didn't get much priority. Because of that mistake, the small number of Spitfires and Hurricanes always seemed to be at the right place at the right time when the Germans came over.

After seeing the slide show and the Ops room, you can stand on the balcony and look down at the Spitfire and Hurricane in their sandbagged pens. The view is partly blocked by a Bofors anti-aircraft gun, but that only makes it more realistic. Starting equipment and mechanics are standing by and you stay there longer than you had planned because you can almost smell the moist dawn air and at any moment you expect those Rolls-Royce Merlins to start coughing and belching and the airframes to shake into life as they did some forty-odd years ago.

There are some that argue as to which, the Spitfire or the Hurricane, was the more decisive aircraft in the Battle of Britain. It is not really the right question, and therein lies another tale—a tale of the competition between two companies for over a half century and of two men, both brilliant yet of different minds, without whom the war itself might have turned out very different. The story starts just after the turn of the century with Noel Pemberton-Billing and T. O. M. Sopwith, neither of whom are the main protagonists of this story.

Pemberton-Billing was one of those Edwardian pioneers of English aviation who started out flying rather crude boxkites. Down in Southampton on the coast, he became involved in seaplanes and in 1912 he founded a company to build them; he named it Supermarine. Seaplanes were not the mainstream of aviation development, but Supermarine became a small but formidable design firm in the field.

A Spitfire and a Hurricane at dispersal, ground power plugs attached and ready to scramble.

Sopwith, early in World War I developed the Pup, one of the first all-round fighters. That led to the Triplane and the Camel and the Snipe, and Sopwith's was becoming a world-famous name in aircraft manufacture. In the background loomed the bulk of Vickers-Armstrong, a huge armaments manufacturer—sort of the Krupps works of Great Britain. Vickers, as a large company, aimed big and they saw their products grow from the clumsy gun buses of 1915 to the large boxy bombers of 1918 such as the Vimy.

With the end of World War I, as when all wars end, military funding dried up and new markets were needed. Creating an image and garnering publicity would be necessary to begin to obtain commercial sales. The Daily Mail newspaper had proferred a 10,000-pound prize for the first transatlantic flight. It might as well have been for a flight to the moon, but that prize could make the company that won it. Sopwith had designed and built the prototype Atlantic, a large single-engined biplane which, if they could win the prize, would be a natural for one of the first commercial transports.

Raynham and Morgan, in their Martinsyde Raymor, on May 18, 1919 were actually the first away, but they crashed on takeoff. They tried again a few months later and crashed again. By then the prize had been won and a third attempt in order to come in second didn't make a whole lot of sense and so they leave our story. The Martinsyde Company didn't last much longer.

Second away, and on the same day as Martinsyde's first attempt, was the Sopwith Atlantic. It was flown by Kenneth Mackensie-Greve and Sopwith's chief test pilot, one Harry Hawker. They very nearly made it. Engine failure forced them down two-thirds of the way across. In fact they were thought dead because the Danish freighter *Mary* that hauled them out of the sea had no radio and it was over a week before their rescue was known.

Meanwhile, out of the wings stepped Vickers and their Vimy, flown by Alcock and Brown, that conquered the North Atlantic. A rather damp Mackensie-Greve and Hawker were feted for their heroic survival along with the celebrations for Alcock and Brown. Sopwith's ended up with only their waterlogged prototype—it actually floated and was later recovered, refurbished and sold—but there were no orders forthcoming for more Atlantics. They hadn't made the kind of splash they were after and they were now getting into desperate financial shape.

Like many another company before and after, Sopwith's declared insolvency and reorganized. Starting off in the same building with the same staff commenced Hawker Aircraft Ltd.—partly to capitalize on Hawker's name and partly to confound the creditors. Hawker died just two years later while flying a Nieuport Goshawk, although it was later discovered that he had tuberculosis and may have collapsed in the cockpit before the crash. The company, however, had hired a young draftsman named Sidney Camm, who turned out to be one of the great airplane designers of all time. Hawker's slowly but surely prospered during the two decades between the wars as Camm's mind and pencil produced a steady stream of Furys, Harts, Hinds, Nimrods and the lot.

Supermarine faced the same financial squeeze, but found a different niche. They, and a young engineer they hired named Reginald Joseph Mitchell, had two ideals—flying off water and speed and more speed. The Schneider Trophy went to the fastest seaplanes so Supermarine was able to hang in there with their reputation for the fastest of racing planes and a steady dribble of orders for the slowest of flying boats and patrol aircraft.

Off in the wings, Vickers plugged along making tanks and guns and such ghastly looking airplanes as the Valetta and the Vildebeest—the latter looking much like its namesake.

By the mid 1930s, both Sidney Camm at Hawker and R. J. Mitchell at Supermarine had reached the same conclusions: that war with Germany was inevitable, that it wasn't far away and that airpower might well decide the issue. Both convinced their managements to proceed at risk. The Hurricane and the Spitfire designs were both started without Air Ministry contracts, and each designer turned his talents loose—but in different directions.

Mitchell at Supermarine was totally single-minded and would brook no compromise with speed and maneuverability. England had to have the fastest fighter to survive and his Schneider Cup experience said that meant compound curves, aerodynamic purity, and above all, thin wings. That is why the Spitfire has such a narrow track and a landing gear that folds outwards; the wing spar was just too thin to take the landing loads if the gear was further outboard. That fanaticism over the thin wing also led to that uniquely graceful elliptical planform that was the hallmark of the Spitfire. Aerodynamicists had long known that an elliptical planform is theoretically the most efficient shape, but even Mitchell at Supermarine felt that the added construction difficulties would be a bit much. Thus the early design sketches of the Spitfire show a straight tapered wing.

The Air Ministry finally came out with contracts and they did get one thing right. With inspired legerdemain, someone estimated that it would take 18 pounds of lead to down the new bombers. The fighter pilot would only have, at the probable future high combat speeds, only a few seconds on target. A simple calculation then led to their insistence on eight machine guns for any new fighter. The eight-gun fighter was a radical step from the two pea-shooters that had been standard ever since World War I. Clearly, eight guns wouldn't fit into the fuselage and to put them in the wing outboard of the gear meant making the wing thicker, something Mitchell refused to do.

The aerodynamic efficiency of a wing, however, is not a function of actual thickness; it is a function of the thickness-to-chord ratio—the chord being the distance between the leading and trailing edges of the wing. Thus Mitchell could keep his wing proportionately "thin" by maintaining a large chord fairly far outboard while he increased the thickness to fit in the gun breeches—by dropping the tapered wing and making it elliptical. So somewhere in the bowels of the Air Ministry, an unnamed civil servant briefly joins the drama as the inadvertent cause of that beautiful elliptical wing and also behind the devastating firepower that both the Spitfire and Hurricane carried.

Meanwhile, at Hawker, Camm took a different approach. He reasoned that Britain would be facing armadas of enemy aircraft and he knew the bureaucracy well enough to expect that the government wouldn't put out large production orders until the eleventh hour. Compromise to allow producibility was mandatory in his mind. Thus the Hurricane, instead of compound curves and stressed aluminum skin, still had a steel tube fuselage with wooden formers and linen covering over the aft fuselage. But parts could be built by retread furniture and car makers all over England and then assembled in jiffy-made jigs in dispersed shadow factories.

By the summer of 1940, the Spitfire could outfly the Germans and maintain local air superiority, but there were always far too few of them. They were a bear to manufacture, production was slow and development problems hindered deployment. A minor but interesting example was that the unusually high rate of climb could cause the guns to

The attackers that failed: a Messerschmitt Bf 110G with a primitive radar antenna, a Junkers Ju 88R, and a Heinkel He 111H.

jam on humid days since the moisture in the gun barrels would freeze before it could evaporate. The problem was eventually eliminated by gun breech heaters but the initial solution was the simple expedient of taping over the muzzles with duct tape before each flight to keep the cold air out during the climb. The flapping blurs you see on closeups of wing guns firing in aerial movie scenes are the remnants of the duct tape.

The Hurricane, on the other hand, had a tough time on a one-to-one with the Messerschmitts, but there were far more Hurricanes than Spitfires and the Hurricanes hit the bombers, harrassed and distracted the Messerschmitts and generally caused more than a great deal of discomfort shooting up everything in sight. Britain needed both aircraft. With only one of them she would have been in much worse trouble. Together, with the Spitfire's performance and the Hurricane's numbers, they were able to hold things together during that critical summer of 1940. Mitchell and Camm made separate and different design decisions, but it was the two different decisions that were necessary and that were a crucial factor for the survival of Britain.

And where was Vickers during all of this? They knew that war was coming; that was their business. They also knew that they were short of the kind of talent needed, so they simply bought out Supermarine in order to obtain Mitchell's brain. Those Spitfires you see on film or at the museums are actually Vickers-Supermarines. And it was some Air Ministry civil servant again that assigned the name Spitfire when they issued the contract for the prototype. The ever single-minded Mitchell, when he learned of it, was heard to utter the hardly erudite remark, "Just the sort of bloody silly fool name they would give it"—a silly fool name that became immortal. Mitchell lived to see his prototype fly, but he never saw the Spitfire in combat. He was only forty-

The deadly Messerschmitt Bf 109E; the Stuka dive bomber behind it was mincemeat for the Hurricanes and Spitfires.

38

two years old when he died prematurely from cancer in 1937. Camm lived through the war but died shortly afterwards.

Strange how those companies' and those two individuals' fates and fortunes crossed and recrossed through the years and how the world could well have been so different without them. Vickers, in addition to Supermarine, went on to pick up Bristol, Percival, English Electric and some others and became the British Aircraft Corporation. Hawker merged with Siddeley which had bought out Avro, and picked up Gloster to become Hawker-Siddeley. In the 1970s British Aircraft and Hawker-Siddeley combined and along with de Havilland, Blackburn and Folland, all became just divisions of the giant British Aerospace Corporation— an era had come to an end.

Go down to the ground floor and you can examine the fighter pens more closely. They stand face to face with the planes that came, but were never able to stay. A Heinkel He 111H and a Junkers Ju 88R start the row and down a ways is a Messerschmitt Bf 109E that was their main and formidable protection. This particular Bf 109 fought and survived through the Battle of Britain with Jagdgeschwader 51, but on November 27, 1940 it was jumped by Spitfires over the Thames estuary. The cooling system was shot up obliging the pilot, Leutnant Wolfgang Teumer, to make a belly landing at RAF Manston, discretion being the better part of valor. The Ju 88 arrived in a more unusual manner: it was flown to Aberdeen by a defecting Luftwaffe crew in May 1943.

There are some less common machines in the hall. A Boulton-Paul Defiant is there; a strange single-engined fighter with a four-gun, bomber-type power turret behind the pilot. In World War I, the Sopwith 1 1/2-Strutter, the Bristol Fighter and others used that configuration (*sans* turret) with great success, but in the flight regimes of 1940, to expect an aircraft with the same engine as the single-seat fighters to compete while lugging around an extra ton or so of ironmongery was preposterous. They also couldn't afford the added weight of any forward-facing armament. Thus the Defiant was adequately gunned while running away, but it made attacking a bit awkward. About the only option appears to be to come up alongside and fire broadsides like the old sailing ships: fire on the uproll! Still, in an odd way it is an attractive, if sinister looking, black beast. This one is the only Defiant left in existence, having been flown by No. 307 Squadron in 1940—No. 307 Squadron was piloted by expatriate Poles who would fly anything in order to get a crack at the Germans.

Covering the earlier days are an Italian Fiat C.R.42 Falco with its Warren truss struts and a Gloster Gladiator, looking as much like a bulldog as Churchill himself. Biplanes should have been scrapped by 1940, but under the exigencies of war, the Fiat served in North Africa, and two squadrons, RAF 247 Squadron at Exeter and Fleet Air Arm 804 Squadron at Wick, actually flew Gladiators operationally during the Battle of Britain. To go up against Bf 109s or Hurricanes in biplanes takes more than a bit of courage. This particular Fiat C.R.42 was sent to Belgium as part of a small Italian contingent to show the flag and cooperate with the Luftwaffe. It was, not surprisingly, shot down by a Hurricane, but was rugged enough to be rebuilt for the museum.

A Westland Lysander, with a strut-braced high wing and fixed gear, looking much like an enlarged Stinson, arouses little interest as compared to the fast fighters. Its paint scheme as an Army cooperation machine—the hazardous, but unromantic occupation in which it originally served in 1940— doesn't help. The Lysander is not a very romantic or exciting looking airplane. More's the pity, because this Lysander served later in the war with 161 Squadron; the outside ladder below the rear cockpit gives that away. And the aircraft of 161, and its sister 138 Squadron, worked for the S. O. E., the Special Operations Executive!

They were the ones that went into occupied France and Norway, flying at tree top height on dark nights to avoid detection, landing on dark, too-small pastures lit only by the headlights of an old Renault and a few torches. They dropped off radio batteries, code books and supplies of explosives—and, yes, secret agents—and picked up maps and downed pilots and resistance fighters that the Gestapo were getting too close to. They kept their engine running and halted for only a few moments; the outside ladder was to allow passengers to scramble out and escapees to board in the minutes before the German acoustic detectors and ground patrols could locate them. Which missions this particular Lysander flew are not known, but some of the exploits of the two squadrons of Lysanders are: Squadron Leader Murphy being shot as German soldiers closed in during the turnaround, but managing to get airborne, bleeding all the way home; Squadron Leader Hodges picking up a fleeing Frenchman with the Germans right on his tail— the Frenchman being Vincent Auriol, later President of France; and Flight Lieutenant Bridger who blew a tire on landing. While his passengers exchanged places, Bridger calmly drew his pistol and shot out the other tire. He liked things symmetrical and managed to take off on the two flats. Many a Lysander of 161 Squadron returned to base with the scrape marks from a French church steeple on its belly and twenty yards of grape vines dragging from its landing gear. Many didn't return at all. The Lysander is not a very romantic or exciting looking airplane. On our last visit, we noted that someone has removed the ladder.

An unsung hero, the Westland Lysander. The ladder that sped embarking during midnight missions to resistance fighters is no longer attached.

The sinister looking, if rather useless, Boulton Paul Defiant between a Bristol Blenheim and an obsolete but noble Gloster Gladiator.

Down at the end of the hall are two flying boats. One is a Supermarine Seagull biplane amphibian, successor to the Walrus, and the other a big, four-engined Short Sunderland flying boat. They were the ones that went out over the North Sea or the Channel to search for the fighters and bombers and Lysanders that didn't make it back.

The humorous but welcome sight to a downed pilot in the North Sea: a Supermarine Walrus (actually a Seagull V).

A small contingent of Italian Fiat C.R.42s was sent to France. This one was not surprisingly forced down in Suffolk. A Bf 110G is in the background.

4

A Pilgrimage

The grass strip has one fuel pump, a grown-like-Topsy collection of hangers along one side, and on most weekdays, little likelihood of an aircraft being visible. But go into the first hanger and another world opens up. Edwardian and vintage aircraft are crammed chock-a-block in roughly chronological order; a view of varnished struts, doped linen, polished brass—and greasy drip pans. They drip oil! No stagnant shells, these airframes fly as their designers prayed for them to some sixty or seventy years ago when they were first coaxed and cajoled into reluctantly leaving the earth.

For this is Old Warden Aerodrome and the home of the Shuttleworth Trust, the finest collection of flyable flying machines in the world. On the last Sunday of each summer month the hanger doors open to the misty dawn air and the stillness is broken by the crackle and rumble of Gipsys and Hermes, Kestrels and Mercurys. But go anytime you have the chance, because even dormant they contain images for the aviation buff that is beyond compare.

A 1937 Swallow 2, a British Aircraft Company version of the Klemm L 25 taxies up to the gate at Old Warden.

43

From London you can take the A1 to Biggleswade, but we prefer the M1 to exit 13 and then the back roads. There is something about wandering along the narrow lanes of the Bedfordshire countryside in the early morning that acts like a pleasant time machine. That is if you remember to drive on the left side of the road—otherwise terrifying would be a better characterization. Taking the A5140 you pass Cranfield, which in its day was one of the centers for the development of English aviation. It still contains a major technical institute. If you can talk your way in, one of the first attempts at a solar-powered airplane sits there forlorn, having been beaten to success by Paul McCready's crew in Pasadena; they having already won the Kremer prizes for both the first manpowered flight and the first manpowered flight across the Channel.

The time machine works even more as you wind across the B603 and the B658. Out of the mists on your left rise the huge ghostly hangers of Cardington which once housed the R 100 and R 101 airships before they went the way of the Akron, the Macon, the Hindenburg and the rest. The story of the R 100 as well as the development of English aviation through the 1920s and 1930s is well told in Neville S. Norway's book *Slide Rule.* Norway was Barnes Wallis' assistant during the design of the R 100. After the cancellation of the English dirigible program, Wallis went to Vickers to design the Wellington, while Norway became one of the founders and the chief engineer of Airspeed, Ltd. Airspeed built a number of excellent light twin-engined aircraft. The Airspeed Oxford was an outstanding performer of its day and became one of the RAF's principle multi-engine trainers while one example of the Airspeed Envoy became the royal family's personal aircraft. Unfortunately, war loomed on the horizon. While that meant huge sales of trainers, it also meant a government–negotiated contract with limited profit and thus the early losses in setting up the company could never be repaid. Airspeed, in deep financial yogurt, was bought out by de Havilland, its major competitor.

After the war, and somewhat bitter over the cancellation of the successful, privately-developed R 100 (due to the crash of the government-designed R 101) as well as his later loss of the Airspeed company, Neville Norway emigrated to Australia and in his retirement took up writing. He had plenty of previous practice. During the earlier Airspeed period, Norway had amused himself and preserved his sanity by writing fiction in his spare time. It wouldn't have been suitable for such a frivolous pastime to be connected with a director of a struggling-to-be-reputable aircraft company; his worried bankers would not have understood. So airplane designer Neville S. Norway wrote under the pseudonym of his middle name—his full name was Neville Shute Norway! And as Neville Shute, he became world famous. *On The Beach* is perhaps most familiar to Americans as the Gregory Peck/Ava Gardner/Fred Astair movie about the aftermath of nuclear war. Another, *No Highway in the Sky,* ended up on film with Jimmy Stewart as the absent-minded aeronautical engineer and *A Town Like Alice,* became a series on public television's Masterpiece Theatre. But his earlier books such as *Landfall, Steven Morris, Most Secret,* and *Pied Piper,* drafted or based on his experiences back in the old Airspeed days, rank Neville Shute as one of the great writers of the classic aviation novel. He was one of the very few, along with perhaps only Earnest K. Gann and Antoine de Saint-Exupéry, who could truly capture the emotions of fliers and of flight.

Only a few miles further on and you will reach Old Warden. Clayton and Shuttleworth had been a heavy machinery company since 1842, and in World War I they produced Sopwith Camels under license. In fact, if the recent arguments that it was really some sharp-eyed Aussie ground gunners who shot down Baron von Richthofen are incorrect, then it was B7270, a Camel built by Shuttleworth, that got him. Being the scion of a wealthy family, Richard Ormonde Shuttleworth had both the money and the love of aviation to begin collecting and maintaining the earliest of aircraft when they were still only ten or twenty years old. Love of aircraft and country caused him to join the RAF with the unfortunate result that in 1940 he was killed in an accident in, of all the dogs in the world, a Fairey Battle. During the war, Shrager Brothers Ltd. ran an overhaul shop at Old Warden that kept Procters and Harvards running to train the new RAF fledglings. They even had their own Home Guard platoon to protect the field from ne're-do-wells and enemy parachutists. It was after the war that Shuttleworth's mother set up the trust, and those who love aviation are forever in her debt.

In the first hall are the earliest treasures: a Blériot with Constructor's Number 14 and similar to the Channel-crossing machine; a 1910 Deperdussin monoplane which could not be considered overpowered with its 35-hp Anzani Y-type engine; and a 1912 Blackburn which was stored in 1914 and discovered in 1937 buried under a haystack. Thank goodness the cows weren't hungrier, because the Blackburn represents the oldest authentic British flying machine that remains in flying condition. Both the Blériot and the Deperdussin were used by flying schools at Hendon in the early pioneering days and were placed in storage at the onset of World War I. Only after decades of deterioration in forgotten garages were they discovered and carefully restored to flying condition. Only the Avro Triplane and the Bristol Boxkite, with their reams of wires, are replicas, having paid their dues in the making of the movie *Those Magnificent·Men in their Flying Machines.* Ironically, while the Avro is a replica, it contains an authentic Avro engine whereas the Avro Triplane at the British Science Museum is authentic but has a replica engine in it. Whether painstakingly built from yellowed plans and old photographs or lovingly restored from a haystack, seeing these ancient craft circuit the field can only be described as magnificent.

This Blackburn Monoplane of 1912 is the oldest authentic British aircraft in flying condition.

Flying those pre-1915 aircraft can also be called an ancient art, for they handle quite differently than what is familiar today. Top speed was generally barely above stalling speed and, with their high drag levels, should the engine fail—a not infrequent occurrence back then—the nose had to be dropped instantly to prevent loss of flying speed. More critical was their pathetic roll control capability, perhaps only ten percent of the control effectiveness of a modern aircraft. A wing drop due to turbulence was a serious matter and took hard-over controls for a hold-your-breath period before the craft would right itself. The Blackburn was one of the slightly better aircraft in this regard. Lavavasseur's Antoinette was one of the few aircraft that evolved from the wing-warping approach to the aileron and then reverted back to wing-warping again. The Antoinette's structure was so flimsy that the aileron would twist the whole wing thereby essentially cancelling out the roll forces the aileron put in. That was a bit much, even for the aviators of that era to put up with. Sit on the fence and watch those craft motor by in the afternoon sky; they are symbols of a heroic and more peaceful time.

World War I came and the incredible change in aircraft in just those few years can be seen in the next hanger. An Avro 504K, a Sopwith Pup, an S.E.5a, and the two-seaters, a Bristol F.2B and a German L.V.G. C.VI, show the airplane becoming a real machine, if unfortunately for less than altruistic purposes. The Bristol Fighter, the Brisfit, was built in 1918 and, while this example did not see active service in World War I, it flew with No. 208 Squadron in Turkey during the 1920s in one of England's many peace-keeping actions in the Near East.

It is from between the wars that more of the fascinating machines came about. De Havillands galore fill the hangers; Moths, Puss Moths, Tiger Moths, Hornet Moths, and non-Moths, a tiny D.H.53 Humming-bird, a Dragonfly and its larger sister, a Dragon-Rapide. The D.H.60X

Patience, skill, and time are applied to restore this vintage 1917 German L.V.G. C.VI light bomber.

A Bristol Fighter and an S.E.5a. The wing-mounted Lewis gun is visible atop the S.E.5a. A Hucks starter is on the chassis at right.

Moth, G-EBWD, was built in 1928 and purchased by Richard Shuttleworth in 1932 for his personal use. Thus G-EBWD probably holds the record for having been based at and continuously flown from one aerodrome, Old Warden, for longer than any other airplane in the world. The de Havilland D.H.51 was one of only three of that type built. It was a precursor to the Moth series and this one is no hanger queen either. It was built in 1924 and exported to Kenya shortly thereafter.

Richard Shuttleworth's personal de Havilland D.H.60 Moth has been flying out of Old Warden for over fifty years, probably a record for an aircraft's home base. An authentic Blériot is on the right.

As *Miss Kenya,* VP-KAA remained airworthy, flying around East Africa for some thirty-five years before being purchased back by de Havilland's and sent to Shuttleworth for a "working retirement."

Geoffrey de Havilland was one of those versatile early pioneers who built his own airplane, designed his own engine for it, and then taught himself to fly in it while simultaneously test flying the beast. In 1908 his first machine, not surprisingly, crashed but his second flew quite well. The Royal Aircraft Factory was being egged on by Cody and others, but had little experience and not much authority or funds available to develop aircraft. They hired the brilliant twenty-five year old and bought his machine for 400 pounds. De Havilland designed several machines for the Royal Aircraft Factory before he left to work for the Aircraft Manufacturing Company. While the airplanes were made by Airco, the numbering system used de Havilland's initials, and they are almost univerally called "de Havillands"; the de Havilland company itself wasn't founded until 1920. The D.H.2 was one of the fairly successful single-seat pusher gun buses that held off the Fokker scourge in 1916. It was actually quite a snappy aircraft considering the pusher configuration. Another de Havilland, the D.H.4, became memorable, not as just a World War I light bomber, but for being the aircraft most predominantly used by air mail pilots in the U.S. for the next decade; then anonymous pilots like Charles Lindbergh cut their teeth flying the night mails in D.H.4s.

Recognizing the need for good commercial aircraft in order to stay in business after World War I, de Havilland also concluded that the D.H.53 Hummingbird was too small and the D.H.51s, such as *Miss*

One of the three 1924 D.H.51s built, Miss Kenya *spent the next thirty-five years in Africa before returning to England; it remains airworthy to this day.*

Kenya, too large. With the Moth he hit exactly the right formula and the series of Moths that followed dominated the training and light aircraft flying in Europe until the beginning of World War II.

Of all the de Havillands, there is one that stands above all in my mind. Mentioned earlier was the special thrill of seeing for the first time a rare and favorite aircraft. At Shuttleworth is the one surviving de Havilland Comet. Not the premature and ill-fated D.H.106 jet transport of the early 1950s, but the original D.H.88 Comet of 1934. A sleek, low-winged, twin Gipsy Six powered, all wood two-seater, *Grosvenor House* was one of only five D.H.88s ever built. It has to be one of the most beautiful aircraft of all time. The first three were built especially for the 1934 MacPherson Robertson London-to-Australia Air Race. Flown by C. W. A. Scott and T. Campbell Black, *Grosvenor House* won the 11,300 mile race from Mildenhall to Melbourne outright in the incredible time of 70 hours and 54 minutes.

But then, the D.H.88 Comet was an incredible machine for its day. Powered by two underslung Gipsy Six engines of only 230 hp each, the Comet could do over 230 mph while carrying enough fuel for almost 3,000 miles at a crack. Part of its success was de Havilland's aerodynamic genius at squeezing every chip off a drag coefficient. The Comet also incorporated an early type of controllable-pitch propeller. The French-built Ratier propeller was actually a fairly primitive form of two-position design. It was set to the takeoff position on the ground by using a bicycle pump to compress air into a container in the spinner. At a speed of 150 mph or so, outside air pressure on the spinner opened a valve and vented the compressed air. This allowed springs to change the pitch to the high speed position. It was a one-shot "Mickey Mouse" deal, pumped up before each flight, but it enabled the Comet to get off the ground with its huge fuel load. One sincerely hopes that both propellers switched pitch at about the same time and without unduly startling the pilot.

The race itself was not without its adventures. After overcoming them and getting most of the way, Scott and Black put down at Darwin, Australia with their worst problem, rapidly failing oil pressure on one engine. By luck, a London newspaper had a phone line open to a local reporter to get up-to-the-minute race results. Scott managed to borrow the line and get relayed through to the de Havilland factory at Stag Lane. With Frank Halford, designer of the Gipsy Six engine on the other end, Scott described his trouble. Halford figured that there was a good chance that most of the problem could be in a defective oil pressure gauge and anything else that was wrong with the engine would take too long to fix in the middle of the race. Over the scratchy, static-filled connection from half-way around the world, Halford told Scott to pour in some extra oil, crank her up and don't look at the gauge. The flaming red *Grosvenor House* landed in Melbourne to pick up the 10,000-pound prize for first place and went on to become one of the most famous of all long-distance racers.

It is sitting on saw horses now, nearing the finish of probably the most complex, expensive, and thorough antique aircraft restoration projects ever attempted—due to years of unfortunate neglect elsewhere. Even incomplete and on sawhorses, it still looks like the thoroughbred racing

The superb de Havilland D.H.88 Comet, Grosvenor House, *winner of the 1934 London-to-Australia air race.*

machine that it is. It also looks like something else. For if you stand back, you can see in its lines and veneered wood construction the shadow of the de Havilland Mosquito Geoffrey de Havilland would use his experience with the Comet to build, seven years after its famous flight, a wooden war plane to race back and forth to Berlin. And *Grosvenor House* should be back in the air again by the time you read this chapter.

In the midst of all sorts of staid biplanes, the 1930s in England brought out the best in sleek looking monoplanes. Both the Percival D.3 Gull and the Miles Hawk Speed Six at Shuttleworth would class as true "Smiling Jack" type airplanes. Jean Batten, like Amy Johnson, was a secretary. A native New Zealander, she made her way to England, and again like Amy Johnson, learned to fly and got her mechanic's license as well at Stag Lane. She also bought a well-used de Havilland Moth. On her first two attempts to better Amy Johnson's record, she was forced down in Karachi and in Rome. On her third try, in 1934, she made it to Australia in the tiny and now much-repaired Gipsy Moth in a little under 15 days. She had beaten Amy Johnson's record by more than four days. Not content, she turned around and flew back in 17 days and 15 hours, completing a record round trip. Jean Batten was the pride of Auckland. She received enough money in awards and from selling the Moth, that on her twenty-sixth birthday in September of 1935 she bought one of the brand new Percival Gulls.

With some reasonable experience, as well as the Gull, G-ADPR, now under her belt, Jean Batten went off on one record-breaking flight after another. The little Gull Six could do over 150 mph for 2,000 miles. In 1935 Jean Batten flew solo from London to Brazil in a little over 61 hours. While being her own mechanic, she was not unfeminine. A French ground crew was amazed to see her off-loading spare parts and tools but carefully repacking two evening gowns at a refueling stop in Senegal during which she had just done her own engine maintenance. Her response was that if the engine failed over the South Atlantic, she wouldn't have much use for the tools and spares, but if she made it she would need the evening gowns for the receptions.

In 1936 she set the fastest solo record for a pilot of any gender from England to Australia at 5 days, 21 hours and 3 minutes. Not content, she went on to New Zealand setting that solo record. In 1937 she reversed her route and set an Australia to London record with the Gull, knocking three hours off her outbound time. Jean Batten's London to New Zealand record with the Gull stood until 1980. In that year, as Judith Chisholm beat that record, she was met at the airport in Auckland by the woman who had set the first one forty-four years before in the trim little Percival Gull.

The only surviving Miles Hawk Speed-Six, an exquisite, high speed private aircraft of the '30s. The Miles is on long-term loan to the Shuttleworth Trust, Bedfordshire.

Impressed into the RAF during the War, Percival Gull G-ADPR was used for much less exotic work around town until peace returned and the Percival company retrieved the machine from the RAF and sent it to Shuttleworth. It rarely flies very far from pattern at Old Warden these days—but it could.

There are a dozen more historic aircraft at Old Warden ranging from a tiny 1923 Wren with its two-cylinder, three-horsepower(!) engine to the Mark V Spitfire with its 1,500-hp Merlin. And if you like biplanes, you can drink a fair number of pints at the local pub arguing which crackles better, the 640-hp Rolls-Royce V-12 Kestrel-powered Hawker Hind or the 840-hp Bristol Mercury radial in the silver Gloster Gladiator. There is only one way to resolve the issue and that is to return to Shuttleworth and listen to them again.

5

Twelve O'Clock High

The square, squat two-story building is still there. A bunch of slightly bent antennas sprout from the roof and a pipe-railed balcony runs around the outside of the upper deck. If it is a drizzly, low overcast day, which it probably is in this part of Cambridgeshire, you can almost hear the drone of high octane piston engines and expect to see someone run out on that balcony to fire a Very pistol. A few yards away is a B-17G Fortress, machine guns and plexiglas wet with moisture. Further out on the grass verge and blurred by the mist is a twin-engined biplane, a de Havilland Dragon Rapide. It all looks real, and it is. You are at Duxford Airfield, about 60 miles northeast of London and only a short drive from Cambridge or Shuttleworth.

A damp and foggy morning before the Boeing B-17G Flying Fortress coughs into life. A Dragon Rapide, a Beech 18 and a Broussard await their daily rounds.

53

Duxford is not as well known an airfield to Americans as Biggin Hill or Croyden, but it has been around a long time. De Havilland D.H.9s of No. 119 Squadron flew out of there in 1918. They were followed by Snipes and Siskins and Bulldogs and eventually by Spitfires and Typhoons. In 1942 the Yanks came along with their P-51 Mustangs and P-47 Thunderbolts, and, after the shooting was over, the whines from the early Meteors and Javelins replaced the snarls of Merlins and Cyclones. Today, Duxford is the home of the Imperial War Museum's aircraft collection. The Duxford Aviation Society and the Russavia Collection also base their aircraft at Duxford. It is an expanse of tarmac and a dozen hangers that hold more aluminum memories than most any other place you can find. If you are lucky enough to get there on the right half dozen days each year, they will even fly some of them for you.

Outside of the hangers are the larger and newer "spam-cans." The multi-purpose TSR-2 twin-jet tactical fighter (proving that not just Americans can have political fiascos) and one of the Concorde prototypes, both stark white, dominate the ramp. A Hawker Hunter, Handley Page's Victor and Avro's Vulcan—part of the evil looking series of 1950s "V" bombers—an English Electric Canberra and an F-100D Super Sabre from this side of the ocean are samples of the jet types. From further back in time are the propeller-driven machines. The Avro Shackleton MR.3 patrol bomber looks like a Liberator with class, but with a boxer's broken nose due to the rather weird nose turret. A Boeing B-29 Superfortress stands not far from its predecessor, the B-17G Flying Fortress. Some of these aircraft did more than just fly around. The B-29 flew thirty combat missions out of Okinawa with the 307th Bombardment Group during the Korean War while the Canberra carried out raids on Egyptian airfields during the Suez episode in the late 1950s. Several airliners including a Vickers Viscount and a Super VC-10 stand alongside one of those first commercial jet airliners, the star-crossed de Havilland D.H.106 Comet.

Inside the row of hangers, de Havillands are all over the place. The most memorable is, of course, the Mosquito. With his thirty years of experience in wood structures, and knowing that aluminum would be in short supply, Geoffrey de Havilland went back to his 1934 design of the Comet racer and came up with a startling idea. He calculated that he could design a light bomber that could outperform a contemporary fighter and, without the weight of armament, could survive based on speed alone. He was right. The Mosquito was a thorn in Germany's side. It would bomb selected targets in broad daylight, frustrating Messerschmitt pilots who could only pound on their instrument panels as the Mosquito pulled steadily away from them. From mid-1941 to early 1944 the Mosquito was the fastest airplane in the RAF inventory and as such was used for all sorts of special missions. It ran the "ball bearing express," flying through the night carrying precision parts made in Sweden across occupied Norway and the North Sea to England—and occasionally having aboard a huddled passenger who didn't give his name or purpose.

Other Mosquitoes flew high altitude photo-reconnaissance missions searching out Germany's intentions and installations. It was after one of those missions that, down in a little room in a photo-interpretation center, Flying Officer Babington-Smith puzzled over something unusual. A tiny, blurred image had caught the flying officer's eye. It appeared to be that of an airplane, but the proportions didn't seem quite right. It was, in fact, something never seen before. The photograph had been taken by a high-flying Mosquito over an obscure Baltic coastal island called Peenemunde. Flying Officer Babington-Smith had just looked at a picture of a V-1 flying bomb! Alerted, other aircraft would visit Peenemunde carrying more than cameras. Later Mosquitoes would pinpoint bomb the V-1 launching ramps in France and the low countries. Constance Babington-Smith knew her airplanes. An aviatrix and the daughter of a director of the Bank of England, she had written for *The Aeroplane* before the war and later would write definitive histories of aerial photo-intelligence and of British test pilots and experimental aircraft.

Meanwhile, the Mosquito was too much of a high performance and versatile aircraft for the unarmed concept to last for long. Fighter and fighter-bomber variants were armed with all sorts of cannons and rockets. Also equipped with radar, they began to supplant the Beaufighter as a night fighter. With Coastal Command they shot up shipping and E-boats off the coast. The Mosquito's precision at very low level bombing was almost supernatural. Operation Jericho, when Mosquitoes bombed the prison in Amiens with such skill that over 200 captured members of the Maquis escaped through the breached wall,

On its ski-ramp launcher, a V-1 buzz bomb hides under the trees from prying Mosquitoes. Imperial War Museum, Duxford Airdrome, Cambridgeshire.

ruining the day's plans for the local firing squad, has been told many times before. Lesser known was an attack on March 21, 1945 when Mosquitoes of No. 464 Squadron destroyed the Gestapo building in the middle of Copenhagen which contained the files on Danish resistance fighters. The buildings on either side weren't damaged. For sheer vindictiveness, or perhaps stemming from that dry English sense of humor, bombing a parade in Berlin in January 1943 at which Goering was to preside may have been a bit much. Certainly returning that same afternoon to pinpoint another affair at which Goebbels was to speak was. The raids were highly successful, and even if their featured speakers managed to be elsewhere at the precise moment, they were certainly more than annoyed at the Mosquitoes. The trees of England provided the wood for the long-bows that enabled her to win the battle of Agincourt in 1415. In 1940 those same trees provided the wood for another kind of long-bow, one that flew and which had much the same effect in another battle. One can stand and admire the Mosquito at Duxford for a long time.

As the war was ending, de Havilland began looking towards the future. If his propeller-driven machines were among the fastest in the world, so would be his new jets. They are lined up at Duxford—Vampires, Sea Vampires, Venoms, Sea Venoms and Sea Vixens; they all look like P-38 Lightnings with stovepipes. De Havilland stuck with the twin-boom configuration for jet fighters for nearly 20 years.

De Havilland was also looking forward to getting back to developing commercial aircraft and, with the same drive in that arena, he set his team to develop the world's first commercial jet airliner. His research department was performing tests in wind tunnels and in the air on the swept wing and other advanced forms that would be most suitable for the new jet engines. De Havilland had test flown all of his aircraft until his age, the size of his company, and the complexity of the new aircraft took him out of the cockpit. Now his son, Geoffrey de Havilland, Jr., headed the company's flight test unit. On September 27, 1946, while practicing for an assault on the world's speed record with the experimental D.H.108 swept wing, tailless research aircraft, the machine suddenly disintegrated and Geoffrey de Havilland, Jr. was killed. At the time he was travelling faster than any man had travelled before. He was the second of the elder de Havilland's three sons to die in a crash of one of his airplanes.

De Havilland buried himself in his work. His jet fighters were successful and his Comet jet airliner entered service with BOAC in 1952 making Douglas DC-7s and Boeing Stratocruisers look like dinosaurs. But within two years, three Comets crashed under mysterious circumstances. In one of the most intensive investigations ever made, including the deliberate destructive testing of a whole airframe, the cause was pinpointed—metal fatigue at a stress concentration point due to the cycling of loads from fuselage pressurization. The Comet was flying at higher altitudes and doing so more frequently than airplanes ever had before. First it was transonic critical Mach number problems at low altitude in the swept wing D.H.108 that had killed his son. Now pressurization-induced metal fatigue at high altitude had killed another 150 people. The technical problems were solved and the Comet was redesigned as the Comet II, but it was too late. The stigma remained and the Boeing 707 and the Douglas DC-8 were already taking over the commercial skies. The Comet at Duxford is a Comet II.

Sir Geoffrey de Havilland died in 1965 at the age of 83. From the D.H.2 gun bus and the Gipsy Moth to the Mosquito and the Vampire, his aircraft were always setting the standards of performance and probing beyond where anyone else had been. He probably designed more great airplanes than any other one man. He achieved great triumphs— and endured great personal tragedy as the price for them.

Other aircraft abound at Duxford and one of the more unusual is the Saunders Roe S.R.A./1, one of the only jet-powered flying boat fighters ever built. With a shoulder wing, a nose scoop for its twin 3,850-lb thrust Vickers Beryl turbojets, and a vertical fin that looks like it came off a Beech Baron, it must have made one hell of a speedboat. How one would expect it to compete with a conventional jet fighter while lugging around a deep hull, step and all, takes some imagination. It was designed with the latter part of the Pacific War in mind, so I expect someone thought it would only have to face the, by then, obsolete Japanese Zero. It actually performed exceedingly well and was noted for making 500-mph runs on the deck at air shows in 1947 and 1948 until that same anonymous someone figured out that there was no mission for it. The program was cancelled and the only S.R.A./1 in existence sits forlornly at Duxford. Still, buzzing a seaplane fly-in in Maine with it sounds like a great idea.

The collection of aircraft at Duxford goes all the way back to World War I with with examples of the Royal Aircraft Factory's B.E.2c and R.E.8 and a SPAD VII. World War II is represented by the familiar Spitfires and Hurricanes as well as a Corsair, a Bf 109 and a Hawker Tempest. Less familiar is the Fairey Firefly, a two-seat Fleet Air Arm fighter, underpowered as were most of Fairey's machines. A very rare bird from the beginning of World War II is the Westland Whirlwind. With its two underslung engines, it was one of the first of the scream-along-the-telegraph poles, shoot-up-the-road types.

Not all the airplanes are hot fighters. The smaller aircraft are also represented, having been extensively used for liaison and training and for being just plain jacks-of-all-trades. The Austers and Miles and Percivals are from England, while a Beech Traveller—the Staggerwing in mufti— and a Cessna 195 come from the U.S. A French-made Fieseler Storch represents the other side. The English kept to the biplanes, such as the Moths, Parnalls, Avro Tutors and Hawker Tomtits until late in the 1930s and then suddenly switched to the cantilevered low wing

One of the only jet-powered flying boat fighters ever built, the Saunders Roe S.R.A/1 stands behind a Hawker Tempest II.

Ungainly, if not outright ugly, a Royal Aircraft Factory R.E.8 reconnaissance aircraft of World War I.

as on the Miles, Percivals, and the Moth Minor. For some reason, they rarely went to the strut-braced high wing which became almost universal for the smaller light planes in this country. One of the few exceptions is the series of Auster A. O. P.s. A. O. P. stood for Airborne Observation Post and they were ubiquitous for artillery spotting and tactical reconnaissance. If an Auster looks vaguely familiar, there is a reason.

C. G. Taylor, president of the Taylor Aircraft Company, was responsible for the design of the original Cub, but in 1937 the company became Piper and the Taylor Cub became the Piper Cub. Taylor set up a new company, the Taylor-Young Airplane Company and developed a similar small plane called the Taylorcraft Model A. With Piper being a tough competitor in the U. S., Taylor began to push the export market. Soon the airplane was being built under license in Leicester by Taylorcraft Aeroplanes Limited. Further development led to the installation of the English Cirrus Minor engine and the name was changed to Taylorcraft-Auster when a proposal for a light observation machine was presented to the British Air Ministry. That led to a never-ending series of Auster A. O. P.s, while in the U.S. Taylorcraft went out of production in the early 1950s. Under the skin though, the early Auster was a Taylorcraft.

Another, if more unusual, STOL observation aircraft is the Cierva C.30A autogyro. Don Juan de la Cierva invented the practical autogyro in Spain during the 1920s. The rotor in the autogyro is unpowered and while the machine cannot rise or land vertically, it can come fairly close, particularly if it is heading into any kind of a wind. While never used extensively, Cierva's autogyros were built under license in England as the Avro Rota and a number were used by the RAF and based at Duxford and Halton. The unpowered rotor in the autogyro got around many of the problems that plagued the early helicopters until after World War II and after which the helicopter completely displaced the autogyro. Halton Airfield is now somewhere under the concrete of Heathrow.

For those who prefer the security blanket of a second engine, there are at Duxford one of the last of Neville Shute Norway's Airspeed Oxfords, an Avro Anson and a Beech Expeditor, the last being a lend-lease version of the sturdy old Twin-Beech. By the way, if you examine them from the front, you may finally observe that all U. S. engines rotate counterclockwise while English ones always turn clockwise. I assume that is due to the same underlying reason that we drive on opposite sides of the road. Come to think of it, the stripes on English ties go from upper left to lower right while ours go the other way. There must be some deep philosophical significance to all of this. Actually, the Griffon and the Sabre turn counterclockwise and there is not much significance involved other than to point out the curious things that may catch your eye while you look at old airplanes.

One of Neville Shute Norway's Airspeed Oxfords, an early World War II trainer and light transport.

Inside the next hanger, a B-25J Mitchell and a Bristol Blenheim are being restored while hammering sounds emanate from the huge innards of the Short Sunderland's hull behind it; the huge Sunderland is also being rebuilt from the keel up. A Junkers Ju 52/3m trimotor sits there with its corrugated skin looking as if it came off a boxcar. It sits nose to nose with another B-17G Flying Fortress.

Nestled under the wing of the Flying Fortress is a North American P-51D Mustang in just about the same relationship that they had back in 1944. The Mustang started off as a private venture by North American and while the airframe and the wing in particular were highly advanced, the first versions were powered by an Allison engine with rather mediocre results. England considered importing the Mustang to supplement its limited numbers of Spitfires and Hurricanes. They sent over a Rolls-Royce Merlin engine to see if it would fit and thus cut down on the need for spares for a different engine. The marriage of the Merlin to the Mustang was more spectacular than if they had been designed for each other and Packard was given a license to produce the Merlin over here. It was the incredible range and endurance of the Merlin-powered Mustang combined with its speed and firepower that protected the Fortresses and enabled them to penetrate deep into Europe without devastating losses.

Nowadays when anyone can fly in a Boeing 747, a plane twice the Fortress' size and at twice its speed, for just a few hundred dollars, the Fortress looks small and slow. It looks a bit drab and strange with its dull paint, tail wheel and machine guns sticking out of various turrets and hatches. But in 1943 and 1944, 10 men boarded each of them every dawn. Hundreds of B-17 Fortresses would start up from fields like Duxford all over England, form up into formations stretching across

The North American P-51 Mustang, when flying escort, was a "Big Beautiful Doll" to the tired crew of the B-17 Fortress.

the morning sky and fly through hundreds of miles of flak, Bf 109s and Fw 190s in the first real test of massed daylight precision bombing. The strategic results are still argued, but to those ten men in their aluminum can, breathing oxygen through a hose, struggling to maintain formation and trying to keep track of the Mustangs and the Messerschmitts, the argument didn't matter. The only thing that mattered was making it through one more mission in *Galloping Gertie* or *Sweet Sue* or whatever other good-luck and skimpily-clad charm they had carefully painted on the Fortress' nose.

Outside again, a restored old firetruck and an Austin 40 Sedan are parked by that squat tower building. Walking to the parking lot past the other B-17 Fortress and the Rapide, it is still overcast and drizzling; it looks like about 800 and 2. You still expect to hear a droning sound growing from the southeast and see a Very pistol flare arc upwards from the tower.

6

Yo-Ho-Ho and a Bottle of Rum, Six .303s and a 500 Pounder

Well west of London on the low plains of Salisbury and near the town and cathedral that bear that name, stands a circle of giant stone monoliths. The day is grey and the stones exude a strange aura. It is a time for the casting of the runes and of strange Druid rituals which we modern mortals know not of. A speck appears on the horizon, not yet really noticeable but distracting the subconcious. The speck grows rapidly and then it flashes overhead, low between the overcast and the nearly treeless plain. For a few seconds the sound is a deafening roar as if the spirits of Stonehenge have arisen. In an instant it is gone, its swept wings and red-hot tailpipe but a blurred impression. Three thousand years of man's development coincide for that brief instant. In reality, it is but a young and overly enthusiastic pilot from nearby Boscombe Downs or Yeovilton beating up the countryside. And we, certainly, will not be the ones to report his transgressions, for it is Yeovilton that is our destination.

The Royal Navy is known, and not without reason, as the Senior Service, and it has been the backbone of English military strength since before the days of Nelson. That illustrious history is carefully preserved at Greenwich in the form of the huge Naval Museum, a pleasant boat ride east from London. Greenwich was, due to the might of English seapower, essentially the center of the world. Our modern aviation sectional charts are still referenced to Greenwich and it is rather fun to stand astride the zero meridian mark on the floor of the observatory up the hill from the Naval Museum.

While the Royal Navy had its share of ultra-conservative "battleship admirals," it also had a number of forward thinkers who did some of the earliest pioneering on the use of aviation as a part of seapower. That is why we have headed west over the Salisbury plains this trip rather than east to Greenwich. An hour's drive southwest from Stonehenge

A Blackburn Buccaneer strike aircraft stands silent guard at the entrance to the Fleet Air Arm Museum.

on the A303 and a marked turnoff to the south just before Ilchester will find the Royal Naval Air Station at Yeovilton. It is a working air station and one can stand by the fence and watch Harriers and Sea Kings plying their trade. It is also the home of the Fleet Air Arm Museum.

As early as 1912 the Royal Navy was experimenting with flying float-planes off the water and biplanes off crude planked runways built atop the turrets of capital ships. The place of honor at the entry to the museum is held by *Jabberwock,* a Sopwith Baby on plywood floats. The Baby is actually a derivative of the earlier Sopwith Tabloid which was constructed in 1913 as a land-based racing machine. It was later put on floats and with Howard Pixton at the controls it won the 1914 Schneider Trophy race for seaplanes. When World War I started, the Royal Navy saw a need for a small, fast, scouting craft. The Schneider-winning Tabloid with beefed up gear and a Lewis machine gun mounted to fire upwards through an opening in the upper wing (they didn't have interrupter gear yet) became a naval scout, the Baby. Some 400 were manufactured, but ironically most were built under subcontract by Blackburn or Fairey, since by then Sopwith was overextended making Camels.

A number of other biplanes grace the exhibit hall, but strikingly, most are not of World War I vintage but date from World War II. Parsimonious budgets and an antediluvian bureaucracy left the Fleet Air Arm with biplanes long after they were obsolete everywhere else.

The Fairey Swordfish is a good case in point. A three-seat, single-engined biplane, affectionately known as the Stringbag, the Swordfish

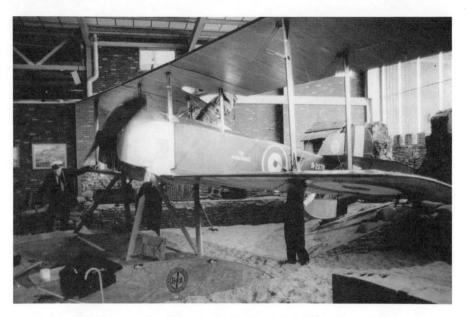

One of the first Naval aircraft, the Sopwith Baby Jabberwock *on floats.*

should have been obsolete by 1935, yet it remained the Royal Navy's primary carrier-borne torpedo bomber well into the early 1940s. Remember that it was during this same period that the U. S. Navy's Douglas Devastator monoplane was massacred by the Japanese at the Midway, being obsolete for attacking against the firepower of modern ships and aircraft. Yet the Swordfish battled on in the Atlantic and the Mediterranean under awful conditions and performed some incredible feats in the bargain.

In November of 1940, in one of the early naval operations of the war, Swordfishes of the Fleet Air Arm made a surprise night attack on the Italian fleet base at Taranto inside the heel of the boot of southern Italy. The damage, in terms of ships sunk and to the psychology of fear instilled in the Italian admirals, was such that the Italian Navy was never again a force to be reckoned with; they were essentially out of the war from that night onwards. This was a year before Pearl Harbor and it was the first major battle by a fleet of aircraft against a fleet of ships and it set the stage for the future of both. Their tactics and the effects of the attack were studied carefully by others. One of the keenest students was Admiral Yamamoto, who shortly afterwards planned the Japanese attack on Pearl Harbor. Yamamoto never sent the Swordfish commander a thank you note for the advice.

Some Swordfish adventures at first appear to be fish stories. Would you believe that three Swordfishes, each with only one torpedo, could sink four ships? The three Swordfishes departed the coast of Egypt on August 20, 1940—1940 was a good year for Swordfishes—after reports had come in of enemy shipping activity to the west. Captain Oliver Patch, flying the lead machine headed well out to sea, then west and then back south again to avoid detection. Skimming over the wave tops, they spotted a German submarine on the surface heading for Bomba Bay on the coast of Cyrenaica, part of what is now Libya. Lieutenant J. W. G. Wellham peeled off and sunk the sub while Patch and Lieutenant N. A. F. Cheeseman pressed on to investigate where the sub might have been heading. At the entrance to Bomba Bay, they spotted another submarine and a depot ship tied up to either side of a destroyer and all in the midst of transferring supplies. The two Swordfishes split up and attacked from both sides simultaneously. One torpedo hit the sub and the other struck the depot ship. Both blew up and they took the destroyer down with them. Four ships for three torpedoes is being remarkably frugal.

The most critical mission taken on by Swordfishes however, occurred the following year. The German battleship *Bismarck,* escorted by the heavy cruiser *Prinz Eugen,* escaped from the Baltic via Norway in May of 1941, sunk the British flagship *Hood* and broke free into the North Atlantic. The *Bismarck* did sustain some damage in the melee and secretly turned toward Brest on the west coast of France. She could be repaired there and no longer having to pass through the narrow Channel or the Shetlands or Faroe passages, could sortie from Brest into the Atlantic. Perhaps accompanied by the battle cruisers *Scharnhorst* and *Gneisenau,* also then in Brest, the *Bismarck* could wreak havoc amongst the Atlantic convoys and strangle Britain. The situation was so desperate that Churchill ordered the Royal Navy to drop everything, even to leaving troop convoys unattended, to find, and at any cost, to sink the *Bismarck.*

Force H, a small task group which included the carrier HMS *Ark Royal,* left Gibralter and steamed northwest; a Catalina flying boat had spotted the *Bismarck* in the Atlantic heading for Brest and safety. On the evening of May 26, 1941 and in appalling weather, a flight of Swordfishes under the command of Lieutenant Commander Eugene Esmonde got off the deck of the *Ark Royal.* The Swordfishes were equipped with new magnetically-fuzed torpedoes. Through breaks in the clouds, Esmonde spotted a ship and dived for the attack, but the new magnetic fuzes were faulty and they exploded on contact with the water when launched. It was a good thing, since the ship they were aiming at was the cruiser HMS *Sheffield* which, unbeknown to the pilots, had steamed ahead to try to harass the *Bismarck.* The skipper of the *Sheffield,* under some understandable stress at the time, was not pleased.

Reloaded with conventional torpedoes, embarrassed at the earlier fiasco, and with that indomitable courage against all odds that it seems the English manage to drag up when all seems lost, the Swordfishes under Esmonde sortied again into the setting sun and deepening storm. Photographs from the *Ark Royal* show the takeoff in a whole gale with the deck pitching over forty feet up and down, conditions where tie-down much less takeoff would be harrowing. In the midst of the storm and under a 900-foot ceiling, these antiquated 120-mph biplanes found the king of the modern German Navy, one of the most powerful and well-gunned ships afloat—and attacked. The foul weather was such that the fifteen aircraft had lost formation in the clouds, so no coordinated attack was possible. Forming up in random twos and threes, sometimes alone, and in the face of scores of machine guns and automatic cannons, they held steady at 90 feet and 90 knots; at 900 yards each dropped its one torpedo. Returning to the *Ark Royal,* three of the Swordfishes were so badly smashed up by what could be dubiously called a landing under those conditions that they just swept the pieces over the side. Another Swordfish made it back with 127 separate holes in her; all in the three man crew were wounded. The few torpedoes that may have hit the *Bismarck* appeared to have had no effect on the monster; an inconvenience at most.

That wasn't the case, however. One of the torpedoes had nicked the *Bismarck's* stern and the next morning she was found steaming slowly in circles, her rudder jammed hard over. This allowed just enough time for the nearly out of fuel battleship *King George V,* a few smaller ships, and the dotty old battleship HMS *Rodney* to reach the scene. The *Rodney* was a barely post-World War I retread just out of mothballs (so was her pulled-out-of-retirement Captain, Frederick Dalrymple-Hamilton). She was enroute to Canada for overhaul. The *Rodney* was considered barely capable of making an Atlantic crossing without breakdown, much less do any fighting. Regardless, when Churchill gave his "all ships" command, she had left her convoy to help find the *Bismarck.* Under radio silence even the Royal Navy had lost track of the *Rodney* until she showed up at just the right time and place. Her superannuated Captain had "outpsyched" the Germans as to the *Bismarck's* probable route. The antiquated *Rodney* had steamed alone for thirty-six hours at flank speed—her engineers holding down her boiler's safety valves— and added her rusty but badly needed old 16-inch guns to the salvoes that would destroy the *Bismarck*— a job that the valiant sorties of the Stringbags had made possible.

A year later, on the morning of February 11, 1942, Lieutenant Commander Esmonde received an urgent call to lead another attack. Reconnaissance had spotted the battle cruisers *Scharnhorst* and *Gneisenau* trying to slip through the Channel from Brest back to Germany. The six antiquated old biplanes of Esmonde's flight went out to attack the remaining bulk of the German Navy; the two battle cruisers, the heavy cruiser *Prince Eugen,* six destroyers and thirty-four E-boats. The Luftwaffe had more than one hundred fighters overhead and the dozen Spitfires that could get to the scene to fly cover couldn't stop them all. The attack was a heroic but glorious failure. Some of the Swordfishes managed to close with the ships through a wall of flak, but every one

Painted in Lt. Cdr. Eugene Esmonde's colors, the indomitable "Stringbag," the Fairey Swordfish.

of the Stringbags in the flight were shot down. The German ships made it back to Germany. It didn't do them much good in the long run; they were bottled up and sunk in harbor later in the war.

Lieutenant Commander Esmonde had spent the previous afternoon, February 10, 1942, at Buckingham Palace. He had been awarded the Distinguished Service Order from King George V for having led the *Ark Royal's* Swordfishes in the attack on the *Bismarck* the prior year. For the attack on the *Scharnhorst*, Esmonde was to receive another medal from King George V—a posthumous Victoria Cross. It is no wonder that the Swordfish, dilapidated old Stringbag that she was, is revered by all Englishmen who sail and who fly. The Swordfish on display at the Fleet Air Arm Museum is painted in the markings of the late Lieutenant Commander Eugene Esmonde's machine.

Another World War II biplane at the museum is the equally-beloved Supermarine Walrus. As crusty as its name, the single-engined pusher amphibious flying boat, while armed with depth charges and a machine gun or two, really made its name as a rescue airplane. Its forte was landing in atrocious conditions and picking up downed pilots from the ditched landplane fighters that were buzzing over the sea during the early days of the war. The rather absurd looking Walrus was referred to as the "air arm of the Salvation Navy." This particular example has an equivalently absurd background. At one point in its career, Walrus N-18 was provided to the Irish Air Corps. On its delivery flight, N-18 got separated from its two wing-mates in bad weather and couldn't make it across the Irish Sea. It put down in the water and eventually taxied the rest of the way across. In 1942, N-18 recrossed the Irish Sea to Cornwall. This time it made it by air all the way, but with its crew unaware that the pilot was under house arrest for some now-forgotten indiscretion and they were flying in a stolen airplane.

There are two machines that are not represented at the museum but which should be, the Sopwith Triplane and the Gloster Gladiator. Early in World War I, the then Royal Naval Air Service, as well as the Royal Flying Corps, had ordered French SPADs. The RFC had also ordered some of the revolutionary new Triplanes from Sopwith, but later decided that they had better standardize. As the first Triplanes were being delivered in February 1917, the RFC traded them to the RNAS for their order of SPADs. As the war on the western front got desperate, a contingent from the RNAS was sent to assist.

The "Black Flight" became famous. Their Sopwith Triplanes were not actually painted black, just the usual dark brown-green with a black cowl, but they were named *Black Maria, Black Prince, Black Roger, Black Death* and *Black Sheep.* Flown by Canadians in the Royal Naval Air Service, the "Black Flight" of Naval Ten accounted for eighty-seven German aircraft in the months of May, June and July of 1917. The Sopwith Triplane totally outclassed the Albatros D.IIIs then in service with the Germans, but by November 1917, already obsolete, the last Triplane was retired to be replaced by the Camel. The Sopwith Triplane developed a famous reputation and had a large effect, both on the design of aircraft (it inspired the Fokker triplane) as well as on the morale of the British ground troops. Yet only 150 Sopwith Triplanes were ever built and their total service life was less than 12 months—and we talk of the pace of modern technology.

The only authentic Sopwith Triplane known to exist is at the RAF Museum at Hendon, which is really unfair. Perhaps they would be willing to trade back again. Actually, there may be one other. A Sopwith Triplane with the number N5486 was used in Russia in 1917 and there are photographs extant of it flying on skis. Rumors are that N5486 still exists at the Russian Air Force's Red Banner Academy at Monino. Whether they or the RAF are more likely to trade is probably moot.

The Gladiator, or rather the Sea Gladiator—identical to the Gloster Gladiator except for the hook and some other minor changes—does spend most of its time at Yeovilton but it is actually based at Shuttleworth up at Old Warden. It was the mainstay of the English carrier forces during the late 1930s. For many of the exploits of the early part of the war, little actually remains, but they are represented by exceptionally well done paintings, photographs, models and dioramas. Such is the case here; particularly of note being the oft-told story of the defense of the little island of Malta. Tiny and ill-prepared, its strategic location in the middle of the Mediterranean was important to both sides. After the initial battles, the sole air defense of the island of Malta consisted of three Gladiators, aptly named *Faith, Hope* and *Charity*; three clapped-out old biplanes against the might of the Italian and German Air Forces. Yet with literally string and baling wire they held out for months until reinforcing Hurricanes arrived. *Faith,* the only one to survive, still exists, albeit only as a fuselage, in the National War Museum at Valletta, Malta.

The Supermarine Seafire, the carrier version of the Spitfire, is represented at the Fleet Air Arm Museum, as is the later Hawker Sea Fury with its monsterous five-bladed propeller. Of somewhat earlier vintage is a Fairey Fulmar, a two-seat fighter looking like, but with somewhat better performance than, the Fairey Battle. Fortunately, the Fulmar never got into too many scraps and was thus saved the ignominious reputation that the Battle got; the Fulmar ended up being mostly used for patrol work.

There are more Grumman aircraft at Yeovilton than at any one place outside the U.S. A deep blue Martlet is there and for those not familiar with English nomenclature, that is a lend-lease Grumman F4F Wildcat. Its successor, an F6F Hellcat fighter as well as a TBF Avenger torpedo bomber (a far cry from the Swordfish) are also included. Representing the competition is a Vought Corsair. It is not generally recognized, but during the middle and latter part of World War II some forty percent of the Fleet Air Arm's aircraft were of U.S. manufacture. They were used principally for convoy escort, protecting the life-blood

It takes a massive propeller to absorb the 2550 hp from the Bristol Centaurus in the Hawker Sea Fury.

of the British Isles. For example, in 1943 the Martlet was the most numerous fighter in the Fleet Air Arm, outnumbering the Seafire 117 to 98.

A number of the aircraft at the museum saw actual combat. The Grumman Martlet, AL246, had been purchased by France, but while being shipped over, the fall of Dunkirk caused it to be diverted to the Fleet Air Arm. Along with AL259, it is believed to be the first American-made aircraft with the FAA to down an enemy aircraft. They are given joint credit for shooting down a Junkers Ju 88 which was attempting to bomb fleet installations at Scapa Flow in the Orkneys on December 25, 1940. The Douglas Skyraider saw action at Suez in the 1950s and the Hawker Sea Fury was one of the few piston-engined fighters to ever shoot down a jet; WJ231 downed a MiG-15 while with 802 Squadron during the Korean War.

The early part of the post-war years are represented by a Westland Wyvern and a Fairey Firefly, the last of the propeller-driven carrier machines; the de Havilland Sea Vampire, the first jet to operate off a carrier, provides the transition to the jet age. The British jet fighters of the 1950s were some of the sleekest aircraft ever built. The Supermarine Attacker F.1, even with its conventional tailwheel, is a most aesthetic machine as is the Blackburn Buccaneer of some years later and which now graces the front gate of the museum. The Fleet Air Arm may be the junior part of the Senior Service, but in its brief fifty or so years it has certainly borne up to that Navy's traditions.

World War I in full fury, a gaggle of Sopwith, Fokker, Albatros and SPAD biplanes with some triplanes on hand as well.

7

The Royal Fortunes

Drive along the Scottish moors, sit on the crumbling walls of Urquart Castle on the shore of Loch Ness and look for a glimpse of the monster, or perhaps have lunch at the Inn of the Seven Heads; the ruined castle at Raven's Roost nearby tells the rest of that story. Perhaps one doesn't think of aviation connected with a country such as Scotland, but one should.

By the way, it took a while, but we think we now have the terms straight. Britain is the island, of which the English are the southerners, the Welsh the westerners, and the Scots the northerners. Great Britain is the political entity that covers the three regions, namely England, Wales and Scotland, (albeit with historical reluctance on the part of some inhabitants of the latter two). The United Kingdom adds Northern Ireland (albeit with even more reluctance from some of them). The British Isles adds the Republic of Ireland, but only geographically. We provide this diversion to preclude while in Scotland the accidental use of the term English when one really means British; it could dramatically reduce the temperature, and hence the consumption of beverages during a discussion of aviation.

Scotland has its own history of aviation not well known to Americans. One of the first true scientific experimenters into flight was Percy Pilcher. Pilcher was a contemporary of Lilienthal and Octave Chanute and during 1895 and 1896 started a series of gliding flight experiments; his first glider was named "The Bat." He visited Lilienthal in Germany twice and after Lilienthal's death continued with experiments into the problems of control. Pilcher was an engineer and, like Lilienthal, his experiments were scientific and stepwise. His fourth and most successful glider was named "The Hawk" and in 1896 he was making flights of over 200 yards. The Australian, Lawrence Hargrave, pioneered in controlled kite experiments and in 1899 visited Britain. He gave a lecture on his results at a meeting at which Pilcher presided. Pilcher started constructing a new glider incorporating some of Hargrave's ideas and was planning to add a power plant to it after initial gliding tests. Before he could complete it, on October 2, 1899, Pilcher was killed during a practice flight in his old Hawk. If not for Hargrave's isolation in Australia and Pilcher's untimely death, the development of early aviation, and the United Kingdom's role in it, could have been quite different.

Pilcher's Hawk represents one of the first aviation acquisitions by a museum. In 1909, it was obtained by the Royal Scottish Museum and has been exhibited there at Chambers Street in downtown Edinburgh ever since. Obtained the same year was a large scale model of a Wright Model A Flyer from its builder, T. W. K. Clarke and Co. of Surrey. Between the wars more aeronautical equipment was gathered and in 1971, with the gift of a Spitfire and three Royal Navy jets, something had to be done, and that is when facilities at East Fortune were obtained.

East Fortune is an airbase. Not well known to most Americans, it first became operational in 1915 so it ranks along with College Park and Le Bourget as a pioneer airport, although it officially closed as an active airfield in 1961. During that half-century it saw much of the development of Scottish and British aviation. The present East Fortune facility, which opened in 1975, is an out-station of the Royal Scottish Museum. It is, however, only open during the summer months and selected holidays during the rest of the year, so plan accordingly.

Take a pleasant half hour drive east of Edinburgh out the A1 and turn left at the signpost onto the B1347 to get to the museum. You will be driving along the south side of the Firth of Forth, which of course is why East Fortune was chosen in 1915 as an airbase. While Scotland seems remote from Europe on a Mercator's projection, on a globe one can see its strategic control over the North Sea and the only sea lanes

One of the Royal Navy's Hawker Sea Hawk fighters.

out of northern Europe besides the narrow English Channel. That is why the main base of the Royal Navy has been away up at Scapa Flow in the Orkneys and why it and the Firth of Forth have been so important to British seapower. East Fortune was designed to protect Edinburgh and the Firth from German airships that would probably be coming from the southeast. The first defense consisted of the noble efforts of two Sopwith Scouts and a Henri Farman. The latter was barely flyable in the cold, wet and fierce winds of the area. If you think they are bad, try landing today up at Kirkwall in the Orkneys in a modern light twin and you will understand why the Scots developed the wool sweater and Scotch whiskey.

By 1916, the Farman and the first Scouts had been wrecked, but a group of B.E.2c's had arrived and things built up from there. During the war years, East Fortune played host to Bristol Scout Ds and Beardmore (Sopwith licensed) Pups, Nieuport 12s and 24s, and Sopwith Camels and 1 1/2-Strutters. In a more permanent contribution to aviation, many of the first fleet trials in the early use of aircraft in conjunction with ships and early "aircraft carrier" experiments were done out of East Fortune. "Carriers" is placed in quotes, since some of these experiments dealt with things like Sopwith Pups taking off from wooden ramps built atop the gun turrets of cruisers and battleships. Just what the recoil of those eight and fourteen-inch guns would have done to an airframe's rigging can be imagined. Yet Sopwith 1 1/2-Strutters based at East Fortune were operated off the battleships *Bellerophon* and *Warspite* and battle cruisers *Courageous* and *Glorious,* some unsung heroes at the controls. Early air-dropped torpedo trials were also performed there using Sopwith Cuckoos and other such beasts and the museum has photos and artifacts from those experiments.

Much of the World War I activity at East Fortune, however, was with lighter-than-air ships, it being a strategic site for coastal patrol in both non-rigid airships as well as the early rigid machines. The first operations were with the 200-foot long Coastal (C) class machines, while later the 262-foot North Sea (NS) class airships were added. The stories of those patrols during 1917 and 1918, contained in the museum's literature and materials, are absolutely hair-raising. Those gas bags had suspended gondolas mounting a machine gun or two, were filled with hydrogen (slightly inflammable as the *Hindenberg* later learned), and powered by not very reliable petrol engines (the couplings to the propellers were fond of breaking, occasionally allowing the prop to slice up the gas bag's skin). Even more absurd were the Submarine Scout Zero (SSZ) class airships. Those had an envelope only 145-feet long and were more or less powered and controlled from a B.E.2c or Maurice Farman aeroplane fuselage with wings and tail removed and suspended beneath the hull by various and sundry cables and wires. The SSZ airships actually stood anti-sub patrols. The C and NS machines would go out from East Fortune with six and ten-man crews for 24-hour patrols over the inhospitable North Sea to protect convoys or act as eyes for the British Fleet. While a far cry from the Goodyear machines of World War II, by late 1918 as many as six C or NS airships would be active out of East Fortune simultaneously. Not all returned.

By the end of World War I, East Fortune was the equivalent of our later Lakehurst, New Jersey, as a premier airship base. With the return of peace, many minds turned to the problem and adventure of trying to link the two hemispheres by air. East Fortune became the starting point for one of the most incredible, yet mostly forgotten, pioneering flights: the round trip crossing of the Atlantic by the rigid airship R 34.

It was in December of 1918 that the British Admiralty proposed such a flight to examine the potential of airships for commercial transatlantic use. If the next several months had not been used up in bureaucratic wrangling between different parts of the government as well as several private companies, including the Cunard Steamship Line, the R 34 might have been the first to fly the Atlantic. As it was, by the time the problems were resolved, the U. S. Navy's NC-4 had hopped its way across and Alcock and Brown completed their non-stop flight just three weeks before the R 34 was ready.

The R 34 departed East Fortune at 2 A.M. on July 2, 1919 with 8 officers and 22 men (plus 2 carrier pigeons and 2 stowaways—a cat

The airship R 34 left East Fortune on the morning of July 2, 1919 for the first round-trip crossing of the Atlantic.

which belonged to the base and a crew member who had earlier been bounced to make room for an American observer). It also carried 4,900 gallons of petrol, 230 gallons of oil, 3 tons of water ballast and about 1,950,000 cubic feet of hydrogen! It was overcast and raining when the airship—643-feet long and nicknamed "Tiny" by her crew—cruised up the Firth of Forth at all of 66 mph. North of Glasgow violent turbulence was encountered and the ship barely cleared the Scottish hills. The ship ran for hours through the fog and rain. Whenever it took a nose-up or down attitude, fuel began to leak out of tank vents and the smell of petrol pervaded the ship. In the afternoon of the next day the water jacket of the starboard wing engine sprang a leak. It was repaired by using the crew's ration of chewing gum, aboard as a substitute for smoking.

By the morning of July 4th, the R 34 approached Newfoundland, but only 2,200 gallons of fuel remained. A radio message saying that they might not make it all the way was misinterpreted as being definite. Major Fuller, who had arrived earlier by ship to direct the ad hoc American ground crew, drove frantically from New York up to Boston where it was thought that the R 34 might try to land. All through July 5th, the R 34 crept over the Nova Scotian pine forests and down through Maine, usually only 500 feet or so above ground, groping her way through more fog and rain. In the afternoon, violent winds were encountered, but after getting through this, "Tiny's" commander, Major G. H. Scott would not give up. He radioed that they would still try to reach their goal, Mineola Field, Long Island. Major Fuller, driving furiously back down the Boston Post Road, could not reach Long Island in time, and there was no one else at Mineola with experience in handling airships to coordinate the American ground crew. This was solved by Major J. M. Pritchard, another officer on board, parachuting out of the R 34 onto Mineola Field and directing the ground crew in grabbing the cables and walking the R 34 to her mooring. While still struggling out of the parachute's harness, a reporter had run up and asked Pritchard an inane question regarding his first reaction to the U.S. His response was, "It's hard!" Major Pritchard has the honor of being the first man to arrive in the U.S. by air from across the Atlantic, no matter how dubious and slightly insane the method of arrival. The R 34 had cut it a wee bit close; she was found to have only 140 of her original 4,900 gallons of fuel remaining.

The ship was reprovisioned and refueled while the crew was wined and dined in New York. Departure was not planned to occur for a few more days, but on the afternoon of July 9th a storm was approaching New York and the tie-down system was at best rudimentary. With frantic last minute preparations, the R 34 managed to get away by 11 P.M. just before the storm arrived—with mascot cat "Wopsie," but minus stowaway Ballantyne (who returned by sea with the advance party) and one of the two carrier pigeons. The latter were to be used for emergency communications, but one had escaped in New York. For you animal lovers it was picked up two days later, exhausted but well, 800 miles out in the Atlantic by the SS *West Kyska*.

Despite more storms, rain and headwinds, unusual going eastbound, at 6:20 A.M. on the morning of July 13th they descended towards the airbase at Pulham, Lincolnshire. There may have been some premonition by a perverse ballast handler that the R 34 and its crew would never receive the permanent recognition that they deserved. As their descent was braked, the water ballast was dumped on top of the welcoming marching band as it was striking up to play "See the Conquering Hero Comes." Despite its somewhat damp and inauspicious arrival, the R 34's achievement was magnificent. In an utterly primitive craft, they had made a round trip over the North Atlantic in a dozen incredible days in 1919.

In addition to the airship memories, the museum at East Fortune has some 30-odd aircraft as well as considerable memorabilia to commemorate the flying from this area. A number of de Havillands represent the marque. The D.H.80A Puss Moth has quite a record of it's own. In 1930 it was flown to Australia, taking only four weeks and four days for the journey. The landing gear legs on a Puss Moth or a Hornet Moth are worth a look. Both those aircraft had relatively low drag for the era and since the practical flap had not yet been developed, their flat approach made landing on the typically short fields of the day rather tricky. A lever in the cockpit could rotate the streamlined landing gear strut cover broadside as a bizarre drag-brake to steepen the approach; it beats opening the door.

Both a D.H.84 Dragon I and a D.H.89A Dragon Rapide are in the museum. Very similar twin-engined biplanes, the latter held ten passengers to the former's six. A de Havilland D.H.82A Tiger Moth completes the prewar fraction while a D.H.104 Dove shows what the postwar replacement for the Dragon Rapide looked like. After running out of propellers (and two-digit numbers) a D.H.112 Sea Venom and a D.H.115 Sea Vampire represent the jet-engined contingent. The Sea Vampire was the first jet aircraft in the world to land and take off from a carrier—December 3, 1945. If you look at it carefully, you may notice that for all its streamlined, twin-boomed looks, the fuselage pod is still made from a plywood shell—the Mosquito's legacy. Still, the Vampire must be one of the only jet fighters that went operational with a wooden structure. A D.H.106 Comet 4C represents the largest jet there. Used for charter work after being released from RAF Transport Command, the poor Comet, while an excellent airplane, could not recover from the reputation it received after the early crashes of the Comet I.

Several one-of-a-kinds are at the museum. A General Aircraft GAL 42 Cygnet is one of only eleven that were built and this is the sole surviving example. It is a two-seat monoplane trainer. Unusual for 1936

Ill-fortune plagued the de Havilland D.H.106 Comet airliners.

was the tricycle gear; they were used to train RAF crews who were
to fly lend-lease Douglas Boston bombers which also had that rather
strange configuration for the times—a wheel at the front instead of at
the back where everyone knows the third wheel should be. Another
one-of-a-kind is a Spartan Cruiser III (no relation to the Spartan aircraft made in the U.S.), which was a small, low-wing, trimotor
monoplane transport of 1935. It was a contemporary and competitor
of the Dragon series from de Havilland, but with considerably better
performance. Unfortunately, only the forward fuselage section is on
display, having been salvaged from the Hill of Stake where it pranged
in on January 4, 1938, the rest of the machine having been too ravaged
by time and the hill to be restored.

One of those many midget Mignet Pou du Ciel, Flying Fleas, is also
on display. Almost always underpowered (the example here was originally powered by an Austin Seven automobile engine—which could
barely power an Austin Seven) and marginally controllable, the Mignet probably killed more pilots per flying hour than any other aircraft
barring the Me 163 Komet (of which there is also an example at the
museum). On a much more pleasant and aeronautically sound footing
are the English Electric Lightning—a Mach 2 machine with that unusual
over-and-under engine configuration—and a Hawker Sea Hawk carrier
jet fighter. Production of the Fieseler Fi 156 Storch, that stilt-legged
STOL liason plane used by the Germans in World War II, was trans-
ferred to Morane-Saulnier in France during the occupation, which is
why the French used them during the later 1940s and 1950s. The aircraft here has a bit of a history. It served with L'Armée de l'Air in French
Indo-China and was at Dien Bien Phu prior to the debacle there. How

The English Electric Lightning was the first British Mach-2 fighter.

it got out and back to Europe and thence to Scotland is not well documented.

The field at East Fortune is quiet now. The crackle of the rotary engines of the Sopwiths and the whining snarls from the Bristol Beaufighters are not heard, nor is there a shadow from an overhead airship. It is a small museum there, but it contains those memories.

While in the vicinity, drive up to the Strathallan Air Museum. The Strathallan is a private museum about an hour and a half north of Edinburgh. Take the M9 northwest and you can stop for a respite at Stirling Castle (you will also pass some good small woolen mill outlets on the way). Continue up the A9 to Auchterarder and cut off to the north on the small road just out of town.

It is likely to be raining, so check in advance to be sure they are open. If not, the rather active parachute club in the next hanger will direct you to the nearest pub to warm up. Strathallan has a number of aircraft that are still in flying condition, including one of the few Avro Lancaster bombers remaining. It is one thing to see a Lancaster in a museum, but outdoors on a grass field, much less in the air, it is something else again. It stands higher than a B-17 and is much more massive.

A rare British Aircraft Swallow, a low-wing training monoplane, and a Miles Magister trainer are also both in flying condition. The collection contains several very rare aircraft; some of the few Fairey Swordfishes, Bristol Bolingbrokes, and Fairey Battles in existence dwell here. A number of de Havilland jets and a Hawker Hurricane and Sea Hawk also grace the field. While an even smaller collection than at East Fortune, it is well worth visiting and an enthusiast's stop on a tour through Scotland. You can return to Edinburgh by heading east on the A823 through the wild hills of Glen Eagles and then down the M90 and over the Firth of Forth Bridge. And while driving back, thoughts of those aircraft and flights will compete with thoughts of a hot drink and a warm bed, much as they must have to the pilots of those machines so long ago.

An Avro Shackleton sits in the grass behind one of the remaining de Havilland Comet airliners.

8

Le Prieuré de Saint-Martin-des-Champs

If one asks which aircraft's flight most impacted the recognition of the potential of the airplane, then the Wright Flyer or Lindbergh's *Spirit of St. Louis* would certainly top the list. But while the Wrights showed that flying was possible, they were closemouthed and it wasn't until 1908 that recognition dawned on the world outside the small circle of early flyers. Even then there was great skepticism—witness their attempts to sell a Flyer to the army. And while Lindbergh caught the imagination of the world, his flight was really just one, if the most emotionally charged one, in a series of continually growing long distance adventures. Demonstrably, it was Blériot's 1909 crossing of the English Channel. That was the flight that took the airplane out of the class of amazing toy and into the realm of world-changer.

Previous flights, when they actually made it off the ground, usually went around in a circle. If they went from A to B, well B wasn't very far from A and half the time the plane paused en route for various reasons of temperment. Blériot's flight was quite different. Perceptive individuals saw well beyond the ballyhoo and recognized that flight for what it portended. It meant that A and B could be tolerably far apart and that mountains and bodies of water, and yes, political boundaries might never mean the same thing again. The ever-astute H. G. Wells observed ". . . in spite of our fleet this is no longer, from the military point of view, an inaccessible island." Thirty years later, at the very same location as Blériot's flight, that was exactly the point at issue.

So sneak away from your tour guide at Notre Dame and take a ten minute walk north. A few blocks past the bizarre modern art center (with it's external structure that should have been banned from so beautiful a city as Paris), stop in front of No. 27 Rue Saint Martin. It is the Conservatoire National Des Arts et Métiers; the science students scurrying around will point out the doorway at the back of the courtyard which is the entrance to the Musée National Des Techniques. The rooms are dark with high ceilings, almost like a cathedral; and in a way it is—a

Number 27 Rue Saint Martin, the *Musée National Des Techniques.*

cathedral to man's quest to understand and remodel his world. The buildings have been been around since the late 1700s. Inside of them steam vehicles, ancient brass telescopes and old clockworks mark the inevitable advance of technology. Dimly lit and dusty, hanging from the ceiling, is the original Blériot XI *la première traversée de la Manche.*

The Blériot XI's lines are familiar from the many sketches and photos that one has seen, yet up close it is a curious mixture of frailty and squat strength much like the man who flew it across the Channel. He nearly didn't make it, in several respects. At the time, Louis Blériot was a manufacturer of acetylene lamps for the early horseless carriages, a business which the advent of the electrical generator was about to place in the same category as making buggy whips. That didn't matter much because, in any event, he was paying little attention to the business. He had devoted everything to flying, but so far he had not the reputation, and certainly not the finances, of the Voisins, Deperdussin, Levavasseur, or the Farmans. Blériot knew his latest design would be successful, but he was just about broke. He had also broken more bones in flying accidents than just about anyone else then still alive. And Hubert Latham with one of Leon Levavasseur's Antoinettes was way ahead in preparations to win the Daily Mail's 1,000-pound prize. Latham had tried once already, but had landed in the drink halfway across and was now awaiting a replacement Antoinette. Blériot hadn't yet paid the

La première traversée de la Manche—the original Blériot XI in which Louis Blériot crossed the English Channel.

bill for the 3-cylinder, 25-hp Anzani engine that was already installed on his plane and he was being hounded for payment.

Then a strange event took place. Early in July, his wife was visiting friends in Paris and saved an overenthusiastic child from falling off the edge of the apartment's high balcony. The next day the boy's father, a wealthy Haitian planter named Laraque, stopped by to express his thanks to Madamme Blériot. Laraque mentioned his admiration for her husband's exploits in the air and of his own interest from afar in aviation. When Laraque heard of Blériot's dilemma, he wrote out a check for 25,000 francs on the spot—without collateral—to stake Blériot for his attempt and prevent repossession of the Anzani.

By July 24th both Latham (for his second try) and Blériot were ready. The weather had been bad for several days, but in the middle of the night the wind began to abate. There are two stories as to what happened next. One goes that Alfred Leblanc, an ex-balloonist and friend of Blériot's couldn't sleep and when the wind began to drop at about 2:30 in the morning, he woke Blériot, urging him to start right away. The other claims that it was Blériot who couldn't sleep, being in some pain from a burned foot caused by a minor incident with an exhaust pipe some days earlier. Tired of tossing and turning, Blériot went out at about 2 A.M. and drove around in a friend's motorcar to relax. As the wind dropped he drove straight to the field to get moving.

Regardless, at 4:35 A.M. on July 25, 1909, just as dawn was breaking, Blériot was off. Poor Levavasseur. Poor Latham! Levavasseur was to awaken Latham if the weather broke, but Levavasseur had had little sleep for several nights what with all the frantic preparation on the replacement Antoinette. He had already been up twice to check the

82

then still miserable weather and had finally dozed off again. Latham and Levavasseur both awoke with despair to the sound of Blériot's Anzani heading away.

Blériot, however, did not have an easy time of it. Ten minutes after takeoff he lost sight of land in the morning haze and outdistanced the French destroyer stationed in the Channel to assist the pioneers. Lost and with no instruments, he tried to climb while he maintained what he thought was about the right direction. The Anzani began to overheat. Then he ran into rain for a time which made the visibility even worse. Actually, most modern observers believe that was the best thing that could have happened. The early Anzani was not a very well developed engine, constantly prone to overheating, and it is likely that the ad hoc evaporative cooling from the rain kept it running those few extra minutes. Blériot saw the cliffs of Dover and struck land quite far to the northeast of his plan. He turned left along the cliffs and thirty-seven minutes after departure he landed in a field just outside the town of Dover. The world would not again be the same.

From out of the crowd and festivities at the landing site stepped some English customs officials. After vigorous discussion, they rose to the occasion and provided a note to Blériot. The note certified that they had ''. . .examined Louis Blériot, master of the vessel *Monoplane,* lately arrived from Calais and that it appears. . .that there has not been on board during the voyage any infectous disease demanding detention of the vessel and that she is free to proceed.'' Not bad for on-the-spot improvisation; the formalities must be observed. Leblanc and Latham each went on to make their own records. Leblanc set the world's speed record at 67.9 mph in 1910. A few months earlier, Latham had set an absolute altitude record for aircraft—all of 508 feet. Barring those lucky exceptions who lived to a ripe old age, Hubert Latham was one of the few of the early flyers who did not die in the crash of his flying machine; he was a better pilot than he was a marksman. Latham was killed in 1912 while on safari in French Equatorial Africa. He was clobbered by a wounded and rather irate Cape Buffalo before he could get in a second shot.

There are two other aircraft at the museum. One is Robert Esnault-Pelterie's R.E.P. monoplane of 1908. It was far advanced for its day having a welded steel-tube fuselage covered in now-dulled red muslin, which led to a fair degree of streamlining. The single main wheel with outrigger wheels at the wingtips was a novel touch. Much more important, it was Esnault-Pelterie with his R.E.P. who pioneered a new control concept; a stick to operate both the ailerons and elevators with a pivoting foot bar for the rudder, rather than the various and sundry separate wheels, levers and sliding seats used until then. From that concept evolved the control system in universal use today.

The other aircraft is Louis Bréguet's 1911 Avion. It appears to be a relatively standard biplane, but remember that this was 1911, not 1916.

The technology changed a great deal during that period. The 1911 Bréguet represents the beginning of the change from the experiments of the pioneers to the "practical" aircraft of World War I. In September of 1911, Louis Bréguet flew the craft across Morocco from Casablanca to Fez in 2 hours and 50 minutes. The airplane was becoming practical.

The Musée National Des Techniques has only three airplanes in its collection. They are three very special airplanes.

Robert Esnault-Pelterie's 1907 monoplane, the R.E.P. A.

One of the first military production airplanes, Louis Bréguet's 1911 Avion.

9

City of Lights, Sky of Stars

Paris is a city for contemplation, for sitting quietly and observing the world with all its variations and idiosyncrasies. On a bright spring day, as a good *boulevardier*, one should sit at a small table at an outdoor cafe near the Eiffel Tower, sip Pernod and watch life, particularly in the form of pretty girls, stroll by. The contrail of a jet heading out from Charles de Gaulle or Orly provides a different train of thought, so do not dally too long on the banks of the Seine.

Take the suburban S.N.C.F. train from the nearby station at L'Invalides to Meudon-Val-Fleury, about a half hour west of the city. As you leave the small station at the sleepy town, cross the square, sit down at an outdoor table at the little cafe and there sip Pernod. You see, there will likely be no one else around—certainly no pretty girls—and definitely no signs to a museum. After the Pernod and ordering a pack of Galois, there is a chance that you may obtain directions. They are to cross back over the square, but to the right of the station, walk up the hill on the Rue Louvois and bear left on Rue Roudier. Jog left and then right onto Rue D'Alembert through a quiet residential area and after a pleasant 15-minute stroll, reach what appears to be a park. The fence and the silent, somber guard indicate that this is not a park. The sign by the Entrée de l'O.N.E.R.A., roughly translated, indicates that if you step off the white path, you will be arrested as a spy. Meudon has been the center of aeronautical research for the French Government for decades. Following the path takes you through beautiful woods. Behind the trees are the shapes and sounds of wind tunnels and laboratories mixed with those of birds and insects who must wonder at who are we to dare to enter their God-given realm of the sky. At the end of the path are the artifacts of those who did dare; the original Musée de l'Air.

At the turn of the century, the French had the largest and most active group of experimenters in the world trying to achieve flight. Ader and

85

his steam contraptions, Santos-Dumont and his hybrid balloons with wings and a dozen others were trying hard but couldn't hit that combination of sufficient power to weight and recognition of the need for control that would set man free from the surface of the earth. That took the brilliance and inspiration of the Wright brothers, but from 1903 to 1907 only vague and not-to-be-believed rumors of their flights reached Paris. Then in 1908 Wilbur Wright showed up with a Wright Flyer to seek sales in Europe, while Orville remained back in the states still trying to convince the Army that the airplane was not a hoax and likely better than a horse for reconnaissance. Initially at Hunaudieres and then at Auvours, Wilbur went cruising around for a half hour at a time while all the rest of the world's achievements to that point could be added together and still be counted in seconds. Alberto Santos-Dumont summed it all up; "We are like children." Far from being jealous, most French aviators treated Wilbur as a hero, for now they were no longer uncertain; they knew flight was possible. French aviation exploded at an incredible rate since they had the base of numbers and experience, and now a clue as to the necessary techniques—and enthusiasm without bounds. Within three years, France had more aviators and more successful aircraft than probably the rest of the world put together. That history is at Meudon.

At the place of honor inside the entry, hangs Ader's "Avion III." Twin, four-bladed, feather-like propellers extend from the leading edge of the bat-shaped arched wing. Underneath sits a bathtub housing the contraption of a steam engine and the pilot. It was one of several machines that Ader built and actually flew, and did so as early as 1897! Most of the occasions were on a circular track and tethered to a center pole, but during free flight attempts, space was seen under the wheels for a few seconds at a time. That is why the French claim to have been the first to fly. It is really a matter of definition. With no constraints on the definition, then the first to fly was some unnamed Neanderthal who jumped off a cliff flapping his arms; details of the outcome being not particularly germain, although pertinent to his relatives. If the definition is lifting off level ground by motor power for however short a hop, then Ader was indeed the first. If the definition, however, is that what was demonstrated was the solution to all the fundamental questions of flight and that from then to today is merely evolution, then it is unquestionably the Wright brothers; the achieving of sustained, controlled flight. Clearly the Ader designs could never have achieved that. As a guest in a foreign country, and if you want to enjoy the Pernod, I would not bring up these nuances of the subject.

The explosive growth that followed 1907 shows in an amazing display behind the Ader. Antoinettes, Farmans, both Maurice and Henri's, and Vuia's strange but pioneering four-wheeler are on the floor while overhead are early experimental gliders, including Chanute's and Biot's originals and a replica of one of Lilienthal's. The quest to change the

Levavasseur's elegant Antoinette surrounded by Farmans, Voisins, Blériots and others.

airplane from a toy to a practical machine shows here and the variations and configurations in that mass of string and wire and linen are almost limitless.

The original Demoiselle, Santos-Dumont's first really successful airplane is there and all ultralight enthusiasts should come to pay homage. If you remember the movie *Those Magnificent Men in their Flying Machines,* the Demoiselle is the one flown by the amorous Frenchman, the tiny high-winged machine with the pilot sitting essentially on the axle with his nose just short of the propeller. In reality, it was one of the best flyers of the age and was certainly inexpensive enough. The ever-altruistic Santos-Dumont gave away the plans to any and all who wanted them.

Allen Wheeler, in his charming book *Building Aeroplanes for 'Those Magnificent Men',* describes what the aircraft of that era were like and how they flew. A great deal of research went into making the replicas for that film as accurate as possible with the necessary, but well concealed, exception of installing modern engines. Accuracy was difficult for most of the information needed was hard to come by. Not in the case of the Demoiselle. Santos-Dumont had documented the design with exceptional care, and both his records and drawings as well as the aircraft itself were available at Meudon. But when it came time to test the most accurate of the replicas, it just would not fly no matter how hard and how long the burly test pilots bounced it across the grass. Going through Santos-Dumont's notes for the dozenth time, the problem and the solution became simultaneously obvious. They hired a new pilot with the necessary special characteristics. In the actual flying scenes in the film, the Demoiselle is flown by Ms. Joan Hughes who, even made up as a man, weighs only 112 pounds, the same as the diminutive Santos-Dumont.

Santos-Dumont, a wealthy expatriate Brazilian, was the most successful and the acknowledged leader of the early French pioneers. He had started off building balloons and then provided power and control for them by strapping rudimentary airframes and engines underneath. He was reasonably successful and on a number of occasions he would fly over Paris, tether his proto-airship to a chimney, and climb down to have lunch at his club. He knew, however, that it would be the successful heavier-than-air craft that would create the real future of aviation. He continued his experiments and his large and clumsy Model 14bis is generally considered to have made the first successful European flight. By 1910 he was at the pinnacle of aviation and his Demoiselle was being built and flown by many early aviators.

Santos-Dumont, however, was a strange romantic and idealist. He could not bear to see this pure and spiritual conquering of the sky put to evil use. As he saw the military become interested, he became concerned and then morose. He gave up his preeminent place in French aviation and later spent World War I closeted inside his Paris apartment almost as a recluse. He never designed another airplane. After the war had ended, he returned to his native Brazil. In 1932 there was an incipient revolution, a not uncommon event in that part of the world. From the window of his hilltop villa, Santos-Dumont could see Brazilian biplanes dropping bombs on other Brazilians. That night he committed suicide.

Further into the museum, the rapid pace of development becomes more apparent. Several Blériots are on view including a 'IX and an 'XI. At Meudon several of the early monoplanes, Morane-Saulniers and the Deperdussin B, can be compared to their contemporary biplanes, the Voisins and a Wright Baby—one of the few authentic Wrights in existence. Another Deperdussin, the Monocoque, was the first aircraft to exceed 200 km/hr and it shows the streamlining and advanced construction that was available even in 1913. Early Nieuports and the Farman Longhorn and Shorthorn trainers compete for space.

The Fabre Hydravion takes a bit of description. To say that the first successful seaplane was a twin-boom canard pusher monoplane doesn't quite convey the designer's somewhat bizarre approach. While the wing is a large braced single mainplane, the forward elevators are biplane. The three airfoil-shaped floats are in a tricycle arrangement and there are two vertical fins above the upper elevator looking like flags but which likely contributed inversely towards directional stability. More unique is that the twin booms are arranged one over the other rather than what might be considered the more usual side by side position, the pilot straddling the upper one amidships much like sitting on a split-rail fence. The configuration has not led to much in the way of direct derivatives down through the years to say the least, but it was the first aircraft to rise off water, an achievement not at all to be belittled. This was off the Seine, outside of Paris in 1910, well before Curtiss' suc-

The Deperdussin Monocoque was the winner of the 1913 James Gordon Bennett race. A Caudron G.3, a Farman and other struts and wires hang overhead.

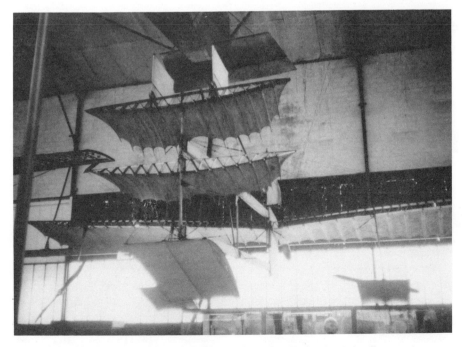

The world's first successful seaplane, Henri Fabre's 1910 Hydravion *is hardly recognizable as an aircraft; neither is which end is the front.*

cess. The U. S. Seaplane Pilots Association entitle their annual award, the "Fabre." Fabre, probably wisely, did not stay in aviation, but went back to building fast patrol boats and thus lived to the ripe old age of 102. He died in 1984. While his initial configuration may appear a bit weird to us, there could have been no better reward for his pioneering than his living to see the Boeing and Martin Clippers, the Latécoères, and even the Lake Buccaneers and EDO float mounted machines of today.

World War I dominates the rear half of the hall, and a full-scale diorama depicts a French airbase of the period. The operations and maintainence shed is actually a theatre and one can spend hours watching silent film coverage of actual operations and combat during World War I. One has no idea that such footage still exists, and while some is scratchy and jumpy, it leaves an image and understanding in the mind that no *Dawn Patrol* type movie can truly accomplish.

Alongside the "shed," a Voisin LA 5B2 gunbus is being readied for takeoff; the "mechanic" is loading his machine gun, or perhaps he is taking aim at the Pfalz D.XII that is diving down from the ceiling along with a Fokker D.VII. Several Caudrons, including a twin-engined G.4, and a Bréguet 14 bomber are getting ready to take off with their Nieuport 11 and 29C1 and Sopwith 1 1/2-Strutter escorts standing by. It is quite a display.

On October 5, 1914, a Voisin LA 5B2 made the first aerial victory on the Western Front.

By the way, have you ever wondered about what ever happened to Armand Deperdussin? After all, he was one of the important builders during the pre-World War I era and his Schneider-winning and record-setting aircraft were among the most successful of that period. Then nothing more is heard of Deperdussin and his aircraft. In France, however, the term for "Incorporated" or "Limited" is "Société Anonyme" or just "Société." Deperdussin teamed with Louis Blériot and designer Louis Béchereau and incorporated. They formed the "Société Pour Avions Deperdussin" and that company became unforgettable under its acronym—SPAD! The SPAD series of fighters were amongst the sturdiest and fastest of World War I. The SPAD VII and the similar looking SPAD XIII were probably the most formidable and we have all seen the picture of Eddie Rickenbacker, the U.S's leading World War I ace, bundled up in the cockpit of his SPAD mount with the Indian Head insignia on the side. The SPADs are deceptively small airplanes. The double bay wing with very short cabane struts and little clearance between the fuselage and the top wing (the pilot could look over or slouch and look under the wing) make the airplane appear much larger than it really is. In actuality, the SPAD has a wingspan a foot or so shorter than a Nieuport's and is much smaller than say, an S.E.5a. The SPAD XIII could hit 135 mph compared to the 115 mph of a Sopwith Camel and while it may not have been quite as maneuverable, no one was ever able to pull the wings off a SPAD, something that could not be said for many machines of that era.

What of Deperdussin himself? The company changed its name to "Société Pour Avions et es Dérives" to preserve the initials after Deperdussin left the firm. He departed somewhat hurriedly when stockholders began to question the whereabouts of all the wartime profits. Deperdussin watched much of the future development of aviation from behind bars since neither the company's stockholders nor the judge had appreciated his "creative accountingsmanship."

Other rare aircraft abound at Meudon; a Packard-Le Pere C-2 which the U. S. shipped over towards 1919, a Hanriot, a German D.F.S. and a Junkers J 9 cluster around the floor. An early de Havilland D.H.9 and an earlier Blackburn represent the English and some of the first helicopters and autogyros are both amusing and puzzling, but all are fascinating. A number of early balloons and the gondolas for several early airships and one from a German World War I Zeppelin, machine guns, steamship type controls and all, line the wall or are suspended from the ceiling.

Alas, as of 1985, Meudon had been closed to the public. Have patience, for the aircraft are being refurbished and more being added to what is already the most impressive collection of aviation during its formative years that exists in the world. The aircraft are being moved, however, to the Musée de l'Air's main facility at Le Bourget where the post-World War I aircraft are already located.

One would have hoped that they could have remained at Meudon, awkward for both the tourist and the museum's logistics as that might have been. One likes to think that the ghosts of those early pioneers— they that had nothing but their courage and intuition to go on and yet did so much— could remain at Meudon and look out the windows and through the trees to those wind tunnels and laboratories. They could watch the testing of the shining and streamlined supersonic derivatives of their labor—and perhaps perform some occasional poltergeisting!

10

Departure Into History

Le Bourget's spot in our memory bank is the night of May 21, 1927 when Lindbergh and his diminutive *Spirit of St. Louis* dropped out of the night sky onto an airport mobbed with a hundred thousand cheering Frenchmen. But Le Bourget was more than that one night. It was a major crossroad of the air routes of Europe at a time when most U.S. cities barely boasted a cow pasture, much less scheduled airline service. Le Bourget was the entry into Paris; the "new" terminal building was built in 1937.

As time goes on, however, airports become obsolete, incapable of handling the ever-expanding traffic and larger aircraft; surrounded by growing suburbs and unable to expand they drift into memory. Newark is still around, but it gave up the centerpiece to La Guardia, which in turn was superseded by Idlewild—known to all but sentimentalists as Kennedy. Newark is at least still sharing New York's load. Grand Central Air Terminal in Glendale, once Los Angeles' major port, is now a shopping center. And London's once famous Croyden is also long gone, although if you look carefully to the right when driving down the A23 from London to Brighton, you can still spot the distinctive square control tower that was Croydon's symbol. The tower and the old center terminal building are now built into what is apparently a large warehouse.

Le Bourget has fared a bit better. It is still a working airport, but only for the aircraft factories that surround it and a few hardy business airplanes. Thus with no commercial airlines, you can't get an airport limousine to it. Instead, take the Paris Metro, with it's Talouse-Lautrec signs, to the Gare de L'Est. Buy a second-class ticket (you save 1 franc, 40 centimes—only the French would have two different classes of cars on a subway). Out front where the bus lines end, take a No. 350 north through the suburbs of Paris; it still stops at the terminal at Le Bourget.

The terminal is empty, but the doors are sometimes still open and if so, walk inside. Its roof is high and the decor Radio City Music Hall Modern. The exits to the ramp are locked, but some wag has left a set of flight destination boards hanging on the panel above and behind the counter: Marseille and Marakesh, Lyon and Lisbon. As you walk back to the exit, your heels echo off the tile floors. You sense that if you looked back over your shoulder you might see Marlene Dietrich and Peter Lorre deplaning from the evening flight from Berlin. Or perhaps that shadow is Antoine de Saint-Exupéry heading off on the night mail to Morocco and to his writings which have gone down as the deepest insight into the souls of men who fly.

But not all is imagination. Outside and to the right is the entrance to the Musée de l'Air and the reality of that history. Through the unprepossessing lobby and a rather well-equipped book shop, one ends up on the airport ramp. Turn left since straight ahead are the rockets and missiles for those who like that sort of stuff. Further down is where the interesting machinery begins. *Salle* A is filled with strange and exotic aircraft, unlikely that one of them has ever been seen by an American before entering here. The center of the hall is dominated by three aircraft that mean much to the history and spirit of French aviation. Just after the time of Alcock and Brown's crossing of the Atlantic in their Vickers Vimy, a wealthy French-American, Raymond Orteig, offered the huge sum of $25,000 as a prize for the first to fly between New York and Paris non-stop in either direction. Impractical in 1919, it wasn't much less so in 1927, but by then aircraft were a bit sturdier. A number of groups on both sides of the Atlantic began to prepare for the attempt. René Fonck actually attempted it in 1926, but his Sikorsky tri-motor crashed on takeoff and two of the four-man crew were killed.

The "new" terminal building at Le Bourget now forms part of the Musée de l'Air.

As winter turned into the spring of 1927, the next to try were Davis and Wooster in a Keystone Pathfinder, also a trimotor, and they also were killed in a crash on takeoff. Flying the Atlantic was certainly not yet much easier than in 1919. Far better prepared and equipped, however, was the team of Nungesser and Coli. Captain Charles Nungesser was already a well-known and beloved national hero. A World War I ace with 45 enemy aircraft to his credit, he had been wounded over a dozen times, mentioned in dispatches about as often, and had received most of the medals that France had to offer. Captain François Coli was no less experienced. Looking a bit like a pirate with his black eyepatch from his World War I injuries he was, in addition to being a flier, an experienced ship's navigator. Together they made a formidable team. They would have to be, because they intended to fly from Paris to New York—east to west—the hard way into the prevailing winds.

Their aircraft was no less formidable and well prepared, at least for the day. Pierre Levasseur had been building aircraft for the French Navy. Note that this was Pierre, not Leon. Leon Levavasseur, builder of the Antoinettes of two decades earlier, has an extra 'va' in his name although one finds it missing in quite a number of references. Pierre Levasseur's aircraft factory was still manufacturing airplanes into the 1930s and it was a Levasseur PL-15 seaplane that on October 30, 1939 was the first French aircraft to sink a German submarine. The two were obviously not related, much less the same person.

Since Nungesser and Coli had little money of their own, they prevailed on Levasseur's patriotism and pocketbook to defend France's honor. Fonck was out of the running and at least two strong American teams (and rumors of some unknown third individual) were well underway. Levasseur, in just a few months, made extensive modifications to an existing design and came up with the PL-8. Named *L'Oiseau Blanc,* the *White Bird,* the Levasseur PL-8 was a rock-sturdy looking biplane with a 48-foot span, the highly reliable, water-cooled Lorraine-Dietrich 12-cylinder W-configured engine and a number of intriguing features. The underside of the fuselage from the cowl back to the wing was almost a shallow hull shape to aid in ditching should that unhappy eventuality ever be faced. The short, stubby landing gear could be dropped after takeoff to save weight and drag; they planned to belly in on landing and could even lock the propeller horizontally to minimize damage. A worthwhile proposition, but a bit risky since it was gear collapse on takeoff that had caused both the Fonck and Davis crashes.

At dawn on May 8, 1927, Nungesser and Coli took off from Le Bourget, circled the field, dropped the disposable landing gear and climbed out toward the west. They were never seen again!

It was on May 20th, only two weeks later, that the rumored unknown individual, an obscure mail pilot named Charles Lindbergh, barely cleared the trees at Roosevelt Field on Long Island and headed eastbound. Lindbergh was actually nervous about his possible reception. France was in national mourning for its two lost heros, but Lindbergh couldn't wait since the teams of Clarence Chamberlain and Admiral Richard Byrd were both about ready to go. He needn't have worried. One hundred thousand people were jammed onto Le Bourget field on that night of May 21, 1927, shedding tears as only the French can—tears of joy for Lindbergh mixed with those of sorrow for their lost heroes.

Throughout the rest of 1927 and 1928 another two dozen or so attempts at crossings were made. A few like Byrd and Chamberlain made it; most did not. Some, like Hassel and Courtney and Haldeman were forced down and rescued or turned back and made landfall. The rest form a long list of "lost at sea" and the toll of missing Fokkers and Stinsons and Sikorskys finally caused the French Ministry of Aviation to ban transatlantic attempts.

The Ministry of Aviation may have banned them, but there was no way that they could stop French aviators from avenging Nungesser and Coli—and France's honor—from the fates. Jean Assolant was a Sergeant Pilot at Le Bourget and was part of a team testing the new Bernard 191. He was quick to recognize the machine's capability. Bernard was a small company and Assolant was able to convince them that the publicity for their new machine was worth the risk. Assolant took off from Orly on a supposed routine test flight and without registration or flight plan flew to Southhampton, England. There the Bernard, now painted bright yellow and named *L'Ouiseau Canaris*, the *Yellow Bird*, was quickly and quietly shipped to New York and thence to Old Orchard, Maine, from where many of the transatlantic attempts were being made.

The Bernard 191 was a big, wooden, single-engine monoplane with a cantilevered plywood wing. With a 56-foot, 8-inch span, the Bernard

Assolant's bright yellow Bernard 191, Oiseau Canari, *which made the first transatlantic crossing by the French.*

looks somewhat like a giant Cessna 195. The two takeoff attempts were both hairy. On their first try, the 600-hp V-12 Hispano-Suiza coughed and sputtered on the differently blended U. S. gasoline; probably insufficient Cognac in the mix. They made it off, but decided to jettison their fuel, land and try again. After much tinkering with timing and mixture, on June 13th, 1929 they were ready for a second attempt. On this takeoff the tail would not come up and as they neared the end of the runway, the Bernard staggered into the air trying to pitch up into a stall. Assolant heaved forward on the stick to keep the nose down. His navigator, René Lefevre, tried to help on the controls. As they soggily passed 1000 feet, the third crew member, Armand Lotti—needed aboard to work the radio and because he had put up most of the additional cash needed for the flight—could only start dumping the radio overboard to lighten ship.

What did help the tail-heavy trim was when a stowaway, a young American "cub" reporter named Arthur Schreiber, crawled forward out of the tail cone. The ensuing conversation was not recorded for posterity. The Bernard ran into storms in mid-ocean and was blown quite south of the intended course. They finally reached Cape Finisterre and were forced to land on the Spanish north coast. With a day's rest and a couple of stops they made it to Le Bourget on June 16, 1929. Assolant, Lefevre, and Lotti were greeted as heroes; French honor had been restored. The other two aboard, stowaway Schreiber and mascot Rufus (a baby alligator) were not so honored. The French Ministry of Aviation conveniently forgot about their ban on transatlantic flights.

But the east-west run, the hard way that Nungesser and Coli had been attempting, had still not been conquered. The Bréguet factory had built some of the best single-engined bombers of World War I and had continued that design concept through the 1920s. A Bréguet XIX, No. 1685, had already set several European long-distance records, including nonstop Paris to Aswan, Egypt and Paris to Omsk, Russia. With Bréguet's chief test pilot Dieudonné Costes and Lieutenant Commander Joseph Le Brix, the big Bréguet, now painted green and named *Nungesser-Coli,* left Paris on October 10, 1927. They went non-stop to St. Louis, Senegal and from there flew to Natal, Brazil for the first crossing of the South Atlantic. They cruised throughout South America, up through Central America and on to New York. From there they flew to San Francisco where the Bréguet was put on a steamer to cross the Pacific. It was reassembled in Japan and spent six days hopping across the far and near east returning to Paris on April 14, 1928. They had circumnavigated the globe, albeit using a ship for a quarter of the way, but nonetheless it was an incredible achievement.

When the improved Bréguet XIX Bidon came out, Costes was convinced it could make the Paris-to-New York westbound run. Unfortunately, neither Bréguet nor Hispano-Suiza, who made the 650-hp 12Nb engine to be used on the ship, had the ready funds for such a project.

The Bréguet XIX, Nungesser-Coli, *made the first crossing of the South Atlantic. The landing gear that Nungesser and Coli dropped from their ill-fated* L'Oiseau Blanc *rests at left.*

The 1930 Bréguet XIX Super Bidon Point d'Interrogation *which made the first east to west flight from Paris to New York.*

In another of those strange episodes where a wealthy patron, apparently distant from the aviation scene, suddenly appears on the stage at just the right time, an anonymous check for the equivalent of about $50,000 showed up at the Bréguet offices. After the flight it was found to have been due to Costes' persuasion of that anonymous patron. All those chic French women who had been buying François Coty's perfumes had built the fortune from which Costes had garnered the donation.

The Bréguet factory added some improvements and fuel capacity and built the special Super Bidon. Quite attractive compared to some of its contemporaries, it is more of a sesquiplane than a biplane. Painted bright red and with a large white "?" on its side—not perhaps a sign of excessive confidence—the *Point d'Interrogation* took off from Le Bourget on September 1, 1930 with Costes and his navigator, Maurice Bellonte, aboard. On the evening of September 2nd, after 37 hours and 17 minutes

The sinister all-black Caudron C.714R was built for an attack on the world speed record in 1939; the onset of war denied it a place in history.

in the air, Costes and Bellonte landed at Curtiss Field on Long Island. Out of the crowd stepped a now not unknown airman, Charles Lindbergh, to greet the weary flyers. Nungesser and Coli had been vindicated.

There, surrounding you in the center of *Salle* A of the Musée de l'Air, are the dark green Bréguet XIX *Nungesser-Coli,* the gawky bright yellow Bernard *L'Ouiseau Canaris* and the crimson Super Bidon sesquiplane *Point d'Interrogation.* Dwarfed by them all is a small stand with two busts on it that you might not notice. On the floor in front of it are some pieces of wood and wire and a pair of wheels. It is the landing gear from the *L'Ouiseau Blanc* that Nungesser and Coli dropped after takeoff—but a few yards from where you are standing—while they circled to the west and into the darkness and mystery from which they never returned.

Back toward the doorway of *Salle* A there stand on pylons three exquisite racing aircraft from the 1930s; a Potez 53, a Caudron-Regnier C.366 and the Caudron C.714R. The C.714R, all black with a highly-tapered wing, narrow, inverted engine and low set-back cockpit, is one of the meanest looking flying machines ever made; surely the mount for a villain in the pulp magazines of the era. The Caudron C.460 no longer exists, but it was roughly similar looking. For those who don't remember bad news, the C.460 was the Caudron that came over to the U.S. in 1936 and picked up both the Greve and Thompson Trophies, making the monster Laird-Turners and Wedell-Williams' appear as dinosaurs.

Hanging from the ceiling are a Morane-Saulnier MS.230 and a Dewoitine D.530, both of that strange class of parasol-winged fighters

A stubby Russian Polikarpov I-153 Chaika hot from the Spanish Civil War, one of the few biplanes with retractable gear.

of the early 1930s that only the French and the Poles seem to have gone in for. Over by the wall is the fuselage, *sans* wings, of a 1919 Farman Goliath, looking for all the world like a tramcar. With wicker seats and curtains, you expect to see a sign saying Powell and Market Street on the side rather than *Isle De France* and F-HMFU. But remember, they were flying daily passenger runs from Paris to London in the 1920s. And they were doing it with a city-center to city-center time of only about an hour more than today, albeit with somewhat less frequency and dependablity, although that last point is arguable. A rare 1927 Schreck FBA 17 HT4 two-seat biplane flying boat with a cricket insignia is against the other wall, with another dozen aircraft spaced around the hall.

Hall B represents World War II and by the entryway one is greeted by a Russian Polikarpov I-153 Chaika, not something one sees every day. A rather stubby biplane with single "I" struts and a gull upper wing, it is one of the few biplanes besides the Beech Staggerwing and some Grummans with retractable gear. It still has the sliding shutters on the cowl intakes of the big radial engine to protect it from the cold of Siberia (and Finland and Manchuria where many found their way). This one clearly came across the Pyrenees one way or the other when the Republicans lost the Spanish Civil War—remember *For Whom The Bell Tolls?*

The center of the hall is dominated by a Yakovlev Yak-3 chasing a Dewoitine D.520 chasing a Morane-Saulnier MS.406. All three are mounted on pylons in flying attitute which makes for a dramatic, if

A Yak-3 chasing a Dewoitine D.520 chasing a Morane-Saulnier MS.406. A Messerschmitt Bf 109 and a Focke-Wulf Fw 190 take off in the background.

not particularly geographically or militarily understandable, display. Particularly since the Messerschmitt Bf 109 (actually a Spanish license-built HA-1112) and Focke-Wulf Fw 190 are displayed taking off in the opposite direction across the room. The Yak-3 is quite a nice, relatively small and neat machine. The Dewoitine 520 was an outstanding aircraft and for its day would have given anything else in the air a run for its money as a fighter. Unfortunately, the French Aviation Ministry was in such disarray in the late 1930s that they gave more contracts for prototypes and service test aircraft than just about everybody else put together. They were just never able to get their act together on production so there were too few of anything, particularly the good ones.

The MS.406, on the other hand, looks like it was hammered out of old Cinzano signs. It has the worst sheet metal work around—not the resoration, it was that way from the start. It is somewhat reminiscent of a Curtiss P-40 that's been through a Chinese laundry. The Moranes, however, fought with great courage, if little leadership, in trying to hold back the Luftwaffe in 1940 as their predecessors did a quarter of a century earlier. Several American and English World War II aircraft are also in the hall and a rather nice Fieseler Storch and an old Morane-Saulnier 230 round out the display.

The post-war years and the early experimental jet aircraft in *Salle* C represent considerable novelty and imagination, some of it perhaps rather misplaced. The Leduc 010 and 022s are rare and exotic, for example, but represent the dead-ended investigation into piloted ramjets. They were both air dropped, ramjet-powered aircraft with the pilot sitting, or perhaps lying—certainly quivering—in the inlet pod with the annular air inlet surrounding him. It gives a great view, but it is not clear how he ejected—surely not through the hot section! In an effort to make the ramjet more practical and get away from the need to be

One of Leduc's early creatures, the 010 had the pilot seated inside the ram-jet's nose stinger looking out through little portholes.

air dropped, the experimental delta-winged Nord 1500.02 Griffon was developed. Its huge intake and fuselage width are to support a SNECMA Atar 101 turbojet which is in the center of an enormous ramjet. It worked; when the beast was cut in, the Griffon could hit Mach 2.7. The SO-9000, Trident I, was another strange beast of an early experimental jet. It has two 400-kg Turbomeca turbojets out on the wing-tips and a 4500-kg rocket in the fuselage. The SO-6000 was France's first jet aircraft and while perhaps on the stubby side and clearly not a Learjet, it did its job well.

While these aircraft may be a bit on the peculiar side, the Mirages and Mistrals and Mysteres and Ouragans in Hall D are not. They were up there in the first line and appeared not just in the ranks of the French Air Force but in others on several continents, sometimes on the oppos-ing sides in the same war and sometimes across the line from some American-made aircraft. Probably one of the best displays is the third Mirage jet fighter. The first two are normal, a Mirage III-A and a III-V1. On the third, the skin and structure are made of plastic! You can see right through it and examine the equipment, plumbing and all the other accouterments that go into a modern jet fighter. It is like being able to touch one of those cutaway drawings and it is one of the best technical exhibits around.

There are also some interesting small experimental aircraft in the hall. The Hirsch HR-100 is a rather attractive 1950s experimental prop-driven twin used for gust absorption research using swivelling wingtips and a system of interconnected double flaps, ailerons and elevators, while the Hurel-Dubois H.D.10 is a small 75 hp-probe into the ultra-high aspect ratio wing. It has a wing with a 40-foot span and about a 14-inch chord with more moving parts than a 727's. The Payen Pa-49 Katy was 20 years ahead of Bede. Built in 1953, it was an experimental, 160-kg

All the plumbing and paraphernalia in a modern jet fighter are visible through the transparent plastic skin of this Mirage.

The Cierva C.8 was made in 1928 using an Avro 504N body. A C.30 and the balloon-assisted, four-rotor fantasy of Oehmichen are in the background.

thrust jet-powered, single seat delta wing. Paradoxically, it had fixed gear. It is different.

The last hall covers light and sport aircraft and spans the gamut from old Caudron and Blériot biplanes to sexy new Scintex Super Emeraudes and Wassmer Pacifics. It is so crammed with aircraft from a sub-floor

A Blériot-SPAD 54 built for the civilian market of 1922. Behind is a Caudron C.60 and a de Havilland Dragon Rapide discharging jumpers.

pit up to the ceiling that it is almost impossible to photograph an individual aircraft. The upper levels are inhabited by a large number of sailplanes. Particularly attractive is the D.F.S. Habicht, a shoulder gull-wing German design from 1936 which was noted for sailplane aerobatics. A de Havilland Rapide is also hanging from the ceiling with the ''jumpers'' just coming out the door.

The Musée de l'Air has a vast holding of aircraft that just cannot fit into even as large a facility as at Le Bourget. Groups of *Ailes Anciennes* are located all over France where they assist in restoring aircraft belonging to the Musée de l'Air and displaying them and others in the local areas. Groups are located at Dijon, Saint Nazaire, Strasbourg, Toulouse and other locales. There are also another two-dozen or so military and Resistance museums and private collections that contain old airplanes scattered around France.

One of the most active groups is the Réseau du Sport de L'Air, the counterpart of our Experimental Aircraft Association. The amateur aircraft movement in France is extensive and the RSA maintains a collection at the Musée Aéronautique de Champagne at the Aérodrome de Brienne le Château. The aircraft range from the tiny Mignet Pou du Ciel to an immense Nord Noratlas transport. The bulk of the collection, however, consists of those limited-production or homebuilt low-wing lightplanes that only the French seem able to make so charming. Jodels, Brochet Pipistrelles, Castels and small Caudrons abound. A rare Leduc RL-19 and Lemaire RL-1 are in the collection and unusual pri-

A Heinkel He 111 is one of several dozen 1940s and 1950s aircraft located outdoors at the Musée de l'Air, Le Bourget, Paris.

vate aircraft are also located at the field. Each July the RSA hosts an international homebuilt aircraft rally and Brienne-le-Château becomes a mecca for hundreds of aircraft from all over Europe. Not all are small homebuilts. At the 1985 meet, the last airworthy French Meteor jet fighter flew in to take its place in retirement at the museum.

Back at Le Bourget and the Musée de l'Air, one can stroll down the ramp as evening falls and wander through a large, if random, arrangement of aircraft. A Heinkel He 111, a Junker Ju 52/3m, and a Boeing B-17G are amongst the World War II types present, as is, curiously, a Short Bermuda flying boat. Jet fighters are all over as well as one of the innumerable Concorde prototypes. A trio of Sud-Aviation SO-4050 Vautour IIs are in "V" formation. The Vautour was an early 1950s twin-jet light bomber-recon aircraft. With its bicycle landing gear and low-slung nacelles it is reminiscent of a cross between the old Martin "Middle River Stump Jumper," their B-26 modified to test such landing gear concepts, and a Boeing B-47.

You might also take a moment to look down at the ground. You are standing at the same spot where Caudrons and Nieuports were parked in 1917, where passengers and crews for Bréguets and Latécoères and Farmans trod in the '20s, where Nungesser and Coli and Costes and Bellonte departed from and where Lindbergh taxied to a stop, where Junkers Ju 52s deposited triumphant German generals and Douglas C-47s deposited triumphant Allied generals. It is the same ground and the same air; only the times have changed—by a little bit.

11

L'Audacieux

Most pilots believe in the old saying that the most dangerous part of a flight is the drive to the airport. Nowhere is that more true than when attempting to get to a remote airfield in a foreign country, particularly in France. Their notions of lane discipline and signalling have a certain Gallic charm and *sang-froid* which is utterly terrifying to all but Boston taxicab drivers. The trip to the Jean Salis Collection is more than worth the adventure.

If you have nerves of steel, get your rental car from one of the dealers on Boulevard Charles de Gaulle in downtown Paris. Brave your way to the Periphique Ouest (an exquisite name for a beltway), and then take the A6 south toward Fontainebleau and Lyon. Those of you who are cowards can take an airport bus to Orly and pick up your car there as the A6 goes right by Orly, but think of the thrill that you are missing and all the new and eloquent French swear words you will not learn. About a half-hour south, take the exit for Mennecy, the N191 through Fontenay-le-Vicomte and continue on to the small town of la Ferté-Alais. Just before you enter the town (that means after you get into the town, make a U-turn and go back to where you now know the beginning is) make two sharp rights and in a half mile you will see a sign to the *aéro-drome* on your left.

Climb the hill and go back seventy years. The Aérodrome de la Ferté-Alais is a grass strip on a low plateau. On your left are some old stone farmhouses with peaked roofs, some of which have sandbagged revetments! If they look familiar, most of the French movies and television shows with World War I aviation scenes have been filmed here. The nearest building holds a small but delightful restaurant where you can sip apertifs, hum *Lili Marlene* and believe yourself to be Jean Paul Belmondo—or maybe Snoopy! One actually expects Snoopy, with begoggled helmet and swagger-stick, to come up to the bar at any moment and ask directions to Pont-à-Mousson.

106

But this is real. In those hangers is one of the finest collections of antique aircraft in the world—and most of them are in flying condition. Jean-Baptiste Salis started collecting airplanes not long after World War I, although many were destroyed during the replay twenty years later. When he died in 1967 his son, also Jean, and most of the antique aero buffs in central France continued the tradition such that now, la Ferté-Alais is a center for antique aircraft in Western Europe.

Leopoldoffs, Polikarpovs, Stampes and other arcane biplanes abound; in fact there are eight Stampe S.V.4Cs in flying condition. During the 1930s, in the transition to the monoplane, the U. S. and England went to either the strut-braced cabin, or the low wing, wire-braced monoplane. For some obscure reason, the French went instead to the cabane or parasol wing. Basically that is a biplane with the lower wing removed, or just forgotten. There must be over a dozen Morane 138s, 185s, 230s, 317s, 341s and Dewoitine D.27s, all looking like someone stole half their mainplanes. They are nonetheless charming and highly maneuverable aircraft. Beautifully restored and painted, they are quite a sight in the air. They were in the same class as, say a Stearman, of which there is also an example at la Ferté-Alais and which has one of the most beautiful examples of restoration possible. Another example of an American airplane of the World War II era is a Piper L-5 in olive drab with Free French insignias. It looks as if it is awaiting its midnight mission to bring messages to the Resistance. One expects to see one of their dented and dusty old black Citroen *Traction-Avant*s next to it with armed and bereted *Maquis* clinging to the running board. Actually, all old Citroens are dented and dusty; I think they came straight from the factory that way.

The serial number 1 Morane-Saulnier MS.185 of 1930. The replica Blériot XI in which Jean Salis recreated the Channel crossing is at left.

107

A Pilatus P-2, with its strange, finned-spinner, propeller pitch control.

Outside are some more-modern machines from the late 1940s and 1950s. The twin-engined Marcel Dassault 311 was used for training navigators and bombardiers just after World War II; the D-18S Twin Beech next to it did the same thing over here just a few years earlier. A Swiss-made Pilatus P-2 from 1944 is an attractive low-wing trainer with a 465-hp Argus engine; it would be a contemporary of our T-6 Texan. The Pilatus has a peculiar feature on its nose. The spinner is made in two separate pieces. The aft part shrouds the propeller hub as expected, but the front cone has a dozen radial strakes. The rotational drag on those strakes provides the torque for the propeller pitch control mechanism. Novel, anyway.

A few of the aircraft are replicas, mostly World War I Nieuports, Fokkers and S.E.5s and all having seen rigorous combat in *l'aviation flics.* The Blériot XI is the replica built by Jean Salis, Sr. and in which he recreated Blériot's famous Channel crossing in 1954 and again in 1959. Another outstanding replica is of the 1913 Deperdussin Monocoque. A shoulder wing, wire-braced, bullet-like monoplane, the original (at Meudon) was the first airplane to exceed two hundred kilometers per hour and two miles a minute. The varnished wood veneer, laid up diagonally, would put a cabinetmaker to shame and shows the advanced construction that was available even in 1913.

Most of the aircraft at la Ferté-Alais are originals, however, not replicas, even including the wrecks. If you can gain entry into the back hanger off in the woods, you will find dozens of airframes and engines dating to who knows when. If you need a connecting rod for a Le Rhône Monosoupape rotary, there may be one laying in the pile and that's probably the only place in the world where there is one. Numerous aircraft are being restored including a Farman, a Caudron-Aiglon, a Fieseler Storch, an attractive low-wing Mauboussin Corsaire and several more Moranes.

The Deperdussin Monocoque was the first airplane to exceed 200 km/hr. This replica was made for a French TV series.

A number of Bréguet XIV bombers of 1918 were converted into early mailplanes; this one was used by Latécoère.

Back in the main hangers are a trio of Bücker biplanes, a Salmson Cri-Cri, and a Bréguet XIV biplane bomber from World War I that was converted to an early transport by Latécoère. Not satisfied with such conversions, Latécoère started building their own transports. The Latécoère 17 at la Ferté-Alais is probably the only one in existence. The reason may in part be that it offends all ones aesthetic sensibilities. For some reason, French designers of larger aircraft in the late '20s and early '30s—Farman, Latécoère, Bloch and others—insisted that not only could they make a barn door fly, to prove it they made the airplane look like a barn door. That is strange, because the smaller French aircraft were, by and large, beautiful-looking machines. However it is prob-

The Latécoère 17 reached new limits of the ugly that could still fly.

ably fortunate for our beliefs in aerodynamics, and likely our sanity, that no Amiot or Liore-et-Olivier bombers or transports of that period have survived.

The Latécoère 17 has a bulbuous fuselage with a 600-hp engine half its diameter stuck on its nose. The wing is a large thick parasol, the preposterous rudder must have come off the Hughes flying boat, and the wheels from a kiddy-car. Offensive as that may seem, Laté. 17s were routinely flying thousands of passengers all over Europe while we were working county fairs. Along with the Farmans and Bréguets and others, the Latécoères built up a major airline infrastructure well before World War II. The Laté. 17 at la Ferté-Alais is actually a semi-replica utilizing major components of a Norduyn Norseman.

Another amazing beast of an airplane is an Antonov An-2. Still used in Russia, it is one of the largest single-engined biplanes ever built. This example made its way from the East via Czechoslovakia and was used as a jump plane for parachutists before winding up at la Ferté-Alais. Also from Russia comes a Polikarpov of 1927. A biplane with more grace is the de Havilland D.H.89 Dragon Rapide, which sits as gracefully as a dowager awaiting a glass of sherry.

But they don't sit long, at least not in the summer months, because these planes are flown, and flown with the same *joie-de-vivre* that they were some fifty-odd years ago when they were new. La Ferté-Alais is a private field and only open to the public on certain summer Sunday afternoons. So call ahead if you are in the area and with some appropriate timing and luck, see if you can get a chance to sip some wine and partake of the past. It is not often that you can lean against a post and watch a flight of Stampe biplanes, or a Fokker, an Albatros, an S.E.5 and an authentic Morane A.1 chase themselves across the late afternoon sky.

Time to head back to Paris. As you leave la Ferté-Alais and swing from the country road onto the cloverleaf ramp to the A6, that bug spot on the windshield turns into a sighting ring. The Renault's engine is powering a Nieuport not a rental car and the 3.8 liter in the machine in front is not in a Mercedes. It's an Albatros! *Alerte! L'Escadron de Chasse* is engaging and the adrenalin is flowing. You will need all of it to get through the Sunday night traffic around the Arc-de-Triumph to return the rental car.

The Antonov An-2T, one of the largest single-engined biplanes ever built, is still used for bush flying in Eastern Russia.

12

One Hundred Years From Waterloo

The Battle of Waterloo was Napoleon's final defeat, although few can recall where it is or who his English adversary was. It must have been Wellington because Nelson was a sea captain and Waterloo was definitely on land. In fact it is only nine miles south of Brussels. Being a small country next to some not always friendly large neighbors leads to rather pockmarked fields and a propensity towards military history. Whenever Germany wanted to attack France (or in prior centuries the other way around), they had this habit of ignoring impediments like the Maginot line and running around the flank through places like Flanders, which unfortunately is mostly part of Belgium. It does, however, lead to well-filled military museums as there is considerable impedimenta left cluttering up the countryside after the war is over. That was particularly true in World War I where much of the trench line, and the air war overhead, was encompassed by Belgian borders.

From the sixteenth century town square of Brussels, walk the few blocks to the main rail station and take the subway (the Metro that is—the cabs are too expensive) several stations east to Merode and the Parc du Cinquantenaire. A block back you can see the Victory Arch in the park and just to the right is an entry to the Musée Royal De l'Armée et d'Histoire Militaire. As would be expected, it is filled with Napoleon's leftovers from Waterloo and the glories of the last few centuries of man's more colorful ways of doing himself in.

The Brussels Air Museum is inside there just a few dozen feet away, but it requires some astuteness to locate unless one speaks fluent Belgian. Actually, there are two Belgian languages: Flemish, which is somewhat like Dutch, and Walloon, which is rather like French. Unless you are very knowledgable, it is better to stay in English. To speak Flemish to a Walloon would be *gauche*. The English will be useless, however, as no one will likely speak it. Repeating a few words over and over and using hand motions and sputtered engine sounds will try to convey the

The main hall of the aviation collection at the Palais du Cinquantenaire.

message that it is airplanes in which you are interested. If you are doing this by the small bookstand, the proprietor will point to a door to the right. Since that door has the universal and unmistakable male and female symbols indicating the *toilette,* you may conclude that your sounds and motions have inadvertently communicated that you are suffering from an obscure form of gastro-intestinal distress. Open the door and in the corridor inside there are two signs; the male/female sign points left and what is clearly an airplane sign points right and your perseverance has paid off. I assume that the sequence of signs is a subtle form of Walloonian humor. Actually there is another more-conventional entrance and this was merely a short-cut. The bizarre route of entry is quickly forgotten because once inside, rare aircraft stretch into the distance. The air museum is contained in one very large hall that was originally built for an exposition with large areas of glass held up by Eiffel-towerish wrought ironwork. Go immediately up to the balcony to get an overview and to examine one of the finest line-ups of World War I aircraft in the world.

A Maurice Farman MF.XI holds the place of honor at the end of the balcony. A two-seat pusher gun bus type with twin booms holding onto the twin rudders, it is one of those machines from early in the war which has so many struts and wires that one is hard pressed to determine just what is holding on to what. It is, however, quite dignified in its way. To its right is an extremely unusual and one-of-a-kind Bataille Triplane undergoing restoration. Built in 1912 by César Bataille, it was one of

A Maurice Farman MF.XI light bomber from 1914 holds center stage at the upper end of the hall.

the first indigenous Belgian aircraft and represents the then still pioneering stage of aircraft development. The three wings have a large amount of stagger and while the forward half of the fuselage is quite well streamlined, the rear half has exposed longerons a la Blériot. There is also an authentic Blériot XI of the same vintage. It is interesting to compare the Bataille's handwheel pitch control with the Blériot/Esnault-Pelterie control column which led to the conventional control systems of today.

Down the side balcony is the main line-up of a dozen World War I flying machines, most with the elaborate squadron insignias of the era. There is something quite different about these machines as compared with World War I aircraft at most other museums. At RAF Hendon, the Musée de l'Air in Paris and others, the machines are spotlessly restored. Here, they show wear and tear and look as if they have just returned from a patrol. Whether that is deliberate or just due to the shortage of funds that all museums suffer from is immaterial. In fact it is particularly nice, because they appear as they actually would have back in 1916 or 1917. They might just be cooling down while their pilots sip some coffee or armagnac before the next sortie.

A Hanriot-Dupont HD-1 pursuit in Belgian colors heads the row, followed by a Nieuport 17C1 scout and their two seat adversaries, a Halberstadt C.V and an L.V.G. C.VI with their Maxim and Parabellum machine guns mounted on the rear upper decking. England is represented by a Sopwith Camel, a Sopwith 1 1/2-Strutter and a Royal Aircraft Factory R.E.8, in order of increasing clunkiness. A Caudron

A SPAD XIII and a Sopwith Camel head this lineup of World War I biplanes.

G.3 and a Voisin LA 5, one a pusher and the other a tractor, but both with twin booms, make the SPAD XIIIs superb lines even more perfect. The R.E.8 crashed on August 18, 1918, just before the Armistice, but wasn't damaged too badly and was later restored. The Sopwith Camel was built by Clayton and Shuttleworth. While the finishes may be a bit dulled by time, the elaborate World War I paint schemes on cowls and wheels and the individualistic squadron insignias—shooting stars, thistles, and birds of prey—still convey the *esprit de corps* of their crews.

The variations in engines can be clearly seen as the ships are all lined up in a row: the massive, half-exposed Benz water-cooled in-lines on the Halberstadt and the L.V.G., a somewhat neater installation of the Hispano-Suiza in the SPAD, and the ridiculous Clergêt and Gnôme rotaries in the Sopwiths and Nieuports. To have the crankshaft stand still while the cylinders and the rest of the engine whirls around cannot be a sane way to produce power. Actually it was, considering when you stop and think about it, that all piston engines are an absurdly complicated way of converting hydrocarbons to thrust. The problem in 1916 was quite simply metallurgical. No one knew how to make light cylinders that would hold together with only a 90-mph airflow to cool them. That essentially ruled out the radial or the in-line or horizontally-opposed air-cooled engines. The water-cooled devices were heavy, complex and not a little prone to stopping from bullet holes in the plumbing. But those ludicrous little rotaries kept cool from the cylinders thrashing around, acted as their own flywheels, and had pretty fair power-to-weight ratios. So what if the early ones had no throttle (the only options were full speed or off which made taxiing a delight) and gyroscopic moments that led to peculiar handling characteristics to say the least. They also had the habit of causing chronic "distress" to the pilot due to constant exposure to the castor oil which was mixed into the fuel for lubrication. But nothing could cavort through the sky like a rotary-engined Nieuport.

A gaudily-painted Hanriot-Dupond HD-1 in front of Nieuports, L.V.G.s, and Albatroses.

Past the Caudron G.3 with the built-in head wind, is the gondola and other paraphernalia from a German Zeppelin Type R. At the end of the balcony is one of Louis Schreck's FBA Type H two-seat, single-engine flying boats; sort of a Lake Buccaneer of 1915. This FBA was based in Calais and actually flew North Sea and English Channel patrols. FBA, by the way, stood for Franco-British Aviation, a consortium that predated the Concorde business arrangements by some 50 years. A nice Morane-Saulnier MS.315 parasol-wing trainer of 1933 and a raft of sailplanes cover the far end of the hall.

On the main floor, a quartet of Stampe S.V.4Bs are arranged at the entrance. The Stampe biplanes from the 1930s and 1940s were designed by Alfred Renard and are essentially Belgium's only indigenous civil aircraft built in significant numbers. They were used as trainers for two decades or so and are reminiscent of the de Havilland Moths in overall configuration (and there is a D.H.82A Tiger Moth there to compare them to). Stampe OO-ATD was one of the first made, with manufacturer's number 4. In July 1941 it was stolen by Michel Donnet and Leon Divoy, two Belgian pilots, who managed to elude the Germans and fly the little biplane to England and freedom.

Belgium did manufacture some military aircraft during the 1930s. The specially-formed Avions Company built under license Firefly and Fox biplanes, two of Fairey's better machines. By 1935, Renard had designed and built a very sleek parasol-wing reconnaissance plane, the R.31, which looks very similar to the Faireys or Hawkers of the era, but with

116

One of the authors gets briefed on the Stampe S.V.4s by a docent at the Musée Royal de l'Armée, Brussels.

no lower wing. None now exist, but a large and attractive model of it stands next to the Stampes.

One of the more attractive English aircraft on display is the rare Percival IV Vega Gull from the late 1930s. It is a rather sleek, low-wing, four-seater with spatted gear. Another interesting comparison is between it and the boxy Fairchild 24 from the same period just a few feet away.

A number of other trainers and utility aircraft, such as a Miles Magister and an North American AT-6 are on the floor. Representing the light twins are a de Havilland D.H.89A Dominie, the military version of the twin-engined Dragon Rapide biplane (which are still running around Australia and which for the life of me I cannot see any difference between) and an Airspeed 40 Oxford, one of Neville Shute Norway's last designs. Not so light a twin is the Douglas DC-3, which gives you an idea of the floor space in that one hall.

Several small alcoves lead off the main floor, of which two are particularly worth stopping at. The first is a small snack bar where one can buy a beer and rest one's feet. Looking at antique aircraft while sitting and sipping beer is a civilized pleasure not available in most U. S. museums. The second is the Sabena exhibit.

Sabena is the Belgian national airline and is worth flying; their food and service are outstanding. Sabena is such an elegant sounding name for an airline. Of course it is not a word, it is another one of those acronyms. In this case it stands for "Société Anonyme Belge d'Exploitation de la Navigation Aérienne." One enters the Sabena alcove by walking through the nacelle from a Boeing 707, which is a nice touch. The wicker seats, artifacts and photographs from the airliners of the between-the-wars era are fascinating. As one of those small European countries with a far-flung colonial empire, the route structure that was in operation in the 1930s is incredible. In the 1920s, Sabena's predecessor, LARA, was flying hydroplanes from Leopoldville to Stanleyville in the Congo, a distance of over 1,000 miles (with lots of stops of course). By the mid 1930s, regular service from Brussels to the Congo in Handley Pages and Fokkers was underway. The mail run took five and one-half days, but it still beat the steamship.

In addition to a dozen or so familiar World War II and just-thereafter propeller-driven machines, is a Fairchild C-119 Packet, which is not even common in the States. You may remember Jimmy Stewart carving one of the booms off a Fairchild to make a homebuilt in the desert in the film *Flight of the Phoenix*. A remarkable number of jet fighters are also crammed onto the main floor. There is a complete collection of Republic F-84s: an F-84G Thunderjet, an F-84F Thunderstreak and two RF-84F Thunderflashes. I have never figured out how or why the USAF kept the same type-number for those three. Look at them closely and I doubt if one can find a half-dozen parts in common amongst them; I suspect it was done to delude the Congressional Budget Office. An English Hawker Hunter Mk.IV, a Canadian CF-100 Canuck, a Swedish SAAB J-35A Draaken, a French Dassault MD 450 Ouragan and a U. S. North American F-86F Sabre represent a truly cosmopolitan roundup of the jets of the 1950s and a fitting completion to an outstanding flight line.

The Percival Proctor IV Vega Gull, a long-distance record setter.

13

Windmills, Tulips and Old Airplanes

Schipol Airport, outside Amsterdam, familiar as the background scenery for a half-dozen recent thrillers, is the gateway to Holland. Actually to the Netherlands, since North and South Holland are just the two provinces west of what was the Zuider Zee, now an inland lake growing rapidly smaller as the Dutch keep making the North Sea bottom part of their real estate. Like any gateway airport, Schipol is modern, hustling and bustling. Not like Amsterdam itself which, with its canals, flower vendors, and cobblestoned old streets, is one of the most charming cities in Europe.

Before becoming totally enchanted with the city and the surrounding countryside's picturebook landscapes of windmills and fields of flowers, make a stop at the Aviodome. Across the airport building complex from Schipol's terminal, it contains a small, but elegant, collection of old aircraft and memorabilia. It is a bit far to walk, but you can catch a local bus at the stop just across the road from the terminal building. Several of the buses go by the Aviodome on the way to the highway. Try Nos. 5, 9, 10 or a little *platt-deutsch* and you will probably get an answer back in American English.

You can't miss the Aviodome; it's just like its name implies, a big white geodesic dome. Besides, the DC-3 parked out front is much too clean to be in service. KLM was a great customer of Douglas' and used every model from the DC-2 through the DC-10. In fact they were the only commercial user of the DC-5. Everyone tried to come up with a replacement for the DC-3, but nobody ever could, not even the Douglas people themselves. They tried in 1939 with the DC-5, a high-wing twin about the same size as the DC-3, but the ubiquitous DC-3 was irreplaceable. Douglas finally talked KLM into buying half of the production run of a whole dozen DC-5s and the U. S. Navy took the other half. It is a shame that none are left, but inside the museum is a collection of photos of the DC-5 along with a large amount of other early KLM memorabilia.

That's to be expected since KLM is the Netherland's flag carrier. It is also easier to fly KLM than pronounce it; KLM stands for *Koninklijke Luchtvaart Maatschappij*. But for all that, KLM has had since the 1930s one of the longest route structures in the world. Remember the Dutch East Indies and the Dutch West Indies; that's how people got there. KLM was also a pioneer in using the latest air transports available, starting with de Havillands and the whole series of Fokker transports to the Boeing and Douglas jetliners of today.

There is one of those old airliners in the Aviodome, a Fokker F.VIIa. The F.VIIa was quite successful and with a "minor modification" (adding two more engines to make it a trimotor) became the even more well known F.VIIb. The most reknown example of an F.VIIb was the *Southern Cross* in which Charles Kingsford-Smith made the first transpacific crossing as well as the first non-stop flight from Australia to New Zealand (there is no place to stop between Australia and New Zealand) in a flight as harrowing as Alcock and Brown's crossing of the Atlantic. The *Southern Cross* holds the place of honor at the Commonwealth Museum in Canberra, Australia.

Walking through the cabin of the Fokker F.VIIa, you can ponder the changes in airline travel in the past fifty years. Some things change slowly, however. We did a gulp and double-take as we entered the cockpit of the F.VIIa. Bolted to the ceiling is what is clearly the backplate of the rotating antenna for an old Lear Orienter low-frequency ADF (automatic direction finder). That brought back memories of stumbling all over the San Fernando Valley at night in "Charlie," our old Cessna 180, trying to hit the Burbank outer compass locator with one of those electronic Frankensteins—while these guys found Indonesia and Australia with the damn things.

Painted as the first Fokker F.VIIa used by KLM and lost in a May, 1940 attack on Schipol Airport, this F.VIIa was in service from 1928 to the mid-1950s.

They not only found those places, they set records doing it. Second place in the 1934 MacPherson Robertson London-to-Australia Air Race was won by a KLM DC-2. Only the de Havilland D.H.88 Comet, especially built for long distance racing, came in ahead of it, with a stripped Boeing 247 in third and the rest of the racers straggling in behind or never getting there at all. But K. D. Parmentier and J. J. Moll, flying the KLM DC-2, were not racing pilots in a racing plane. They were airline pilots carrying a full load of passengers in an airliner on a scheduled run! When they reached the end of the line at Batavia, they dropped their last paying passenger and just kept on going to Melborne. That's class! The third-place Boeing 247, flown by Roscoe Turner and Clyde Pangborn, now hangs in the Smithsonian's National Air and Space Museum in Washington.

Fokker and Koolhoven were the two major Dutch aircraft manufacturers, with Fokker being the much larger and better known. Fokker was not only a brilliant designer and a man of much personal courage, but an exceptional businessman, with little fear in that area as well. His first successful machine was the *Spinne* which he flew in 1911 when he was just 21 years old. A replica is in the museum while the original is being restored alongside it. The diminutive *Spinne* monoplane has a stick-like fuselage with a kingpost above and a long skid between the gear like the Avro 504, all of which is laced with a complete network of wires. It does remind one of a spider's web.

With much larger possibilities for sales in Germany than in the Netherlands, Fokker moved there and set up a factory at Schwerin just before World War I. He began building monoplane fighters, of which the Fokker Eindekker E.III (the ''E'' for Eindekker or monoplane) was the most famous. Thence followed a series of biplanes, culminating in the notorious D.VII as well as the Triplane Dr.I and at the very end of the war, the high-wing D.VIII monoplane. Fokker was the most common name in German aircraft and even Albatroses and Pfaltz' were generically called ''Fokkers'' in the press. Yet at the end of World War I, Fokker was still less than thirty years old. And he had a problem. Germany would be in disarray for years to come and reparations would ruin the economy. Aircraft production would be severely limited if not completely banned. His Fokker D.VII already had the dubious honor of being singled out in treaty documents as being specifically forbidden. Clearly it was no place to try to run an airplane business. So Fokker hurriedly loaded everything in his factory that wasn't bolted down—and much that was—onto railroad cars; the tracks went past his factory. Blueprints and records, tooling and materials, half-built D.VIIs, machinery and engines were bundled into freight cars; six 60-car trainloads of them. The borders were supposedly closed, but Fokker solved the transit, customs, and clearance problems in his usual inimitable way. In the confusion of war's end, he simply bribed every railway

Tony Fokker's first aircraft, his Spinne. *A replica, the pieces of the original under restoration are at right.*

and customs man he came across such that his six trains, carrying the bulk of his factory, steamed merrily and safely across the border into his native Netherlands.

One problem remained. He didn't have an airplane—at least not the prototype F.II that he hoped to make the foundation for a future commercial aircraft business. The F.II was under guard at a German airfield near Schwerin. Fokker's colleague, Bernard De Waal, snuck back to Schwerin in a true-life cloak and dagger adventure, complete with false beard, dark glasses and midnight rendezvous' with trusted friends still at the old factory. De Waal promptly stole the F.II from under the noses of the guards, taking off directly out of the hanger. If that wasn't enough, the aircraft was in need of maintainence and shortly the engine began to cough and fail. De Waal put the plane down safely in a field, but he was still in Germany. The police who arrived on the scene were suspicious, but would have to check out the cock and bull story that De Waal was feeding them. They left a guard and De Waal whiled away the time by repairing the clogged carburetor. Then with some even more improbable story about damage to the engine if the oil cooled off too fast, he convinced the guard to help hand-prop it for him. As the engine started, De Waal rammed the throttle home and with a startled and angry guard chasing after him, managed to take off and turn west again. The engined failed once more, but this time the forced landing was on Dutch soil; Fokker was back in business!

Fokker continued to assemble D.VIIs from the airframes and components he had smuggled out as he began the design of newer models. The most successful of his military aircraft was the C.V, whose active life spanned most of the period between the wars. A very attractive

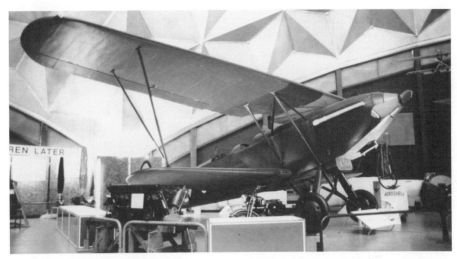

The Fokker C.V-D soldiered on from 1925 to the beginning of World War II. A rare survivor is painted as one destroyed defending Haamsted Airfield.

two-seat biplane made in a number of variations, the C.V-D in the Aviodome is powered by a Rolls-Royce Kestrel. Fokker C.Vs served all over the world from Scandinavia to the Dutch East Indies and were sold to a dozen air forces; even the Bolivian Air Force had a squadron of C.Vs. It was a Fokker C.V that rescued Umberto Nobile off the polar ice pack after his dirigible, *Italia*, went down on a polar attempt in 1928. The C.V soldiered on until the start of World War II. The machine on display (originally No. 634) is painted in the colors of No. 618, one of the old biplanes which fought valiantly to stem the German invasion in May 1940. No. 618 was finally destroyed during an attack on Haamstede Airfield by Messerschmitt Bf 110s.

Meanwhile, the F.II had become the grandfather to a whole series of Fokker transports of one, two, three, and eventually, four engines which formed the backbone of European air transportation. Two of our favorite Fokker designs do not exist at the museum and must be remembered from the photographs and models on display. One is the D.XXI, a dainty fighter of the Curtiss P-36 school, but with panted, fixed gear. Some fought in Holland in 1940, but their most famous use was by the Finns in their winter war with Russia. There is an authentic Fokker D.XXI at Luonetjarvi Air Force Base in Finland.

No examples of the other type remain. It was the Fokker G.I, which was revolutionary when it first flew in 1936. The G.I was a twin-boomed, two-seat fighter, something like an early P-38 Lightning, or rather more like the XP-58 Chain Lightning from nearly a decade later. With eight machine guns protruding from the nose, the G.I was rightly called *La Faucheur*—The Grim Reaper. Only a few G.IAs and twenty-three improved G.IBs had been built when war started. Some of those were destroyed by surprise on the ground, but the rest fought hard and literally until the end, when only a single machine remained in one piece. Even that one was not yet done for. A year later, two Fokker factory pilots managed to distract some German guards and escape in it to England. Stealing airplanes away from the Germans seems to be a Fokker tradition.

To see what a Fokker G.I or D.XXI looked like, one must travel an hour or so southeast from Amsterdam to the Kamp van Zeist airbase at Söesterberg. The twin radial engines of a late 1930s Lockheed 12A, parked in the grass and painted in Dutch colors, tell you that there is something special here. Pass the Republic Thunderstreak, a Catalina flying boat and its later replacement for patrol work, a Lockheed SP2H Neptune. A Douglas C-47 marks the entry to the Militaire Luchtvaart Museum.

A Douglas C-47 and a Lockheed SP-2H Neptune guard the entrance to the Militaire Luchtvaart Museum, Soesterberg.

If not for the Dutch insignias, one expects Amelia Earhart or Howard Hughes to be flying this immaculate Lockheed L-12A.

124

Two well-lit and attractive buildings house the collection. The building on the right contains a small coffee shop where your can rest up after your travels and talk airplanes. More important, it contains the major treasures of the collection. The Grim Reaper, the Fokker G.I, has its eight machine guns aimed at you as you enter the hall. Since no authentic G.Is survived the war, the one on display is a replica. More accurately, it is a full scale mockup of a G.IA made originally for a Dutch TV program. Nevertheless, surrounded by figures of pilot and ground crew preparing for takeoff, it is an impressive exhibit. Reviewing its armament and performance figures, one recognizes that had there been two dozen squadrons of G.Is available in 1940, instead of less than two dozen G.Is in total, the blitzkrieg into the low countries could have met with quite a different fate. The stubborn Dutch have never been tolerant of invaders of their homeland. In 1574, the specially-built and heavily-armed shallow-draft boats of William of Orange were the weapon that destroyed the Spanish invaders. In 1940, the Fokker G.I could have had the same effect had there been enough of them. Perhaps that can be considered an exaggeration. Perhaps a few squadrons of 300-mph heavy fighters with eight guns concentrated in each nose would have had little effect on the tanks concentrated on the narrow roads and dykes. Perhaps they would have had little effect on the unarmed Junkers Ju 52 transports overhead laden with paratroops. Perhaps.

The diminutive Fokker D.XXI is also a replica. It was cleverly made from an AT-6 Texan's airframe and if you crawl underneath, you can see the AT-6's wheel wells, clearly unusable with the D.XXI's fixed and spatted gear. Enough parts from an old airframe have since been located and within a few years an authentic Fokker D.XXI should be sitting in that spot.

With that row of nose guns, the Fokker G-IA (replica) aptly deserved the title La Faucheur— *'The Grim Reaper.'*

One of the authors with a replica Fokker D.XXI.

The automobile and the mannequins portray the era in which this Farman HF.20 flew.

Other aircraft in the hall range from Farman HF.20, de Havilland Tiger Moth, and Dominie biplanes to Spitfire, Mustang, and Mitchell aircraft from World War II. The second hall, a large hanger, contains the newer aircraft as well as the restoration facilities. An authentic Fokker D.VII from World War I is being painstakingly restored and will soon take a place of pride in the main building. An AT-6 Texan has been left with its fuselage skin removed to form a full scale cutaway showing its structure and innards. The Dutch manufactured a number of American and British jets under license and imported others. A dozen Thunderjet, Sabre, Hunter and Meteor jet fighters cluster around the spacious floor.

Before leaving the museum complex, examine the collection of engine and airframe parts in the main building. These are not sample pieces supplied by the manufacturers. They have come to the surface as new lands have been drained and reclaimed with new dykes in the Zuider Zee and other areas. They come from British, American and German aircraft: bombers that didn't make it home from a bombing mission over Germany, fighters that hesitated just a little too long when closing on those bombers, dive bombers that went in just a little too low. The parts are bent and broken. They could each tell a story. Perhaps as more land is reclaimed, enough parts for a Fokker G.I will be found to construct one of those valiant machines.

As sad as it is that there are no G.Is left, even more of a shame is that there are no pre-war Koolhovens of any type known to exist. Koolhoven was a much smaller company than Fokker, lived in that company's shadow all its life, and was eventually taken over by them after World War II. Koolhoven manufactured some attractive light aircraft and light transports during the between-the-wars era and also built a mix of attractive, as well as totally ugly, fighters. There is only one Koolhoven of any type known to exist in a collection anywhere, and that is in, of all places, an automobile museum.

About a half-hour south of Soesterberg, just off the E-37 and right after you cross the river Maas is the National Automobiel Museum at Raamsdonksveer. The museum is located behind (and we think owned by) the European Toyota assembly plant. If your tastes in machinery are catholic, then by all means visit it, since it is one of the finest and most extensive antique automobile collections in the world. One can stroll through some sets of turn-of-the-century or 1920s streets or sit

The only Koolhoven in a museum and likely one of the only Koolhovens left anywhere; an Fk.43 'flies' over an old fire truck at the Het Nationaal Automobiel Museum.

at an indoor "outdoor restaurant" and have coffee while viewing Bugattis, Daimlers, Mercedes, and hundreds of other vehicles and rolling stock. Hanging from the center ceiling, however, is a Koolhoven Fk.43. The Fk.43 was a single-engined, high-wing monoplane, roughly similar to a Fairchild F-24. At least it appears to have a landing gear made by the same demented ironmonger that made the Fairchild's. In its day, however, the Koolhoven Fk.43 was quite a good performer and the few built saw light commercial service throughout northwestern Europe during the rebuilding of that area in the late 1940s. Take a look at it, its the only Koolhoven left.

Circle back to Amsterdam and pay a last visit to the Aviodome before returning home, as there are still more aircraft to see there. The Blériot XI has constructor's number 54; Blériot's cross channel flight made the 'XI a best-seller in 1910. Several additional Fokkers are in the museum ranging from a 1925 S.IV currently being restored to the more modern S-11 Instructor, an S-12 used for boundary layer control experiments, and the S-14 Mach-Trainer. Representing the close ties between the Netherlands and England are a Supermarine Spitfire Mk.9c, a Hawker Hunter and a Hawker (Armstrong Whitworth) Seahawk. The Hawker Seafury FB.51 and the Gloster Meteor on display were built by Fokker under license.

Several U.S. aircraft are also on the floor including a nondescript Piper L-4 Cub. The Cub, however, has a somewhat suspicious history. U. S. records show that an L-4 with constructor's number 12732 was delivered to the U. S. Army Air Corps in early 1945, sent to Tacloban in the Philippines for spotting work, and did not survive the war. Yet a

A Fokker S.11 Instructor and a Grumman S-2N sit in front of the Aviodome's geodesic roof on the road around Schipol.

Piper Cub with no known history, but with the same constructor's number 12732 was discovered in Belgium in 1947 registered as OO-GEI. Now at the Aviodome with Dutch registration PH-NLA, one wonders what stories it could tell. Somewhere there may be an ex-GI of entrepreneurial talents who just might be able to explain how that Cub erased itself off the U. S. Army's books, transmigrated ten thousand miles and transmuted nationality.

In addition to other complete aircraft, both authentic and replicas, are the cockpit sections of a North American B-25D Mitchell, a de Havilland D.H.104 Dove, and a Sud Aviation SE.210 Caravelle 3 which are enjoyable to look through. Even more enjoyable is the circa World War II Link blind-flying trainer. A far cry from the electronic cockpit simulators of today, a large number of now more-elderly pilots painfully learned to navigate in the dark and stay right side up in those quaint blue boxes on a pedestal. Give it a try while you are there; it's operational, but one may find that, as with video games, the 12-year-olds on a school tour of the museum do better on a Link than most adults. Slightly humbled by both the aircraft of the past and the 12-year-olds, one exits the Aviodome for the bright blue sky outside—and the scream of a KLM 747 as it breaks ground enroute to Bangkok or Batavia.

14

To Be or Not To Be

After strolling through Tivoli and taking a leisurely walk down the Amagertorv, almost everyone who visits Copenhagen takes the bus tour to Helsingor—Shakespeare didn't take spelling seriously and he called it Elsinor. Don't! Get a rental car instead so that in addition to visiting Hamlet's castle you can drive a short distance west along the Nordre Strandvej and spend time at the Danmarks Tekniske Museum.

It is a small museum, as proportionate to a small country and it has all the quaintness, charm and touch of humor that is typically Danish. Old fire engines and diminutive steam locomotives, arcane electrical apparatus and even some models of large windmills abound. While the windmill normally connotes Holland, it was actually Denmark that around the turn of the century developed the modern electricity-producing windmill; in 1985 windmills were Denmark's third largest export product to the U. S. After all, the wind is about the only indigenous energy source that Denmark has. Perhaps with all that wind, minds turned toward the sky. While there are only a few flying machines at the Danmarks Tekniske Museum, they are particularly worth seeing.

Just because the bulk of the technical literature originates in the big countries that have the resources to dominate various arenas, we tend to forget that brains and perseverance are not necessarily distributed in some ratio to land area. Hence we sometimes also forget the contributions that citizens of the smaller countries, sometimes quite isolated and with little resouces, have made to the advancement of science. Remember that both Tycho Brahe and Nils Bohr were Danes, and there is a crater on the moon named for one and a nuclear research institute for the other.

The same pioneering was true in aviation. One of the first powered flights ever was by Jacob Christian Ellehammer. An engineer by training, he built several gliders around the turn of the century and in 1905, constructed an 18-hp monoplane with semi-cylindrical wings. While that first machine was not successful, his second did much better. In September of 1906 on the little island of Linholm, his new biplane achieved a flight of 42 meters and got several feet in the air. There is an actual photograph extant of him clearly off the ground.

That 42-meter flight was one of the longest yet achieved outside of the Wright brothers and one must remember that while the Wrights flew in 1903, only rumors and not their technology had yet reached Europe. Admittedly Ellehammer's machine was tethered and flying in a circle, but Ellehammer did recognize the need for control. He suspended himself in a cradle and could adjust the center of gravity by swinging his body, much like a hang glider pilot does today. Actually, Ellehammer's machine was not a true biplane, but should rather be called a semi-biplane. The lower wing was a conventional braced structure with spars and ribs, while the upper wing was more of a sail or semi-parachute. While not spectacular, Ellehammer's hops provided a major stimulous to the progress of the other pioneers; progress that was to suddenly burst forth in 1908 after the Wilbur Wright visit, and then leave the U. S. and the Wrights in the comparative dust for the next twenty years.

In a small country, one must be a jack-of-all-trades. Ellehammer not only built that biplane, he also performed some of the first experiments in the world on the helicopter. His machine is quaint and it doesn't look as if it could fly. On the other hand the latter point also applies to most modern helicopters and they would look a lot more attractive if they were quaint. In fact, I have serious doubts that helicopters actually fly; even as an aerodynamicist, I have always suspected that it is just some crude form of levitation. Only those machines with wings (preferably two), a propeller (preferably wood), and a reciprocating engine (preferably radial), truly fly, but that is just an opinion.

One of the first aircraft in Europe to actually leave the ground; the Ellehammer Type II reached an altitude of 18 inches in 1906.

Ellehammer's, and one of the world's, first experimental helicopters dates from 1911; it wasn't successful.

Ellehammer's helicopter is actually fairly well thought out. The use of counter-rotating blades helps overcome the lack of cyclic pitch. The conventional propeller and controls might have made it near workable, but the power-to-weight ratio needed for a helicopter put the practical machine fifty years into the future.

Ellehammer was not deterred by either the limitations of his semi-biplane or the lack of success with his helicopter; he continued his experiments and developed a 30-hp triplane, unfortunately also not very successfully. It was, however, the first true triplane. He went on in 1909 to develop a monoplane using the same engine. Thus Ellehammer experimented with the monoplane, the biplane, the triplane and the helicopter. None were very successful, but they were part of that glorious beginnings of flight. The biplane, the monoplane, and the helicopter hang side-by-side and you can get a good view of them from the balcony at the Danmarks Tekniske Museum. They form a tribute to a lone and, outside of his native country, nearly forgotten pioneer.

A Farman Glenten canard biplane sits alongside them, portraying how developments were then proceeding outside Denmark. But the end aircraft in the row is one that takes the breath away, at least for the lover of flying boats. The Donnet-Leveque Maagen 3 must be the most beautiful flying boat of the early years, if not of all time. There is just no comparison between it and the generally klutzy-looking machines of its era. The machines of pre-World War I and even into the 1920s were pioneering wonders, but beautiful is not the descriptor that would normally come to mind for them.

The Maagen is a diminutive, two-seat biplane with a single pusher prop. The hull is suspended beneath the lower wing a little way by short

One of the most exquisite flying boats of all time, the Donnet-Leveque Maagen at the Danmarks Tekniske Museum, Helsingor.

struts. The proportions are pure grace; the fuselage hull has the lines of an early slender speedboat and the varnished, laminated wood is of the quality one sees in high-priced Danish furniture. It is hard to describe beauty in words, but from any angle, the Maagen just looks perfect. It would be wonderful to fly one today, or even just to see it fly. There are only six aircraft at the Danmarks Tekniske Museum; any one of them makes the visit worthwhile.

While in Copenhagen, take time out from eating for a few minutes and also visit the Tojhusmuseet, the Royal Arsenal Museum. It is just off the Fredricksholms Kanal and next to Christiansborg Castle, right in the midst of all the sightseeing you would be doing anyway. The Tojhusmuseet is in King Christian IV's armory, built around 1600, and while there are only three aircraft on display, again their rarity makes it worth the trip.

The Avro 504K is not actually all that rare, but the Berg und Storm BS.III and the Hawker Dankok are very rare indeed. In fact, both are the only ones of their type in existence. The Berg und Storm dates from 1910. It was one of those machines that bridged the gap between the pioneers and the "practical" machines of World War I. It is a 40-hp monoplane with a tail that looks like an Antoinette, wings reminiscent of a Blériot and a landing gear that, while it has the single braced centerpost of an Antoinette, is so far forward that it is nearly under the propeller. It was the first airplane of the Danish Air Force.

One of the few of Hawker's machines that didn't fly all that well, at least initially, was the Woodcock. Changes were made and the satisfactory Mk.II was adopted by the RAF in 1924 to replace the Sopwith Snipe which was getting a bit worn, having served since the tail end of World War I. Some 62 Woodcocks were built and served until about 1928; none are left. Simultaneously, Hawker was active in trying to export their products, and they convinced the Danish Air Force of the Woodcock's intrinsic worth. Some additional modifications were made, including shortening the span of the lower wing and the Danecock (or Dankok) was born. The Hawker factory built three of them and an additional dozen were made under license in Denmark.

It is a stubby biplane, although the fairly wide landing gear made it attractive to pilots who dislike crosswinds. The 385-hp Armstrong Siddeley Jaguar IV engine is completely exposed and both the reasonable power-to-weight ratio and the ailerons on both sets of wings made it quite an aerobatic airplane. Number 158, hanging in the museum is one of those made in Denmark and the original intent was for the squadron to be used for the defense of the Copenhagen Naval Base. They served until 1936 when they were replaced briefly by Hawker Nimrods. In any event, it is doubtful if either would have been able to defend the base in 1940 when Germany attacked. While neither the Dankok nor the Woodcock ever saw combat, they are still reminders of that time between the wars when the biplane fighter was king and the pilot wore a scarf.

If you are ever driving down the west coast of Jutland—don't ask why you might be driving down the west coast of Jutland—be sure to stop at Stauning Airport. If you ask at the small terminal building (there are one or two flights a day from Copenhagen), the dispatchers and attendants likely will not speak English nor know what you are talking about. So walk next door to the small building housing a little restaurant for some pastries and coffee. The woman behind the counter won't know what you are talking about either. But her ten year old daughter will; most young people are learning English in school. She will translate and her mother will get her father and somewhat reluctantly he will drop what he is doing and escort you across the field and unlock a moderate-sized hanger.

It is here that another point about visiting foreign air museums comes home. The first plane inside the door was a pale blue de Havilland Hornet Moth with the sponsoring liquor company's advertising on the side. On a small stand nearby was a map showing the route it had flown back in the early 1930s; forgotten now is whether it was from Denmark to South Africa or to Singapore or to some other equally unlikely place. While our bored attendant waited, the two of us began jabbering together trying to decipher the text; clearly we were interested and impressed with whoever had flown that frail and ancient craft so far so long ago.

The next thing you know our reluctant guide was all over us with a great big grin, talking away incomprehensibly, pointing out this, emphasizing that, opening cowls and cockpits and dragging the distaff half into a baggage compartment to expain something (I hope that is what he was doing). The point is that those in other countries, particularly smaller countries, are as proud of their achievements in aviation as we are of ours. Sometimes there may be a little bit of uncertainty or hesitancy about these strange Americans. But with a little sincerity and honest interest in their aviation, the doors and the grins open wide. It was hours later when the little girl came in with instructions to get her dad back to work. That was fortunate as it was the only polite way we were going to extricate ourselves anyway.

Further into the museum hanger are several S. A. I.s. S. A. I. was one of the few Danish aircraft companies manufacturing original designs and they produced a series of aircraft with the initials KZ. S. A. I. is the abbreviation for Skandinavisk Aero Industri; the KZ stands for designers Kramme and Zeuthern. In any event, the KZ II-T is a rather nice open cockit, two-seat, low-winged trainer dating from 1937 and similar to the Ryan PT-21. The KZ II Koupe, while based on the same structure and with the same wings, is quite a different looking machine. It is a side-by-side enclosed monoplane with a sightly 'humped' curve to the fuselage lines. Quite a few were later used in Sweden as trainers.

The KZ III is more of an Aeronca-looking machine that was designed in 1943 during the German occupation for use as an air ambulance; it was capable of of carrying one stretcher. The second prototype was actually smuggled out of Denmark to Sweden where it underwent flight tests. As soon as the war ended it went into production as a light personal aircraft and trainer.

The distaff half examines an S.A.I. KZ II Koupe used for training in both Denmark and Sweden in the 1940s.

Carl Johannsen's CAJO 59, a two-seat amphibian powered with two 60-hp Walter engines.

The fuselage (and the parts awaiting restoration) for the only existing KZ IV are in the hanger. The KZ IV was a very attractive light twin. While a monoplane, the 130-hp inverted Gipsy Moth engines, long wing and spatted fixed gear remind one of a de Havilland Rapide with one less wing. Also first designed as an air ambulance, the twin-tailed machine would carry six at a dignified 130 mph.

Another unusual twin is the CAJO 59, its name based on that of its designer, Carl Johannsen. The CAJO is a small twin-engined, two-seat amphibian looking somewhat like a scaled down Grumman Widgeon. It was essentially a homebuilt and it would be nice to get hold of the plans. With its high wing holding two inverted 60-hp in-line Walter engines and with a simple retractable tricycle gear, it might prove an inexpensive alternative to the out-of-sight prices that a current amphibian demands.

One of the more attractive singles is a rare Miles M.28 Mercury 6. It has the tail of an Ercoupe and the nose of a de Havilland, but the cockpit, with its gull-winged doors is strictly Miles. If you are an *aficionado* of the English aircraft of the 1930s, take a closer look. When war started, some English officers unofficially approached Miles and articulated the need for a better light "hack" for communications and liaison work. Miles added a third central fin and rudder for better low speed control, beefed up the gear for the military-issue clods that would be flying it and went to more standard doors—and out came the Miles M.38 Messenger. There may be a dozen Miles Messengers left around Britain and even an example in Brussels, but there is only one Miles Mercury in a museum, OY-ALW, and it is probably the only Mercury left in the world.

One aircraft that anyone would love to fly is the Focke-Wulf Fw 44J Stieglitz. The Stieglitz, of which less than a dozen still exist, is one of those classic radial-engined aerobatic biplanes like the Bücker Jung-meister, Waco Taperwing or Stearman, that demand that the pilot fly the airplane but in return provide that sense of exhilaration that only comes with flying an open cockpit aerobatic biplane. We must remember to rob a bank someday.

The museum at Stauning is private, the home of the Dansk Veteran-Flysamling (Antique Flying Club), although it is hoped that in the future it will be open more generally to the public. While it may be hard to get a chance to drive through Jutland, if you do, try to time it for the right weekend in late June. That is when the KZ & Veteranflyklubben hold their annual fly-in, and nearly every flyable antique north of the Alps and east of Greenwich will head for Stauning. You ought to meet them there.

You can return to Copenhagen by the once-or-so a day airliner, by car, or better yet by the excellent Danish railway. If you take the latter, you can stop at Egeskov on the central island of Fyn, not far from Hans Christian Andersen's home at Odense. At Egeskov is the Veteran-museum and another two dozen antique aircraft await. Besides a number of S. A. I. KZs of various models and several SAABs, there are some other pretty rare beasts. These include a Hollaender AH.1, a General Aircraft Monopar ST-25 and a Moelhede Petersen XMP-2 (which we mention as a test of aviation esoterica). At Egeskov, and as rare in this country, are a Lockheed 12A, a smaller version of the first Electra, and a Fairchild PT-26 Cornell trainer.

The sleek Miles M.28 Mercury Six with its gull-wing canopy at the Dansk Veteranflysam-lung, Stauning.

137

If you continue back to Copenhagen by train, be advised that the train goes on a ferryboat to get from Fyn to Sjaelland and Copenhagen. Now since ferryboats are short and fat and trains are long and skinny, the train is uncoupled into several shorter lengths and shunted onto parallel tracks on the ferryboat. The trip takes an hour or more, so you can go to the upper deck and have a sandwich and beer and stroll outside. Don't dally too long, however, or you may have to race downstairs as the train pulls out, hop on the first car you can grab and then search the corridor until you find your compartment and your luggage. You may not! It may then come as a surprise to you that there had been more than one train on the ferryboat and you are on the wrong one. We provide that advice based on experience; but there are a great many nice places to visit in Denmark, even if unplanned, and so what if you miss your connections at Copenhagen. Who knows, you might even find another hidden airport with antique airplanes.

15

The Main Line

If you do much travelling through central Europe, then sooner or later you will have a few hours to kill at Frankfurt's Rhein-Main Airport. Frankfurt, like Atlanta or Denver, is a regional hub. Thus if the weather turns sour or the French air traffic controllers go on strike (I think its every other Thursday) things begin to jam up. Actually, it is not a bad airport to get stuck at. It is large, modern and expansive—a far cry from when Rhein-Main was the starting point for the famed Berlin airlift; when Harry Truman decided that Berlin would stay an open city come hell or high water. The DC-3s and DC-4s lined up in solid rows at the old Rhein-Main terminal. In good weather or soup so solid that birds couldn't fly, they loaded up and flew circuits to Berlin's Templehof Airdrome some 275 miles away. They did something airplanes had never done before—they supplied a whole city by air and kept it alive.

Rhein-Main has changed in the forty years since then, but if one does get stuck there for a while, there are several choices. You can plunk down in a chair, be uncomfortable and take a chance on dozing and missing your flight. You can go into one of the bars, be comfortable and take a chance on dozing and missing your flight. Or you can visit Dr. Muellers Sex Shoppe. Actually, the authors have never visited it (at least each swears that to the other), but from secondhand reports and the amount of advertising around the airport, it appears to be a potentially viable third option.

Actually, you have a fourth choice; just look up! You see, the Air Classik Collection does not have a permanent home and so the caretakers did a very wise thing. Where else would you expect to find airplanes but at an airport. So with only modest funds and support, they distributed the collection around Germany's major airports, not just at Frankfurt, but at Berlin-Tegel, Düsseldorf, Hannover, Koln-Bonn, Munich and Stuttgart.

A Bücker Jungmann, a de Havilland Tiger Moth and a Stampe S.V.4C line the balcony at Frankfurt Rhein-Main Airport.

At Frankfurt, go up the staircase at the center of the upper level and there are a half-dozen aircraft, including a Bücker Bu 133B Bestmann, a de Havilland D.H.82A and a Klemm Kl 35D hanging from the ceiling as well as a number of models and artifacts. Even more enjoyable is to take a stroll out of doors and along the rooftop of the center pier where the iron machinery is kept. One can approach quite close and have a chance to examine some interesting aircraft in great detail.

A Junkers Ju 87 Stuka stands just outside the door. The Stuka epitomizes all the *Sturzkampfflugzeuges* and the machines of war; the Ju 87 is truly a bird of prey. The inverted gull wings, panted fixed gear and chin radiator lead to a terribly ugly, but unforgettable, appearance. It is said that during a tour of the U. S. in 1932, Ernst Udet, a World War I ace and later a general in World War II, watched a display of Curtiss SBC Helldivers (the original biplane, not the later World War II SB2C). They were being used to perfect the techniques for dive-bombing against ships for the U. S. Navy. He took both the idea and two brand-new Curtiss F11C Hawks back to Germany for testing; the idea was adopted.

The Stuka was an integral part of the blitzkreig, tied together with the tank columns and the motorized infantry carriers. No matter that the Stuka was totally useless when confronted by Spitfires and Hurricanes in the Battle of Britain. That was a year later when they were fighting without air superiority, a hundred miles from base, and against heavily defended targets. In that situation they were wiped out; in the

The arch-typical bird of prey, a Junkers Ju 87 Stuka from the Blitzkreig through the low countries, France and Poland.

summer of 1940, a sortie to Britain in a Stuka was a suicide mission. But earlier in Poland or Belgium or France, or in 1937 as it destroyed Guernica in Spain, the Stuka was one of the most feared weapons in the world. It is fairly large for a single-engined airplane and angular in every respect. The slotted flaps, ailerons and dive brakes, plus the high overall drag gave it perfect control and accuracy in a dive. One views it sitting there fifty years later with very, very mixed emotions.

A less threatening Messerschmitt Bf 108 stands nearby. It is a rather elongated four-seater with retractable gear and a 240-hp Argus eight-cylinder engine. A Bf 108 Taifun will still give a Beech Bonanza a run for its money. Its performance of 189 mph with a range of 620 miles was spectacular for the late 1930s. So much so that Nord in France made them under license through the 1950s as the Nord 2002; it would be a nice machine to own even today.

A Junkers Ju 52/3m also adorns this elevated "ramp." A great many must have flown out of here during the 1930s and 1940s; Junkers made something like 4800 of them. The boxy trimotor, with its corrugated skin, appears to have been designed by the same guy who designs most airport hangers. It was gawky on its fixed gear and had control forces similar to a tug-boat's, but it was the "DC-3 of Europe" in those days, and not just of Europe. The Ju 52 was the last in a whole series of tri-motors built by Junkers throughout the 1920s and '30s.

One of the most notable from its effect on aviation was the Junkers G 31. The G 31 was similar to the later Ju 52/3m, but was a bit smaller and still retained an open cockpit. The all-metal corrugated skin concept created a breakthrough in load carrying capability and fuselage cargo space. Due to that breakthrough—and two strange characters—a small grass strip in a nearly unheard-of valley in New Guinea became, in 1934, one of the three most active airports in the world. Gold supplied the motive. "Shark-Eye" Park had discovered gold in the Bulolo River Valley in 1922, but the valley was almost inaccessible except by foot; a two-week trek through the jungle—longer if the headhunters got restless. It was, however, only a half-hour by air from the coast to the gold fields. Cecil J. Levine came up with the harebrained idea that an airplane could provide the primary support for the gold fields. So a small fleet of Junkers, with hatches cut into that corrugated ceiling, formed the world's first major air cargo operation. In an almost continuous flow for nearly a decade, the G 31s carted in tools, supplies, workers, horses, oxen, small trucks, and eight monstrous dredges—6 million pounds each—every nut and bolt of them carried by air to be assembled on site. During 1931, the four Junkers G 31s in New Guinea carried more freight in one month than the total of all the world's airlines put together did for the whole year. The rusting dredges are still there; the gold isn't. The Junkers proved that you could move anything by air.

As World War II came along, the G 31's offspring, the Ju 52 continued to prove that. They supplied, fed, bombed, dropped parachutists, towed troop gliders, whisked (albeit at a sedate speed) Hitler and his generals around, and did a thousand and one jobs and the ugly beast did them well. The Iron Annie was beloved by the pilots who flew her; sometimes love is blind. Actually the Ju 52 here is a Spanish license-built CASA 352; one of the problems with losing wars is that one loses so much that one later has to go out and scrounge up the pieces again.

An Me 262 Schwalbe sits on the roof at Frankfurt looking less like a swallow and much more like the shark that it was. It was the first jet fighter to really see active service. We should be very thankful for Hitler's paranoia. First he halted work on it as being redundant; the V-1 buzz bomb and V-2 rocket would end the war and thus the Me 262 would be a waste of funds. Then he ordered it to be converted into a high-speed penetrater bomber—sort of a super Mosquito—to be able to get through and bomb London in revenge for what German cities were going through from the 8th Air Force's B-17s. Without that idiocy, things might have taken quite a different turn. The confusion and contradictory directions delayed the production and introduction into service of the Me 262 by over a year and that year was critical. The Me 262 was over 100 mph faster than the P-51 Mustang or the Mk XIV Spitfire, the fastest propeller-driven fighters we had at the time. Of the Allied jet aircraft, the experimemental Bell Aircomet and the Gloster E28/39 were just that, and the first decent Allied jet fighter, the Gloster Meteor, wouldn't be available in quantity until much later. No, if the Me 262 had shown up in force in 1944 instead of in limited numbers

Fortunately the Messerschmitt Me 262 Schwalbe got into production too late to do much damage to Allied bombers.

under silly operational constraints in the spring of 1945, the history of the air war might have been quite different. One can stand on the roof at Frankfurt and sense the incredible power that that machine had as compared to its contemporaries and only be glad that the fates work in the strange ways that they do.

The last aircraft on the "ramp" is a familiar figure, one of those old, ubiquitous C-47s, the army's DC-3. Down below, DC-8s and 747s and Airbuses are taxiing back and forth, loading passengers and losing luggage as airlines do everywhere around the world. It's the continuous hustle and bustle of any large airport and people go their busy way without regard for the weather or giving anything else a second thought. But that DC-3 was flying back when there wasn't weather radar—there wasn't any radar. It wasn't pressurized and spent most of its life plugging along at 12,000 feet pushing its way through whatever weather the good Lord put in front of it. It didn't have inertial navigation, VORTACs, area-nav, or Loran. Usually, it just had a rather wretched low-frequency ADF and the pilot's pair of ears, but it made all that followed possible. It carried ammunition and vital cargo and VIPs and toilet paper; it flew the hump in Burma and the flats of Kansas; it carried the supplies that kept Berlin free and one got me from college to my first summer job in Buffalo. And somewhere in the world, it is still carrying people or cargo or chickens, still earning its living. It has earned much more than that. Over its wing and beyond the tower, an L-1011 breaks ground and the P. A. system is announcing our flight; one doesn't want to leave.

So next time you are trudging through an airport terminal in Germany, stop hunching over and looking at your suitcase and your shoe-

Douglas C-47s once took off from here in weather that grounded the birds during the Berlin airlift. A Messerschmitt Bf 108 Taifun is parked alongside.

laces. Look up; you may be missing some great old airplanes. Or you can always go over to Dr. Muellers.

Now one of the more enjoyable aspects of Germany is the Oktoberfest in Munich. When you have had your fill at the Hofbrauhaus, walk over to the Marienplatz, the square with the huge town hall and its famous Glockenspiel, the mechanical clock with the parading figures. Then go through the Viktualienmarkt, the outdoor food market, nibble some weisswurst and leberkäs, and continue south down the Reichenbachstrasse a block or two and turn east to cross the bridge, the Cornelius-Brücke. On an island in the middle of the Isar River is the Deutsches Museum, part of which was fortunately not destroyed during World War II.

The Deutsches Museum is one of the finest technical museums in the world and is particularly notable for its hands-on training exhibits. It is outstanding if you have a 12-year old in tow; the operating exhibits that explain physics are ones that even we can understand. But we are interested in airplanes and the display starts in the courtyard. The EWR-Sud VJ-101C next to the entrance was an early l960s tilt-engine V/STOL experiment similar to our X-19. A Lockheed T-33 and an F-104 also guard the entrance.

The treasures are upstairs in the aviation hall. The earliest machines are hanging from the ceiling, the rarest of which are an authentic Lilienthal Type 11 monoplane glider from 1895 and a Type 12 biplane glider from 1896. Lilienthal was one of the few pioneers who took a scientific and step-by-step approach to understanding the issues and problems associated with flight. He was also, as a true scientist, willing to share his results with others, including the Wrights and Pilcher. Lilienthal's gliders were essentially what we would now call hang-gliders. He was killed when one them stalled; he was one of the first

144

to encounter that phenomenon. Lilienthal's death had a profound effect on the Wright brothers and it is generally believed that the Wrights went to the canard configuration in an attempt to come up with a design that would not stall.

A number of early German flying machines also hang from the ceiling, several of them of the Taube configuration. The Etrich Taube was one of the more successful ones and formed the origins of the Luftwaffe at the beginning of World War I. The Taubes are easily recognized by their swept-back wingtips. An authentic Blériot XI and a Grade Libelle also grace the ceiling.

There is another rare, but more familiar airplane hanging there. It is a Type A Wright Flyer of 1908, and thank goodness that it was not destroyed during the war. While there are a number of replicas floating around, there are actually only six authentic Wright flying machines in the whole world. The Smithsonian has three: the original 1903 Flyer; a 1909 Military Flyer that the Wrights finally managed to sell to the U. S. Army; and the *Vin Fiz*, a 1911 machine in which Cal Rodgers managed to stumble across the U. S. in 49 days and 19 crashes. There is a modified Type B at the Air Force Museum at Wright-Patterson, a

A 1909 Grade Lanzpreiz hangs between an Etrich Taube, a Wright Model A Flyer and a Blériot.

Baby at the Musée de l'Air in Paris, and this Wright Type A in Munich. They are all that are left of one of the greatest legacies ever provided to man—the ability to fly.

World War I is represented by a two-seat Rumpler C.IV, a Fokker Dr.1 triplane (actually a replica) and the notorious Fokker D.VII. You know, many times we look but we do not see, as Sherlock Holmes would have said. We stare at the Fokker Dr.1 and D.VII carefully, trying to pin down what it is that is different from other World War I aircraft. There are no wires; those diagonal bracing wires that crisscross between wings and struts and fuselage on all the others. Designers back then were beginning to understand the laws of aerodynamics. It was the slow progress in structures and materials that held them back. By 1917, Fokker was using a rather thick airfoil that had both good lift-to-drag characteristics as well as enough thickness to allow a hefty wing spar. The prototype Dr.1 actually had cantilevered wings with no struts or wires. When the high command saw it, they refused to believe that it was safe and a long argument ensued. Fokker finally gave in and put struts between the wings to appease them, even though they were, in fact, totally unnecessary. While he gave in on the struts, he steadfastly refused to continue the facade and add the silly wires to either the Dr.1 or the D.VII.

Germany was badly constrained during the 1920s by the terms of the Treaty of Versailles, and so most of the craft from that era are gliders.

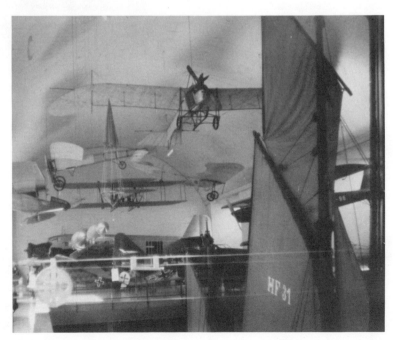

Lillienthal gliders, Taubes and Blériots; the Wright Type A is one of the six authentic Wright flying machines left in the world.

146

A lot of future Luftwaffe pilots received their first training on those gliders. A few powered exceptions which are on display are a Junkers F 13 and an A.50 of 1928 and 1931, respectively. Actually, Germany started developing military aircraft during that period and had negotiated a secret treaty with Russia. During the late 1920s and early 1930s there was an extensive secret base at Lipezk about 250 miles southwest of Moscow where Germany tested their new aircraft and trained future pilots. It is quite a cloak and dagger story and is why the Luftwaffe suddenly burgeoned in the mid 1930s out of apparently thin air.

The infamous Messerschmitt Bf 109E of that period stands out on the floor. They were manufactured by the Bayerische Flugzeugwerke, hence the "Bf" designator. It wasn't until 1941 that, as a reward for his brilliant designs and the fact that he had managed to essentially take control of the company, Willy Messerschmitt's "Me" initials started appearing. The "E" or Emil was the version available at the start of the war and throughout the Battle of Britain. The Bf 109 was as dominant an aircraft in World War II as the Fokker D.VII was in World War I.

The design philosophy was simple; put the smallest airframe possible behind the biggest engine available. The concept worked extremely well. It was nearly as fast as a Spitfire and actually had a smaller turning radius. Unfortunately, the Messerschmitt prototypes had trouble with stresses that caused rumors even though they were later fixed. It was then as strong as was necessary, but pilots are a pretty superstitious lot and their concern remained throughout the war. Even though the Bf 109 had a theoretically smaller turning radius than the early Spitfires, their pilots treated them a bit more cautiously while the Spit's pilots would pull the stick into their gut and turn inside the Messerschmitts. A real advantage for the Bf 109, however, was the fuel injec-

Tony Fokker's infamous D.VII in lozenge pattern camouflage is admired by one of the authors. Behind is a Junkers Ju 52/3m.

147

tion system on the Daimler-Benz engine. With it, the Bf 109 could fly inverted whereas the Spitfire's Rolls-Royce Merlin had a conventional carburetor which would cut out under negative "Gs." That's why when entering a dive the Spitfire either lost its engine for several seconds or went into that flamboyant, but actually time consuming, half-roll into a dive; either of which took a little longer than the power-on noseover that the Messerschmitt could do. As an aside, that evil-looking snout in the center of the Bf 109E's spinner is not the muzzle of a cannon; it is nothing more sinister than a cooling air inlet for the generator. The Messerschmitt spitting shells from its nose in movies about the Battle of Britain is an artistic liberty. The Germans had development problems with the cannon installation and most Bf 109Es had plain vanilla machine guns in the wings. It wasn't until the Gustav, the Bf 109G, came out in 1942 that the firing-through-the-hub cannon problem was solved and that was well after the Battle of Britain was over.

The Germans were good at concentrating their resources. They ran a tough competition, picked the best they had, and then never deviated. Thus Germany had only one standardized fighter, the Bf 109. Everyone could build them and everyone could fly them. It was only later in the war that Germany added the Focke-Wulf Fw 190 to its arsenal. The Bf 109 was in manufacture in one country or another for over two decades and more of them were manufactured than any other fighter in the world. It was to no avail; the stamina, spirit, Spitfires and radar of the British and the overwhelming mass of equipment from the U. S. did them in. Today there are less than 30 Bf 109s left out of the 35,000 or so produced. Half of those are license-built and surplused-off Spanish Hispano HA-1112s that never saw combat. The Bf 109 at Munich, AY+YH, was made by Messerschmitt and it did see combat—ironically in Spain with the German pilots of the Condor Legion.

Being only one hundred kilometers north of Lake Konstanz where the Zeppelin factory was located, the tradition of the dirigible is strong in Munich. Both the *Graf Zeppelin* and the *Hindenberg* were familiar sights overhead in the 1930s. None are left and they would be a bit big to fit inside a building anyway. In their place there are several detailed exhibits, including a complete diorama of the original Zeppelin factory at Friedrichshafen, as well as a considerable display of artifacts and memorabilia and some very large models. At the time of the Zeppelins, the Texas oil fields contained essentially the world's only supply of helium. Since the U. S. considered it a strategic and irreplaceable commodity, which indeed it was, we refused to sell any to Germany. Thus Germany was forced to use highly inflammable hydrogen as the lifting gas for the Zeppelins. They believed that by using great care and discipline, the use of hydrogen could be accomplished safely. They were wrong. That famous photograph of the *Hindenberg* going down in flames at Lakehurst, New Jersey on May 6, 1937, depicts the death knell of the Zeppelin. They were enormous and glorious machines, a tribute to the art of engineering, but for want of helium they went the way of the dinosaur.

A number of Germany's last vain, but incredible, efforts are at the end of the hall; the Me 262-A1 Schwalbe and the Me 163-B1 Komet. The Komet was that radical stubby flying wing designed by Professor Alexander Lippisch, who had been playing with glider and propeller versions of such things for a number of years. This time, the work of Dr. Helmuth Walter on rocket engines came into play, and the Me 163 was the first, and essentially only, rocket-powered aircraft ever to see operational service. Walter's work was a continuation of Opel's experimental rocket-powered aircraft of the 1930s and there is one of the only Opel rocket gliders in existence at the Munich museum.

An interceptor that could do 600 mph and climb at 16,000 feet per minute in 1944 could have wreaked total havoc with Allied bombers. On top of that, the Me 163, with it's rather rather rotund fuselage and simple structure, was designed in a way that it could be produced very quickly and cheaply. Fortuitously for Allied bombers, the Me 163 had a few defects; the principal one was a general propensity for blowing up. Even if the rocket engine stayed in one piece, the handling characteristics were atrocious and if the pilot did manage to get to altitude, it was unlikely that he would hit anything—the ultra-fast Komet was armed with only one slow-firing cannon. Stuffed with only six minutes of fuel, the Komet had little chance for a second pass. It then landed on a skid and sat around for an hour waiting to be carted back to a hanger for refueling, being fair game for Typhoons during that time. The Me 163 is perhaps tied with the Mignet Pou du Ciel in killing more pilots per flying hour than any airplane since 1910. It has to go down as one of the worst aircraft ever designed. That so many have survived to be displayed in museums is probably due to a certain sense of individuality within the European culture which makes good Kamikaze pilots hard to find. But the Me 163 was a failure mainly because the base technology just wasn't well enough developed in 1944 for what they were trying to achieve. That was forty years ago. Rocket and aircraft technology has changed a great deal since then. Perhaps what the Komet represented was really a preview of the air combat of the future.

The Dornier Do 335A-1 at Munich (although actually on loan from the Smithsonian) was another unusual aircraft. It was one of the few push-pull fighters ever built, and about the only one that wasn't a twin-boom type. The Do 335 had two Daimler-Benz 12-cylinder engines, one fore and one aft, with the pilot somewhere in the middle. It was a way to get twin-engined power without the drag of two separate nacelles or twin booms. It was fast, with a top speed of 474 mph, but it had too many development bugs that couldn't be worked out in the last days of the war. The last of all this silliness was the Bächem Ba 349, one of the only living examples of which is at Munich. It also had an early

Walter rocket like the Komet, but this beast took off vertically and after its brief mission the pilot bailed out, no pretense being made of trying to land the thing. The first manned flight, by the (immediately-after-takeoff) late Oberleutnant Lothar Siebert, was short and spectacular. Before another volunteer could be drafted, the war came to an end.

The old European railroad cars are different from Amtrac's and have a certain class which we perceive from watching too many old mystery movies. You know the cars, the ones with the aisle down one side and the eight-passenger compartments on the other. It is pleasant to sit in one, sip some Bavarian beer and watch the windmills, the locomotives, and in particular, the Hansa HFB-320 biz-jet with its swept forward wings, and some Dorniers and Lockheeds go by. Of course they don't go by very fast because the rail car is standing still; it's the coffee bar in the courtyard of the museum, but it is still a pleasant place to sit and watch the world go by.

16

Vantaa Lahestymislennonjohto 119.1

Fortunately, some words migrate in various but intelligible forms from language to language. Musée, museo, mussee are all recognizable. So if you are wandering through Vantaa Airport at Helsinki—a peculiar enough pastime—and spot an art-deco logo, an arrow and the word *Museo,* there is a fighting chance that there is an air museum around somewhere.

Unfortunately, the route of the arrows is not too clear and *Museo* is about the only word that has migrated into Finnish in recognizable form. Finnish is not a Germanic language; it isn't even in the Indo-European group. It is Finno-Ugric of which the Magyar tongue of Hungary is about the only possible near relation. If you speak fluent Hungarian, you may not have too much trouble. Actually, Ostyak is a closer dialect, but none of our companions were born by the lower Irtysh River of northwest Siberia. Thus we had to resort to the time-honored method of gesturing frantically and making sounds somewhere between that of a Pratt and Whitney and a sick penguin. Presumably that is why we ended up in the clinic, the rest room and going through customs twice the wrong way. Finally, we were just pushed out of the building through a side door—this all accompanied by lots of good-natured grins, equally incomprehensible gestures and a great chorus consisting of mostly *t*s, *v*s, and *k*s. I think they were saying something like, "more crazy Americans—and they let them fly airplanes yet."

Now next to every large airport terminal is a multi-story parking lot—usually under construction. Either it is, or the terminal is. If you are running late for your flight, then they both are. But next to the parking structure at Vantaa Airport you can spot a twin-boomed de Havilland D.H.115 Vampire jet fighter trainer. Along with the Vampire is a Folland Fo.141 Gnat, which was an imported-from-England standard jet fighter of the Finnish Air Force for many years. Sure enough, there it

151

is; *Ilmailumuseoyhdisys Ry.* — at least that is what the card says at the entry—The Exhibition of the Finnish Aviation Museum Society.

Inside, however, must be the most curious museum configuration in the world. It is ten feet wide, a hundred or so feet long, and shaped in a curve. You see, it is built under the up-ramp of the parking garage. This makes it difficult to display aircraft in simulated natural settings. In fact, it makes it impossible just to leave their wings on. All this doesn't matter; it just adds to the charm. The Finns love flying and are as avid pilots and sailplane enthusiasts as they are runners and sports car rallyists.

These are just temporary quarters and the Society is working hard to find a more suitable, if less bizarre, permanent facility for the future. Much of their stock of vintage aircraft is in storage, but many aircraft are scattered at nine other airports and military bases. One can hunt around at almost any airport in Finland and find something, although many locations outside of Vantaa and the Technical Museum at Tampere are on military bases and require some type of advance visit approval.

Actually, a number of rare machines are displayed in the Vantaa terminal itself; a Junkers A.50 two-seat, open-cockpit, low-winged monoplane looking like a Ryan with corrugations, a VL Sääske biplane and a VL Pyry monoplane are there amongst others. The Junkers A.50 Junior is older and more historic than one first realizes. Built in 1931, it was one of the world's first all-metal aircraft to see production. This example is also the machine in which Vaino Bremer flew around the world in 1931! An incredible flight in such a tiny machine and as unfamiliar to us as it is famous in Finland. Bremer continued to fly his little Junkers A.50 until 1966, surely one of the longest-term love affairs between a man and his airplane.

Two young docents in what appeared to be Civil Air Patrol-type uniforms had met us at the door of the museum and ushered us in with large smiles and waves. I think we had been their only customers that quiet weekday. Here the total lack of verbal communications means little. Several fuselages are arranged along the curve of the outboard wall while the inner one is lined with propellers and engines. Cases of models and dioramas depict the chronology of Finnish aviation and every square inch of wall space is covered with photographs. You don't have to be able to read the legends; the pictures speak for themselves and two points come home.

One is the amount of pioneering in Arctic flying that the Finns accomplished. Like Wien in Alaska and Hassell in Canada, the Finns were flying up in the Arctic Circle in the 1920s and 1930s in open cockpit biplanes at way below zero temperatures in weather conditions that only a Lapp or a reindeer could tolerate. With no navaids or radios, navigation must have been by carrier pigeon as much of the landscape

152

One of the authors examining a fuselage in the old museum under the ramp to the parking garage.

of Finland consists of identical-looking lakes with the space in between covered with pine trees. Mail, medical supplies, camp equipment and mapping were the staple of the little planes and big men. One of our favorite photos shows a Santa Claus-costumed pilot clambering out of the most disreputable looking of biplanes on December 18, 1935, delivering a sack of Christmas presents to a remote camp at Lord-knows-where. The grin on his face and the ice in his beard tell the whole story of that flight.

The other point is Finland's air wars. Most of us only remember that she was the only country to pay back all of her World War I debts and that somehow she was on the German side in World War II. Now being a tiny, independent country in-between such giants as Germany and Russia does not provide restful sleep for either prime ministers or average citizens, but that, along with the ambient temperature, does breed a built-in toughness. So when great big Russia attacked little Finland in 1939, the bear found a tiger and the photos and artifacts at the museum tell the story.

The story starts much earlier, back in 1917 in the midst of the Russian Revolution. The Finns took the opportunity to break away from Russia and fight their own war of independence to form their own nation, Finland. On March 6, 1918, Swedish Count Eric von Rosen flew his Thulin D to Finland and presented it to the Finnish forces of General Gustaf Mannerheim. Since this was the second Swedish aircraft to be donated, the Finns decided that with two flying machines, they now had an air force. On March 10, 1918, just four days later, a commander was appointed to head the *Ilmailuvoimat*, the new Air Force. Thus the

Finns were one of the first countries to form an independent military air service. Count von Rosen had painted his Thulin D with his personal good luck sign, a blue swastica. This symbol was adopted by the *Ilmailuvoimat* as their national insignia. It was unfortunately to be confused by many with the black swastica adopted by Nazi Germany a decade and a half later.

Aircraft were rounded up from all over; some purchased, some borrowed and some captured such that shortly the new air force had a motley collection of 47 aircraft of 19 different types. Fortunately, the war ended before the logistical nightmare became unbearable. By 1920 the Ilmailuvoimien Lentokonetehdas, a government aircraft factory, was set up to standardize things and a license was obtained to build German Hansa-Brandenberg W 33 floatplanes as the I.V.L. A 22.

When tension with Russia, who needed room to protect their flank around Leningrad, got out of hand in the late 1930s, Finland again gathered aircraft from all over—Morane 406s from France, Blenheims from England, Fokker D.XXIs from Holland, and Fiat G.50s from Italy. As the Winter War of 1939-40 started with Russia, the Swedes again came bearing gifts. Swedish volunteers arrived with a dozen Gloster Gladiators and Hawker Harts, acquired in some obscure and devious manner from the Swedish Air Force. Germany, looking for help to distract the Russians, provided Curtiss Hawk 75s and a bunch more Morane 406s captured in the fall of France.

Many of the aircraft were not suitable for the Arctic conditions, particularly the Fiats, but the fixed-geared, maneuverable-as-hell, Fokker D.XXIs ate up the Russian Ratas and Polikarpovs hot from the Spanish Civil War. The Russian was fighting under orders and his last general had probably been purged by Stalin. But the Finn was fighting for his homeland; Helsinki was not much over a hundred miles from the

One in four Polikarpov I-16s was the two-seat UT-1 trainer, spoiling its lines but training pilots to handle the tricky fighter; this one was captured in Soviet Karelia in 1941.

154

border. Odds were typically five to one. The front moved around so much that sometimes the outlying fields didn't know whose lines they were behind. A good part of the time the Fokkers flew on skis and used any patch of snow for an airfield.

By the spring of 1940, the Russians decided that they were getting nowhere and the Winter War ended in an armistice. In June 1941, the Russians again decided that the Germans might come around the northern flank and in what was to become known as the Continuation War, Finland was back in combat with Russia. There weren't enough Fokkers left, so the Finns tried to buy anything they could get. About the only thing left was the dreadful Brewster Buffalo, which we didn't want and which the British wouldn't take any more of. In the Pacific theatre, the takeoff checklist for a Brewster Buffalo included the last rites; the Japanese munched up every one in Malaya within weeks.

The Finns loved them; they were the fastest, heaviest- gunned fighter they had ever seen, and in low level attacks they shot up the Russian infantry and harrassed their tanks. Up higher they took on the newer Yaks and Stormoviks. The Brewster was built like a rock. If you ran out of ammunition, you could always chew up a bomber's rudder with the Buffalo's propeller, an amusing way of extending a sortie, and that was done at least once. The odds were even worse than before. On one occasion, Eino Juutilainen encountered twenty-two Russian fighters while on a lone reconnaissance patrol; he attacked and shot down three of them! On display at the museum is the fin of Lieutenant Hans Wind's Brewster 239, the export version of the Buffalo, admittedly a marginally better version than the domestic one. The fin is decorated with markings showing Wind's thirty-eight kills. It is hard to believe that a Brewster Buffalo ever shot down thirty-eight of anything. Not surprisingly, there are no original Buffalos left. If you must see a Brewster Buffalo, there is one remaining VL Humu at the Aviation Museum of Central Finland at Tikkakoski. When the Finns couldn't get any more Buffalos from the U.S., they began making their own version as the VL Humu and they look about the same. Even with the Buffalos and Humus and the loan of Messerschmitt Bf 109s from Germany (who else could the Finns get airplanes from, Russia was our ally), numbers eventually tell and another armistice was finally called in 1944. The Finns are made of stern stuff, however, and the country rapidly recovered to become one of the productive, creative, and pleasant to visit places in Europe.

As we left the little temporary museum, we stuffed a few Finnmarks into the little box with the slot in the top. We couldn't read the sign, but the meaning of the box, like *Museo*, is universal. It was to hope that the day would come a little closer when their new air museum could be built. Maybe the next time we go back, all those rare Valmets and Haukkas and Saaskis will be together again where they belong. The two CAP-types smiled; they knew what we were thinking. Language isn't all that important.

But now we have to rewrite this whole chapter. You see, between the time of our visit and the writing of this book, they got their new museum building. No longer constrained by the parking lot ramp, the new building provides for the display of the aircraft as they were meant to be—at least with their wings back on. Still on the airport grounds, but a long walk or a short ride from the terminal is their new home. Planes that were in storage or packed away have now moved into their new home, including the two-seat trainers, the VL Pyry II and the VL Saaski II, from their hangings in the airport terminal, although Bremer's Junkers remains there to point the way.

VL stands for Valtion Lentokonetehdas, an aircraft company that manufactured small-to-moderate sized aircraft from the 1920s to the present. Another VL machine in the museum is the very attractive biplane Tuisku which was used as a trainer from 1933 until 1949. This example is nicknamed Sugar Lump, the funds to purchase it having been donated by the Finnish sugar company Suomen Sokeri Oy. The Saaski II is a somewhat similar looking machine whilst the Pyry II is a low-wing monoplane reminiscent of a Vultee Vibrator.

Two incredibly rare machines are now on display. The first is an I.V.L. A.22 Hansa, actually a W 33 Hansa-Brandenburg floatplane manufactured under license by Ilmailuvoimien Lentokonetehdas. Hansa-Brandenburg floatplanes are instantly recognizable by being about the only airplanes to have flown satisfactorily with the vertical fin and rudder under the fuselage rather than their more commonplace position on top where you can paint the license number. The configuration actually made a lot of sense for a floatplane. The floats put the fuselage high enough that there is enough room for the fin underneath (and besides, if at high angles of attack it struck the water it would probably serve as a useable water rudder). More important, it provided a clear

The new Finnish Aviation Museum building at Vantaa Airport outside Helsinki.

Funds for this VL Tuisku were donated during the war by a sugar company, hence its nickname, Sugar Lump.

field of fire for the rear gunner. The basic concept dates from 1916 or so and Hansas were produced by both Austria and Germany throughout World War I and in both biplane and monoplane versions. Remarkably durable and practical machines, they soldiered on doing miscellaneous missions in a number of countries until the mid-1930s, long after they had paid their dues. Several Hansa-Brandenbergs were involved in the rescue searches for the airship *Italia* in 1928, long after they should have been retired. The aircraft on display, numbered 4D2, was made in 1922 and is the only Hansa-Brandenburg known to exist. It is actually one of the two sent in pieces by Hansa to Finland as patterns for the licensed-built machines.

The second rare machine is a Russian Polikarpov I-16UTI. The I-16 Rata, the Rat, with retractable gear and a 750-hp radial engine, was Russia's first monoplane fighter. They saw their initial combat on the side of the Republicans in the Spanish Civil War. The little Gee-Bee like pursuit, with the trailing edge of its wing almost touching the leading edge of the stabilizer, could raise havoc with Franco's Fiat C.R.32s on loan from fellow-dictator Mussolini, but there were far too few of them to turn the tide. The arrival in Spain of some Messerschmitt Bf 109s from Mussolini's compatriot ended the few remaining.

The Rata was also a little too much like a Gee-Bee and not all pilots are Jimmy Doolittles. The high landing speeds, with no flaps and poor over-the-nose visibility, caused a huge attrition rate in landing accidents. The need for extensive training to handle the beast meant that fully one out of four I-16s produced was the UTI two-seat trainer version. The second cockpit spoils the lines of the stubby open-cockpit fighter a bit, but even so it is clearly one of the hot machines of its era. The little Ratas, piloted by determined Russians, helped hold back the Germans pushing east in 1941 and 1942 until reinforcements of Yaks and Ilyushins could take their place. That was no mean feat for a 1932 design.

A number of small sport planes also grace the Finnish museum. The tiny Eklund Te-1 was built by Torolf Eklund in 1948 as a single-seat amphibian, although the limitations of a 40-hp engine later encouraged the weight-saving change to a straight flying boat. OH-TEA was the only one built, but if one can't afford a Lake, this would be a fine way to pretend. A collection of sailplanes and motor-gliders cover the ceiling and cases of artifacts clutter the room with more additions to hopefully come later. We doubt if our little donation had made any difference in building the new facility, but knowing the Finns, we expect that next time even more of those priceless machines will have moved onto the stage they deserve.

Vantaa Lahto Aluelennonjohto 121.3.

(The opening and closing phrases mean Contact Vantaa Approach and Departure Control respectively.)

I.V.L. A.22 Hansa, serial number 2, was a license-built Hansa Brandenburg that served from 1922 to 1936.

17

Of Struts and Wires and Of Boats That Fly

Lago Bracciano, a volcanic lake some 35 km northwest of Rome, has connections with aeronautics which started in Paris in 1804. That was barely twenty years after the Montgolfiers started the enjoyable, if totally impractical, sport of ballooning. To honor Napoleon's coronation as emperor, Jacque Garnerin, Paris' chief balloonist, launched six unmanned balloons from the Place de Notre Dame. Five ended up in the countryside as expected. The sixth drifted across France, over the Alps, and down the spine of Italy to crash into Nero's tomb on the outskirts of Rome. This particular balloon's display was a *papier-mâché* emperor's crown, part of which was torn off by the stile on the *Tombe di Neroni*. Much too improbable for coincidence, this clutching away of the crown by the ghost of another emperor, eons dead, was clearly an evil omen. Garnerin spent a fair period of time hiding from a furious Napoleon. The lightened balloon doubled back north and fell into Lago Bracciano to the consternation of the local fishermen.

Not perhaps an auspicious start, but by the 1890s Vigna di Valle, on the west shore of Lago Bracciano, became the site for Italy's early observation balloon development. For the next three-quarters of a century, it was home for both military and rescue aircraft squadrons. During World War II it became an Italian "Peenemunde," if one stretches the analogy a bit, with experimental glide bombs and remote-controlled torpedoes cluttering up the lake and again perplexing the local fishermen. Then on May 24, 1977, with nine jet fighters of the *Frecce Tricolori* aerobatic team spewing red, white and green smoke trails over the lake, the home of the Museo Storico dell'Aeronautica Militare was officially dedicated.

Play gladiator through Rome's traffic and take the Via Claudia across the now calmer countryside to Vigna di Valle. You will probably have to leave your passport or library card with the guard at the gate to ensure

159

A seaplane crane and a memorial to the Italia *stand silent tribute to the past.*

that you eventually leave as the museum is on a military reservation.

The lake is bright blue with the hills on the far shore fading into the mist. The memory of much of Italian aviation history, at least for most Americans, has also faded into the mist. Here one can sit on the shore of the lake, alongside some Fiat and Piaggio jets, and relax while contemplating the courage and daring that lives in that history. The crane that used to lift Caproni and Savoia seaplanes from the water sits there silently. On a small promontory, also silently, stands a monument to the men of the fallen airship *Italia*.

Leonardo da Vinci, besides painting churches and the Mona Lisa, sketched some of the first potential flying machines. It is therefore appropriate that full-scale models of his concepts frame the entryway to the museum. The first propellers to actually turn at Lago Bracciano, however, were not on a flying machine. Some of the earliest tests of high-speed hydrofoils were made on the lake. The Barchino Idroplano, with its twin 6-foot propellers, hit 70 km/hr on the lake in 1907. Replicas of a Wright Type 4 and the Curtiss Triad flying boat as well as an authentic two-seat Blériot XI also grace the entry hall.

Almost forgotten, overshadowed by the vastness of the western front during World War I, are the exploits of the early Italian pilots. Flying crude machines over the rough terrain of northern Italy, they fought violent battles against the Austro-Hungarians. The SPAD VII and the Hanriot HD-1 at the museum may be familiar types, but the Ansaldo S.V.A. 5 is extremely rare. The Italians, in the Ansaldo S.V.A. 5, came

One of the only multi-engined World War I aircraft left in the world, the three-engined Caproni Ca.33.

up with the fastest pursuit aircraft of World War I. It could easily hit 145 mph. The Ansaldo's Warren-truss struts and triangular rear fuselage make it easy to identify. This particular S.V.A. 5 actually participated in a raid on Vienna in 1918.

The pursuits, however, are dwarfed by the twin-boom, tri-motored Caproni Ca.33 biplane towering over them. The Ca.33, one of the only multi-engined World War I aircraft extant, is a case in point. Like Sikorsky in Russia, Caproni in Italy had started developing multi-engined machines before the war began; the Ca.33 of 1916 derives from the Ca.30 of 1913. The configuration is unusual with a tractor engine at the front of each of the twin booms and a pusher between them behind the fuselage. These machines actually made raids over the Alps, the front gunner and the two pilots huddling behind their little windshields. The rear gunner deserved a medal just for going aboard. His position was standing up in a bird cage on a platform above the pusher engine, just in front of its propeller. This gave him a clear 360° field of fire over the wings and tail, deafness for life, and a permanent case of pneumonia.

Entering the next hall are the only Ansaldo AC.2 parasol monoplanes, Weber A.VII Ethiopias, and IMAM Ro.43 catapult floatplanes left. There is also a one-of-a-pair Fiat C.R.32 biplane from the Spanish Civil War era; the other is in Madrid. But behind the Warren-truss struts, wheel pants and crisscrossed wires of the C.R.32, the wall glows crimson from the reflections off a sight that is breathtaking.

There are seven seaplanes left in the world as legacies from that most demanding of all air races, the Schneider Trophy race. Jimmy Doolittle's Curtiss R3C-2 is in the Smithsonian. A Supermarine S.6A is at

R. J. Mitchell Hall in Hampshire and the S.6B is at the Science Museum in London. The remaining four—all in the traditional Italian scarlet racing colors—are lined up in a row at the Museo Storico.

First in line is the 1926 Macchi M.39 of Mario de Bernardi. Since its inception, the Schneider Cup had been a bash between the English and the Italians, with the brash Americans holding sway in the mid-twenties and the French rarely ever finishing. Doolittle had won in 1925 and thus America would host the 1926 race at Hampton Roads, Virginia. The English were unprepared and hoped the race would be postponed. The Italians were equally unprepared, but in December 1925, Mussolini unexpectedly announced that Italy would win the 1926 race. Mario Castoldi, Macchi's chief engineer, was ill with fever over the Christmas weekend when Mussolini's call arrived. Castoldi went straight from his sick bed to the Varese factory and began to sketch the design of what would become the fastest airplane in the world.

By July, the first of the five Macchis was delivered. Disaster hit during the summer with both Americans and Italians losing aircraft during practice flights. By early November, preparations at Hampton Roads had commenced in earnest on what was already perceived would be one of the hottest and closest competitions yet. The U. S. had two sleek Curtiss biplane racers, the more powerful R3C-4 in the hands of their best pilot, Lieutenant George T. Cuddihy. The nearly as fast R3C-2 would be flown by Lieutenant Frank Schilt. The third Curtiss had crashed in practice so a much slower, but probably reliable, Curtiss Hawk on floats would be driven by Lieutenant William Tomlinson.

On the Italian side, the three M.39s would be flown by Lieutenant Adriano Bacula, Captain Arturo Ferrarin and Major Mario de Bernardi.

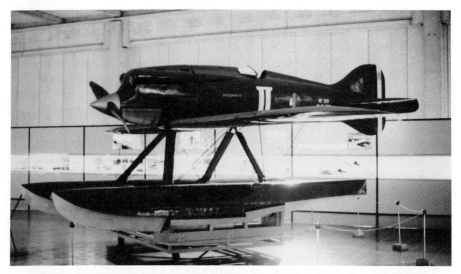

The Macchi M.39 in which Mario de Bernardi won the 1926 Schneider Trophy race at Hampton Roads, Virginia.

The three Macchis were all the resources they had. The other two machines had crashed previously and their one remaining spare engine had already contributed part of its inards to keep the others flying. During pre-race trials Ferrarin's machine threw a rod and the odds were swinging further against the Italians. But Il Duce had commanded that they win the race. More likely, by then the crew had their wind up and belts tightened and were going to give it all they had regardless of dictators, broken engines or the U. S. Navy. They worked straight through the night and by the next day had made one engine out of the remains of Ferrarrin's and the spare in a precursor to what would be the Supermarine S-6's midnight episode five years later.

The Italians race their airplanes like they race their cars, and with scant regard for prudence. The Schneider Race was actually a time trial; the aircraft did not take off simultaneously. They raced against the clock, but started at five-minute intervals such that there would usually be something in the air to provide continuous excitement for the spectators. There was some leeway allowed in the starting times, expanded by 1925 to fifteen minutes to provide for getting the evermore cantankerous racing engines started and to get airborne.

The Italians developed a last-minute plan. De Bernardi was to damn the torpedoes, run the race with the throttle firewalled, and hope his Fiat engine remained in one piece. Bacula would throttle back to conserve his engine and match the pace of the slower Hawk of Tomlinson. That way if everybody else dropped out with engine failure—in 1919 nobody successfully made it to the finish line—Bacula could speed up on the last lap and be sure to win. Cuddihy, in the Curtiss R3C-4, was clearly the tough one to beat. Ferrarin was given the job to stay on Cuddihy's tail and try to rattle him into abusing his engine or cutting a pylon. At worst, Ferrarin could try to dive in front of him at the finish line. Unfortunately, the protocol had Ferrarin, as the first of the guest team, departing five minutes ahead of the American, Cuddihy. So Ferrarin took a calculated risk. When his starting time came, he "had trouble" with his engine. Cuddihy's turn came five minutes later. He took off immediately for fear of overheating; those racing engines were all marginally cooled, especially when sitting still. Suddenly, Ferrarin's "trouble" disappeared. His engine roared to life and he was airborne right behind Cuddihy; it was no longer a time trial—it was a race!

Lap after lap, fifty feet over the bay, the Macchi of Ferrarin screamed along only yards behind the Curtiss' tail. Ferrarin was pushing Cuddihy past every red-line on the gauges. Schilt, in the other Curtiss, the R3C-2, had a float bracing-wire break and the vibration made the plane barely controllable. He had to slow down and just watch Ferrarin, Cuddihy and de Bernardi, now also airborne, go blasting by.

The hasty overnight repairs to Ferrarin's engine showed on the fourth lap. He finally had to dead-stick in, but he had done his job well. Cuddihy's engine, pushed too hard by Ferrarin, quit shortly after and the U. S. Navy's best pilot and fastest plane had to glide onto the water two miles short of the finish line, out of the race. Mario de Bernardi's engine, running flat out with all its gauges also in the red, managed to hold together. On the last lap he brought the Macchi right down to the surface to streak across the finish line at an average speed of 246.5 mph, a record for seaplanes. Schilt came in second, vibration and all, while Bacula, as planned, beat out Tomlinson's Hawk for third. The Italians had done what no one believed they could do. Four days later, de Bernardi removed all doubts by setting a world's absolute speed record of 258.87 mph in the bright red Macchi M.39 that now sits at Vigna di Valle.

Next to the M.39 are two Fiat C.29s, one minus its wings. Italy lost the 1927 race at Venice to the English. For that race, the Italians had developed four separate machines, but to no avail. The radical ones crashed or weren't ready in time, the Macchi M.67s retired with engine failures and a leftover M.52R could only come in second. The Fiat C.29s, beautiful as they are, never made it past the starting gate.

But behind them stands one of the most awesome propeller-driven airplanes of all time, the incredible Macchi-Castoldi MC 72. The MC 72's revolutionary supercharged Fiat A.S.6 engine consisted of two supercharged V-12s arranged in line-astern with each half coupled to one of a pair of giant counter-rotating, fixed-pitch propellers. This led to a 51.1 liter, V-24 powered beast that, between the blower and ram air, produced 3,100 hp out of only 2,050 pounds. The side of the

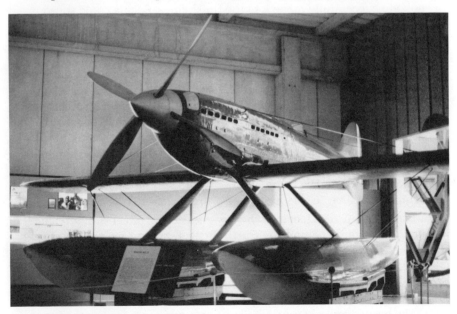

The awesome Macchi-Castoldi MC.72, its scarlet fuselage lined with exhaust ports, remains the fastest propeller-driven seaplane ever built.

MC 72's fuselage appears to be one long row of exhaust ports stretching into the distance.

Unfortunately, plagued by a late start and a number of misfortunes, the Italians could not be ready in time for the 1931 race. Perhaps unsportingly, but financially necessary, the English held the race all by themselves and retired the trophy with the third win in a row. The Italians may have been badly disappointed, but the Schneider was only a Cup and they weren't going to waste their time and their airplanes. In April of 1933, Warrant Officer Francesco Agello flew the MC 72 to a speed record of 423.82 mph.

In 1934, Agello again took up this engine-on-wings and achieved a then absolute speed record of 440.68 mph; for the next five years, the MC 72 was the fastest airplane in the world. The Macchi-Castoldi MC 72 sits silently at Vigna di Valle awaiting all comers, for it still holds the world's speed record for propeller-driven seaplanes. There are no challengers. Recognize also that that speed is within twenty percent of the present world's record for any propeller-driven airplane, modern technology, retractable landing gear, laminar flow airfoils and all. And the Macchi-Castoldi did it on floats, on a lake, fifty years ago.

While the MC 72 represents one of the end points of the development of the propeller-driven airplane, the Caproni-Campini N.1 parked just behind it represents the very beginning of a different era. In the 1930s, both Germany and Italy began experiments on the jet engine. Frank Whittle in England hadn't yet received much support and the U. S. still thought the gas turbine was, with luck, only good for power

The Caproni-Campini CC.1 was the world's second jet aircraft to fly. It was impressive, elegant, and slow.

stations. Heinkel, in Germany in 1939, was actually the first to get one flying. Italy came next with the N.1.

The Caproni-Campini N.1 is an attractive machine, looking somewhat like those low-winged Lockheed and Northrop radials of the 1930s but without a propeller. The fuselage is quite large, since it contains a 900-hp Isotta-Fraschini radial to drive the compressor. The state of metallurgy in Italy in the 1930s was such that making turbine blades for the temperatures involved was somewhat beyond them. This hybrid engine actually produced about 1,600 pounds of thrust compared to only 1,100 or so from the Heinkel-Hirth, but the concept also required the large and heavy aircraft to carry it. Mario de Bernardi was the test pilot on August 28, 1940 when the Caproni-Campini first took to the air. Too large an airplane with too heavy an engine for the thrust produced, the Caproni-Campini N.1 had the less than blistering top speed of 220 mph, somewhat slower than a Fiat C.R.32 biplane and half that of the MC 72. De Bernardi must have been bored stiff. The N.1 did make a non-stop flight from Milan to Rome to gather support, but all it gathered was dust while the *Regia Aeronautica* turned their attention to such futuristic ideas as monoplane fighters. Whittle and other more farsighted folks, however, viewed it as another sign that the days of the propeller were numbered.

It was the trimotors, however, that were the mainstay of the Italian transport and bomber fleets. Actually a goodly number of the bombers were visibly conversions of transport designs. The design requirements would have led to a twin-engined configuration in the U. S. or England, but Italian radial engines were a bit under-size and thus the propensity for trimotors. Four trimotors remain at Vigna di Valle.

The Savoia-Marchetti S.M.82 and the Fiat G.212 are both fairly large machines, noticably bigger than a Junkers Ju 52/3m. The S.M.82 Marsupiale was built in fair numbers and the Germans borrowed fifty or so for use as transports in the Mediterranean. While they are both the only ones of their type left, the CANT Z.506S is both unique and different. It is a trimotor on floats. Cantieri Riuniti dell'Adriatico was an offspring of a shipyard in Trieste, hence their proclivity for seaplanes of one kind or another. CANT's chief designer Zappata worked throughout the 1920s for Blériot in France. Mussolini couldn't see wasting good Italian talent in France and prevailed on Zappata to return to Italy; part of his reward being the 'Z' for Zappata in CANT's numbering system. The Z.506S Airone was one of Zappata's best. A number of them, including the museum's Airone, soldiered on in the Adriatic until the 1960s.

The most familiar trimotor in the hanger is a Savoia-Marchetti S.M.79. Officially named Sparviero (Sparrowhawk), the characteristic hump behind the cockpit housing the upper gunner led pilots to call it the *Gobbo Maledetto* (the Hunchback). The hump and the underslung gondola housing the ventral gunner *cum* bombardier—its hard to have a

A stocky 1937 Macchi MC 200 fighter nestles under the wing of a Savoia-Marchetti S.M.79 Sparviero.

greenhouse nose in a trimotor—make it readily recognizable both as an S.M.79 and as a converted transport design. The original was to be an eight-passenger, high-speed transport and the plan was to enter the prototype in the 1934 MacPherson Robertson race to Australia. Like so many Italian projects it just wasn't ready in time. Nevertheless, some 1,300 S.M.79s were built between 1934 and 1944. While that isn't very impressive by the standards of most of the World War II protagonists, for the *Regia Aeronautica* it was mass production.

Armed with two free-swivelling 12.7-mm machine guns for the gunners, another 12.7-mm fixed above the pilot's visor to make him feel heroic, and a 7.7-mm Lewis gun—a drum fed Lewis gun in 1940!—sticking out a side window, a flying fortress it was not. The carry-thorough spar of the low wing and the ventral gondola, both legacies from its transport ancestry, led to a short bomb-bay. That, in turn, constrained it to a rather small bomb load stored vertically; they sort of tumbled out during the bomb run. Yet it was a reliable and generally useful airplane for bombing villages in Libya and towns in Spain.

The Germans and Russians learned a lot from those precursor combats, but the Italians kept getting the wrong message. They never caught on that while the Fiat C.R.32s and 42s and the S.M.79s did fine under most conditions, whenever they ran into a gaggle of I-16 Ratas or a Curtiss Hawk, things turned to worms. The result was that the *Regia Aeronautica* stuck to underpowered and undergunned light bombers and highly maneuverable, if slow, open-cockpit fighters for their war production buildup. Italian designers developed some outstanding fighters that would have given any of their contemporary Hurricanes or Moranes a run for their money. But the *Regia Aeronautica* could never make up its mind, allowed too many to be developed and then didn't have the production capability to manufacture more than a handful of each. With this mixed bag of an excess of old airplanes and too few modern machines of too many different types, they were eaten alive as an air force by 1942. This is not to say that individual machines and pilots didn't engender a healthy respect in their British counterparts. More than one English capital ship went down in the Mediterranean under attacks pressed home by S.M.79s with torpedoes slung underneath.

Several examples of those better fighters are on display between the trimotors. The Macchi MC 200 Saetta was a good radial-engined machine by late 1930s standards, perhaps in the same class as a Seversky P-35 or a Grumman F4F. When the Daimler Benz DB601A V-12s became available in 1940, the top speed of its descendent, the MC 202 Folgore, reached 360 mph which put it up there with its antagonists of 1940. By 1942, the Macchi MC 205 Veltro would clip along at over 400 mph. While remaining undergunned by British standards, they still retained the superb maneuverability and control feel of their obsolete predecessors.

The Aerfer Sagittario and Ariete represent early jet fighters of the mid-1950s and lead the way outdoors to where the more-modern Fiat and Aermacchi jets are lined up. But before leaving the museum itself, there are some cases of memorabilia to examine; one deals with airships and the other with long-range flying boats. They also deal with a story of two men, their pioneering flights, and the enmity and antagonism that led to the undeserved disgrace of one and fame and reward for the other; the disgrace lasting forty years before being rectified while the fame and reward was much more ephemeral and not as long enjoyed.

Italy pioneered in the development of the semi-rigid airship. The driving force behind this effort was Umberto Nobile. Nobile had visions of his airships exploring far-flung corners of the world and of eventually leading them into commercial passenger service. Much of his work was done at Vigna di Valle.

His opportunity came in 1926, when Norwegian explorer Roald Amundsen, who had beaten the ill-fated Scott expedition to the South Pole, decided to be the first to fly over the North Pole—walking there having already been accomplished by Peary. Amundsen, his permanent crustiness increasing with age, wanted one last great success. To find some land mass in the then still hardly-touched polar regions, and have it named for him, could be his great finale. The problem of money was solved when the wealthy American, Lincoln Ellsworth, agreed to stake him for the privilege of going along on this lark over a few thousand miles of frozen wasteland in the primitive aircraft of the 1920s. As they examined each airplane, they became convinced that this might not be too bright an idea. Then they discovered that one of Nobile's airships, the used but still servicable N-1, might be for sale. Nobile jumped at the chance. Here was funding, a pioneering flight, and a chance to prove his ideas.

On any expedition, like a military campaign, a clear chain of command and a well integrated team is mandatory. The Amundsen-Ellsworth-Nobile Polar Expedition in the N-1, now christened the *Norge*, had a confused command structure with a Norwegian polar expert who knew nothing about airships, an Italian airshipman with no experience in the Arctic, and an American financier with little but money to contribute to either. The crew was made up of half Norwegians and half Italians who couldn't communicate with each other.

The *Norge* was also too small for such a trip and weight would be critical. More important, there was almost no experience in the world in flying airships in Arctic conditions. Nobile flew the *Norge* from Rome to England and then across the North Sea to Norway. From Oslo, the *Norge* made its way to Leningrad, up to Vadsoe, and from there across the Arctic wastes to King's Bay on Spitsbergen. Merely getting to the base camp had taken the *Norge* across forty degrees of latitude and had been a major accomplishment in itself.

Amundsen was already there, having gone ahead by ship. A surprise was that another group of polar explorers were also at King's Bay. Richard Byrd and Floyd Bennett had shipped their Fokker F.VIIa/3m trimotor to King's Bay by boat and now posed a threat as to who would be the first to fly over the Pole. Amundsen wasn't rushing; he didn't really think that the heavily loaded Fokker on its little skis would be able to get off from the deep snow. They did get off and Byrd became the first to fly over the North Pole. Amundsen didn't show his great

The Norge *just before departure of the Amundsen-Ellsworth-Nobile Transpolar Flight, King's Bay, Spitzbergen, May 1926.*

disappointment. He was looking to discover new lands and more than just a dash to the Pole, but the seeds for future troubles were sown.

Just two days later, on May 11, 1926, the *Norge* took off; 770 miles to the north was the Pole. Just before 1 A.M. on May 12th, in the permanent light of summer, the *Norge* slowly circled around the North Pole. Amundsen and Ellsworth dropped small Norwegian and American flags; they had accepted Nobile's pleadings about minimizing weight. Nobile took out a giant Italian flag which Mussolini had given him to drop at the Pole. The friction between the factions grew.

But now the real exploration began. Peary, when he came back from the first trek to the Pole, thought that he had seen mountains off in the distance. Surely there was another land mass up there to balance the continent of the Antarctic. Hour after hour the *Norge* droned forward; the barren and bitter-cold ice pack stretched on forever. The weather began to worsen and ice formed on the hull, but still they saw no sign of land; they never would for there was none. Natale Cecioni, the chief engineer kept watch on the engines while the chief rigger, Renato Alessandrini, crawled over the catwalks and even outside the hull in that frigid air to ensure things were going well. They weren't. Ice was weighing the marginal *Norge* down. Ominous twangs were heard as some of the ice, flaking off the hull, was falling into the propellers and being flung into the fabric skin.

Slowly the *Norge* limped on. Over thirty-six hours after the liftoff from Spitzbergen, the Alaskan coast north of the Yukon was spotted. What with preparations and all, they had been up for over 48 hours, but the end was not yet in sight. They cruised past Point Barrow where, by coincidence, polar explorers George Wilkins and Norwegian-American Ben Eielson had been waiting for days for the weather to clear in order to start their Stinson for some polar flights of their own. Wilkins and Eielson cheered and waved, but they weren't seen by the *Norge* as it droned above them groping its way between the clouds.

The Norge *making its forced landing at Teller, Alaska, on May 13, 1926 after successfully traversing the North Pole.*

Facing the *Norge* were mountains shrouded in rain, snow and fog, and a wrinkled coastline that was hard to follow. Slowly they maneuvered down the Bering Strait, half the time lost and blind. Nobile, Hjalmar Riiser-Larsen, Amundsen's Norwegian navigator, and the key Italian crew members were almost dead with fatigue. A landmark showed up, but as they turned into the bay toward a small settlement they realized that it wasn't their destination, Nome. Instead, it turned out to be a small gold mining camp named Teller. That didn't matter. What did matter was just getting down before they collapsed or crashed. With arm motions to the Eskimos and the few settlers on the ground, the ropes were dropped. While the *Norge* was badly damaged in the ensuing impromptu grounding, the first crossing of the Arctic had succeeded.

Nobile was hailed as a hero, and rightly so. His flying of the primitive and overloaded *Norge* through the worst of conditions an airship could encounter was nothing less than superb. Mussolini ordered Nobile, now promoted to general, to give a lecture tour through the U. S. Amundsen was furious. He hadn't discovered any new lands to be named after him and now the press were treating him as just a passenger. Never a particularly dispassionate man, he lashed out in speeches and articles at Nobile, accusing him of being an incompetent hired skipper who had nearly wrecked them several times. Nobile held himself above the bitter attacks and only came out with straightfor-

Disassembling the frame of the damaged airship Norge *at Teller, Alaska, May 1926.*

171

ward descriptions of the flight and his machine. Nobile and Amundsen later reconciled, the friction likely aggravated by Ellsworth, but those early attacks by Amundsen, believed by some, would come back to haunt Nobile two years later. For now, though, Nobile had more important things to think about. Construction of a much larger airship had started before he had left Italy. With such a ship, he could accomplish a true scientific exploration of the whole Arctic.

Nobile did not yet realize that things back home were not going well. The new Under Secretary for Air was General Italo Balbo, one of Mussolini's key aides. He considered the airship a dead end and was envious of Nobile. Balbo cancelled the new airship and had the parts scrapped before Nobile could get home. Nobile was now stuck with the last of the too-small N-class ships. With financial help from the city of Milan, Nobile began to outfit the ship he would call the *Italia*. General Balbo did all he could to scuttle the project from behind the scenes.

Nobile prepared with care, seeking advice from every polar explorer he could contact. He became close friends with Rudolf Samoilovich of the Arctic Research Institute in Leningrad, who provided invaluable help even while containing his considerable forebodings. By the spring of 1928 and with a completely Italian crew, including Alessandrini and Cecioni and three others from the *Norge*, Nobile was ready to start. Pope Pius XI presented Nobile with a cross to place at the Pole.

The flight to Spitzbergen was one of the worst that Nobile had ever been through. Taking a more easterly course than in 1926, having stopped in Milan for departure celebrations, they encountered severe weather over Czechoslovakia, Germany and Finland, but Nobile built his ships well and the *Italia* made her way to Vadsoe where they moored for the night. The next day they departed for the old base at King's Bay

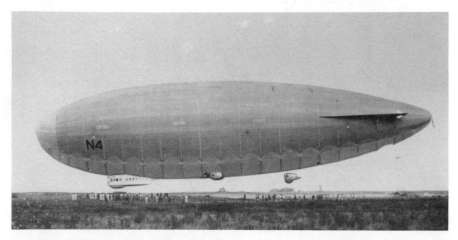

The first flight of the airship N 4, the Italia, *at Ciampino airport, Rome, June 3, 1927, its tragic flight to the Pole less than a year away.*

The Italia *being backed out of a hanger at Stolp, Germany on its flight to the Arctic.*

on Spitzbergen, being buffeted by blizzards a good part of the way. The support ship *Citta di Milano* was already there although there were no support aircraft as had been requested; Balbo had squelched that.

While Nobile wanted to go to the Pole again, he was planning much more than that; a whole season of exploration of the entire polar cap. On May 15, 1928 the *Italia* took off on her first polar voyage. This initial trip went northeast from Spitzsbergen, past the northern tip of North-East Land to Franz Josef Land and almost all the way to Severnaya Zemlya, north of central Siberia, thence southwest to Novaya Zemlya and back to Spitsbergen. On this "preparatory" trip, the *Italia* and her crew had flown 2,500 miles in 69 hours and had viewed 20,000 square miles of previously unexplored Arctic wilderness. It was a feat of exploration that in accomplishment per unit time was unheard of. Perhaps the airship was the ideal way to explore the Arctic. But the *Italia* had encountered that worrisome ice again and her performance limitations were becoming increasingly obvious.

Every day of the good, by Arctic standards, weather was precious, so during the permanently-light early hours of May 23, 1928, the *Italia* lifted off once again. This time she turned northwest and twelve hours later Cape Bridgeman, the very northern tip of Greenland, hove into view. Eight hours later the *Italia* was slowly circling over the North Pole. This time there were no experienced Norwegian explorers, no wealthy American financiers; it was an Italian success. Czechoslovakian scientist Franz Behounek and Swedish meteorologist Finn Malmgren were

View aft from the cabin of the Italia *over Bear's Island, May 14-15, 1928 on its next-to-last flight.*

exceptions because they were the best experts in their respective fields. Another Italian flag was dropped onto the Pole as was the huge cross which the Pope had asked Nobile to place there. The cross was so heavy that even the massive Natale Cecioni had trouble hoisting it out the door.

Not all was going well, however. The weather and the trip had been taking their toll and the *Italia* was not in the best of shape. There had been discussions for several hours about whether to continue on to Alaska, head toward Severnya Zemlya, or go back to Spitzbergen. The last was the shortest distance, but they had reached the Pole rapidly because of strong winds out of the southeast. That would mean bucking stiff headwinds all the way back. Malmgren had been watching the weather carefully and he was convinced that the pattern was changing and within a few hours the wind would veer around. The route to Spitzbergen should have, in fact, the most favorable winds. That finally convinced Nobile and with a last toast to the Pole beneath them, the crew of the *Italia* settled down for the long, grinding return to base—and flew into the teeth of a raging gale. When they could see the ice below, they discovered that their ground speed was all of 26 mph. Hour after hour went by without any decrease in the headwinds. Even today it's tough to forecast the weather in the Arctic. Malmgren's prediction of the changing pattern was basically correct; he was just off by twenty-four hours as to when it would occur. Rarely would a meteorologist have to pay as high a price for blowing a forecast.

Snow, ice, and turbulence were all building up. To slow down would decrease the loads, but they would get nowhere, while to speed up would risk structural damage. They had little reserve lift or ballast and

174

that gnawing plunk of ice being flung from propellers onto the hull could be heard ever more frequently. Those not engaged tried to catch some sleep up in the hull. Alessandrini was inspecting valves to make sure ice wasn't blocking them and the motor engineers like Ettore Arduino huddled in each nacelle, kicking the straining engines. Natale Cecioni was at the wheel. Suddenly the *Italia* began to settle by the stern. Cecioni hauled full up on the elevators, the engineers rammed their throttles home and an attempt was made to dump what little ballast remained. It was to no avail. Within moments, the *Italia* smashed into the ragged ice cap. The cabin was scraped off the hull and dumped onto the ice. Lightened, the half-collapsed hull floated rapidly up and to the east and with it went Alessandrini, Arduino and the others to their still-unknown fate.

One other, the center motor mechanic Pomella, was dead. Nine men were now castaways on the ice in the midst of a blizzard. Nobile had been at the front of the cabin and received the worst of the injuries with a broken arm and a broken leg. Cecioni also had a broken leg and Malmgren a banged up shoulder, but the rest were in fair physical shape. As important, most of their supplies had been spilled onto the ice nearby. Miraculously, the emergency radio—tubes, batteries and all—was laying there still in working order.

In an ironic coincidence, word that the *Italia* was overdue reached Oslo in the midst of a testimonial dinner for another polar flyer, Captain George Wilkens, the one who had waved up to the old *Norge* from Point Barrow two years before. A goodly percentage of the world's population of polar explorers were all sitting in the same room and there then began one of the longest ordeals of Arctic rescue ever undertaken.

For a week, while once each hour Biagi's plaintive distress call went unheard, no one knew the fate of the airship and its crew. Some of the survivors felt that there was no hope of being found, even though the crash site was only a few-dozen miles short of North-East Land. After long debates and some feeling of abandonment by those who stayed, second and third in command, Commanders Adalberto Mariano and Filippo Zappi, started a long march south over the jagged ice pack to try to reach help. Meteorologist Malmgren, the only survivor with Arctic foot-slogging experience, went with them.

Then late on the evening of June 3rd, 1928, over a week after the crash, a Russian radio operator in a small town near Archangel, over 1,200 miles away, was relieving his boredom by scanning the 30-meter band. Garbled, static-ridden, and in a foreign language, but prefaced with the Morse code's universal distress signal came Biagi's faint repeated call, "S.O.S., *Italia*, Nobile." They were alive! The rescue sprang into high gear. Arctic explorers and pilots from all over the north headed for King's Bay to join what was to become an unprecedented, if completely disjointed, rescue effort.

Hjalmar Riiser-Larsen's Hansa-Brandenberg being shipped to Spitzbergen for the Italia *rescue expedition.*

The Swedish base at Spitzbergen; Hansa-Brandenbergs are at the shoreline while a Junkers is tied to a supply ship.

From Norway came two Hansa-Brandenberg seaplanes of World War I vintage. One was flown by Amundsen's compatriot and navigator from the *Norge,* Hjalmar Riiser-Larsen. The city of Milan, not General Balbo, sent one of the new Savoia-Marchetti S.55 flying boats piloted by long-distance flyer Umberto Maddalena and his long time co-pilot Fausto Cecconi. Also from Milan came Major Luigi Penzo in a twin-engined

Dornier Wal. From Russia steaming north came the heavy ice-breakers *Krassin* and *Malygin*, both carrying Junkers on skis. From Sweden came several Heinkels and Fokkers and the Finnish airline Aero Oy, now Finnair, sent a Junkers F.13 seaplane. King's Bay was becoming a veritable O'Hare Airport with more aircraft than had ever been seen before in the Arctic. Ships in the area, except for the Russian's, were too thin-hulled to make much progress through the ice pack, but Italian *Alpini* ski troops from the *Citta di Milano* and Norwegian trappers with sledges and dogs began making their way across the forbidding ground of northern Spitzbergen.

Several times the survivors on the ice could see or hear aircraft in the distance, but it is one thing to see an aircaft in the sky and quite another to spot a few men and a small tent, even if colored red with dye marker, mixed amongst hundreds of square miles of jumbled ice pack. It was June 20th when Umberto Maddalena and Fausto Cecconi, after innumerable search flights in the Savoia and now being helped by radio directions from Biagi, finally spotted the stranded men.

Getting the survivors off the ice, however, would not be easy. There was not enough open water for the seaplanes and the few flat spots on the ice pack were too small and rough for all but the slowest and smallest of the ski planes. On June 23rd, two Heinkel He 5 floatplanes and a Fokker C.V-D on skis from the Swedish Air Force Base at Linkoping circled the survivors. While the floatplanes remained overhead, Lieutenant Einar Lundborg managed to land the small two-seat Fokker biplane on the ice. He could squeeze only one person aboard in addition to his observer, Lieutenant Birger Schyberg. Nobile had foreseen the possibility that they might not all be rescued at once. He had made a list of the priority for departure, with himself and radioman Biagi last. The Swedish commander back at Linkoping, however, had given very pragmatic orders to Lundborg to rescue Nobile first. He was the most seriously injured. In addition, it had been clear that the various factions back at King's Bay were uncoordinated and confused. Even injured, Nobile could get things organized. Nobile refused to leave, arguing that the also-injured Cecioni should be first. Lundborg argued back that he had his orders and regardless, the Fokker couldn't handle the huge Cecioni in addition to Schyberg. Besides, he could be back in a few hours without his observer and could then take Cecioni. At one point a frustrated Lundborg was said to have shouted that this wasn't an Italian costume opera. With the other castaways encouraging Lundborg—they had great sympathy for their commander who had been in serious pain for weeks—Nobile allowed himself to be carried into the rear seat of the Fokker. It was a decision he was to regret for the rest of his life.

Lundborg returned shortly as promised. As he landed, the Fokker C.V-D, somewhat nose-heavy with an empty rear seat, stubbed a ski and flipped over. The number of stranded was back up to six again.

Stranded survivors of the Italia *on the ice flow rest on the wreckage of Einar Lundborg's ski-mounted Fokker C.V.*

Clearly an even slower and smaller airplane was needed. It was July 6th before Schyberg could get back with a tiny de Havilland Moth on skis. He took back his boss, Lundborg, but the landing and takeoff had been so perilous and with the weather turning bad, they gave up any other attempts; the remaining five men were left alone on the ice once again. It was July 12th before the Russian icebreaker *Krassin*, pounding her way through the ice with Nobile's friend, Rudolf Samoilovich, on the bridge, was able to reach them.

The *Krassin* had already rescued the party that had tried to hike back. Zappi and Mariano had made it by foot about half-way to land. Meteorologist Malmgren's experience had kept them alive. At one point, Malmgren managed the remarkable feat of getting them food by shooting a polar bear with his Colt revolver. But Malmgren would never make another weather forecast. With his damaged shoulder weakening him, he had perished on the ice before the *Krassin* arrived.

There was another week of cleanup, gathering in various other rescue parties stuck in sundry locations around the northern end of the islands, but the drama was far from over. The other rescue pilots had been appalled when they originally learned of Lundborg's orders to take out Nobile first. Practical as it may have been, they knew it would lead to repercussions. An ice flow and the remains of an airship may not be the *Titanic*, but the tradition that a captain is the last to leave the ship would be hard to overcome. They didn't know just how serious those repercussions would be.

Mussolini, Balbo, and the Fascist government were embarrassed at the failure of the expedition and the success of rescue efforts by other countries. To lesser egos it wouldn't have mattered. Arctic expeditions are nothing if not risky and there is no shame in one having failed, but in their minds a scapegoat had to be found. Accused of cowardice in leaving his men on the ice, Nobile was returned to Italy virtually a prisoner. The public remembered Roald Amundsen's vitriolic outbursts against Nobile after the *Norge* flight two years earlier. Hearings, yellow journalism, exaggerations and downright lies followed and Nobile, his enemies coming out of the woodwork, was doomed. He had been the first to traverse the polar reaches, had been to the Pole twice, had accomplished incredible explorations in a painstaking, professional manner, had handled the unwieldy airships with skill, courage and brillance, and had endured uncounted hardships. For most of the rest of his life, he was to be an outcast in his own land. Today, his papers, artifacts from those adventures, and some of the pieces taken off the ice by the *Krassin* are carefully maintained at the Centro Documentazione Umberto Nobile at the Museo Storico at Vigna di Valle.

General Italo Balbo was, however, even if reprehensible, quite correct. The airship was likely a dead end, even if in the 1920s it appeared to be the only machine with the range and reliablility for long-distance commercial and military use. Ironically, it was the exploits of the aircraft partaking in the *Italia* rescue that helped show their potential future capabilities. Balbo pressed the development of the airplane in Italy, particularly the flying boat. To publicize the Italian Air Force and the Fascist regime, Balbo wanted to make a showing. After the *Italia* debacle and the loss of the Schneider Cup, some spectacular achievement was vital. By the early 1930s, however, almost every two points on the earth worthy of a dot on a map had been connected by someone's long distance flight. Clearly one more by a single airplane wouldn't rate a column on page 12, much less a headline. But a flight *en masse* would be something else. It would prove the airplane's practical capability and impress the world with Mussolini's prowess; that those could be bombers instead of transports was the subliminal message.

Balbo had at his disposal the resources of the entire *Regia Aeronautica* and he selected the Savoia-Marchetti S.M.55 as the plane for the job. The peculiar S.M.55 with its twin hulls, push-pull engines, and wire-braced booms towing several rudders and tailplanes, was actually a quite reasonable machine. It certainly couldn't be mistaken for anything else, assuming the viewer was sober and without double vision.

Twenty-four Savoias, each with color coded fins, along with spare aircraft, men and support vessels, were assembled. They were to fly in three-plane *V* formations, with four groups of *V*s making up each squadron; the two 12-plane squadrons to fly within sight of each other. Balbo would fly the lead plane of the first *V* of the first flight. His flying boat had the humble license of 'I-BALB.' On July 1, 1933 this huge formation took off from Orbetello for Amsterdam, Scotland and Reykjavik. Flying through fog most of the way, keeping the huge formation intact was no mean feat. The Savoias pushed their way west, most of the time only a few-hundred feet above the angry waves of the North Atlantic. They reached Labrador safely, having avoided storms around Cape Farewell, Greenland. From there they continued to New Brunswick and

Display models of Italo Balbo's massed fleet of Savoia-Marchetti S.M.55s.

thence to Montreal. After bouncing their way through thunderstorms over Lake Erie, they tightened up into a precise formation and thundered across the Chicago World's Fair; twenty-four flying boats in precise *V*s on *V*s.

The return flight involved stops at New York, New Brunswick, the Azores and a greeting by Mussolini back in Rome. For all one may consider Balbo the villain in the previous drama, one has to recognize the organizational and political skills that he possessed and was willing to risk. He had moulded 100 pilots and crewmen into a perfectly trained team. His squadron consisted of 24 flying boats with 48 Isotta Fraschini engines, 288 carburetors and 1,728 spark plugs and he kept men and machines running for 6 weeks over 12,000 miles of ocean and wastelands. Mussolini made Balbo Italy's first air marshal.

Sipping capucino on the shore of the lake outside the Museo Storico, one can contemplate the vagaries of fate and wonder about what ever happened to them all. Nobile suffered for half a lifetime. Unable to respond to criticism in the censored world of Facism, he had to suffer in silence. With the help of his friend in Leningrad, Rudolf Samoilovich, Nobile spent five years in Russia consulting on airship design. Political conditions in Russia then went rapidly downhill and Nobile was well advised to depart promptly. With help from friends in the Vatican, he managed to get a job teaching aeronautics for several more years at a small Catholic school near Chicago. During that time, Samoilovich was shot in one of Stalin's purges. Nobile's friends and those in most avia-

Umberto Nobile (rt.) and Roald Amundsen with Nobile's mascot Titina (who survived both the Norge *and* Italia *flights) and unidentified American little girl.*

tion circles knew the truth about the *Italia* episode, but the general public did not and Nobile could not speak out for fear of reprisals to his family. He returned to Italy and while things got a bit better after the war, myths die hard.

Then, on the 50th anniversary of the flight of the *Italia*, May 24, 1978, a ceremony was held at the Museo Storico at Vigna di Valle. With senior representatives attending from the many countries that had participated in the rescue, General Umberto Nobile was celebrated as the pioneering airship designer, pilot and Arctic explorer that he was. The years of tribulation were over and Nobile finally received the honor due him. He died two months later at the age of ninety-three. In that same spring of 1978, the Russians launched a modern new 1,200-ton Arctic oceanographic research vessel—and christened it the *Rudolf Samoilovich*.

Roald Amundsen, the polar explorer, first to reach the South Pole, that anachronistic, bitter, crotchety, hard old man, died somewhere in the Barents Sea between Norway and Spitzbergen. With one last Arctic adventure in the cards, perhaps called by some unwrittten code of honor, and with the old jealousies hopefully forgotten, Amundsen went to rescue Nobile. He departed Tromsoe, Norway in a Latham 47 flying boat on June 18, 1928. With another Norwegian explorer and a French crew, he left to search for the *Italia*. Several months later, a ship spotted a blue-grey wingtip float bobbing in the waters off Fugloy Island. The float and one of the fuel tanks was all that was ever found of the Latham. Amundsen never found a northern landmass to be named after him.

Air Marshal Italo Balbo met a glorious Fascist hero's death. His aircraft was shot down over North Africa in 1943. Of course, given the chaos in any war zone, particularly when you are losing, plus the fact that Balbo was well disliked by a goodly number of his men, there is more than a little suspicion—in fact a preponderance of evidence—that he was actually shot down by guns from his own *Regia Aeronautica.*

Rescue pilots Lundborg, Maddalena, and Penzo all died in airplane crashes; Penzo hitting the Alps on the way back from Spitzbergen and Maddalena three years later. Maddalena was enroute from Milan to Rome to start another long-distance flight across the Atlantic when a propeller disintegrated, tearing his aircraft apart. In the Borgheze Gardens off the Via Veneto in Rome there is a row of marble busts, mostly of dignified Romans; the one with the helmet and goggles is of Fausto Cecconi. Ever the copilot, Cecconi went down in the right-hand seat alongside Maddalena. Amundsen's friend, navigator from the *Norge* days and Hansa-Brandenberg search pilot during the *Italia* episode, Hjalmar Riiser-Larsen, went on to become head of the Norwegian Air Force.

That big bear, Natale Cecioni, Nobile's helmsman, saved his money and bought a farm outside of Rome. His son married the daughter of motor engineer Ettore Arduino, one of those who had disappeared when the bag of the *Italia* drifted away during the crash, never to be seen again.

And what of the high-speed racing team of the Schneider Trophy days; Ferrarin, Bacula, Briganti and the rest? They all died in aircraft accidents and crashes of one form or another. All that is except Mario de Bernardi, winner of the 1926 Schneider and holder of world speed records with the Macchi M.39 seaplane racer. He went on to become a reknown test pilot and also one of the world's great aerobatic pilots. After World War II, de Bernardi sponsored the development of several light aircraft and continued giving aerobatic displays as Italy's premier pilot. That is, until one day in 1959. On that day he was performing an aerial display at an airport outside of Rome. He completed his usual flawless routine, swung into an approach, landed, taxied back in front of the applauding crowd and swung his little aerobatic machine into its parking place. But he didn't shut down the engine. After watching the idling propeller ticking over for several minutes, a mechanic wandered up to see if he could help with anything. He couldn't; de Bernardi was slumped over the controls, dead of a heart attack at sixty-seven. Perhaps in that last moment as he set the brakes and reached for the mixture shut-off knob, he wasn't smelling the haze of Rome or hearing the buzz of the diminutive aerobat's engine. Perhaps instead he was smelling the salt air of Hampton Roads and was being deafened by the roar of those bellowing Fiats in their bright red beasts on floats.

The Castle of the Count

The country around Lake Maggiori in northern Italy reminds one of good food, red wine, Mussolini, smugglers, *Carabinieri*, and seaplanes. It was at Lake Maggiori and nearby Lake Como that Italian aviation developed around the early seaplanes of Caproni and Savoia-Marchetti. In case you are ever in the area, let us explain how to find the Caproni Museum at Vizzola Ticino.

From Arona or Varese, head south for Somma Lombardo. From there on, whenever you come to an intersection with a sign saying *Aeroporto*, turn the other way! You see, Milan has built a great big modern airport and like Washington's Dulles Airport, it's away out in the boonies. The Milanese authorities are so proud of their airport that there is a sign pointing towards it at every road junction from the Alps to the Yugoslav border. Unfortunately, that is not the airport you are looking for. Never fear, keep heading west and south towards Malpensa. Sooner or later, you will be rolling down a narrow, tree-lined, two-lane road with a long brick wall on your left. Suddenly there is a break in the wall and a faded sign saying "Caproni." Slam on the brakes and swerve left through the gap. Don't bother to signal, Italian drivers in that area would only find it confusing. The dirt road leads through a small wood and into the twilight zone. You will emerge at an empty grass airstrip with a row of clearly very old, low, brick hangers. On the lintel above the first hanger you can still make out the engraving, "Caproni Aeronautica 1911."

Originally a factory, then a museum, the hangers and airfield have been there for over 75 years.

It will likely be a warm and still day with one of those pale yet bright blue skies that only northern Italy seems to provide. The museum should open on Sundays at 10 A.M. and while it is much later than that, the door is still locked. Don't worry, excessive promptness is considered one of the few possible vices in these parts. Sit under a shady tree, or better yet, if you were smart enough to bring along some bread and cheese and wine, sit at one of the benches and enjoy a late breakfast in the sun. Man need not always proceed at the breakneck speed of the airplane. Soon the caretaker will arrive carrying his bread, cheese and wine. With a gracious *Buòn giorno*, he will bid you enter and then retire to his meal and to read in the local paper of the latest change of government (I think its every other Wednesday). You will then likely be alone with some of the rarest airplanes in the world.

The museum is dark and dim after the outside sun, and the aircraft are dusty and jam-packed into one very large room. Count Gianni Caproni founded in 1908 what was to grow into one of the most prolific aircraft and industrial organizations in southern Europe. Well over 100 different aircraft types were built during the 60 years of active production, but Caproni produced all sorts of other equipment and machinery as well.

These included the Isotta-Fraschini engines which powered other aircraft in addition to his own, including several of the Schneider Cup racers that gave the Curtiss' and Supermarines a run for their money; the 1,400-hp, 18-cylinder *W*-configured engine was an engineering masterpiece of its day. A number of engines from the Isottas back to early Anzanis are on display between and under the aircraft.

Caproni's organization got so large that he formed a half-dozen subsidiaries, each specializing in different classes of aircraft. With their different names, it is hard to keep track of them. Reggiani built some excellent World War II fighter planes, although they were not produced in large quantities. Bergamaschi and SAIMAN were also Caproni subsidiaries. Fortunately, Caproni was a compulsive saver; he saved all of his automobiles as well as one of each Caproni aircraft type that he could. Many were destroyed by the war or lost because the one and only example crashed. Others were just too big for anyone to find a place for. Nevertheless, examples of quite a few survive. The Ca.1, Caproni's first plane is one of them, but like several others is in storage at another site and not readily available for viewing.

The earliest aircraft on display is a Caproni Ca.6 from 1910, which is not too far from the beginnings of Caproni or of aviation. The Caproni Ca.18 near the entry door is a wire-braced monoplane, similar to the early Moranes. It actually flew with the fledgling Regia Aeronautica in 1913—prior to the beginnings of World War I. Even earlier, Italy had provided a "first" which foreshadowed things to come. On November 1, 1911 a flight of nine miscellaneous Italian aircraft hand dropped some two-kilogram grenades on Turkish installations at Taguira Oasis

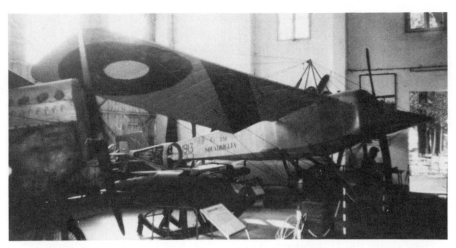

The Caproni Ca.18 scout of 1913 used a 100-hp Le Rhone rotary; to the left is the nose of an Ansaldo A.1 Balilla.

in Libya during some now-forgotten Italo-Turkish squabble. The Italians thus attained the dubious distinction of inventing aerial bombardment.

Another aircraft of World War I vintage is the Ansaldo A.1 Balilla. It is a single-seat fighter biplane with twin machine guns and is powered by a 220-hp SPA 6-cylinder liquid-cooled inline engine. On the other hand, the Ca.53 is a rather large multi-seat, single-engined triplane of 1917 vintage. Its covering is completely missing, but other than that, it is intact. That actually makes it quite interesting as one can examine every rib, wire and cable; sort of a giant stick and tissue model airplane.

Caproni seemed to go in two directions at once. From the later part of World War I on through the 1930s, he built some of the largest, lumbering flying boats and bombers ever to fly, adding wings and increasing size every chance he could. Some flew well, but many became white elephants to say the least; the gigantic and classically humorous Ca.60 nine-winged flying houseboat being the most notorious of these occasional lapses. These monsters now exist only in faded photographs mounted on the walls between the rather large and strange propellers and wheels which hang or lean beside them.

During this same period, Caproni was also developing some fine light and medium aircraft. There are two Ca.100s, one on wheels and the other on floats. From just a short distance away, you would swear that they were de Havilland Moths, and in fact they were based on the Moth's design, but with quite a bit of difference in the details.

More original, and I think much more attractive, is the Ca.113. It is a graceful biplane of the Waco or Travel Air type powered by a 240-hp Walter Castor radial engine. A few special versions used the 370-hp Piaggio Stella VII radials and in the hands of pilots like Mario de Bernardi and Tito Falconi they were capable of spectacular aerobatics. De Bernardi, in fact, won the aerobatic trophy at the 1931 Cleveland Air Races in a Ca.113 while on a goodwill tour of the U.S. As with their racing cars, the Italians seem to be able to become almost a part of their exotic machinery.

Caproni continued to build light aircraft after World War II. The Ca.193 is a five-seat light twin which maintained Caproni's reputation for unconventional configurations. It is a mid-wing twin with two Walter Minors in a pusher configuration, twin rudders, and the passenger compartment well forward *a la* Aero Commander. With a 160-mph cruise and 1,200-lb useful load, it should have been a competitor of the early Aero Commanders and Piper Apaches. It was the last airplane to be designed and built by the Caproni factory at Vizzola.

Not all of the light planes at the museum are Caproni's. Mario de Bernardi had designer Luigi Pascale build a light aircraft for a post-war production run that did not come to pass. Built for him by Partenavia in 1957, only this one MdB.02 survives. It is a diminutive low-winged, two-seater looking a bit like an Ercoupe with a single fin. The Lombardi F.L.3, on the other hand, looks more like those few low-winged Aeroncas of the late 1930s and the Macchi MB 308G is a dead ringer

The diminutive Savoia-Marchetti S.M.56 single-engined, two-seat flying boat.

for a Tripacer. The SAIMAN 202-M, made by another of Caproni's subsidiaries, is a particularly attractive two-seat, low-wing trainer.

Do not get the idea that conventional light aircraft are the only things
on display. Savoia-Marchetti was one of the great builders of flying boats
and amphibians. The S.M.56 is a truly charming little two-seat biplane
amphibian with a single tractor engine. The S.M.80 was originally a
similar aircraft, but some five years newer and this time a monoplane.
What is on display marked as an S.M.80 is actually an SM.80bis; *bis*
meaning modification and in this case not a minor one. The fuselage
was extended to hold four people and the single tractor engine replaced
by a pair of pushers.

When we left the museum, what had been an empty grove of trees
and an abandoned grass runway were now covered with people.
Unbeknownst to us, the monthly flying meet of the local radio-
controlled model glider club had commenced. While the 30-year olds
flew their models, the old men sat under the trees and played pinocle
and the grandmothers looked after the toddlers. Those old men would
have been alive and could have watched the Ca.6s and Ca.9s take off
from this field. The models that their sons fly have aerodynamics far
superior to any aircraft in that museum and carry electronics that were
beyond conception when the Caproni Ca.36s were flying. I wonder what
the grandchildren, playing now in the same field, will see during their
lifetime!

Alas, we discovered that the Vizzola Ticino museum was slated to
close, although our limited Italian precluded getting any details. (My
parents, as good naturalized Americans, spoke only English in the
house—except when we kids were bad and tempers flared. Thus our
only Italian consists of swear words. This is not very useful in an aviation museum, but seems serviceable when skirmishing with taxicab
drivers in Rome.) Good fortune, though. We later discovered that the
collection has found a new home. In the near future, a new Caproni
Museum will open, appropriately, at the Count Gianni Caproni Airport
at Trento, not far to the east of Milan.

While in the vicinity, one should visit the Leonardo da Vinci National
Museum of Science and Technology. Finding the museum in the center
of Milan is easy enough. Just take a taxi; finding it by car or public transport is hopeless. It is after you arrive that the difficulty begins. Each
time that you ask for directions to the aeronautical collection, you will
be routed through various staircases, underground passages and out
doors to other buildings. The museum is located in what was an old
Olivetan Monastery. In the 380 years since the first building was constructed, the monks and those that followed added on in a less than
organized manner. After passing rows of old locomotives, one finds a
lone North American Texan. Surely, that can't be all, so you open the

last door. Several jet fighters frame the entry to one last building and that is the destination.

The lower floor is devoted to ships and contains a row of old speed-boats, several complete small ships and the actual bridge from the liner *Conte Biancamano*. A few aircraft are on the lower level, but most are

A Nieuport 10 Bébé, a Breda Ba.15 and a Magni Vale line up under a 1909 Forenon-Savoia (Farman) at the National Science Museum, Milan.

The Ricci 6 of 1919, a diminutive, civilian "derivative" of the military triplanes of a few years earlier.

This Ambrosini Supersette, I-PAIN, set a number of long distance records.

on the upper floor and several are either quite rare or unique. A series of record-setting and aerobatic small aircraft includes the Ambrosini Supersette, I-PAIN, a Pasotti F.9 Sparviero, the Muegyetemi M.24, I-TITI, and a SAIMAN 202-M. Even more unusual is the Ricci 6 of 1919. Ricci apparently decided to make a scaled-down version of the World War I triplanes for amateur use; there are pigeons with larger wingspans.

With no wings at all is the battered fuselage of the second, and last, of the Caproni-Campini jets of the late 1930s, the CC.2. Both the Magni PM3 Vale and the Breda Ba.15 are the last examples of their types left in existence. The Vale is a particularly attractive and unusual aircraft. Of plywood monocoque construction, it is remarkably streamlined and graceful for a strut-braced, high wing aircraft of 1937. The Vale was also noted for its aerobatic capabilities.

A Nieuport 10 Bébé comes from World War I and representing an even earlier time is the Forenon-Savoia, a copy of a 1909 Farman. You can go even further back into the history of flight at the Milan museum. You see, they also have many of Leonardo da Vinci's original drawings and documents. One can't go much further back to the origins of flight than that.

18

Where the Sava Meets the Danube

On the road to Belgrade's Surçin Airport, just before you reach the terminal building, you can see a very strange structure on the right that looks somewhat like an unfinished concrete mushroom. It is an unfinished concrete mushroom. Someday, however, it will also be one of the truly special air museums in the world. Originally planned to be completed by 1980 or so, in 1986 it still had some way to go; admittedly not an unusual circumstance. Be patient until it is opened, because the Vazdahoplovn Savez Jugoslavije will be a rare treat.

There are three reasons why it is special. The building that houses it is not an impressed hanger or rectangular box; it is a three-story work of art with the stem of the mushroom to contain a theatre, bookshop and special exhibits, while the overhanging second and third floors will hold the primary exhibits. With glass walls surrounding the circular rim, one will be able to look down on the airport. The larger and more modern and durable aircraft will be stationed outside in a park-like area around the building.

Art has its price and in this case it is one of the reasons for the delay. The outside glazing was originally designed to be of large triangles of plastic. Unfortunately, the plastic turned out to have problems and a switch to glass had to be made and that required structural changes. Airplanes aren't the only things that run into development problems when you press the state of the art. Meanwhile the aircraft—some 94 of them of 62 types, plus 24 sailplanes and a stack of engines, propellers and armament—are stored in the basement, the Jugoslav Air Transport. hangers and anywhere else with some room, waiting for the day when they can see the sky for which they were designed.

Too small a fraction of the air museums around the world are located at airports, but those that are, generally are there more for convenience than anything else. The second special feature of the Yugoslav Air Museum is that it will be truly integrated with the airport with live

190

A Sabrejet in front of the Vazdahoplovn Savez Jugoslavije, *under construction at Surcin airport, Belgrade.*

air traffic control radar displays and tower and approach radios piped in. The visitor will have the ability to see history's and today's aviation side by side.

But there is a further reason why this museum is special. There are a few defected MiGs and surplused An-2s floating around the west and there are some leftover lend–lease Bell Aircobras and at least one embarrassed Lockheed U-2 sitting behind the Iron Curtain. Yugoslavia, however, being a border country, has been in close contact with both sides. Thus where else can you see side by side a Hawker Hurricane and a Yak-9; a DC-3 and it's unlicensed sibling, the Lisunov Li-3; or an Ilyushin Il-14R and an F-86 Sabrejet? That is what makes this museum truly unique.

Being on the border has a price, and Belgrade has been on some border for a few thousand years. The Sava and Danube Rivers have always been natural barriers—between the Romans and the barbarians, the "civilized west" and the Saracens, and countless others. The fortified point where the rivers meet (and where the remains of multitudinous generations of forts are located) formed the start of Belgrade. That is, however, a somewhat precarious location for the average citizen and Belgrade has been destroyed more times than the historians can count. So while the tourist in search of quaint towns with old churches or places to ski (with obscenely delicious food at absurdly low prices) will go to Sarejevo or Dubrovnik, plan to route yourself thru Belgrade and be there when its museum opens.

Aviation started surprisingly early in Yugoslavia, although communications at the time were such that few in the west ever heard much about it. It wasn't even Yugoslavia then; Yugoslavia didn't become a unified country until the sorting out of World War I. You have to look under names like Serbia in early *Jane's All The World's Aircraft* to get any information and then not much. The pioneer Serbian designer and aviator was Ivan Saric. In 1910 he built the Saric I, of which a replica has been constructed. The Saric II, a Blériot-like machine was fairly successful and its remains still exist. When the museum started collecting in the 1950s, Saric was still alive and he donated not only the remains, but all his notes, drawings and original tools and photographs. When the museum opens, the centerpiece just inside the entrance will be an exact reproduction of Saric's shop with the original accoutrements surrounding the restored Saric II. That is truly the way to honor a pioneer.

While many Yugoslav aircraft were purchased from other countries, an indigenous and ingenious aircraft industry operated through the middle of the century, of which Ikarus was the leader. They started up in 1923 in Novi Sad, or New City, not far from Belgrade, and in 1926 commenced building French Potez 25s under license. By 1935 they were building their own designs such as the IK-2 fighter. The French influence shows. It had a semi-cantilever shoulder wing with an iron foundry's conception of wing and landing gear struts. It looked much like a Fairchild 24 with a few machine guns stuck here and there, at least from the photos and models which are all that exist at this point.

Ivan Saric's No. 2 of 1911 is the oldest Yugoslav aircraft in existence.

Around the rim of the mushroom, the shape of things to come is beginning to take place as more aircraft are moved into position. A Spitfire V and a Hurricane IV are by the outer rim and several helicopters huddle near the core. A Focke-Wulf Fw 190 and a Messerschmitt Bf 109 are there to compare with their P-47 and P-51 Allied counterparts.

Seemingly, the Russians decided in 1939 that one way to stop the panzers of the blitzkrieg was to put wings on some of their tanks. Nothing approaches the flying tank more than the Ilyushin Il-2 Stormovic. One hears stories of those eastern front combats, but one has to see a Stormovic to believe it; it is a far more formidable hunk of machinery than, for example, the Ju 87 Stuka. Cannons of various sizes, all large, stick out from several places such that you don't even notice the machine guns. Russian designs have generally been aimed more at offense than defense, but the shortage of pilots and aircraft led to the desire to protect both when slugging it out over the treetops with a panzer. Tap the underside of the cowl and you will bruise your knuckles; it is steel, not aluminum. The Stormovic carried over 1,500 pounds of armorplate. The steel skin extends back to beneath the wing and the oil and glycol coolers could be retracted into it for brief periods to shield them during combat. The Stormovic was originally designed as a single-seater, but the need for rear defense led to its redesign into a two-seater. Such were the pressures of war that as soon as the prototype was accepted, squadron trials and training were accomplished on the first pre-production batch—by flying them into the Battle of Stalingrad! One of

A flying tank, the Ilyushin Il-2 Stormovic; only a handful survive.

the outstanding aircraft of World War II, over 35,000 are believed to have been built. It was truly a moose.

On the other hand, the Yak-3 is a small, simple and straightforward fighter, clearly in the same arena as the Bf 109 and a lot more attractive. The Yak-3 was designed for minimum maintenance to allow for the vast stretches of the Russian plains and the logistic burdens that geography imposed. Omitting "frills" was one way to keep maintenance down and performance up. For example, the only gyro instrument in a Yak-3 is a turn and bank; there is no artificial horizon. If you couldn't fly instruments on ball, bank, and airspeed, you didn't deserve to be a Russian pilot. Besides, you weren't supposed to be up in the clouds, but down on the deck supporting the troops and thus presumably able to maintain visual contact even in a blizzard. The Yak-3 is dwarfed by the P-47D Thunderbolt next to it.

During World War II, a small Free French contingent of fighter pilots operated Yak-3s as a detachment in the Soviet Air Force. Known as the Normandie-Niemen Regiment, these expatriates fought on the eastern front and into the Balkans. Towards the very end of the war, they were given the opportunity to make their way back to France. On June 20, 1945, the squadron of French-piloted Yak-3s helped recapture Le Bourget Airport during the liberation of Paris. One of those Normandie-Niemen Yak-3s still sits at Le Bourget, at the Musee de l'Air; it is the only other Yak-3 outside Eastern Europe.

After the destruction of World War II, the Yugoslavs began rebuilding leftover Yak-3s and -9s and later developed the S-49, which is really a redesigned Yak-9. Once the rubble was swept up and by the early 1950s, some fascinating prototypes were being developed.

Clearly, as speeds increased manueverability would be limited, in part by the human pilot's ability to take 'G' forces. Designer Beselin took a novel approach to the problem, concluding that a prone pilot would

The Ikarus S-49C was a Yugoslav-built version of the Russian Yak-9.

194

The Ikarus 451 Pionyr prone-pilot research aircraft of 1949, a tiny twin-engined tail-dragger.

The Pionyr airframe, with two small turbojets evolved into the Ikarus 451M Zolja; number 177 is a KB-6 Matajur.

allow higher 'G' forces and also allow a smaller fuselage cross section and thus less drag. The Ikarus 451 Pionyr research prototype was the result and it still exists. A diminutive tail-dragger with twin inverted inline engines, it has a slender pod fuselage with a glazed nose for the pilot to gaze out at the world as he lies prone on his couch; whether eating grapes or endeavoring to maintain attitude with little horizontal reference is not recorded.

It was quickly apparent that the jet engine was going to take over from the propeller aircraft and thus Ikarus replaced the 451 with the 451M, Zolja. Similar in size, it gave up the prone pilot idea and replaced the inverted jugs with two small 330-lb thrust Turbomecca Palas turbojets in wing mounts. Again it is a charming and diminutive aircraft, sort of a miniature Gloster Meteor with a tail wheel. Side by side, the two research aircraft are indeed captivating one-of-a-kinds.

Now the U. S. Navy's old aircraft numbering system was merely obscure; Ikarus' was incomprehensible. They apparently began with

195

a straightforward Ikarus 1, Ikarus 2 and so forth. Later they began adding an 'S' in front of those that were trainers. Then somewhere along the road they suddenly jumped to number 451, stopped counting and just started putting letters fore and aft. There is a 451MMT Strsljen and an S-451MM Matica. The latter, meaning Queen Honeybee, is again a completely different airframe than the previous ones that had that magic number. The Ikarus S-451MM is more modern, although also of a similar configuration to a Meteor. One interesting feature is the folding wings, although we are not aware of any Yugoslav aircraft carriers patrolling the Adriatic. Part of the feature is that when the wings are in the up position, the outer halves of the engine cowlings fold with them, automatically exposing the innards for maintenance.

This Ikarus S-451MM Matica set an FAI subclass C-1d record at 466 mph; a Stearman PT-17 is at rear.

The only Fiat G-50bis in existence hides in the basement awaiting restoration; it still has its Croation markings.

Actually, there was one last design, the Ikarus 452, of which one example was built, but which no longer exists except in photographs. It was also a twin jet, but of twin-boom configuration and with one jet engine above the other in the nacelle fuselage. It appears extremely stubby and much like some combination of an English Electric Lightning and a D.H.112 Venom that bumped against the sound barrier. It also represented the last of the line for some unique and unusual fighter aircraft developments.

Down in the basement lurk some other extremely rare aircraft. The only Fiat G.50bis Italian fighter of World War II known to exist is there waiting for restoration as well as—nearly unheard of by Americans—a UTVA 213, a Vajic V-55 and both a Petlyakov Pe-2 and a Polikarpov Po-2. You should not confuse Petlyakovs with Polikarpovs, which are distinctly different aircraft; it would indicate lack of sophistication. Just bluff and hope you don't have to pronounce them.

Yugoslavia is a small country made up by the diplomats by merging the old Balkan republics, kingdoms, and provinces after World War I. It has been overrun numerous times. But there is a pride and dedication to the past, while looking towards the future. It came through in the 1983 winter Olympics at Sarejevo. Clearly it is coming through in the building of their air museum. Wait a little longer, it will be worth it. Or perhaps by the time you read this, a speaker near those aircraft will be crackling with a tower operator's commands: "Ilyushin Alpha Charlie, cleared for take off; Lockheed Zebra Whiskey, turn left after departure." The aircraft near the speaker will not have heard such commands in half a century.

19

Three Gold Crowns

The authors must now make a confession. The one western country with a major airframe industry whose significant aeronautical collections they have not yet visited is Sweden's. Not that we haven't visited Sweden, but rather it was unfortunately before the idea for this book had germinated. It is not for the reason promulgated by our Swedish colleagues: that our time in Sweden was spent on the Westerbrogade eating crayfish and drinking Schnapps. Whichever the reader chooses to believe, the aircraft should not go without discussion because the Swedish contributions to aviation have been significant. Swedish designs, particularly SAAB's, have been at the cutting edge of aeronautical technology.

It was in 1716 that Emanuel Swedenborg designed a "Flying Machine," but like da Vinci and Cayley, it was premature to say the least. For-real type flying began in 1910 as the French influence spread through Europe; Oscar Ask and Hjalmar Nyrop began building Blériot-type machines in the summer of that year. Nyrop's third aircraft was donated to the Swedish government in 1911 for maritime reconnaissance, assuming anyone would be willing to fly over the frigid waters of the Baltic for any stretch of time in such a primitive machine. Nevertheless, it was relatively successful and became Aeroplane No. 1 of the Royal Swedish Navy. The donation was sponsored by a wealthy brewery owner, Otto Emil Neumuller. Aeroplane No. 1 has ever since been known as "The Brewer's Machine." Braumeister Neumuller's faith in aviation went only so far. One of the conditions attached to the donation was that his son should be precluded from being allowed to fly in anything until he in turn had at least two sons; somebody had to run the brewery if the engine conked out. Aeroplane No. 1 still exists in the possession of the Swedish Air and Space Museum.

The Swedish Air and Space Museum doesn't yet have a permanent home, although the museum's supporters are actively pursuing a facil-

The "Brewer's machine" of 1911, donated by brewery owner Otto Neumuller, became aeroplane number 1 of the Royal Swedish Navy.

ity to be located at Arlanda, Stockholm's principal airport. Until then, most of the aircraft are in storage or on loan to other locations. The Royal Swedish Air Force has its own museum at Malmslatt, near Linkoping; other collections exist at Ugglarp and Gothenburg and there are small groups of aircraft on view at other museums at Malmo, Landskrona and Stockholm. In the latter two are the only authentic Thulin machines in the world; an "NA" biplane at the Lanskrona Museum and a "B," a "G," and an "N" at the Tekniska Museet in the Djurgarden in Stockholm Harbor. (Even though we are discussing aircraft, don't miss the 16th century galleon *Vasa* at its own museum nearby.)

Dr. Enoch Thulin was known as the "flying doctor" and had made notable pioneering flights throughout Scandinavia. These included ones from Paris to Landskrona, from Malmo to Stockolm carrying photographs of the Baltic Exhibition for a newspaper, and a presumably profitable one carrying a Baron Blixen-Finecke from Gothenberg to Copenhagen so that he could attend two horse races in the same day. By 1914 Thulin's medical practice had taken a rear seat to aviation in much the same way that Dr. Watson neglected his patients to chase hansom cabs with Sherlock Holmes. Thulin took a more adventurous career than Watson and founded AB Enoch Thulin Aeroplanfabrik and began building civil and military aircraft. He was killed on May 14, 1919 in an airplane crash as were so many of his contemporaries.

During the 1920s and 1930s flying flourished in Sweden, particularly during the short summers. The oldest active de Havilland Tiger Moth

The oldest Tiger Moth still flying, SE-ATI has been training Swedish pilots since 1932. Noted Moth pilot Goran Klevstigh (rear cockpit) and Sven Hugosson, Royal Swedish Aero Club at the controls.

in the world, delivered in 1932, is still flying with the Royal Swedish Aero Club. Factories such as M. F. I., F. F. V. S., and Goetaverken began building aircraft. Goetaverken was, of all things, a shipyard that got into the light aircraft business. Their GV-38 in the Arlanda collection is a delightful, license-built Rearwin 9000-L Sportster. Homebuilts such as the Rieseler RIII, built by Werner Rieseler and Filip Bendel in 1922, covered the fields that the manufacturers did not. Examples of a number of these rare machines are contained in the Swedish collections.

It was in 1936, when Svenska Aeroplan AB was founded in Trollhattan, merging some of the other aircraft companies, that Swedish aircraft design really began to pioneer by world standards. Known by the company's initials, SAAB aircraft were among the best in the world. One of the most interesting is the SAAB 21 of the early 1940s; one of the few remaining examples is at Malmslatt, about a hundred miles southwest of Stockholm. The J-21A, the first production version, was a twin-boomed pusher fighter of exceptional performance. The configuration also led to it being a great gun platform. Initially a 20-mm Hispano cannon and two 13.2-mm machine guns were clustered in the unobstructed nose, later versions adding more and more armament. The J-21A was also the first operational aircraft to have an ejector seat, necessary for the pilot to clear the propeller whirling away a few feet behind his head. The SAAB 21 never saw combat, Sweden remaining neutral throughout World War II. With that armament and a top speed of 398 mph in 1941, the SAAB 21, along with the other aircraft of the

One of the first advertising flights was made in 1923 by hanging signs under this Rieseler R III.

The SAAB J-21A of 1943 was a superb gun platform. Royal Swedish Air Force Museum, Malmslatt.

Flygvapnet, was probably part of the reason why Sweden could retain her neutrality.

By 1945 it was clear that the jet engine would supersede the propeller for pushing airplanes, certainly for fighter planes. The configuration of the SAAB 21 was ideal for installing a turbojet. Thus the liquid-cooled Daimler-Benz DB605 engine was swapped for a de Havilland Goblin. The stabilizer was raised to clear the exhaust, the armament increased to a 20-mm Bofors cannon and four-13.2 mm Bofors machine guns and the SAAB 21R was born. The SAAB 21 thus has the distinction of being one of the few aircraft (along with the Northrop Flying Wing) to fly as both a propeller-driven and a jet aircraft.

The SAAB 29, appearing somewhat like an early MiG-15 and with all the graceful looks of a flying beer barrel, followed soon thereafter. In fact, while the SAAB 29 had no official name, all pilots called it the *"Tunnan"*—which simply means barrel. It was the first operational swept-wing aircraft in Europe. While the SAAB 29 also never saw combat, it provided the *force majeur* behind the UN peacekeeping forces in the Congo and elsewhere during the 1950s and 1960s. The multipurpose SAAB 32 Lansen (Lance) became its heavier stablemate during the 1950s.

In 1949 SAAB began a far-reaching design program. The Swedish Air Force asked for an almost impossible set of requirements; a fast rate of climb interceptor with extreme maneuverablility while simultaneously having nearly STOL performance to operate off dispersed fields. One of Sweden's great defense capabilities is that her fighters, like Switzerland's, are dispersed all over the country. Located at small airfields and even at small bases without runways—they are designed to take off on some nearby highway—they are thus almost immune to surprise attack. To top off the requirements, the aircraft had to have well over Mach 1 capability in level flight. This requirement was in 1949 when only the Bell X-1 could go supersonic in level flight. At that time, most aircraft that had reached Mach 1 had done so in a dive and precious few had returned to tell about it; there was a great deal not yet known about the mysteries of the "sound barrier."

Erik Bratt and his design team at SAAB turned to and met those specifications. They came out with one of the most outstanding aircraft of the early jet age. The prototype SAAB-35 Draken flew on October 25, 1955 using a British Rolls-Royce Avon engine with afterburner. The Draken could hit 1,188 mph (later ones reached 1,320 mph) at 40,000 feet and could still land in less than 2,000 feet. This flying dart had a double-delta planform with the front leading edge swept 80 degrees while the the outer portion of the wing was swept a more conservative 57 degrees! It makes the Douglas A-4 Skyhawk look like a sailplane. Yet its pilots loved it for its ease of handling, tight turning radius, and high rate of roll—only the latter is at all believable after looking at one. The Draken more than lived up to its expectations. Quantities were exported to several countries, including the similar-thinking Swiss. The Draken soldiered on through the 1960s and 1970s, which is why there are a number of examples of this incredible machine on display throughout Europe.

The Draken was followed in the 1970s by the even more advanced SAAB-37 Viggen. This Thunderbolt, for that is what the name translates to, is a canard delta and was designed in various versions to replace both the Draken and the Lansen. Equipped with cannon pods, air-to-surface and air-to-air missiles, and gobs of electronics tied into the Swedish air defence system, it still has performance that outdoes its predecessors—and it is still able to take off and land from 2,000-foot stretches of highway. The Viggen will likely, as did the Draken and the J-21 before it, make any potential aggressor think twice before heading north. Viggens can be seen at several of the Swedish airports (and occasionally parked in the trees near a road), but not as part of museum collections; they are on duty.

We have to get back to Sweden. We need to visit Malmslatt and to hope that the new facility at Arlanda for the Swedish Air and Space Museum gets underway—and we can't forget the crayfish and Schnapps.

20

North of the Alps

North of the Alps, but still so close that you can see them on the horizon, lies the city of Zurich. We have to stop there once in a while to check our numbered bank account. A few minutes south of Zurich's Kloten Airport is the almost adjoining military airfield at Dubendorf and the home of the Museum der Schweizerischen Fliegertruppe. It is an appropriate home for the Swiss Air Force Museum; Dubendorf was the scene of the first air meet in Switzerland in October of 1910. By 1914 it had already become a military base. Even today, jet fighters take off in the background while their forebears sit silently in the museum and others, more patiently, in hangers awaiting a new and larger building.

The oldest aircraft in the museum is a 1912 Rech monoplane (the only Rech in existence) and it represents the days when flying, any kind of flying, around the mountainous terrain of Switzerland was something of an achievement. One of the reasons that the peaceful Swiss remain at peace is to maintain a small but strong military. The first Swiss-made military aircraft were a reminder to their warring neighbors in World War I to keep their arguments elsewhere. On view are the only DH-1 and DH-5s left from that era. Regardless of the familiar appearing nomenclature, they are not de Havillands. August Haefeli had been a designer at the German Ago works and, after returning to Switzerland, he developed the DH-1, an outgrowth of the Ago C.II. Six of the twin-boomed observation craft were built by E. K. W., the Federal Construction Works at Thun in 1916. Far more streamlined than most of the pigeon's-roost twin-boomed pushers of mid-World War I, the DH-1 on view is a partial reproduction using bits and pieces of an original and a great many painstaking hours by volunteer air force personnel.

The Swiss have usually used a mix of imported, license-built aircraft and indigenously designed airplanes based on their own special needs.

The twin-boom Haefeli DH-1 surrounded by by Hanriots, Moranes, the only existing Rech, and a Haefeli DH-5 at the Museum der Schweizerischen Fliegertruppe, Dubendorf.

The two-seat DH-5 represents one of the latter. It was pulled by a 200-hp Winterthur water-cooled V-8 built by the *Société Suisse pour la Construction des Locomotives*—it was not a lightweight. The DH-5 could actually reach over 20,000 feet, something badly needed when the mountains start getting in the way. Haefeli's DH-5s started flying in 1919 and the thrifty Swiss got mileage out of them until the early 1930s.

Also from World War I are one of those infamous Fokker D.VIIs, a Hanriot HD-1 and a Nieuport 28C-1. Both the Hanriot and the Nieuport, with their castor oil spewing rotaries and close-coupled bodies, could hold their own with the Fokker fairly well, except for the Nieuport in a dive. For some inexplicable reason, one of Nieuport's more bewildered designers put the seam for the upper wing covering spanwise across the upper surface about one-quarter of the way back, which is, of course, where the lowest pressure occurs. Other than the occasional ensuing disrobing of the upper wing, both disconcerting and usually fatal, it wasn't a bad airplane.

A dozen other aircraft, including Dewoitines, Morane-Saulniers, Messerschmitts and Bückers are crammed into the small buildings. One of the best displays of aircraft engines and ordnance is in the rear building. Oerlikon is a Swiss company and not a few U. S. rapid-fire anti-aircraft guns in World War II were based on their designs. There are also a large number of display cases full of U. S. World War II artifacts. Many a B-17 or B-24 pilot, his bomber shot full of holes with one or two engines out and wounded aboard, decided that Dubendorf was a

A "pilot" stands by his mount, a 1921 Hanriot; in the background is a Fokker D.VII.

The twin-tailled E.K.W. C-3603 strike aircraft; a Morane-Saulnier MS.406 is at left.

lot closer to Munich or Schweinfurt than was Duxford. If one was going to spend the rest of the war interned, better that it be in friendly, if neutral, Switzerland than down where people were angry at you. Not a few Eighth Air Force pilots came home that way, and left behind the bits and pieces of that flight.

Until the new museum building is constructed, some of those aircraft not in storage are on loan to the Verkehrshaus, and that is but a short hour's drive away at Lucerne. A few kilometers east of that charming town on the north shore of the lake, the Verkehrshaus, the Swiss Transport Museum, is contained in a number of buildings in park-like surroundings. As one wanders between the buildings containing

A Douglas DC-3 appears about to touch down and the Convair 990 Coronado may have to make a go-around.

old trains and cog-railway engines, racing cars and trolley cars, one spots an old DC-3 coming in to land. It is actually on a mount in a courtyard and marks the entry to the aeronautical collection.

The large hall is crammed with over two-dozen aircraft, and over a third of them are one-of-a-kinds! The oldest aircraft in the hall, and the oldest Swiss aircraft in existence is the Dufaux IV. The Dufaux brothers, Henri and Armand, were motorcycle makers; that almost sounds like a parody of the Wright brothers, but it isn't. The Defaux's first few ventures were not very successful, but by the time they reached the 'IV, they were getting pretty good. The Dufaux IV was the first Swiss machine to stay aloft for any really finite period and Armand managed to fly it the length of Lake Geneva on August 28, 1910. They tried to sell it to the Swiss military, but the military felt that it was not very practical, its top speed was all of 78 km/hr, something under 50 mph. The Dufauxs built the improved Dufaux V which the Swiss military did buy, having now decided they were practical, a somewhat improbable set of reasoning given the brief period and small differences between the two machines.

Another Swiss pioneer flyer was Oskar Bider who, with great courage and a heavy overcoat, flew over the Pyrenees in 1913. Later that year he flew over the Alps from Berne to Milan. Both flights were in a Blériot XI which, if you have ever looked down at the Alps from a DC-10, one finds more than a bit courageous; in fact I suspect that much of the time he was looking up at the Alps! Bider crashed trying to fly at night (night flying in alpine country in a Blériot!), but he had enough money and unbroken bones left to purchase a second Blériot. Just as a wealthy horseman would take his own mount with him when he went off to

*The Dufaux brothers built the first successful Swiss flying machines. A 1910 Dufaux; above
is Oskar Bider's Blériot XI.*

war, Bider took his Blériot, a two-seat modified 'XI, off with him when
he went into military service in 1914. Bider and seven others like him
became the beginnings of the Swiss Air Force. Somehow his Blériot survived and it is the machine hanging behind the Dufaux in the Verkehrshaus. Bider himself was killed at Dubendorf in 1919.

While many small countries import much of their aircraft fleet, particularly civil and airline aircraft, they usually want to produce some
of their own fighting machines for self-sufficiency, if not for national
pride, reasons. In 1934 the E. K. W., the Eidgenössische Konstruktions
Werkstätte, produced the C-35 to replace the Fokker C.V-E two-seat
biplane close-support/reconnaissance machine then in service. The C-35
is also a biplane and also of generally attractive appearance. Its Hispano-
Suiza 12Ycrs engine was one of the earliest to mount a 20-mm cannon
between the cylinder banks, but except for that, it was probably not
much advanced over the Fokker. It could, however, reach the respec-
table altitude of 16,400 feet in a little over 8 minutes, which if you fly
in the Alps is a worthwhile characterisic. A French-designed, but
E. K. W.-built, Dewoitine D.27 high-wing fighter, also from the 1930s,
hangs nearby.

The C-35 and the D.27 are both one-of-a-kinds. But another one-of-a-
kind at the Verkehrshaus was originally American; the only Lockheed
Orion left in the world—not the more recent Navy patrol bomber, but
one of those beautiful radial-engined, "Smiling Jack" type speedsters

of the 1930s. The Orion was part of Lockheed's series of cantilevered-winged bullets that included the Vega, the Sirius, and the Altair. While small and of limited passenger carrying capability, they were fast, long-ranged, and reliable. Only one Sirius exists, Lindbergh's float equipped *'Tingmisartoq'* at the Smithsonian. There are a couple of Vegas around including Wiley Post's Winnie Mae and Amelia Earhart's bright red machine, both also at the Smithsonian, but only the Verkehrshaus has an Orion.

While each type in the series appears quite different—the Vega is a forward cockpit, stilt-legged, high-wing machine; the Sirius a low-winged, fixed-gear two-seater with the cockpit set far back; the Altair and the Orion were low-winged, retractable-geared machines—they were all built from essentially the same parts. The depression was on and Lockheed didn't have much cash for tooling for the molded-plywood structure that made those designs so streamlined. The four airplanes actually all use the same wing and tail surfaces and the same fuselage molds were utilized for each. Lockheed just cut the notch for the wing in the top for the Vega and on the bottom for the others (although a few of the last machines produced were made of aluminum).

Swissair used her two "Red Dogs" for fast mail service between Zurich, Munich, and Vienna, another of those routes that in the early 1930s must have made the Orion a boon for spies and couriers. At the time, the Orion had nearly twice the cruising speed of most aircraft in commercial service. Both of Swissair's Orions were sold off in 1936 to make room for larger aircraft. They went to France and from there ended up as makeshift warplanes in the Spanish Civil War. They didn't survive. The Republican forces in that conflict were desperate for aircraft and the Lockheeds, with their speed and range, even if getting a bit old—and therefore not too expensive—made good bargain-basement warplanes.

The Rudolf Wolf Company, a New York burlap firm, suddenly developed a need for aircraft to transport merchandise—burlap bags? Wolf's agents quickly but quietly purchased Varney Airlines' and Northwest's aging Orions. Scouring the country in a cloak and dagger operation, the burlap company made offers owners couldn't refuse and picked up most private Orions and Siriuses and not a few Vegas. The Lockheeds then simply disappeared off the registration lists and reappeared in Spain. As with Swissair's Orions, none of them survived the Spanish Civil War either, which is why there are so few of those old high-speed express Lockheeds left. The Orion on display at the Verkehrshaus is actually Jimmy Doolittle's famous *Shellightning* in which he made a number of long distance record-setting flights in the 1930s sponsored by the Shell Oil Company. The machine is now carefully restored and painted in the bright red colors of Swissair's original "Red Dogs."

As war clouds formed, the E. F. W. (the name had been changed to Eidgenössische Flugzeug-Werke) produced the C-3603, a mean-looking,

Painted as one of Swissair's "Red Dogs," the only Lockheed Orion in existence; a Fokker F.VIIa hangs below it.

twin-tailled close air support fighter- bomber. Very Teutonic in appearance, over 160 C-3603's and a dozen or so C-3604's of slightly more horsepower were produced in the early 1940s (there is another C-3603 at Dubendorf). The C-3603 could clip along at about 300 mph. With an Oerlikon cannon firing through the spinner, two 7.5-mm wing guns and two more 7.5-mm machine guns for the observer in the rear cockpit, they, the weather and the Alps helped keep an island of peace in the middle of the chaos of World War II.

With the jet age dawning, the Federal Aircraft Factory (which is a rough translation of what E. F. W. means) designed a very advanced four-engined delta, the N-20 Aiguillon. The Aiguillon once graced the entry of the Verkehrshaus, but it has disappeared into that twilight zone where old airplanes go until there is enough money and space to restore them—it is scheduled to go to Dubendorf eventually. The design was sufficiently risky that, as Northrop did with their flying wings, a scaled-down test aircraft was built first. The bright yellow Arbalette, with its four tiny Turbomeca Pimenes in nacelles, two above and two below the tailless swept wings, has to be one of the niftiest mini-jets around. It flew some ninety-one test flights and the Aiguillon was built around the data the Arbalette obtained.

Not only was the delta-winged configuration of the Aiguillon advanced for the late 1940s, but the planned engines were also revolutionary. They represented one of the first attempts at afterburning—

The four-minijet-powered E.F.W. Arbalette surrounded by an E.F.W. C-3603, an E.K.W. C-35 and others.

really more a ramjet surrounding the turbojet. A four-engined, delta-winged, heavy jet fighter with afterburner in 1950 would make one spectacular interceptor. Unfortunately, the engine development caused schedule slippages and cost overruns and the N.20 became a political football. Literally on the eve of the full-scale Aiguillon's test flight, the program was cancelled and specific orders were issued that it be disabled and not flown. The Swiss government settled instead for using de Havilland D.H.112 Venoms. A Venom now guards the entry door to the Verkehrshaus instead of the sole N-20 Aiguillon that used to be there—representing what might have been, and the end of any major Swiss military airframe industry.

Further inside the Verkehrshaus is a Comte Gentleman, a delightful four-place cabin monoplane somewhere in between a Puss-Moth and a Piper Pacer in looks. The Soldenhoff S-5 two-seat flying wing pusher of 1931, on the other hand, is a little more on the incredible side, but surprisingly it flew quite well. So far we have only touched on the unique examples, not the "more common" Fokker F-VIIa, the Fieseler Storch, the Zögling glider, or the two Mignet Pou du Ciels—one of which is on skis. When you get tired of walking around the aircraft, you can stand in the full-sized mockup of the tower of Zurich's Kloten Airport and play at air traffic controller while looking down into the aircraft hall—although I expect the speed spread in that pattern would keep you on your toes.

Returning to Zurich's Kloten Airport one notes that, as in Germany, some airports in Switzerland place a few of their old aircraft in the terminal. At Kloten hang a Bücker Bu 131 Jungmann, a Messerschmitt Bf 108 Taifun, and another one of those ubiquitous Mignet HM-14 Pou du Ciels, the last bearing an uncanny resemblance to a potato. Having mentioned the bizarre-looking Pou du Ciel several times before, it is perhaps time to tell its equally bizarre story, even though it was originally and primarily a French machine.

M. Henri Mignet had been fascinated by birds and the thought of flight since his early childhood. Impressed into the French Signal Corps in World War I, he managed to get his hands on a SPAD. While attempting some unauthorized taxiing, he destroyed both the SPAD and any chance of being sent to a flying school. For the next decade, brooding over his episode with the SPAD, Mignet became more and more obsessed and experimented with ever more weird and unconventional concepts. He became convinced that the typical airplane was unsafe, excessively expensive, and being foisted on the world by greedy, incompetent militarists. Conversely, his ideas would lead to the pure, ideal aircraft which "anyone who can nail together a crate" could build and fly. The first point is arguable, the second patently absurd.

Mignet's concepts reverted back to the idea that an aircraft should be intrinsically totally stable—the 'chauffeur' approach which failed at the turn of the century. He had no ailerons or active roll control. Lateral stability was achieved by extreme wing dihedral and upswept

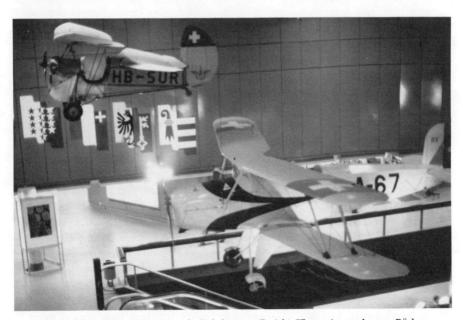

One of those infamous Mignet Pou du Ciels hangs at Zurich's Kloten airport abeam a Bücker Bu 131 Jungmann.

212

tips; an overly-large rudder slid the craft upright or into turns. Fortuitously, almost all Pou du Ciels are single-seaters, because waggling the rudder to get yaw-induced roll leads to a severe wallowing motion, exactly the process used today by fiendish pilots who desire to get their rear seat passengers airsick.

But it was in his concept for vertical control that Mignet's windshield cracked—and in which the seeds of disaster were sown. Of the two stubby, almost tandem wings, the rear was fixed and had no elevator. Vertical control was achieved by pivoting the forward wing on its mounts by a handle hanging down into the cockpit. By the time he reached his HM-14 in 1933, however, Mignet actually achieved a design that could, with some reservations in the definition, actually fly. More important, he had struck a nerve in a vast population that desperately wanted to fly, but were financially unable to. The HM-14 could be built in a garage for ten percent of the cost of a factory airplane and could be coaxed off the ground and remain approximately level by an untrained enthusiast. Mignet's book Le Sport de l'Air was half rambling philosophy and half construction manual, but its 6,000 copy first edition sold out in weeks (woulds't that would happen to this opus). Mignet, by this time probably certifiable, went on an almost evangelical speaking and flying tour, even to miraculously staggering his HM-14 across the English Channel. With almost religious fervor, hundreds of individuals began building the Pou du Ciel, literally translated as Sky Louse, but converted in England into Flying Flea. Clubs were formed— the Glasgow Tramway Employee's Flying Flea Club being a delightful example. Flying Flea races were held with thousands of spectators attending, some of the Fleas actually becoming airborne. The day of the airplane for 'everyman' was at hand. Trained engineers wept and went unheard.

Overweight, underpowered (by any type of motorcycle or lawn tractor engine at hand), and with poorly carved propellers, most Pou du Ciels hopped and bounced but rarely got very far into the air. Astonishingly, the better-built ones actually could fly. They were the unlucky ones because a fatal flaw was still lurking inside the design—a design that wasn't engineered in aeronautics; rather it was voodoo. A good, reasonably-powered Pou' could fly along fine for months when without warning it would suddenly pitch over and crash. The first tragedy occurred on April 20, 1936 at Renfrew, England. Fatalities continued in both France and England at a rate of around one a month until alarmed officials put a full-sized Pou du Ciel into a wind tunnel— fortunately it was small enough to fit.

The problem was Mignet's pivoting wing concept; it was only stable through a limited range. Sooner or later, if through some combination of gusts or control movement a moderately negative angle of incidence was reached, flow interference between the wings led to a pitching moment which no pulling on the controls could overcome. In fact, the one attitude in which a Pou' was perfectly stable was the ensuing vertical dive from which no recovery was possible.

The movement ended as abruptly as it began. The Pou du Ciel was banned from flying by most authorities across Europe. With the exception of Mignet himself and a few diehards who continued into the 1950s to try to perfect the concept, discouraged and forelorn builders packed it in and, to the relief of their wives, gave up their dreams. That is why there are so many leftover Pou du Ciels floating around air museums in Europe, an artifact of a dream that failed.

But the basic dream did not fail, even if the Pou du Ciel did. The younger and more realistic enthusiasts could now begin to get subsidized flight training in conventional aircraft from governments that recognized the need for a reserve of pilots should a war come—and World War II was just over the horizon. More important, a large number of people recognized that the desire to fly was far more pervasive than had been recognized. By the end of the war, with new materials, considerably more experience, and rules and regulations to preclude most fiascos, the homebuilding movement began again—this time on a much sounder basis. Today, the amateur-built airplane movement in France, Switzerland, England, and throughout Europe (as well as in the U. S.), providing the pride of building and the joy of flight to thousands, is healthy, safe, exciting and growing. Most have now forgotten that one of its principal foundations, for all the tragedy involved, was the ugly, ungainly, unsafe potato—the Flying Flea.

21

East of the Alps

East of the Alps and on the banks of the Danube lies the beautiful city of Vienna. Famous for her music and carefree life at the turn of the century, she was the capital of the old Austro-Hungarian Empire. Austria's relations with the Balkan countries, some within her empire and some without, were, however, part of the root cause of the First World War. While one normally thinks of German aircraft in World War I, a considerable amount of early pioneering was done in Austria and the interchange of technology between Austria and Germany was important to the development of aviation in central Europe. The Etrich Taube formed the basis (along with Fokker's Spinne) for the initial use by Germany of monoplane fighters; Igo Etrich was Austrian. The graceful Taube monoplane with bird-like wingtips, overpowered by 1911 standards with a 60-hp Austro-Daimler engine, was sufficiently impressive that the Rumpler company bought the design and began producing them for the German military.

An original pre-World War I Etrich Taube is on view, along with a number of other pioneering aircraft, at the Techniches Museum in Vienna. The museum is on the Mariahilfer Strasse across the park from the Schönbrunn Palace and not far from the Westbahnhof. Buses 52 or 58 or a short taxi ride can reach it from the train station.

Going back in time, the museum also contains an original Lilienthal 1892 glider, part of that series of experiments with which Lilienthal laid the foundations for flight and which the Wright brothers found so useful. Another pioneer who found Lilienthal's work useful was Pischof. The Pischof Autoplan is one of those charming machines of the 1910 era when the airplane was just evolving from the ability to get off the ground to ones that could actually fly somewhere. It was only a few years until that somewhere became the trench lines. The quaintness of the Pischof and the Taube were replaced by the stubborn

Pischof's Autoplan of 1910; front is at left although it probably mattered little.

lines of the Berg D.1 and the Phöenix D.III. A Berg (the type was produced in Germany by Aviatik) is on show at the museum, but the only Phöenix left is in storage up at Malmslatt in Sweden where the type served in the early post-war years. Austria suffered even more than Germany after the end of World War I. Her aircraft industry never recovered, but a glimpse of those halcyon days just after the turn of the century can be seen at the Technisches Museum and, in a broader sense, all about Vienna.

Gyros and Gyros

They are pronounced differently. One, along with *pastitsio* and *moussaka*, placates the taste buds while the other serves to keep airplanes right side up. Both can be enjoyed in downtown Athens. Greece, as with many other small countries, does not have a separate air museum, but keeps some aircraft at its war museum. In the Balkans there has almost always been a war going on, so the military museums tend to get rather crowded. Thus at the Polemiko Moysio, on the Vas Sofia near the Ameri-

216

A Canadian Harvard and a Supermarine Spitfire, photographed from the cockpit of a Curtiss SB2C Helldiver.

can Embassy and with a view of the Acropolis in the background, the aircraft are outside in a courtyard just beyond the sidewalk. Lined up behind them are a series of horse-drawn "tanks" from various turn-of-the-century Balkan wars. They appear to consist of wheeled, cast-iron garbage cans with hand-loaded cannons protruding from them. It probably explains why most old retired Balkan artillery men are generally deaf.

A Farman biplane hangs outside the entry to the Museum. It is a replica of one of the six Farmans that formed the first Greek military squadron, although to what wartime purpose a Farman could be placed is difficult to fathom. While the Farman is surrounded by only a small collection, that collection is graced by one of only four known remaining Curtiss SB2-C Helldivers. The SB2-C dwarfs the Spitfire and North American AT-6 alongside and intimidates the de Havilland Tiger Moth facing it; a Lockheed T-33 represents the jet age. A small collection, but worth stopping for as you walk back from an afternoon at the Acropolis and try to shake off the effects of the *gyros* and *souvlaki*—and the *ouzo* which you had sworn never to drink again.

Further East and Other Places We Haven't Been

We cannot end this chapter without surveying some of the rare and exotic aircraft that exist in museums in Eastern Europe, even though the vagaries of timing and itineraries have precluded the authors from having personally visited them. Both tourist and business travel to the East have become more common and popular, although the rate cycles somewhat based on fluctuations in the politics of detente. But if one can travel east, the experience for the connoisseur would be exquisite. All of the Warsaw Pact countries have aeronautical collections and while data on some museums are skimpy, there is a whole history of aviation and examples of aircraft largely unknown in the West.

Aviation started early in Russia and Sikorsky was building and flying four-engined monster biplanes in 1914 when a wingspread of over forty feet was still considered science fiction further west. The Soviet Union has vast distances between urban centers from the Ukraine to the plains west of Moscow and the difficulties in communicating across Siberia and to the Pacific are unimaginable. The development of aircraft that could handle those distances and weather conditions, as well as military needs, led to an extensive aviation industry from the late 1920s through the present. With only a few wartime exceptions, most of the earlier aircraft and pioneering flights have gone largely unheralded outside of her boundaries.

There are several museums in and around Moscow displaying that history with large assortments of Antonovs, MiGs, Yakovlevs, Ilyushins, and Lavochkins. Many are at the Gagarin Museum which also contains a rare Beriev Be-12 amphibian and several Polikarpovs. The Beriev is of the twin-engined flying boat configuration, with a hull and landing gear reminiscent of a Grumman Goose, but with a gull wing and twin rudders more similar to those on a Martin Mariner. A Sopwith Triplane and a 1934 ANT-40 bomber are also believed to be at Monino as are a number of replicas of early Sikorskies and Tupolevs originally constructed for the making of a movie. Also in Moscow are a number of early jet fighters, along with that embarrassed Lockheed U-2, at the Central Museum of the Armed Forces. Several World War II types, including not a few U. S. fighters that date from better days, and a rare Heinkel 100 are at the Zhukovsky Museum in downtown Moscow. The only known Shavrov Sh-2, used in pioneering flights over the Arctic by Babushkin, is at the Arctic Museum in Leningrad and the Tupolev ANT-25 that flew across the North Pole from Moscow to Oregon in 1937 is at the Chkalovsk Museum, named after the pilot of that flight.

One of the most extensive collections of aircraft in all of Europe is at the Muzeum Lotnictwa i Astronautyki in Krakow, Poland. Polish avi-

Valeriy Chkalov flew this ANT-25, the Stalinskiy Marshrut, *the Stalin Route, from Moscow 5,288 miles over the Pole to Oregon; weather forced it back to Vancouver.*

ation actually started before Poland became, once again, an independent country. At the turn of the century, part of Poland was under German control and the other part, Russian. Two of the group of six trainees sent by Russia to France in 1910 to learn to fly in Blériots and start Russia's air arm were Polish: Bronislaw Matyjewicz-Maciejewicz and Grzegorz Piotrowski. Polish pilots started showing their mettle early. In that same year of 1910, Piotrowski set a world's record by carrying a passenger 23 miles over water from Petersburg to Kronstadt while Matyjewicz reached the record altitude of 4,100 feet. Jan Nagorski is believed to be the first to fly over the Arctic when in 1914 he flew out of Novaya Zemlya searching for a lost polar expedition.

In the confusion created by the Russian Revolution and the collapse of the German Army in 1917 and 1918, Poland and the Polish Air Force were born. Small groups of pilots, soldiers, and mechanics commandeered air bases and scarfed up all the aircraft they could find. The Polish Air Force was formed under fire, fighting Germans and then Russian and Ukranian forces with a mixed bag of several dozen Rumplers, Albatroses, Brandenburgs, and Halberstadts; an occasional Anasal, Nieuport or Bréguet and even a singular and monstrous Sikorsky Ilya Mourometz found service. Many aircraft from that era survive at Krakow, including an Albatros, a D. F. W. C.V, an L. V. G. B.II, a Roland D.VI and a unique Grigorovitch M.15 flying boat from 1917. An Antoinette, a Geest Möewe and an authentic Fokker Spinne date from an even earlier era. Most, of course, are not from those that fought in Poland. They are from the Berlin Air Museum which had one of the most extensive collections in the world. When it was heavily bombed during World War II, the Germans moved the remains to hiding places east of Berlin for safekeeping. They were found by Polish forces and

P.Z.L. in Poland was one of the first developers of the metal stressed-skin structure which gave surprising performance to their high-wing fighters such as the P.11.

taken to Krakow. Another unique aircraft in that collection is Fritz Wendel's specially-built Messerschmitt 209V-1, D-INJR, in which he set a world's speed record in 1939. His record of 469.22 mph for propeller-driven aircraft stood for thirty years until Darryl Greenamyer broke it in 1969 with his hopped-up Grumman Bearcat.

Between the First and Second World Wars, the Polish aircraft factories produced some first-class aircraft. P. Z. L., in particular, was one of the pioneers in metal stressed-skin construction contemporaneous with Jack Northrop's work in the U. S. and when most countries were still using wood or welded steel-tube structures. The P. Z. L.s, L. W. D.s, W. W. S.s, and S. Z. D.s may have unpronounceable names behind those initials, but the aircraft they produced, and which are now at the Krakow museum, represent some outstanding and extremely rare machines.

Aviation also started early in Romania. Trajan Vuia was a Romanian living in France at the turn of the century. He was one of that group of pioneers that included Santos-Dumont, the Farmans and Levavasseur. On February 16, 1903, nearly a year before the Wright brother's first flight, Vuia presented a paper at the Academy of Science in Paris on the subject of flight and his proposed design to achieve it. Three years later, on March 18, 1906 Vuia, in his Vuia No. l, was the first person to take off from level ground by engine power alone in an untethered machine. His flights took place at Issy-les-Moulineaux outside of Paris and, while they were only brief hops, they provided a stimulus to the other experimenters in France. Vuia continued his research and in 1922, his helicopter was one of the first ever flight tested.

Back in Romania, Aurel Vlaicu was also experimenting with flight. He began unpowered gliding flights in 1909, but by 1911 he was flying

A replica of Vuia's No. 1 of 1906 in front of more modern types at the Central Military Museum, Bucharest.

his successful Vlaicu No. 2 in a series of flights around Romania. At the International Air Competition in Aspern, Austria, in 1912, Vlaicu picked up five separate prizes. Vlaicu was another of those pioneers who gave his life trying to challenge the skys. He was killed while attempting to fly across the Carpathian Mountains on September 13, 1913.

The original of Vuia's No. 1 is at the Musee de l'Air in Paris, but replicas of the Vuia and Vlaicu's No. 2 are at the Muzeul Militar Central, the Central Military Museum in Bucharest. Also at the museum are a Lavochkin La-9 fighter, an Ilyushin Il-10 (an advanced Stormovik), and a Yakovlev Yak-11 trainer, the last similar to an AT-6. A very rare Fleet F-10G biplane made its way from the U. S. The Italian Nardi FN.305 is also extremely rare, there being only two in existence—one in Italy and this one in Bucharest. The pre-war FN.305 was a two-seat trainer with retractable gear. It was built with both inverted in-line and radial engines and in most versions had a very aft-set cockpit leading to quite elegant lines.

Several jet aircraft from Russia are at the museum, however Romania itself produced two of the earliest experimenters with jets and rockets. Despite the appearance of his first name, Henri Coandă was a Romanian sub-lieutenant. As early as 1907, Coandă undertook experiments with rockets for use in aircraft. He exhibited the world's first

The Vlaicu II (replica) was a successful flyer for 1911 given the chain drive to dual propellors and control surfaces at both ends.

"jet" engine at the 1910 Paris Air Show. The engine was actually what we would call today a ducted fan. The then existing state of technology was too primitive for it to be practical. Coandă's ability impressed a number of people and although his jet engine concept never got very far, he went off to become a technical director of the British and Colonial Aeroplane Company, later and better known as Bristol Aircraft. He was influential in the design of several of the early Bristol monoplanes and biplanes. Some were conventional, but Coandă was always trying innovations. One of his designs had two rotary engines sideways-mounted on either side of the fuselage and bevel-geared to a single propeller. While that design was not successful, many of his designs of both aircraft and armament installations were. Coandă returned to Romania and continued research in aeronautics. Most of that is now forgotten. His name has gone down in aeronautical engineering circles instead for the Coandă effect—a phenomena of ducted flow.

The second innovator was Hermann Oberth, who was born in Sibiu in 1894. Oberth was one of the first to experiment with liquid-fueled rockets and he authored some of the first technical treatises on the subject, documents which are still referenced at the beginning of any book on the history of rockets and space travel. His work laid much of the

The Industria Aeronautica Romana I.A.R.813, a first-rate, all-purpose trainer and utility aircraft.

foundation for Werner Von Braun's development of the V-2 rocket in Germany twenty years later.

Romania also had an indigenous airframe industry in the the Romanian Aeronautical Industry at Brasov. I. A. R. built biplanes and later turned to monoplanes during the between-the-wars era. They were a prolific firm and produced a large number of designs including some streamlined low-wing monoplane fighters. Few early I. A. R.'s remain, but the museum has has an I. A. R. 813, an attractive, low-wing, two-seat trainer on display to round out its collection.

Both Bulgaria and East Germany have aeronautical collections in their military museums. At the National Military History Museum in Sophia, Bulgaria, is a collection of Russian aircraft. This includes one of those cast-iron Ilyusion Il-2 Stormoviks as well as a Yakovlev Yak-9, which was an outstanding radial-engined fighter plane, quite on a par with a Messerschmitt Bf 109G. The Yak-9 actually had a top speed 20 mph faster than the Bf 109 at low altitudes, but the advantage reversed at heights over 15,000; the Yak-9s spent their time working over ground installations and making the Bf 109s come down to them. The Tupolev Tu-2 is an interesting twin-engined, twin-tailed light bomber while the Yak-23 is a very early jet fighter with the engine mounted low in the nose such that the exhaust warms the pilot's seat.

The Arado 196 at Varna once patrolled the Black Sea for the Bulgarian Navy; there are only three Arado 196 float planes left in the world.

The Bulgarian Naval Museum at Varna on the Black Sea coast has a particularly rare airplane. It is a German Arado 196A-3 single-engined float observation aircraft. The Arado served with the Bulgarian Navy from 1942 until 1956 and was used for patrolling Black Sea shipping. It was a fairly heavy airplane, weighing in at over 7,000 pounds. The Arado also had fairly heavy armament for its type and the Bulgarian one is unusual in that it has an additional cannon over the German versions: two 20-mm cannons and a single machine gun. The Arado 196 became the standard catapult float plane for most of the German capital ships. For some reason, the U. S. concentrated on the central single-float configuration (with small wing-tip stabilizing floats) for its observation float planes, witness the Loening, Grumman, and Curtiss machines. Germany and most of the rest of the world, however, went to twin floats more like the bush float plane of today. The Arado at Varna is temporarily out of view, fortunately for restoration because there are very few observation float planes of any type left, particularly any of the Arados. The only other known Arado 196s are both in the U. S.; one is in storage at the Smithsonian and the other at the Naval Air Station, Willow Grove, Pennsylvania. Both came off the catapults of the German cruiser *Prince Eugen*. It might be worth going to Varna just to see one.

Dresden, in East Germany, has been noted for centuries for its china, glasswork, and crafts. It is also the home of the Armeemuseum der

A flight of Polikarpov Po-2s. The Po-2 was the primary trainer for most of Eastern Europe for thirty years; there is one at Dresden.

Deutschen Demokratischen Republik. The Armeemuseum contains a collection of MiGs including several MiG-17s and MiG-21s. The MiG-17 is an outgrowth of the MiG-15 from the Korean War era while the MiG-21 is a delta-winged intercepter. The Yakovlev Yak-18 is a small, two-seat primary trainer of the BT-13 school while the Antonov An-14 is an unusual high-wing, twin-engined, twin-tailed STOL transport used for all the myriad of purposes that such aircraft are put to; both date from the early 1950s. More unfamiliar to Americans would be the Aero L-29 Delfin and the Polikarpov Po-2. Both, however, were trainers produced in vast quantities. The Delfin, from Czechoslovakia, won a competition among East European countries for a jet trainer in the early 1950s and thousands were produced. The Polikarpov Po-2 was Russian, but served the same role thirty years earlier. The Po-2 bipane, which looks like a squarish Tiger Moth with a radial engine, was designed in Russia in 1924 and was the principle primary trainer in the east for decades. It was produced in Russia until 1944; the Poles kept making them until 1949 as the C. S. S. 13. A Fieseler Fi 103 is one of the only aircraft of German origin remaining at the Armeemuseum.

Czechoslovakia is the other Eastern European country that had an extensive aviation industry and that has air museums of a size that reflects that background. The Zlin aircraft are famous today as some of the best aerobatic aircraft in the world. In the past, however, Aero, Avia, Letov, and others produced outstanding aircraft from light planes to fighters. The Czechs were also sailplane enthusiasts. The Technical

The Aero 45 served as the principal light twin and jack-of-all-trades in Eastern Europe in the years just after the war.

Muzeum of Brno contains a series of Letov, Zlin, VAAZ and KSM gliders and motor-gliders as well as examples of a number of the Zlin trainers and aerobats.

It is at the Military Museum, the Letecka Expozice Vojenskeho Muzea in Prague, that the world's largest collection of Aeros and Avias exists. The Aeros range from a 1922 A-10, a very square-shaped, single-engined transport, to the Brigadyrs and Akrobats of the 1960s. The Aero 45 and the higher-powered Aero 145 were light twins of the post-war era with inverted in-line engines and a round nose similar to a scaled-down Boeing Stratocruiser. It is unlikely that there has ever been one in the U. S., but they were used from Brazil to Indonesia.

Avia, on the other hand, produced some excellent biplane fighters in the 1930s. The Avia 534 was the standard Czech fighter at the time of the Munich crisis. It was probably one of the highest-performing biplane fighters ever built and certainly was the best in central Europe at the time. In 1937, at the Zurich Air Meet, the only aircraft that outsped it was the then new Messerschmitt Bf 109. The Avia 534 was also one of the most attractive biplane fighters ever built; it certainly ranks with the Hawker Fury and the Curtiss Hawk for sheer good looks. The only known Avia 534 is at the Prague museum. Letov was another builder of military aircraft, although certainly not of ones as aesthetic as the Avias. Still, the only Letov S 2 and S 20 biplane attack aircraft of the 1920s are at the Military Museum in Prague.

Also in Prague is the Narodni Technicke Muzeum. While there are a few newer aircraft at the museum, most go back to the beginnings of aviation and the First World War era. Aircraft that represent the only ones of their kind, or nearly so, comprise probably half the collection. These include an Anatra from 1917, a 1919 Bohemia B-5, an early Avia BH-9, the Knoller C.II, a Kaspar Monoplane, and, of all things, a 1918

American Thomas Morse Scout. The Kaspar was built by Jan Kaspar in 1910 from photographs that he had seen of Blériot's Channel crossing adventure. Surely, the Narodni's aviation hall is one of the great treasure houses of old aircraft.

Another museum with an extensive collection of older aircraft is the Kozlekedesi Muzeum, the Hungarian Transport Museum in Budapest. It contains a number of Antonovs, Ilyushins, and Yakovlevs, but among the earlier aircraft are a Brandenburg B-1, a Fabian Levente II, and a

One of the fastest, as well as one of the most attractive, biplane fighters of the late 1930s, the Avia 534.

The all-metal, corrugated skin of the Junkers F-13 gave it, and its multi-engined brethren, outstanding load-carrying and long-range performance.

The P.Z.L. 104 Wilga replaced the 104 Gawron and the L-60 Brigadyr for agricultural and "light-hack" duties in the early 1960s.

Junkers F 13; the last with an intriguing history. The early Swiss airline, Ad Astra, made the mistake of leasing the Junkers without checking the lessee's credentials too carefully. It was used in an attempted coup by Hungarian Royalists in 1921 and Ad Astra never got the Junkers back. The Lloyd 40 from 1914 and the Lampich Roma from 1925 are also pretty rare birds. The Kozlekedesi Museum also contains probably the most extensive collection of Rubik sailplanes in the world. Rubik senior was a prolific designer of high-performance sailplanes from the 1930s to the 1960s; Rubik junior was the inventor of the diabolical Rubik's cube. We much prefer to spend our time with Rubik senior's sailplanes.

Not far away, the MEM Repuloges Szolgalat Collection of the Hungarian Agricultural Ministry includes a number of Zlins, MiGs, several Rubiks on loan from the Transport Museum, and an Aero Super 45 twin originally used as an air ambulance. As one would expect at a museum of the Agricultural Ministry, concentration is on aircraft used in agricultural and remote bush operations. The P. Z. L. 101 Gawron is such a plane and the collection has three of them. Hauled by a 260-hp Ivchenko radial engine, it has a 41-foot span with wing slots and tip plates. The landing gear would appear to allow it to land on lava flows. Having a soft spot for bush planes, we would love to compare one with "Old Charlie."

The names and initials of many Eastern European aircraft may not mean much to any but the aviation historian or fanatic. If you look up their photographs in some thick encyclopedia of aviation, however, they will trigger the desire to hunt up your passport (and to get a new trenchcoat). As visits between East and West grow, perhaps to aviation enthusiasts a Letov, an I. A. R. or a Lavochkin can be as familiar as a Hawker or a Fokker or a Douglas. The love of flight and the adventure of flying are the same no matter what country one is in.

Back in the west are other collections that we must also look forward to. No matter what country in Europe you are in, nor the size of the collection, there is almost always something rare or unique. The only known Curtiss CW-25 Falcon is at the Turkish Air Force Museum in Izmir; the last of the two-dozen Northrop N-3PB float plane fighter-bombers ever built is in the Kongelige Norsk Luftforssvaret Collection in Norway; the only A. I. S. A. I-115 left is at the Museo Del Aire in Madrid; and the last Fairey III-D is on floats at the Museu Da Marinha in Lisbon. If you are standing in the aisle of a bookstore and have read this far, but have not yet bought the book, please do so. The authors need the money for tickets to those places (as well as for new trench-coats) in order to replace this chapter in the next edition.

A Spitfire holds its cowl high, refusing to be embarrassed as the Brussels Air Museum is rented out for a week to an antique show to raise funds.

Appendix A
Understanding European

If not quite a Tower of Babel, the multiplicity of European languages adds a challenge. While there are usually some English-speaking persons at the major museums, that is not true for the smaller ones and, of course, most exhibit explanations and guidebooks are in the local language. We relate to aircraft with names like Thunderbolt, Hawk or Tornado. Names such as Folgore, Lunak, or Pyörremyrsky don't trigger the same reaction, but they should because those names mean exactly the same thing. Table A-1 translates most of the aircraft names and nicknames that you are likely to run into and should provide an idea of the image that the designers or pilots had of their aircraft.

Table A-2 is a small dictionary of key aeronautical words from a majority of the European languages and should serve to guide the reader enough to comprehend most exhibits. Of necessity the list is not comprehensive but a little amateur cryptography should allow one to decipher most major points. For example, if the sign in front of each aircraft starts with something like "Bouwer: Douglas" or "Bouwer: Messerschmitt", then "Bouwer" must mean Manufacturer or Fabricator and it doesn't really matter which. If you paid the taxi driver to the museum with Belgian francs and he didn't complain, then the language must be Belgian. Words such as "helicopter", which is nearly identical in most languages and for which the object is patently obvious, are also not included.

With no disrespect meant to any country, we just could not fit them all in and/or didn't have friends that could translate those languages for us for free. There are a great deal of similarities, so for Danish or Norwegian use Swedish and for Swiss try French or German. For Portuguese, Spanish may help and for Czechoslovakian, Bulgarian, and other Slavic areas, try Serbo-Croatian (Yugoslavian) or Polish. A few minutes spent memorizing the sounds of the Cyrillic (and Greek) alphabets is worth the investment. The majority of the letters, once you figure out which is which, have similar sounds to ours and many aeronautical terms are phonetically decipherable. Much in Romanian can be puzzled out from Italian and English (or Latin if you are classically inclined). For Hungarian (Magyar), you are on your own. We did not include a column in English-English (as distinct from American-English) since such terms as airscrew, alighting gear, or parafin can generally be unraveled or one can query a guide. We do advise, however, that it is generally more difficult to understand English in Scotland, Wales, or Ireland than it is in Denmark, Sweden, or the Netherlands.

In the U. S. and England, most airframe companies are named for their founder, or more accurately, the founder named his fledgling company after himself. Thus we are used to, and can identify with, Cessna, Boeing, Sopwith or de Havilland although occasionally the spelling gets modified as with Lockheed (nee Loughead) or Avro (A. V. Roe). A few are named after their location, such as Bristol or Gloster (originally Glouchestershire), but sooner or later economic pressures cause many to be swept up into conglomerations as with North American or British Aerospace. Regardless, there still remains a word to conjure up an image or memory of the type and family of airplanes involved—a Beech or a Grumman or a Hawker.

That is generally not the case in Europe, particularly in central and eastern Europe, where many aircraft have only initials. That adds a degree of unfortunate anonymity to the airplanes and the people behind them. One reason for the initials is that in the languages involved, the founder's names contained a fair number of syllables and if there were two or three partners, that could take a whole letterhead. Corporations, particularly nationalized ones, can take a whole page, and generally read something like Northern Provincial Locomotive, Refrigerator and Flying Machine Making Institution. Can you imagine radioing the tower that you are Szybowcowy Zakład Doświadczainy Jaskółka; Sugar Papa, Whiskey George Bravo, outer marker inbound. You would be past the missed approach point before being cleared to land. Actually, French company names are about the longest.

Regardless, the use of unfamiliar initials deters a feeling for the organization and the people that built that machine and the other machines in their history that all had some connection—and soul—even if hidden behind that acronym. For those that are curious, we appendix in Table A-3 that alphabet soup and some approximate translation where it is not self-apparent. We also note that, for all our research, sources are conflicting as to whether or not periods are (or were) used between the letters in a number of cases; let future researchers beware. In addition, we have sometimes not spelled out or translated the word for corporation, company, or partnership where the abbreviation in the particular language is fairly common and self-evident; typical are GmBh, AG, AB, SA and so forth.

All of continental Europe uses the metric system of units and thus the reader, if not technically inclined, may not assimilate what the numbers mean. The problem is that most conversion tables go to four or five digits. Unless you are making parts that have to fit, all one wants is a "feel" for what the numbers imply. Who can visualize what 240

232

mph means except that its faster than a P-26 and slower than a P-40, which is really what you want to know. The following is a "poor pilots" approximation:

Meter (m)=3.2808 feet. Multiply by 3 and add a little. A wingspread of 20 meters must be about 65 or 68 feet and an altitude of 3000 meters should be close to 10,000 feet.

Kilogram (kg)=2.2046 pounds. Double and add a little. A 200 kg bomb is near enough to a 500 pounder if you are in the vicinity when it lands and an 1100 kg gross weight is about the same as our Cessna 180's 2600 pounds.

Kilometer (km) and Kilometers/hour (km/u,km/o,km/h—the abbreviation for hours varies in different languages)=**0.62137 miles or mph.** Take about ⅔ the number and knock a bit off to get the range in miles or speed in mph. Three hundred kilometers per hour is close to 185 miles per hour and 1800 kilometers is about 1000 miles.

The **millimeter (mm)=0.03937 inches** (or about 1/32″) and is usually only needed for the caliber of guns. They are usually about 7.7 mm (roughly our 30 caliber) and 12.5 mm (roughly our 50 caliber) while 20 mm and 37 mm (look at your 35 mm film can) are typical for cannons. Meanwhile, a **liter** of petrol is a schnitzel **(1.0567)** more than a **quart** of gasoline, so divide by 4 to get gallons.

While most aircraft in a country's museum will likely come from that country, such is not always the case. Listed below are the registration number prefixes (the 'N' number prefixes) assigned by the major countries to identify nationality of the aircraft. This can be of interest both in the museums as well as around the airports in Europe.

CCCP	Soviet Union	HB	Switzerland	OY	Denmark
CF	Canada	I	Italy	PH	Netherlands
CS	Portugal	LN	Norway	SE	Sweden
D	West Germany	LX	Luxembourg	SP	Poland
DM	East Germany	LZ	Bulgaria	SX	Greece
EC	Spain	N	U.S.A.	TC	Turkey
EI	Eire	OE	Austria	TF	Iceland
F	France	OH	Finland	YR	Rumania
G	United Kingdom	OK	Czechoslovakia	YU	Yugoslavia
HA	Hungary	OO	Belgium	ZA	Albania

With all that information and a lot of arm motions and smiles you should be able to get through any of the museums with pretty good comprehension. The only two other important points are that the symbols for rest rooms and the word for beer are essentially universal.

Table A-1: Aircraft Familiar Type Names

Abeille	Worker Bee	French	Draken	Dragon	Swedish
Aiglon	Eaglet	French	Edelweiss	(type of flower)	German
Aiguillon	Stinger	Swiss	Elster	Magpie	German
Airone	Heron	Italian	Emeraude	Emerald	French
Aladár	A male name	Hung.	Eolio	Wind	Italian
Alcione	Kingfisher	Italian	Esztergom	Town in No. Hung.	Hung.
Alcotán	Lanner (falcon)	Spanish	Etendard	Flag-Standard	French
Alcyon	Kingfisher	French	Fachiro	Fakir	Italian
Alizé	Tradewind	French	Falco	Falcon	Italian
Alouette	Lark	French	Falke	Falcon	Swedish
Aquilon	Northwind	French	Fem Koma	Metal Friend	Hung.
Arbalette	Crossbow	Swiss	Fergeteg	Tempest	Hung.
Ariete	Battering Ram	Italian	Flamant	Flamingo	French
Azor	Goshawk	Spanish	Folgore	Thunderbolt	Italian
Bachstelze	White wagtail (bird)	German	Freccia	Dart	Italian
Baladin	Buffoon	French	Frelon	Hornet	French
Baldo	Fearless	Italian	Futár	Courier	Hung.
Balilla	Hunter	Italian	Gabbiano	Seagull	Italian
Bergfalke	Mountain Falcon	German	Galeb	Gull	Serbian
Besenstiel	Broomstick	German	Gawron	Rook	Polish
Bibbecio	A south-west wind	Italian	Ghibli	Desert Wind	Italian
Bidon	Canteen (soldier's)	French	Gil	Bullfinch	Polish
Biene	Bee	German	Girfalco	Gyrfalcon	Italian
Bies	Bogeyman/daredevil	Polish	Glenten	Kite/hawk	Danish
Bipo	Two-seater (slang)	Italian	Göbë	Wily highlander	Hung.
Biposto	Two-seater	Italian	Greif	Griffon	German
Blitz	Lightning	German	Grifo	Griffon	Italian
Bohatyr	Hero	Czech.	Grünau	Town near Alps	German
Bovin Taupine	Mole (small female)	French	Gyöngyös	Pearl	Hung.
Brigadyr	Brigadier	Czech.	Häbicht	Goshawk	German
Broussard	Woodsman	French	Halcón	Falcon/Hawk	Spanish
Buchón	Pigeon	Spanish	Harakka	Magpie	Finnish
Canguro	Kangaroo	Italian	Haukka	Hawk	Finnish
Capronicino	Little goat	Italian	Hornisse	Hornet	German
Centauro	Centaur	Italian	Humu	Loud Rumble	Finnish
Chaika	Seagull	Russian	Idroplano	Seaplane	Italian
Chauve Souris	Bat	French	Ifjúság	Young Man	Hung.
Cicogna	Stork	Italian	Iskra	Spark	Polish
Cigale	Cicada	French	Jadran	Adriatic	Serbian
Cimbora	Companion	Hung.	Jaskółka	Swallow	Polish
Citabria	Airbatic (backwards)	Amer.	Jastreb	Hawk	Serbian
Cmelák	Bumblebee	Czech.	Jastrząb	Hawk	Polish
Coccinelle	Ladybug	French	Joigny	Pearl	French
Colibri	Hummingbird	French	Junak	Young Man	Polish
Criquet	Locust	French	Jungmann	Cadet	German
Czajka	Lapwing	Polish	Jungmeister	New champion	German
Czapla	Heron	Polish	Júnious	June	Hung.
Delfin	Dolphin	Czech.	Kaie	Jackdaw (bird)	Norweg.
Demant	Diamond	Czech.	Kania	Kite/hawk	Polish
Demoiselle	Dragonfly	French	Kanya	Kite/hawk	Hung.
Diamant	Diamond	French	Karaś	Carp	Polish
Djinn	Genie	French	Kék Madár	Bluebird	Hung.

Kiebitz	Plover (bird)	German
Kolibri	Hummingbird	German
Koma	Friend	Hung.
Kos	Blackbird	Polish
Kotka	Eagle	Finnish
Krajánek	Journeyman	Czech.
Kranich	Crane (bird)	German
Kurir	Courier	Serbian
Kurki	Crane	Finnish
Laerke	Skylark	Danish
Lampart	Leopard	Polish
Lansen	Lance	Swedish
Leone	Lion	Italian
Lepke	Butterfly	Hung.
Levente	Knight/champion	Hung.
Libel	Dragonfly	Dutch
Libelle	Dragonfly	German
Libellula	Dragonfly	Italian
Loisirs	Leisure times	French
Los	Elk	Polish
Luciole	Firefly	French
Lunak	Kite/Hawk	Czech.
Maagen/Magen	Seagull	Danish
Macchino	Machine (flattering)	Italian
Macka	Wildcat	Serbian
Magister	Schoolmaster	French
Malysh	Little Boy	Russian
Marsupiale	Marsupial (possum)	Italian
Martinet	Swift	French
Mascaret	Tidal wave	French
Matica	Queen Bee	Serbian
Medak	Honey Bee	Czech.
Meise	Warbler (bird)	German
Ménestrel	Minstrel	French
Meta-Sokol	Super-falcon	Czech.
Meuse	The river	German
Miś	Teddy bear	Polish
Mistral	A cold north wind	French
Mokány	Spunky	Hung.
Moravia	Czech Province	Czech.
Motyl	Butterfly	Polish
Moustique	Mosquito	French
Möwe	Seagull	German
Myrsky	Storm	Finnish
Natter	Viper	German
Nibbio	Kite	Italian
Ohka	Cherry Blossom	Japanese
Oiseau Canaris	White Bird	French
Orkan	Whirlwind	Polish
Ouragan	Hurricane	French
Pajtac	Little One	Hung.
PAN	(Nat'l.Aerobat.Team)	Italian
Papillon	Butterfly	French
Paukkulauta	Cannonade	Finnish
Pchelka	Little Bee	Russian
Peque	Child/'Little One'	Spanish
Pfeil	Arrow	German
Phalène	Moth	French
Picchio	Woodpecker	Italian
Pilis	Mountain in Hungary	Hung.
Pingouin	Auk	French
Pionir	Pioneer	Serbian
Pionyr	Pioneer	Czech.
Pipistrelle	Small bat	French
Pipistrello	Bat	Italian
Planeur	Glider	French
Pou du Ciel	Sky Louse/Fly. Flea	French
Pouplume	Feathered Louse	French
Poussin	Baby Chick	French
Praha	Prague	Czech.
Pucará	Small fortress	Argent.
Pyörremyrsky	Tornado	Finnish
Pyörretuuli	Whirlwind	Finnish
Pyry	Blizzard	Finnish
Rekin	Shark	Polish
Rhonlerche	Rhone-lark (bird)	Dutch
Roda	Stork	Serbian
Roensegler	Rhone sailplane	German
Rondone	Swallow	Italian
Rubis	Ruby	French
Sääski	Mosquito	Finnish
Saeta	Arrow/Dart	Spanish
Saetta	Lightning	Italian
Safir	Saphire	Swedish
Sagitarrio	Archer	Italian
Salamandra	Salamander	Polish
Saphir	Sapphire	French
Sauterrelle	Grasshopper	French
Schulgleiter	Training glider	German
Schwalbe	Swallow	German
Scricciolo	Wren	Italian
Sęp	Vulture	Polish
Shturmoviki	Storm trooper	Russian
Simoun	The hot windstorm	French
Siraly	Seagull	Hung.
Sohaj	Gallant	Czech.
Sokół	Falcon	Polish
Sparviero	Hawk	Italian
Spatz	Sparrow	German
Specht	Woodpecker	German
Sperling	Sparrow	German
Sroka	Magpie	Polish
Stahltaube	Steel dove	German
Steinadler	Golden Eagle	Austrian
Stieglitz	Goldfinch	German
Storch	Stork	German
Strsljen	Hornet	Serbian
Stuka	Abbr. Attack plane	German
Supersette	Super-Seven	Italian
Szpak	Starling	Polish

Taifun	Typhoon	German		Veltro	Greyhound	Italian
Taube	Dove	German		Viggen	Thunderbolt	Swedish
Tavi	Teal	Finnish		Vihuri	Squall	Finnish
Tempete	Tempest	Danish		Viima	Wind Gust	Finnish
Tigerschwalbe	Tiger-sparrow	German		Vipan	Pee Wee	Swedish
Tiira	Tern	Finnish		Vöcsök	Grebe (bird)	Hung.
Tortuca	Tortoise	Italian		Volksjaeger	People's hunter	German
Toucan	Toucan (parrot)	French		Vrabac	Sparrow	Serbian
Trojka	A 3-horse trap	Serbian		Wal	Whale	German
Trzmiel	Bumble Bee	Polish		Weihe	Kite/hawk	German
Tuisku	Severe snow storm	Finnish		Wicher	Gale	Polish
Tummelisa	"tumbling girl"	Swedish		Wilga	Thrush	Polish
Tumppu	A mitten	Finnish		Wilk	Wolf	Polish
Tunnan	Barrel	Swedish		Zak	'Poor Student'	Polish
Ugar	Luck	Turkish		Zerstorer	Destroyer	German
Uhu	Owl	German		Zögling	Pupil/student	German
Vampyr	Vampire	German		Zuch	Valiant Man	Polish
Vanneau	Lapwing/peewit	French		Zugvogel	Migratory bird	German
Vasama	Arrow	Finnish		Zuk	Beetle	Polish
Vautour	Vulture	French		Zuraw	Crane	Polish

Table A-2: Translation of Key Aviation Terms

ENGLISH	DUTCH	FINNISH	FRENCH
Airport/airfield	Luchthaven	Lentoasema/—kenttä	Aéroport/Aérodrome
Airplane/aircraft	Vliegtuig	Lentokone	Avion
Civil/private	Civielvliegtuig	Sivilli—/yksityiskone	— civil
Airliner	Lyn—	Liikennekone	— de ligne
Military	Militair—	Sotilaslentokone	— militaire
Pursuit/fighter	Jager/Gevechts—	Havittäjäkone	— de chasse
Bomber	Bommenwerper	Pommikone	— de bombardement
Transport	Transportvliegtuig	Kuljetuskone	— de transport
Trainer	Les—	Koulukone	Avion-école
Observation	Waarnemingjs—	Tiedustelukone	Avion d'observation
Experimental	Experimenteel—	Experimental kone	— expérimental
Racing plane	Race—	Kilpakone	— de course
Pusher	— met duwschroef	Työntöpotkurinen	— à hélice propulsive
Tractor	— met trekschroef	Vetopotkurinen	— à hélice tractive
Biplane	Tweedekker	Kaksitaso	Biplan
Seaplane	Watervliegtuig	Vesikone	Hydràvion
Flying boat	Vliegboot	Lentovene	— à coque
Floatplane	Drjvervliegtuig	Kellukekone	— à flotteurs
Glider	Zweef—	Liitokone	Planeur
Sailplane	Prestatiezweef—	Purjekone	— de vol à voile
Wingspread/span	Spanwijdte	Jänneväli/Kärkiväli	Envergure
Wing area	Vleugeloppervlak	Siipipinta-ala	Surface portante
Length	Lengte	Pituus	Longveur
Height	Hoogte	Korkeus	Hauteur
Empty weight	Leeggewicht	Tyhjäpaino	Poids à vide operationnel
Gross/max. wht.	Maximum gewicht	Suurin sallittu paino	Poids maximum
Useful load	Nuttige Lading	Hyötykuorma	Charge utile
Max. airspeed	Maximum Snelheid	Huippunopeus	Vitesse maximale de vol
Cruise speed	Kruis snelheid	Matkanopeus	Vitesse de croisiére
Max. altitude	Plafond/max hoogte	Lakikorkeus	Altitude maximale
Service ceiling	Practische hoogte	Palveluskorkeus	Plafond pratique
Range	Vliegbereik	Lento matka	Distance franchissable
Seats/places	Aantal zitplaatsen	Istuimia/paikkaluku	Nombre de sièges
Piston engine	Zuigermotor	Mäntämoottori	Moteur à pistons
Radial engine	Stermotor	Tähtimoottori	Moteur en étoile
Rotary engine	Rotatiemotor	Pyörivä moottori	Moteur rotatif
Horsepower (hp)	Paardekracht (pk)	Hevosvoimia (hv)	Cheval-vapeur (cv)
Propeller	Luchtschroef	Potkuri	Hélices
Turbojet engine	Straalmotor	Suihkumoottori	Turboréacteur
Thrust	Stuwkracht	Työntövoima	Poussée
Machine gun	Machine geweer	Konekivääri	Mitrailleuse
Cannon	Kanon/boordgeschut	Tykki	Canon
Bombs	Bommen	Pommeja	Bombes
Landing gear	Landingsgestel	Laskuteline	Train d'atterrissage
Cockpit/cabin	Stuurhut/cockpit	Ohjaamo	Habitacle du pilote

ENGLISH	GERMAN	ITALIAN	POLISH
Airport/airfield	Flughafen/Verkehrs—	Aeroporto	Lotnisko
Airplane/aircraft	Flugzeug	Velivolo/aeroplano	Samolot/aeroplan
Civil/private	Zivilflugzeug	— civile	Samolot cywilni
Airliner	Verkehrs—	Aereo di linea	— komunikacyjny
Military	Militär—	— militare	— wojskowy
Pursuit/fighter	Jagd/jagdflugzeug	Apparecchio da caccia	— myśliwski
Bomber	Jagdbomber	Aereo da bombardamento	— bombowy
Transport	Transportflugzeug	— transporto	— transportowy
Trainer	Schul—	Velivolo scuola	— szkolny/trener
Observation	Aussichts—	— d'osservazione	— przestrzesgający
Experimental	Versuchs—	— sperimentale	— doświadczalny
Racing plane	Renn—	— da corsa	— wyścigowy
Pusher	— mit drukschraube	— con eliche propulsiva	Śmigło pchające
Tractor	— mit zugschraube	— con eliche tratora	Śmigło cignące
Biplane	Zweidecker	Biplano	Dwupłatowiec
Seaplane	Wasserflugzeug	Idrovolante	Hydroplan
Flying boat	Flugboot	— a scafo	Łódź latająca
Floatplane	Schwimmerflugzeug	— a galleggianti	Pływać
Glider	Gleit—	Aliante	Szybowiec
Sailplane	Segel—	Veleggiatore	Samolot żaglowy
Wingspread/span	Spannweite	Apertura alare	Rozpiętość skrzydła
Wing area	Flügelflache	Superficie alare	Obszar skrzydła
Length	Länge	Lunghezza	Długość
Height	Höhe	Altezza	Wysokość
Empty weight	Leergewicht	Peso a vioto d'impiego	Ciężar własny
Gross/max. wht.	Fluggewicht	Peso al decollo	Ciężar bratto
Useful load	Zuladung	Carico utile	Obciążenie użytkowe
Max. airspeed	Hochstfluggeschwindigkeit	Velocità massima di volo	Maxsymalna prędkość lotu
Cruise speed	Reisegeschwindigkeit	Velocità di crociera	Prędkość przelotowa
Max. altitude	Flughöhe	Quota massima di volo	Maksymalma wysokość
Service ceiling	Dienstgipfelhöhe	Tangenza pratica	Pulap praktyczny
Range	Reichweite	Autonomia chilometrica	Zakres
Seats/places	Sitzgelegenheit	Capacità posti	Siedzenie/liczba miejsc
Piston engine	Kolbenmotor	Motore alternative	Silnik tłokowa
Radial engine	Sternmotor	Motore stellare	Silnik gwiazdowy
Rotary engine	Umlaufmotor	Motore rotativo	Silnik obrotowa
Horsepower (hp)	Pferdstärke (ps)	Potenza al freno (pf)	Angielski koń-parowy
Propeller	Luftschraube	Elica	Śmigło
Turbojet engine	Luftstrahltriebwerk	Turboreattore	Silnik turboodrzut
Thrust	Schub	Trazione la spirta	Ciag/siła ciągu
Machine gun	Maschinengewehr	Matragliatrice	Karabin maszynowy/strzelba
Cannon	Kanone	Cannone	Armata/karambol
Bombs	Bombe	Bombe	Bomby
Landing gear	Fahrwerk	Carrello d'atterramento	Podwozie samolotu lądowego
Cockpit/cabin	Flugzeugkanzel	Abitacolo	Kabina pilota

ENGLISH	SERBO-CROATIAN	SPANISH	SWEDISH
Airport/airfield	Aerodrom	Aeropuerto/Aerodromo	Flyplats
Airplane/aircraft	Avion/Letilica	Avión	Flygplan
Civil/private	— civilni	— civil	Civilflygplan
Airliner	— punticki/linijski	— de línea	Trafik—
Military	— vojni	— militar	Militar—
Pursuit/fighter	— lovac	— de combate	Jakt—
Bomber	— bombarder	— de bombardeo	Bomb—
Transport	— transportni	— de transporte	Transport—
Trainer	— skolski/za obuku	— de entrenamiento	Skol—
Observation	— osmatracki	— de observación	Spanings—
Experimental	— probni	— experimental	Experiment—
Racing plane	— sportski	— de carreras	Tävlingsmaskin
Pusher	gurac	— de hélice propulsora	Skjutande
Tractor	tractorski	— de hélice tractora	Dragande
Biplane	Drokrilni	Biplano	Dubbeldackare
Seaplane	Morski	Hidroavión	Sjoflygplan
Flying boat	Hidroavion	— de casco	Flygbat
Floatplane	Hidroavion sa plovkama	— de flotadores	Toffelflygplan
Glider	Jedrilicar	Planeador	Glid—
Sailplane	Zracna jedrilica	Velero	Segel—
Wingspread/span	Raspon krila	Envergadura	Spannvidd
Wing area	Krilca	Superficie alar	Vingyta
Length	Duzina	Largo	Langd
Height	Visina	Altura	Hojd
Empty weight	Tezina bez tereta	Peso en vacio	Tomvikt
Gross/max. wht.	Ukupna/max. tezina	Peso máximo	Totalvikt
Useful load	Koristan teret	Carga útil	Nyttolast
Max. airspeed	Max. brzina vazduha	Velocidad Máxima	Topphastighet
Cruise speed	Ekonomicna brzina	Velocidad de crucero	Marschfart
Max. altitude	Max. visina	Altitud máxima	Hogsta flyghojd
Service ceiling	Duzina letenja bez servis.	Techo de servicio	Tjanstetopphojd
Range	Domet/domasaj	Alcance	Rackvidd
Seats/places	Sedista/broj mesta	Número de asientos	Antal platser
Piston engine	Klipni/naizmenicni motor	Motor alternativo	Kolvmotor
Radial engine	Radijalan motor	Motor en estrella	Stjärnmotor
Rotary engine	Rotacioni motor	Motor rotativo	Roterande—
Horsepower (hp)	Konjska snaga (ks)	Potencia caballos (pc)	Hästkraft (hk)
Propeller	Elisa	Hélice	Propeller
Turbojet engine	Turbo-dzet	Turboreactor	Jetmotor
Thrust	Pritisak/operecenje	Empuje	Dragkraft
Machine gun	Mitraljez	Ametralladora	Kulspruta
Cannon	Top	Cañón	Kanon
Bombs	Bombe	Bombas	Bomber
Landing gear	Uredjaj za sletanje	Tren de aterrizaje	Landstall
Cockpit/cabin	Pilotska kabina	Cabina del piloto	Kabin

Table A-3: Manufacturer's Acronyms and Translations

A.E.G.   Allgemeine Elektrizitäts Gesselschaft (Germany—General Electricity Company)

A.I.S.A.   Aeronautiche Industriale SA. (Italy— Aeronautical Industries, Inc.)

CAARP   Cooperatives des Ateliers Aéronautiques de la Région Parisienne (France—Paris Region Cooperative Aeronautical Workshop)

CAB   Constructions Aéronautiques du Béarn (France—Bearn Aeronautical Manufacturing Company)

CAMS   Chantiers Aéro-Maritimes de la Seine (France-Seine Seaplane Dockyard)

C.A.N.S.A.   Construzioni Aeronautiche Novaresi SA (Italy— Novara Aeronautical Construction Company, a Fiat subsidiary)

CANT   Cantieri Riuniti dell'Adriatico (Italy—United Shipyards of the Adriatic)

C.A.S.A.   Construcciónes Aeronáuticas SA (Spain— Aeronautical Construction Company)

CFM   Centrala Flygverkstäder Malmen (Sweden— Malmen Central Aircraft Manufacturer)

C.S.S.   Centralne Studium Samolotow (Poland—Central Aircraft Research Group)

C.V.V.   Centri di Vola a Vela Politechnico di Milano (Italy—Milan Technical Center for Soaring Flight)

C.W.L.   Centralne Warsztaty Lotnicze (Poland—Central Aviation Workshops)

C.Z.L.   Ceskoslovenské Zavody Letecké (Czechoslovakian Aircraft Works)

D.A.R.   Darjavna Aeroplanna Rabotilnitza (Bulgaria— State Aircraft Factory)

D.W.L.   See L.W.D.

D.F.S.   Deutsches Forschungsinstitut für Segelflug (German Research Institute for Sailplanes)

D.F.W.   Deutsche Flugzeugwerke (German Aircraft Factory)

E.F.W.   Eidgenössische Flugzeug-Werke (Swiss— Federal Aircraft Factory)

E.K.W.   Eidgenössische Konstruktions Werkstätte (Swiss—Federal Construction Works)

F.B.A.	Franco-British Aviation (France-U.K.)
F.F.A.	Flug und Fahrzeugwerke AG (Swiss—Flight and Vehicle Works, Inc.)
FFVS	Flygförvaltningens Verkstäd (Sweden— Government Aviation Works)
FIAT	Fabbrica Italiana Automobili Torino (Turin Italian Automobile Fabricators)
I.A.R.	Industria Aeronautica Romana (Romanian Aeronautical Industries)
I.C.A.R.	Intreprindere Constructii Aeronautice Romane (Romanian Aeronautical Construction Company)
IMAM	Industrie Meccaniche e Aeronautiche Meridionali (Italy— Southern Mechanical and Aeronautical Industries)
I.S.	Institut Szybownictwa (Poland—Sailplane Institute)
I.V.L.	Ilmailuvoimen Lentokonetehdas (Finland—Air Force Aircraft Industry)
K.Z.	Kramme and Zeuthen (Denmark—The designers for S.A.I. of a family of light aircraft—the Danish equivalent of Clyde Cessna and Walter Beech)
LET	Letecké Zarody Narodni Podnik (Czechosovakia-National Aviation Works: manufacturers of Aero aircraft)
LFG	Luftfahrtzeug-Gesellschaft (Germany—Aviation Manufacturing Company)
L.K.B.	Letalski Konstrukeijske Biro (Yugoslavia—Aero Design Group—at the Ljubljana Polytechnic Institute)
L.V.G.	Luft-Verkehrs-Gesellschaft (Germany—Air Transport Company)
L.W.D.	Lotnicze Warszaty Doświadczlane (Poland— Aircraft Construction Research Establishment; some translations use D.W.L.)
L.W.S.	Lubelska Wytwórnia Samolotów (Poland— Lublin Airplane Manufacturing Works)
M.B.B.	Messerschmitt-Bölkow-Blohm (Germany—The successor to the old Messerschmitt and newer Bölkow companies and the Blohm and Voss shipyard and flying boat factory.)
MFI	A.B. Malmo Flygindustri (Sweden—Malmo Aircraft Company)
MiG	Mikoyan-Gurevich (Russia—Design bureau named after the two prolific designers.)

M.K.E.K.	Makona Ve Kimya Endustri Kurumu (Turkey— Machinery and Chemical Industries Corporation)
NHI	Nederlanse Helicopter Industry (Netherlands)
O.K.L.	Osrodek Konstruckcji Lotniczych (Poland— Aviation Construction Design Center)
P.W.S.	Podlaska Wytwórnia Samlowtów (Podlasian Aircraft Manufacturing Plant)
P.Z.L.	Państwowe Zakłady Lotnicze (Poland— National Aviation Establishment)
PIK	Polyteknikkojen Ilmailukrerho (Finnish Institute of Technology)
R.A.F.	Royal Aircraft Factory (United Kingdom—during World War I Britain's air arm was then the Royal Flying Corp; only later would the initials get confused with the present Royal Air Force)
RWD	Stanislaw Rogalski, Stanislaw Wigura, and Jurzy Drzewicki (Poland—Named after the design team at L.W.D.)
SAAB	Svenska Aeroplan Adtiebolag (Sweden—Swedish Aeroplane Company)
SABCA	Société Anonyme Belge de Constructions Aéronautiques (Belgian Aeronautical Construction Company)
SAI	Scandinavisk Aero-Industri (Denmark— Scandinavian Aero-Industry)
S.A.I.	Societá Aeronautica Italiana (Italian Aeronautical Company)
S.A.I.A.	Societá Aeronautica Italiana-Ambrosini (Ambrosini Aeronautical Company of Italy)
SAIMAN	Societá Anonima Industrie Meccaniche Aeronautica Novali (Italy—New Aeronautical Machine Industry Company)
S.A.M.L.	Societá Aeronautica Meccanica Lombarda (Italy—Lombardy Aeronautical Engineering Company)
S.C.A.	Stabilimento Construzioni Aeronautiche (Italy— Aeronautical Construction Establishment)
SECAN	Société d'Études et Constructions Aéro-Navales (France—Naval Aircraft Design and Construction Company)
SFAN	Société Française d'Aviation Nouvelles (France—French New Aviation Company)
SFCA	Société Française de Constructions Aéronautiques (France— French Aeronautical Construction Company)

SGTA	Société Générale de Transport Aérien (France—General Transportation Company—The Farman Line)
S.I.A.	Societá Italiana Aviazione (Italy—Italian Aviation Company)
S.I.A.I.	Societá Idrovolante Alta Italia (Italy— Northern Italy Seaplane Company—previously Savoia)
SIPA	Société Industrielle pour l'Aéronautique (France—Aeronautical Construction Company)
SNCA Midi	Société National de Constructions Aéronautiques du Midi (France—National Aeronautical Construction Company: Midi Region. France nationalized her aviation industry in 1936 on a regional basis. The Midi group absorbed the old Dewoitine company and was later absorbed into SNCASE, then into SNCASO and finally became Sud-Aviation.)
SNCAC	Société National de Constructions Aéronautiques du Centre (France—Central Region; the nationalized successor company to Farman and Hanriot)
SNCAN	Société National de Constructions Aéronautiques du Nord (France—Northern Region Aeronautical Construction Company— included Amiot, CAMS, Potez, Bréguet and others)
SNCASE	Société National de Constructions Aéronautiques du Sud-Est (France—South-East Region; the successor to Liore et Oliver, Romano and SPCA)
SNCASO	Société National de Constructions Aéronautiques du Sud-Ouest (France—South-West Region; the successor to Blériot and Bloch)
SNECMA	Société National d'Études et de Constructions de Moteurs d'Aviation (France—National Aircraft Engine Design and Construction Company)
SNIAS	Société National Industrielle Aérospatiale (France)
SPAD	Société pour l'Aviation et es Dérivés; successor to the Société pour l'Aviation Deperdussin (France—Aviation and Related Equipment Company; originally the Deperdussin Aviation Company)
SPCA	Société Provençale de Constructions Aéronautiques (Provence Aeronautical Construction Company)
SRCM	Société de Recherches et de Constructions Mécaniques (France—Mechanical Research and Construction Company)
SSVS	Sezione Sperimentale Vola a Vela (Italy— Sailplane Experimental Group)
SVA	Societá Giovanni Ansaldo (Italy—The Giovanni Ansaldo Company, but the initials stood for designers Umberto Savoia,

Rodolfo Verduzio and Ansaldo himself. The third designer was not commemorated in the initials, thus Celestino Rosatelli quit SVA and joined Fiat which explains the numbering system of Fiat fighters such as the C.R.32 and C.R.42.)

SZD — Szbowcowy Zakład Doświadczlany (Poland— Aviation Research Establishment)

T.H.K. — Turk Hava Kurumu (Turkey—Turkish Aviation Foundation)

UFAG — Ungarische Flugzeugfabrik AG (Austro-Hungary— Hungarian Airplane Manufacturing Company)

VFW — Vereinigte Flugtechniche Werke (Netherlands— United Aeronautical Engineering Works)

VL — Valtion Lentokonetehdas (Finland—State Aircraft Factory)

VZLU — Vykumny a Zhusebi Letecké Ústav (Czechoslovakia—Vykumny and Zhusebi Aviation Establishment)

WSK — Wytwórnici Sprzetu Komonikacyj (Poland— Transport Equipment Manufacturing Center)

WWS — Wojskowe Warszaty Szybowcowe (Poland—Military Aviation Workshops)

American aircraft companies with acronyms for names can also be found in European museums—from Aeronca (Aeronautical Company of America) to WACO (Weaver Aircraft Company).

A Spitfire stands in front of one of its thoroughbred sires, the Supermarine S.6A, at the R. J. Mitchell Museum, Southampton Hall of Aviation.

Appendix B
Aircraft Collections and Locations

The following tables include over 3,000 aircraft in the air museums and aviation collections in Europe. Table B-1 organizes the aircraft by museum to provide the prospective visitor with a view of each collection's contents. Table B-2 cross-references the aircraft alphabetically such that the existence and location of any desired aircraft or type can be determined.

The aircraft are listed by location rather than by ownership to provide a reasonable estimate of what to expect to see at each museum. None-the-less, loans between museums, new restorations replacing old, special exhibits, and the like cause continual variations in what is actually on display. Museum hours and even the museum's location may also change with time. If planning to visit a particular museum (especially a smaller one) or to view a specific aircraft, one should write or phone ahead.

The aircraft information and the basic data format was obtained from the Smithsonian Institution's National Air and Space Museum's most recent museum aircraft data base (August 1, 1983). This material has been updated and corrected based on guidebooks and lists obtained from the museums, personal visits and correspondence, and supplemented with data and notes courteously supplied by Bob Ogden and Gordon Riley. Their works containing aircraft listings (*European Aviation Museums and Collections* and *British Aviation Museums* by Bob Ogden and *The British Aircraft Museums Directory* and the *Vintage Aircraft Directory* by Gordon Riley) are updated fairly frequently and a prospective museum traveller should obtain a latest edition at the first aviation port of call in Europe.

The Smithsonian's coding system, modified as noted, has been used in the lists of aircraft as follows:

1. **TYPE: The Design Firm**—the organization (e.g. Vought) that first designed the aircraft even if someone else (e.g. Goodyear) manufactured the particular example. This is followed by the **Type Number** originally or most commonly used (e.g. DC-3); the actual type number of the particular example (e.g. C-47) is shown following in brackets. The **Type Name** follows, again using the most common usage. Replicas are noted with an (R). Names of individual machines are in quotes (e.g. "Lief Eriksson" or "Santa Cruz"). Other notes are included in brackets where possible. In the alphabetical listing, Table B-2, variants have been grouped with the basic design type.

2. **STATUS:** The Smithsonian's code is used in a slightly modified form:

PV—Public Viewing: usually on view.

RA—Research Accessible: for serious researchers, not on view to general public, or private museums usually closed to the general public; prior arrangements to view is generally required for either.

S —Stored: not accessible, may be crated.

A —Active: still being flown on occasion.

C —Currently undergoing restoration.

X —Displayed in markings not authentic to specimen.

D —Derelict or badly damaged, may someday be restored.

I —Incomplete: if noted with PV, generally means only the fuselage or cockpit is on view.

A numerical suffix differentiates among different locations for museums having multiple sites.

3. **NUMBER:** The civil or military registration number is generally provided, since that would be the number most visible to the visitor. If such number was not available, then the constructor's or manufacturer's number is shown.

4. **YEAR:** If known, the year in which the particular aircraft was manufactured; if unknown, it is a year (marked "c" for *circa*) in which that type of machine was first in general use. If a replica, it is the year of the original, not when the replica was made, to put the aircraft type in perspective with its original contemporaries.

5. **MUSEUM CODE NUMBER:** The Smithsonian's code for each museum has been used with two additions. For museums not in the Smithsonian's data base, the "new" museum has been provided an identifier by adding a suffix to the logically preceeding museum's number, placing the "new" museum in proper sequence without disrupting the basic Smithsonian's numbering. A second one- or two-letter suffix has been added to each museum's number, its country's aircraft registration prefix letter (Appendix A), to identify the museum's nationality. ("CP" is used rather than "CCCP" for the Soviet Union to pragmatically maintain column width; "CP" is officially one of two designators for Bolivia.)

6. **MUSEUM ADDRESSES:** These are generally the official or mailing addresses of the museums; there are cases where the aircraft are located elsewhere. Unless readily apparent or described in the text, obtaining directions locally is advised. While we have endeavored to include all aircraft in all museums, there are some unavoidable omisions, particularly among the smaller and newer museums in Britain, France, and Eastern Europe, the practicalities of deadlines causing those few omissions. The data nevertheless represents the most complete listing yet published in the U. S. and should provide sufficient information for the most dedicated aviation enthusiast.

Table B-1: Aviation Museum Collections and Addresses

AUSTRIA (OE)

160/OE Technisches Museum fur Indistrie und Gewerbe (Technical Museum for Trade and Industry), Maria-hilfer Strasse 212, A-1140, Vienna.

Aircraft Type	Stat.	Number	Yr.
Aviatik D.I (Austro-Hungarian Berg)	PV	101.37	18
Bell 47G-2 Sioux	PV	3B-HO	c55
Berg-Krupka (glider)	PV		32
De Havilland D.H.104 Dove	PV	OE-BVM	57
Etrich II Taube	PV		10
Fieseler Fi 156 Storch	PV	D-ENPE	43
Gumpert G-2 (sailplane)	PV	OE-0017	37
Hutter Hu 17B (Sailplane)	PV	OE-0341	56
Kermer Wien (sailplane)	PV		23
Lilienthal Glider	PV		94
Musger Mg 19A Steinadler	PV	OE-0399	62
Musger Mg 23SL (sailplane)	PV	OE-0766	65
Osterreich Aero Club Austria	PV	OE-0410	59
Pischof Autoplan	PV		10
Schneider Grunau Baby IIB (glider)	S	OE-0064	42

160A/OE Heeresgeschlichtliches Museum (Museum of Military History), Arsenal, Objekt 1, 1030, Vienna.

Aircraft Type	Stat.	Number	Yr.
Albatros B.1	S	20.01	c15
North American AT-6 Texan	S	4C-TE	c45
SAAB 29F (J-29F)	S	29530	c54
Yakovlev Yak-11	S	4A-AF	c52
Yakovlev Yak-18	S	3A-AA	c50

BELGIUM (OO)

165/OO Musee Royal de l'Armee (Royal Army Museum), Parc du Cinquantenaire, Jubel Park 3, B1040, Brussels.

Aircraft Type	Stat.	Number	Yr.
Airspeed A.S.40 Oxford	PV	O-16	c40
Auster Mk.V A.O.P.	S	TW-464	44
Auster Mk.VI A.O.P (8)	S	several	44
Auster Mk.VI A.O.P.	PV	VY990	44
Aviatik C.I	C	227/16	16
Avro Canada CF-100 Canuck Mk 5	PV	18554	c55
Bataille Triplane	PVC		11
Bleriot XI-2 (2-seat)	DI		c13
Boeing 707-329 (nacelles only)	PVI	OO-SJA	c60
Breguet 905S	S	OO-ZJN	c55
Bristol 149 Bolingbroke IV	D	10038	42
Bucker Bu 181 Bestmann	PV	OO-RVD	c40
Caudron C.800	PV	N156	c46
Caudron G.3	PV	2531	c14
Cessna 310B	S	OO-SEL	c54
Chandellon (helicopter)	S		
Dassault MD 450 Ouragan IV	PV	F-TEUQ	c50
De Havilland D.H.82 Tiger Moth	PV	T-24 UR	c36
De Havilland D.H.82 Tiger Moth (2)	S		c36
De Havilland D.H.82 Tiger Moth (9)	S		c36
De Havilland D.H.89B Dominie	PV	OO-CNP	c37
De Havilland D.H.98 Mosquito NF.30	PV	RK952	c44
De Havilland D.H.115 Vampire T.11	PV	XH292	c55
De Havilland DHC-1 Chipmunk (Can)	RA	P-130	c50

Aircraft Type	Stat.	Number	Yr.
De Havilland DHC-3 Otter (Canada)	PV	OO-SUD	c55
Dornier Do 27	PV	OL-DO4	c58
Douglas A-26 Invader (B-26)	PV	N67160	44
Douglas DC-3 (C-47 Dakota)	PV	OT-CWG	43
Fairchild C-119G Flying Boxcar	PV	CP-46	53
Fairchild F-24 (UC-61K Forwarder)	PV	OO-LUT	43
Fairchild F-24 (UC-61K Forwarder)	RA	OO-LMV	44
Farman Shorthorn F.11A2	PV		14
Farman-Voisin (Dabert II)	PVC		
Fiat G.91R/3	PV	30+85	c58
Fieseler Fi 156 Criquet (MS.502)	SD	F-BFCD	c42
Fieseler Fi 156C-3 Storch	PVC	5503	c42
Focke-Wulf Fw 50 (glider)	S	PL-50	
Fouga C.M.170 Magister	PV	MT-24	c58
Gloster G.41 Meteor F. Mk.8	S	R-B2	c50
Gloster G.41 Meteor F. Mk.8	PV	K-K5	c50
Gloster G.47 Meteor (Armstrong-W.)	S	SE-DCH	c57
Gloster G.47 Meteor (Armstrong-W.)	S	SE-DCF	c57
Halberstadt C.V	PV	3271/18	18
Hanriot HD-1	PV	HD-78	18
Hawker Hunter Mk.4	PVX	IF-70	56
Hawker Hurricane Mk.IIC	PV	LF345	c43
Hunting-Percival P.66 Pembroke	PV	OT-ZAD	c56
Jodel D.9 Bebe	C	OO-15	c48
Jonathan Livingston BD-2 (glider)	PV	02	
Kassel 12 (glider)	PV		31
Kreit KL-1	PV	OO-ANP	
L.V.G. C.VI	PV	5141	18
Lockheed F-104G Starfighter	PV	FX-12	c64
Lockheed T-33A Shooting Star	PV	FR-34	c50
Mignet HM-290 Pou Du Ciel	S		c58
Miles M.14A Magister	PV	OO-NIC	c40
Miles M.38 Messenger 2A	S	G-AKIS	44
Morane-Saulnier MS.230	PV	F-BEJO	c48
Morane-Saulnier MS.315	PV	F-BCNT	c32
Nieuport 17C1	PV	N5024	17
Nord N.1002 Pingouin (Bf 108)	PV	F-BERF	c46
North American AT-6C Harvard II	S	EX292	c45
North American AT-6D Harvard III	PV	EZ256	c45
North American F-86F Sabre	PV	5316	c56
Percival P.1 Gull	PV	G-ACGR	33
Percival P.34 Proctor Mk IV	PV	NP171	c44
Percival P.40 Prentice	PV	OO-OPO:	c48
Percival P.44 Proctor Mk V	S	G-AHZY	c46
Piper J-3 Cub (4)	RA		c46
Piper L-18C Super Cub	PV	OL-L87	53
Republic F-84F Thunderstreak	PV	FU-30	52
Republic F-84G Thunderjet	PV	FZ-71	c55
Republic RF-84F Thunderflash	PV	FR-28	51
Rhonschwalbe KA 2	PV	PL-13	
Royal Aircraft Factory R.E.8	PV	326	c17
Rumpler C.V	PVC		c18
S.A.I. KZ III	PV	OO-MAA	c44
SAAB 35A Draken (J-35A)	PV	F16/34	c62
SABCA Junior	PV	11	
SABCA Junior (3)	S		
SABCA Poncelet Vivette	PV	O-BAFH	25
SPAD XIII C1	PV	SP-49	c18
Schempp-Hirth GOE 4 Goevier	PV	OO-ZPJ	
Schneider Grunau Baby II (2)	S		c40
Schneider Grunau Baby II (glider)	S	OO-ZBA	c40
Schneider Grunau Baby III (glider)	PV	PL-37	c40
Schneider Grunau S.G.38 (glider)	PV	PL21	c40

Aircraft Type	Stat.	Number	Yr.
Schreck FBA IV	PV	55	14
Sikorsky S-55 (Chickasaw)	PV	OT-ZKF	c58
Sopwith 1 1/2-Strutter 1A2	PV	88	c17
Sopwith Camel F.1	PV	B5747	c18
Stampe-Renard S.R.7 Monitor	PV	OO-SRZ	c53
Stampe-Renard S.V.4B	PV	V-28	c45
Stampe-Renard S.V.4B	PV	V-64	c45
Stampe-Renard S.V.4B	PV	V-56	c45
Stampe-Renard S.V.4C (SNCAN)	PV	F-BFZC	c45
Stampe-Renard S.V.4D	PV	OO-SRS	c45
Stampe-Vertongen S.V.4 (Divoy-)	PV	4	c40
Sud-Aviation SE-210 Caravelle VI	S	OO-SRA	c60
Supermarine Spitfire Mk.IX	PV	GE-B	c42
Supermarine Spitfire Mk.XIV	PV	GE-R	c42
Tipsy S.2 (Fairey)	PV	OO-TIP	c39
Voisin LA 5B Canon	PV		15
Westland Lysander	C	Y1530	c42
Zeppelin L-30 (nacelles only)	PV		c19

BULGARIA (LZ)

180A/LZ Morski Museum
(National Maritime Museum)
2 Chervenoarmeiski Blvd., Varna.

Arado Ar 196A-3	PV		c39

180B/LZ Voenen Musei (Army Museum)
2 Blvd. Skovelev, Sofia.

Ilyushin Il-2m3	PV		c42
Tupolev Tu-2S	PV		c43
Yakovlev Yak-9U	PV		c47
Yakovlev Yak-23	PV		c50

CZECHOSLOVAKIA (OK)

235/OK Vojenske Muzeum
(Military Museum) Kbely,
Praha 9, 19706, Prague.

Aero 45	PV	OK-DMO	49
Aero 145	PV	OK-KDA	c59
Aero A 10	PV	L-BALB	c23
Aero L-29 Delfin	PV	10010	c60
Aero L-39 Albatros	PV	3905	
Aero L-60 Brigadyr	PV	OK-KOS	56
Aero L-200 Moravia	S	OK-MEE	c57
Aero XL-160	PV	0414	c56
Avia B 534	PV	H-6	c36
Avia BH-11C	PV	L-BONK	26
Avia BH-11K	PV	3	c26
Avia CS-129	PV		
Benes-Mraz L-40 Meta-Sokol (Orl.)	PV	OK-KHN	56
Benes-Mraz M-1C Sokol	PV	OK-BMH	c47
Benes-Mraz M-1C Sokol (Orlican)	PV	OK-BHM	47
Bucker Bu 131 Jungmann (Aero C-104)	PV	A-27	c47
Bucker Bu 181 Bestmann(Zlin)	PV	OK-DRK	c49
Douglas DC-3 (Lisunov Li-2D)	S	2710	c46
Douglas DC-3 (Lisunov Li-2F)	S	3002	c46
Elsnic El-2M Sedy Vic	PV	05	
Fieseler Fi 156 Storch	PV	OK-DPU	c42
Fieseler Fi 156 Storch	PV		c42
Ilyushin Il-2 Stormovik	PV	38	c40
Ilyushin Il-2 Stormovik	PV		c40
Ilyushin Il-10	PV	5271	c44
Ilyushin Il-10 (Avia built)	PV	5502	c44
Ilyushin Il-28	PV	6926	c50

Aircraft Type	Stat.	Number	Yr.
LET L-13 Blanik	PV	OK-4835	
LET L-200D Morava	RA		c62
Lavochkin La-7	PV	"77"	44
Letov LF-107 Lunak	PV	OK-0835	50
Letov LF-109 Pionyr	PV	OK-2209	50
Letov S-20	PV	E-10	c32
Letov S-218	PV	C-49	c30
Letov S-218	PV	C-49	c30
Messerschmitt Bf 109 (Avia S-199)	PV	UC-26	c45
Messerschmitt Me 163B-1 Komet		V-31	c45
Messerschmitt Me 262A (Avia S-92)	PV	V-34	45
Messerschmitt Me 262B	PV	51104	45
Mignet HM-14 Pou du Ciel	PV		36
Mikoyan-Gurevich MiG-15	PV	1720	c50
Mikoyan-Gurevich MiG-15	PV	1585	c50
Mikoyan-Gurevich MiG-15	S	several	c50
Mikoyan-Gurevich MiG-15	PV	1713	c50
Mikoyan-Gurevich MiG-15 (Czech)	PV	2626	c50
Mikoyan-Gurevich MiG-17	PV		c60
Mikoyan-Gurevich MiG-17F	S	several	c60
Mikoyan-Gurevich MiG-17PF	PV	1015	c60
Mikoyan-Gurevich MiG-19P	PV		c60
Mikoyan-Gurevich MiG-19PM		1043	c60
Mikoyan-Gurevich MiG-19S	PV		c60
Mikoyan-Gurevich MiG-21F		0613	c65
Mil Mi-1 helicopter	S		49
Omnipol L.13 Blanik	PV	OK-4835	57
Piper L-4B Grasshopper		10	c42
Polikarpov Po-2	S	SP-BHA	c40
Praga E-114M Air Baby	PV	OK-BGL	47
SPAD VII	PV		c17
Saunders Roe A.19 Cloud (fly.boat)	C	OK-BAK	33
Smrcek VSM-40 Demant	S		58
Supermarine Spitfire Mk.IX	PV	TE565	c42
Taylor E-2 Cub	PV	OK-ATW	c38
VOSLM BAK-01	PV	01	46
VT-116 (glider)	S		63
VZLU HC-2 Heli-Baby	PV	OK-IVA	53
VZLU HC-2 Heli-baby	PV	OK-10	55
VZLU TOM-8	PV	OK-08	
Vega VSB-62 (glider)	S		62
Yakovlev Yak-11	PV	1727	52
Yakovlev Yak-12A	PV	OK-JEN	55
Yakovlev Yak-17	PV	30	c48
Yakovlev Yak-23	PV	HX-51	c48
Zlin L.425 Sohaj 3	PV	OK-0711	55
Zlin VT.425 Sohaj 3	RA	OK-5377	c55
Zlin Z.13	PV	OK-TBZ	37
Zlin Z.22 Junak	PV	OO-FRE	c46
Zlin Z.23 Honja	PV	OK-5629	46
Zlin Z.24 Krajanek	PV	OK-8565	46
Zlin Z.26		UC-36	c48
Zlin Z.124		OK-1725	
Zlin Z.125 Sohaj 2	PV	OK-1768	51
Zlin Z.126	PV	OK-FRS	c53
Zlin Z.130 Kmotr	PV	OK-1240	50
Zlin Z.135 Heli-Trainer		OK-045	c60
Zlin Z.381 (Bucker Bu 181D)		UA-264	c45
Zlin Z.XII		OK-ZBX	c36

235A/OK Technicke Muzeum v Brne
(Technical Museum of Brno),
Orli 20, 60186, Brno.

Aerotechnik Uh. Haradiste A-70	S	proto.	72
KSM Kromeriz KD-67 Gyroglider	RA	19	73
Letov LF-107 Lunak	S	OK-0830	51
Mikoyan-Gurevich MiG-19S	PV	0511	c60

Aircraft Type	Stat.	Number	Yr.
VAAZ Brno XA-66 Aeron	S	proto.	66
VZLU L-8 Praha TOM-8 (fuselage)	SI	proto.	56
VZLU L-208 Praha TOM-208(fuselage)	SI	proto.	57
Zlin Z.35 Helibaby (HC-102)	RA	OK-RVL	60
Zlin Z.226B Bohatyr	PV	OK-MPR	c55
Zlin Z.226T Trener	S	OK-HLK	c56

237/OK Narodni Technicke Muzeum (National Technical Museum) Kosteini 42, 17078, Praha 7, Prague.

Aircraft Type	Stat.	Number	Yr.
Anatra DS Anasal	PV	11120	17
Avia BH-9	PV	Ok-IPF	24
Avia BH-10	PV	OK-AVO	25
Benes-Mraz M-1C Sokol	PV	OK-AHN	47
Bensen B-8W (gyrocopter)	S		68
Bleriot XI "King Kaspar"	PV	76	10
Bohemia B-5	D		19
Bucker Bu 131 Jungmann	PV	OK-AXY	47
Bucker Bu 181 Bestmann	S	OK-DRK	49
D.F.S. Weihe	S	OK-8303	43
Etrich Limusine	PV		28
Fieseler Fi 156 Storch (Mraz)	S	OK-DFJ	49
Janecek Delta-C Glider	PV	JJ-77	77
Knoller C.II	PV	119.15	17
Kunkadlo (Simunek VBS-1)	PV	L-BILG	25
L.W.F. V Scout	PV	4	18
Mignet HM-14 Pou Du Ciel	PV		35
Mrkev Or Racek (glider)	PV	OK-8340	37
Piper L-4H Grasshopper	PV	OK-YIE	43
Silimon IS 30	S	OK-9811	58
Slechta Praha	S		32
Zlin Z.24 Krajanek	S	OK-8560	46
Zlin Z.25 Sohaj	S	OK-8672	47
Zlin Z.125 Sohaj 2	S	OK-8755	50
Zlin Z.125 Sohaj 2	S	OK-8767	50
Zlin Z.130 Kmotr	S	OK-1242	50
Zlin Z.225 Medak (prototype)	S	OK-1781	52

DENMARK (OY)

245/OY Danmarks Flyvmuseum (Danish Aviation Museum Society) P.O. Box 202, 2950 Vedbaek. (A/c stored at 247/OY and elsewhere)

Aircraft Type	Stat.	Number	Yr.
D.F.S. Weihe	RA	OY-VOX	43
De Havilland D.H.89A Dragon Rapide	SD	OY-AA0	44
De Havilland D.H.104 Dove	RA	OY-DHZ	56
Ellehammer 1906 (R)	S		06
Fairchild F-24R 46A Argus III	RA	OY-EAZ	44
Fairchild PT-26 Cornell	PV	253	44
Focke-Achgelis Fa 330 Bachstelze	PV	60127	44
General Aircraft ST-25 Monospar	PV	OY-DAZ	37
Hogslund-Olsen 2G (glider)	S	OY-ATX	46
Hollaender A.H.1	PV	OY-ADO	56
Hunting-Percival P.66 Pembroke	RA	OY-AVA	56
Hutter Hu 17 (sailplane)	PV	OY-AXH	38
Klemm Kl 35D	RA	SE-AKN	40
Lund HL-1	S		60
Miles M.65 Gemini IA	RA	LN-TAH	47
Miles M.65 Gemini IA	S	G-AKDK	47
Moelhede Petersen XMP-2	PV		63
Percival P.31 Proctor Mk.III	SD	OY-ACP	42
Polyteknisk Flyvegr. Polyt II	S	OY-ACP	46

Aircraft Type	Stat.	Number	Yr.
S.A.I. KZ II-S Sport	PV	OY-DOU	39
S.A.I. KZ III	RA	SE-ANY	44
S.A.I. KZ IV	RA	OY-DZU	44
SAAB 17A (B-17A)	PV	17320	44
SAAB 29F (J-29F)	PV	29487	54
Schneider Grunau Baby II	RA	OY-DAX	39
Schneider Grunau Baby IIB	RA	OY-AHX	46
Schneider Grunau S.G.38 (glider)	S	OY-86	46
Sud-Aviation SE-210 Caravelle	S	OY-KRD	60

246/OY Danmarks Tekniske Museum (Danish Technical Museum) Nordre Strandvej 23, 3000, Helsingor.

Aircraft Type	Stat.	Number	Yr.
Donnet-Leveque "Maagen 3"	RA		c14
Donnet-Leveque II "Maagen 2"	PV		13
Ellehammer Biplane	PV		06
Ellehammer Helicopter	PV		c10
Ellehammer Monoplane	PV		09
Farman Svendsen Glenten	PV		10

246A/OY Dansk Veteranflysamlung (Danish Historical Aircraft Association), Stauning Lufthavn, 6900, Skjern.

Aircraft Type	Stat.	Number	Yr.
Aero Super 45	PVA	OY-EFC	c60
Auster J/1 Autocrat	PVC	D-EKOM	c46
De Havilland D.H.82A Tiger Moth	PVA	OY-ECH	c36
De Havilland D.H.82A Tiger Moth	PVC	OY-DVP	c36
De Havilland D.H.87B Hornet Moth	PVA	OY-DEZ	c38
Druine D.31 Turbulent	PVA	OY-AMG	c60
Gumpert G-2 (sailplane)	PV	OY-BLX	c37
Hollschmidt 222	PV	OY-FAI	
Johansen CAJO-1	RA	D-GDFH	
Jurca MJ.2A Tempete	PVC	OY-CMB	c56
Lockheed T-33A Shooting Star	PV	DT-884	c50
Mignet HM-14 Pou du Ciel	PV		c36
Miles M.28 Mercury 6	PVA	OY-ALW	c41
North American AT-6 Texan	PV	31-306	c45
North American AT-6 Texan	PV	16126	c45
Piper J-3F Cub	PVA	OY-ABT	c45
Raab Doppelraab IV	PV	OY-XIT	
Rearwin 9000 Sportster	PVC	OY-AVJ	c40
Republic F-84G Thunderjet	PV	A-057	c55
S.A.I. KZ G1	PV	OY-ASX	
S.A.I. KZ II-K Koupe	PVA	OY-AEA	c45
S.A.I. KZ II-T	PV	OY-FAN	c46
S.A.I. KZ II-T	PVC	OY-FAE	c46
S.A.I. KZ II-T	PVC	OY-FAM	c46
S.A.I. KZ III	PVA	OY-DZA	c44
S.A.I. KZ IV	PVC	OY-DIZ	c44
S.A.I. KZ VII	PVD	D-EBTO	c47
Scheibe Mu 13 Bergfalke II	PV	OY-REX	c50
Scheibe Spatz B	PV	OY-AXU	c61
Schneider Grunau Baby IIB	PV	OY-AUX	c40
Taylorcraft D (Auster I)	PVC	LB381	c40

247/OY Egeskov Veteranmuseum (Egeskov Historical Museum) 5772 Kvaerndrup.

Aircraft Type	Stat.	Number	Yr.
De Havilland D.H.82 Tiger Moth	PVX	OY-BAK	43
Douglas DC-7C (nose only)	PV	OY-KND	57
Hutter Hu 17A (sailplane)	PV	OY-AXII	c42
North American AT-6 (Noorduyn)	PV	FT-380	44
Republic F-84G Thunderjet	RA	52-9792	52
Supermarine Spitfire HF.IX	PV	41-401	c41

248/OY Tojhusmuseet (Royal Danish Arsenal Museum) Frederiksholms Kanal 29, 1220 Copenhagen.

Aircraft Type	Stat.	Number	Yr.
Avro 504N	PV	LBI 110	27
Berg und Storm Monoplane	PV		10
Gloster G.43 Meteor	S	461	c50
Hawker Dankok F.B.II	PV	158	28
Supermarine Spitfire Mk.IX	S	401	44

248A/OY Flyvevabnets Historiske Samling (Danish Air Force Historical Society), P.O. Box 202, 2050 Vedbaek. (A/c stored at various bases.)

Aircraft Type	Stat.	Number	Yr.
Consolidated PBY-5A Catalina	RA	L-857	c43
Consolidated PBY-6A Catalina	RA	L-861	c44
De Havilland DHC-1 Chipmunk	RA	P-127	c52
De Havilland DHC-1 Chipmunk	RA	P-143	c52
Douglas DC-3 (C-47A)	RAA	OY-PBP	c44
Douglas DC-3 (C-47A)	RA	K-681	c44
Douglas DC-3 (C-47A)	RA	K-687	c44
Gloster Meteor F.4	RA	43-461	c50
Gloster Meteor F.4	RA	43-469	c50
Gloster Meteor F.8	RA	44-499	c50
Hawker Hunter F.51	RA	E-401	c56
Lockheed F-104G Starfighter	RA	R-846	c60
Lockheed T-33A	RA	several	c52
North American AT-6 Texan	RA	31-309	c45
North American F-86D Sabrejet	RA	several	c52
North American TF-100F Super Sabre	RA	GT-927	c57
Republic F-84G Thunderjet	RA	several	c55
Republic RF-84F Thunderflash	RA	C-264	c51
S.A.I. KZ VII	RA	O-622	c47
Sikorsky S-55C	RA	S-883	c55
Sud-Est SE-3160 Alouette	RA	M-388	

FINLAND (OH)

275/OH Vesivehmaan Varastohalli (Vesevehmaa Storage Hanger) Kariniemenkatu 28 B 65, SF-01531, Lahti 14

Aero A 11	RA	AE47	27
Aero A 32	RA	AEJ59	c29
Blackburn T.5D Ripon IIF (Finnish)	RA	RI-140	31
Breguet 14A-2	RA	3C30	c25
Caudron C.59	RA	CA50	23
Caudron C.60	RA	CA84	27
Caudron-Renault C.714	RA	CA556	39
Folland Fo.141 Gnat	RA	GN-112	58
I.V.L. D.26 Haukka	RA	HA39	27
I.V.L. K.1 Kurki	RA	1	27
Kassel 12A	RA	13	35
Mikoyan-Gurevich MiG-15	RA	MU-2	c50
VL E30 Kotka 2	RAD	KA-147	31

276/OH Suomen Ilmailumuseo (Finnish Aviation Museum) PL42, 01531, Vantaa Lento, Helsinki.

Adaridy	PV		
Bell 47D	PV	OH-HIA	c49
Convair CV-340/440 Metropolitan	PV	OH-LRB	53

Aircraft Type	Stat.	Number	Yr.
D.F.S. 108-14 Schulgleiter S.G.38	PV	SG-1	44
D.F.S. 108-70 Olympia	PV	OH-OAC	c47
De Havilland D.H.115 Vampire	PV	VT-9	56
Douglas DC-3 (C-47 Skytrain)	RA	OH-VKB	38
Eklund TE-1	PV	OH-TEA	49
Fibera KK-1 (UTI)	PV	OH-368	68
Fieseler Fi 156 Storch	PV	OH-FSA	39
Folland Fo.141 Gnat	PV	GN-106	c58
Heinonen HK-1 Keltiainen	PV	OH-HKA	54
I.V.L. A.22 Hansa	PV	IL-2	22
Junkers A.50 Junior	PV	OH-ABB	31
Karhumaeki Karhu 48 Tavi	PV	OH-KUA	48
Kokkola Ko-04 Super Upstart	PV	OH-XYY	68
Lockheed 18 Lodestar	PV	OH-VKU	40
L.W.L. WWS-1 Salamandra	PV	OH-SAA	39
PIK 3A Kantti	PV	OH-YKA	50
PIK 5B	PV	OH-PAR	50
PIK 10 Paukkulauta (motorglider)	PV	OH-PXA	49
PIK 11 Tumppu	PV	OH-YMA	53
Polikarpov I-16 (UTI)	PV	UT-1	40
SAAB 91D Safir	RA	SF-9	59
SIL Harakka II	PV	H-56	52
Schneider Grunau 9	PV	IL	39
Schneider Grunau Baby II (glider)	PV	OH-BAA	43
VL Pyry 2	PV	PV-27	41
VL Saaski II	PV	SA-131	31
VL Tuisku	PV	TU-178	37
Zlin Z.37 Cmelak	S	OH-CMB	c64

277/OH Keski Suomen Ilmailumuseo (Central Finland Aviation Museum) PL 1, 41161, Tikkakoski.

Avro 504K	PV	AV57	c18
Bell P-39 Aircobra I	RA	AC26	c42
Brewster B239 Buffalo (VL Humu)	PV	HM-671	44
Bristol 142M Blenheim	RA	BL200	44
Cessna F-172H Skyhawk (Reims)	S	OH-CNH	68
D.F.S. 108-70 Olympia	S	OH-143	45
D.F.S. Meise Olympia (glider)	S	OH-OAB	45
D.F.S. Weihe	S	OH-WAB	39
De Havilland D.H.60X Moth	PV	OH-EJA	29
De Havilland D.H.100 Vampire	S	VA-6	53
De Havilland D.H.115 Vampire	PV	VT-8	56
Douglas DC-2	C	DO-1	35
Douglas DC-3 (C-47 Dakota)	PV	DO-4	c44
Fokker C.X (fuselage)	PVD	FK-113	43
Fokker C.X (fuselage, tail)	D	FK-115	43
Fokker D.XXI	C	FR-110	39
Folland Fo.141 Gnat	S	GN-104	c58
Folland Fo.141 Gnat	PV	GN-101	c58
Gourdou-Leseurre B.3	PV	GL12	23
Hawker Hurricane Mk.1	PV	HC452	39
Hunting-Percival P.66 Pembroke	PV	PR-2	56
Ilyushin Il-28R	PV	NH-4	c50
Martinsyde F.4 Buzzard	PV	MA-24	18
Messerschmitt Bf 109F-4	PV	NE+ML	42
Messerschmitt Bf 109G-6	PV	MI507	c44
Mignet HM-14 Pou du Ciel	PV		36
Mikoyan-Gurevich MiG-15	RA	MK-103	c50
Mikoyan-Gurevich MiG-15	PV	MU-4	c50
Mil Mi-1 helicopter	PV	OH-HRC	c55
Mil Mi-4	PV	HR-2	51
Morane-Saulnier MS.50C	PV	MS52	25
PIK 3B	S	OH-199	59
PIK 5B	PV	OH-PAX	56
PIK 5C (glider)	S	OH-PBA	57

Aircraft Type	Stat.	Number	Yr.
Paatalo "Tiira" (homebuilt)	PV		77
Polikarpov Po-2	S	1	37
SZD 10bis Czapla (glider)	RA	OH-209	59
Schneider Grunau Baby IIA (glider)	S	OH-B AD	36
Thulin D (fuselage)	RAI	F1	18
VL (VMT) Pyorremyrsky	PV	PM-1	45
VL Myrsky II (fuselage)	PVD	MY-5	44
VL Pyry 2	C	PY-35	41
VL Viima II (fuselage)	DI	VI-	39
Valmet Vihuri II	PV	VH-18	52

278/OH Hallinportti Ilmailumuseo
(Halli Air Base Air Museum)
35600 Halli.

Aircraft Type	Stat.	Number	Yr.
Bristol 105A Bulldog IVA	PV	BU59	c35
Caudron G.3	PV	1E18	20
De Havilland D.H.100 Vampire	PV	VA2	53
Focke-Wulf Fw 44J Stieglitz	RA	SZ25	c40
Focke-Wulf Fw 44J Stieglitz	A	SZ-4	40
Folland Fo.141 Gnat	PV	GN-103	c58
Folland Fo.141 Gnat	S	GN-113	59
Folland Fo.141 Gnat Mk.F1	S	GN-107	58
Gloster Gauntlet II	A	GT-400	36
I.V.L. C.24	PV	8F4	24
I.V.L. D.27 Haukka II	PV	HA-41	27
Karhumaeki Karhu 48 Nalle	PV	OH-VKK	48
Mikoyan-Gurevich MiG-15	PV	MU-1	c50
Mil Mi-1 helicopter	PV	HK-1	c55
Rumpler 6B	S	5A-1	18
SAAB 91D Safir	S	SF-7	59
VL Saaski II	PVC	LK-1	29
VL Viima I	S	VI-1	35

279/OH Tampereen Teknillinen
(Technical Museum of Tampere)
Itsenaisyydenkatu 21, 33500,
Tampere.

Aircraft Type	Stat.	Number	Yr.
De Havilland D.H.60X Moth	PV	OH-ILA	27
Mignet HM-14 Pou du Ciel	PV	OH-KAA	35
Mil Mi-1 helicopter	PV	HK-2	c55
VL Pyry 1	PV	PY-1	39

FRANCE (F)

285/F Jean Salis Collection
Aerodrome de la Ferte Alais
91590, la Ferte Alais.

Aircraft Type	Stat.	Number	Yr.
Abraham 2 Iris	RAD	F-PBFV	
Agusta-Bell 47G	RA	F-BNFB	c55
Albatros C.III (R)	RAA	F-AZAX	c16
Albatros C.III (R)	RAA	F-AZAV	c16
Antonov An-2	RAA		49
Arsenal Air 100	RAA	F-CBHC	
Arsenal Air 102	RA	F-CABQ	
Auster J/1 Autocrat	RAD	F-BDAK	c46
Beech D-18S (C-45G)	RAA	F-BHMM	c44
Beech E-18S Expeditor	RAA	F-BTCS	c50
Bell 47G	RA	F-WIPA	c49
Bleriot XI (R)	RAA	F-AZBA	c10
Breguet 14P	RAA	F-AZBP	c20
Breguet 14P	RAA	F-AZBH	c20
Breguet 904S	RAA	F-CCFV	c50
Brochet MB 72	RA		49
Bucker Bu 131 Jungmann	RAA	F-AZBU	c35
Bucker Bu 131 Jungmann	RAA	F-AZBZ	c35

Aircraft Type	Stat.	Number	Yr.
Bucker Bu 133C Jungmeister	RAA	F-AZBS	c36
Bucker Bu 181 Bestmann	RAD	F-BCRF	c40
CAP.10	RAA	F-PZLD	
CAP.20LS	RAA	F-PZAJ	
Caudron C.69	RAD	F-AFHH	
Caudron C.270 Luciole	RA	F-AMAC	c35
Caudron C.275 Luciole	RAD	F-ALLL	c35
Caudron C.282 Phalene	RAD	F-AMGJ	c33
Caudron C.601 Aiglon	RA	F-POIT	c35
Caudron C.800	RA	F-CAZX	c46
Caudron C.800	RA	F-CAJK	c46
Caudron C.800	RAA	F-CAZY	c46
Dassault MD 311 Flamant	RA	F-AZCB	c50
De Havilland D.H.82A Tiger Moth	RAA	OO-SOB	c36
De Havilland D.H.82A Tiger Moth	RAD	Several	c36
De Havilland D.H.82A Tiger Moth	RA	F-BGEQ	c36
De Havilland D.H.82A Tiger Moth	RA	OO-EVM	c36
De Havilland D.H.89A Dragon Rapide	RA	F-BHGR	c35
De Havilland D.H.89A Dragon Rapide	RAA	F-AZCA	c35
De Havilland D.H.94 Moth Minor	RAX	F-PAOG	c38
De Havilland DHC-1 Chipmunk T.20	RAAX	WB557	c50
Deperdussin Monocoque (R)	RAA	F-AZAR	c13
Dewoitine D.26	RA	F-AZBC	c31
Dewoitine D.26	RA	F-AZBF	c31
Dewoitine D.520DC	RA	650	c39
Douglas AD-4N Skyraider	RAA	F-WZDQ	c52
Douglas DC-3 (C-47B)	RAA	F-BLOZ	c44
Fairchild F-24R	RAA	F-AZCI	c40
Fairchild F-24R Argus	RAD	Several	c40
Fairchild F-24W	RAAX	4314499	c40
Farman F.400	RAC	F-PBAY	
Fauvel AV.36	RAA	F-CBRS	c57
Fokker Dr.I Triplane (R)	RAA	F-AZAQ	c17
Fouga C.M.8/15	RAA	F-CABN	
Great Lakes 2T	RAC		c32
Jodel D.120	RAA	F-BHTS	c55
Latecoere 17P (semi-R)	RAA	F-AZBD	c26
Leopoldoff L.3 (Colibri biplane)	RA	F-APZP	c37
Leopoldoff L.6 (Colibri biplane)	RAD	F-BBCY	c55
Leopoldoff L.55 (Colibri biplane)	RAC	F-WVZR	c55
Mauboussin M.120	RAD	F-AMHT	c40
Mauboussin M.127 Corsaire	RA	F-PBTB	c48
Mauboussin M.130 Corsaire	RAA	F-PCIZ	c48
Max Holste M.H.1521M Broussard	RAA	F-BXCS	c55
Max Holste M.H.1521M Broussard	RA	F-BVSS	c55
Max Holste M.H.1521M Broussard	RA	F-BVSU	c55
Mignet HM-8	RA		c30
Miles M.14A Magister	RAA	HB-EEB	c40
Morane-Saulnier A1 (R)	RAA	F-AZAP	c17
Morane-Saulnier A1 (R)	RAA	F-AZAN	c17
Morane-Saulnier MS.130E	RAD	F-AZAA	c28
Morane-Saulnier MS.138	RAA	F-AZAJ	c30
Morane-Saulnier MS.181	RA	F-PKFX	c30
Morane-Saulnier MS.185	RAA	F-AZAZ	c32
Morane-Saulnier MS.230	RAD		c48
Morane-Saulnier MS.315	RAD	Several	c32
Morane-Saulnier MS.317	RAD	F-BCNY	c35
Morane-Saulnier MS.317	RAA	F-BCNL	c35
Morane-Saulnier MS.317	RAA	F-BFZO	c35
Morane-Saulnier MS.317	RAA	F-BCNU	c35
Morane-Saulnier MS.317	RAA	F-BCBI	c35
Morane-Saulnier MS.341/3	RA	F-AZCX	c35
Morane-Saulnier MS.341/3	RAD	F-ANVT	c35
Morane-Saulnier MS.505	RA	F-BEJE	c64
Morane-Saulnier MS.505	RAA	F-BAYE	c64
Morane-Saulnier MS.505	RA	F-BAUV	c64
Morane-Saulnier MS.733 Alcyon	RA	F-BLOC	c55

Aircraft Type	Stat.	Number	Yr.
Morane-Saulnier MS.733 Alcyon	RAA	F-BLXP	c55
Navion Rangemaster G	RAA	F-BJSD	c62
Nieuport 11 (R)	RA	N1538	c15
Noorduyn Norseman (UC-64A)	RAA	F-AZBN	c42
Nord N.702 (Siebel Si 204)	RAC	331	c45
Nord N.856A	RAD	Several	c53
Nord N.1002 Pingouin (Bf 108)	RA	F-BFUY	c46
Nord N.1101 Noralpha	RA	120	c48
Nord N.1101 Noralpha	RAA	F-BBGA	c48
Nord N.1101 Noralpha	RA	F-WZBI	c48
Nord N.1101 Noralpha	RAA	F-BLYU	c48
Nord N.1101 Noralpha	RA	19	c48
Nord N.1101 Noralpha	RA	34	c48
Nord N.1101 Noralpha	RA	F-BLQY	c48
Nord N.1101 Noralpha	RA	F-BLQQ	c48
Nord N.1203 Norecrin	RAA	F-BIFU	c49
Nord N.1203 Norecrin II	RAA	F-BMHZ	c49
Nord N.1203 Norecrin VI	RAA	F-BBEP	c49
Nord N.2000	RAA	F-CAYQ	
Nord N.3202	RAD	Several	c60
Nord N.3202	RAA	F-WZBA	c60
Nord N.3202	RAA	F-WZBY	c60
North American AT-6C Texan	RAA	F-AZBE	c45
North American AT-6G Texan	RAA	F-AZBK	c45
North American AT-6G Texan	RAC	F-AZBQ	c45
North American AT-6G Texan	RAC	F-BRGA	c45
North American AT-6G Texan	RAD	Many	c45
North American AT-6G Texan	RAA	F-AZAS	c45
North American T-28A Trojan	RA		c53
Opel RAK-1 (R)	RAX	D-125	
Piel CP.1310 Super Emeraude	RAA	TY-TFE	c62
Pilatus P-2/05	RAAX	F-AZCD	c48
Pilatus P-2/06	RAAX	F-AZCE	
Piper J-3C Cub (L-4J)	RAA	F-BETX	c44
Piper J-3C Cub (L-4J)	RAA	F-BFQD	c44
Piper J-3C Cub (L-4J)	RA	F-BFEF	c44
Piper J-3C Cub (L-4J)	RAA	F-BEGG	c44
Pitts S-1S	RAA	F-WZAF	c70
Pitts S-2A	RAA	F-BYAJ	c77
Polikarpov Po-2	RAC	F-AZDB	c40
Poullin PJ.5B	RAA	F-BAQC	
Republic P-47D Thunderbolt	RAC		c44
Royal Aircraft Factory S.E.5a	RAA	F-AZCN	c18
Royal Aircraft Factory S.E.5a	RAA	F-AZCY	c18
Ryan Navion B	RAA	F-BHBV	c48
S.F.A.N. II (Br. A/C Co. Drone)	RA	F-WBTE	c35
S.F.C.A. Bovin Taupine	RAA	F-AZBG	
S.I.P.A. S.121	RAD	F-BLKH	c53
S.I.P.A. S.903	RA	F-BEPV	c47
S.I.P.A. S.903	RA	F-BGAA	c47
S.R.C.M. 153 Joigny	RAA	F-PIRZ	c60
SPAD XIII	RAC		c18
Salmson 2A2 (R)	RAA	F-WZBK	c18
Salmson 2A2 (R)	RAA	F-WZBJ	c18
Salmson D.6	RA	F-AZAB	c37
Salmson D.6/3	RAD	F-BDJV	c37
Salmson D.7	RA	F-BEAN	c46
Scintex ML 250 Rubis	RAA	F-BJME	c61
Stampe S.V.4A	RA	F-BFRL	c40
Stampe S.V.4C	RA	F-BDOV	c45
Stampe S.V.4C	RA	F-BFZS	c45
Stampe S.V.4C	RAA	F-BEKI	c45
Stampe S.V.4C	RAA	F-BGGP	c46
Stampe S.V.4C	RAA	F-BDOT	c45
Stampe S.V.4C	RAA	F-BDCY	c45
Stampe S.V.4C	RAA	F-BCOP	c45
Stampe S.V.4C	RAA	F-BQCT	c45

Aircraft Type	Stat.	Number	Yr.
Stampe S.V.4C	RAA	F-BDCQ	c45
Stampe S.V.4C	RAA	F-BMMJ	c45
Stampe S.V.4C	RA	F-BBAL	c45
Stampe S.V.4C	RAA	F-BFZJ	c45
Stampe S.V.4C	RAA	F-WZAZ	c45
Stampe S.V.4C	RAA	F-BAHV	c45
Stampe S.V.4C	RAD	Many	c45
Stearman A75N1	RA	F-AZDI	c42
Stearman A75N1	RAA	F-AZCK	c42
Stinson 108 Voyager	RAA	F-BFPM	c47
Stinson SR-10C Reliant	RAA	F-BBCS	c40
Taylor J-2 Cub	RAA	F-AZBM	c39
Yakovlev Yak-11	RA	Many	c52
Zlin Z.326 Trener Master	RA	F-BORP	c59
Zlin Z.326 Trener Master	RAA	F-BPNO	c59
Zlin Z.326 Trener Master	RA	F-BORV	c59
Zlin Z.XII	RA	F-AQIE	c36

286A/F   Musee Aeronautique de Champagne Aerodrome de Brienne-le-Chateau, 10 Brienne-le-Chateau.

Aircraft Type	Stat.	Number	Yr.
Adam RA.14 Loisirs	PV	F-PEW	c50
Beech UC-45 (ex-RCAF)	PV	6250	c44
Breguet 904S	PV	F-CCFT	c50
Brochet MB 50 Pipistrelle	RAD		47
Castel C.25S	PV		
Castel C.310P	PV	F-CRCH	
Castel C.310P	PV	F-CRJF	
Caudron C.282 Phalene	PV		c33
Caudron C.800	PV	F-CBAM	c46
Centre Aviation GA-620 Gaucho	PV	F-PKXH	c64
Chanute Glider (R)	PV		c97
Chapeau EC.19 Planeur (glider)	PV	11	
D.F.S. 108-14 Schulgleiter	PVA	F-AZBJ	c45
Dassault MD 312 Flamant	PV	235	c50
Dassault Mystere IVA	PV	28	c54
Drezair Hang-Glider	PV		
Druine D.31 Turbulent	PVD	F-PMXN	c60
Fauvel AV.36	PV	F-CBZA	c57
Fleury Vedette	PV	1	
Fouga C.M.170 Magister	PV	7	c58
Gardan GY-201 Minicab (Bearn)	PV	F-PJXT	c52
Gloster G.41 Meteor NF.11	RA		c53
Guerchais-Roche SA.103	RA	F-CRQD	c45
Guerchais-Roche SA.104 Emochet	PV	F-CRGE	c45
Jodel D.112	PVA	F-PEVF	c55
Lachassagne AL.07	PV	F-WBBN	
Leduc RL.19	PV	F-PAGT	c52
Lemaire RL-1	PV	F-PPPN	
Lockheed P2V Neptune	PV	147563	c51
Lockheed T-33A Shooting Star	PV	51-4115	51
Max Holste M.H.1521M	PV	91	c55
Mignet HM-360 Pou du Ciel	PV	F-PLUZ	c60
Miroue Dodier Pou du Ciel	PV	F-WTXF	
Nord N.856N Norvigie	PV	F-BNAR	c55
Nord N.2000	RA	F-CABE	
Nord N.2501 Noratlas	PV	31	c60
Piel CP.80	RAD	F-PVQF	c66
S.I.P.A. S.903	PV	F-BGBS	c47
Schleicher ASK-16	PV	F-CEGY	c75
Siren C.30 Edelweiss	PV	F-CCCZ	
Siren C.34	PV	F-CCAZ	
Williams Motorfly	PV	F-WEAZ	

286B/F   Musee de l'Aeronautique de Nancy
Parc de Haye, Nancy.

Aircraft Type	Stat.	Number	Yr.
Augusta-Bell 47G	PV	046	c50
Breguet 904S	PV	F-CCFS	c50
Bucker Bu 181B Bestmann	PV	F-PCRL	
Castel C.25S	PV	F-CRMI	
Cessna L-19A Bird Dog	PV	F-WZXB	
D.F.S. 108-14 Schulgleiter SG-38	PV		c45
Dassault MD 312 Flamant	RA	F-WZXA	c50
Dassault Mystere IVA	RA	23	c54
Fairchild F.24R Argus	PV	F-BEXU	c39
Fouga C.M.170 Magister	PV	F-WDHG	c58
Fouga C.M.173	RA	01	
Guerchais-Roche SA.103	PV	F-CRDI	c45
Lockheed SP-2H Neptune	RA	148334	c60
Lockheed T-33AN	PV	21255	c53
Max Holste M.H.1521M Broussard	PV	198M	c55
Morane-Saulnier MS.505	PV	F-BDQT	c64
Morane-Saulnier MS.733 Alcyon	PVX	186	c56
Nord N.856N Norvigie	PV	51	c55
Nord N.1203 Norecrin VI	PV	F-BBET	c49
Nord N.3202	PV	64	c58
Nord N.3400	PV	100	c60
Sikorsky S-55 (Chickasaw)	PV	SA-59	c53
Sud-Ouest SO-1221 Djinn	PV		c56

286C/F   Ailes de France, Aerodrome de
Luneville-Croismarie, Luneville.

Aircraft Type	Stat.	Number	Yr.
Bison PG-2 (Mauboussin M.123)	RAA	F-PBHQ	59
Breguet 904S	RAA	F-CCFP	c50
Castel C.25S	RAA	F-CRPQ	
De Havilland D.H.82A Tiger Moth	RA	F-AZCS	c40
Fauvel AV.45	RAA	F-CRRM	c60
Jurca MJ.5 Sirocco	RA	F-WLKM	c62
Max Holste M.H.52	RA	F-AZCR	
Morane-Saulnier MS.317	RAA	F-BGKW	c35
Morane-Saulnier MS.317	RAA	F-BBZU	c35
Morane-Saulnier MS.505	RAA	F-BCMQ	c64
Morane-Saulnier MS.733 Alcyon	RAA	F-BHCB	c56
Nord N.856 Norvigie	RA		c55
Nord N.1300	RAA	F-CRII	
Nord N.3202	RA	19	c60
Potez 600	RA	F-PIHA	c38
Stampe S.V.4A	RAA	R-BTXD	c40
Stampe S.V.4C	RAA	F-GDXM	c45

286D/F   Escadrille du Souvenir, Etampes-
Mondesir Airport, Etampes.

Aircraft Type	Stat.	Number	Yr.
Aero 145	RAA	F-AZCL	c59
Bleriot XI (R)	RA		c11
Breguet 904	RA	F-CCFK	c50
Caudron C.600 Aiglon	RAA	F-AZCO	
Caudron C.801	RA	F-CBTK	
Curtiss Wright CW-1 Junior	RAA	F-AZBR	c33
De Havilland D.H.82A Tiger Moth	RA	K2570	c40
De Havilland D.H.100 Vampire	RA	50	c50
Druine Turbulent	RAA	F=PCZT	c60
Guerchais-Roche SA.103	RA	F-CRGB	c45
Morane-Saulnier A1 (R)	RAA	F-AZAO	
Morane-Saulnier MS.504	RAA	F-BCME	
Morane-Saulnier MS.733 Alcyon	RA	F-AZAF	c56
Morane-Saulnier MS.733 Alcyon	RA	F-AZAE	c56
Nord N.702	RA	315	

Aircraft Type	Stat.	Number	Yr.
Nord N.1101 Noralpha	RAA	F-WZBI	c48
Nord N.1101 Noralpha	RAA	F-BYAV	c48
Nord N.1101 Noralpha	RAA	F-BLQR	c48
Nord N.2501 Noratlas	RA	98	c60
Nord N.3202	RA	several	c60
Nord N.3400	RA	108	c60
Nord N.3400	RA	99	c60
North American AT-6 Texan	RAA	F-AZAU	c45
North American AT-6 Texan	RAA	F-AZAY	c45
Piper J-3C Cub (L-4B)	RAA	F-BEGD	c41
Potez 60	RAC	F-AOSE	
Santos-Dumont Demoiselle (R)	RAC		c08
Stampe S.V.4A	RA	38	c40
Stampe S.V.4A	RA	F-BISY	c40
Zlin Z.326 Trener Master	RA	F-BNMU	

290/F   Musee de l'Air et de l'Espace
93350 Le Bourget, Paris.

Aircraft Type	Stat.	Number	Yr.
Ader Avion III	PV		97
Aerospatiale Concorde	PV	F-WTSS	c70
Agusta-Bell 47G	PV	076	c55
Arsenal Air 100	PV	F-ZABY	
Avia 40P (glider)	PV		32
Avia XV A (glider)	RA		37
B.D.M. 01 (helicopter)	PV	F-WEPH	58
Beech D-18S	PV	N61909	c44
Bernard 191 "Oiseau Canari"	PV	F-AJCP	29
Biot Planeur (glider)	PV		c95
Bleriot IX (fuselage)	PV		08
Bleriot XI Monoplane	PV		09
Bleriot XI-2 (2-seat)	RA	878	13
Bleriot XI-2 (2-seat)	RA		13
Boeing 707-328	PV	F-BLCD	c60
Boeing B-17G Flying Fortress	PV	44-8889	44
Boeing B-17G Flying Fortress	PV	F-BGSO	44
Breguet 14A-2	PV	2016	17
Breguet 19 Grand-Raid	PV	1685	26
Breguet 19 Super-Bidon	PV		29
Breguet 901	PV	F-CAJA	c50
Breguet 941S	PV	04	c61
Breguet 1050 Alize	PV	10	57
Breguet III (gyroplane)	RA	F-WFXC	46
Breguet/B.A.C. Jaguar	PV	04	c70
Brochet MB 850	RA		50
Bucker Bu 181 Bestmann	RA	F-WBYU	38
Castel C.242	PV	04	
Castel C.301S	PV	F-CBYM	
Castel-Mauboussin C.M.813	PV	F-CCHM	49
Caudron C.60	PV	F-AINX	21
Caudron C.109	PV	F-PFLN	25
Caudron C.277 Luciole	PV	F-ADFX	35
Caudron C.282/8 Phalene	PV	F-AMKT	33
Caudron C.635 Simoun	PV	F-ANRO	c35
Caudron C.714R	PV	01	39
Caudron C.800	RA	334	46
Caudron C.800	PV	334	c46
Caudron G.3	RA	2531	13
Caudron G.3 Type XII	PV	324	13
Caudron G.3 Type XII	PV	324	13
Caudron G.4	PV	1720	15
Caudron-Regnier C.366	PV		33
Chanute Glider	PV		97
Cierva CB.11 (autogyro)	PV	G-EBYY	28
Crosses Mini Criquet (Pou du Ciel)	PV	F-PVQI	c57
D.F.S. Habicht	PV	F-CAEX	37
D.F.S. Kranich II	RA	1399	39

Aircraft Type	Stat.	Number	Yr.
Dassault MD 312 Flamant	PV	241	c50
Dassault MD 315R Flamant	PV	130	c50
Dassault MD 450 Ouragan	PV	154	c50
Dassault Mirage G.8	PV	01	c63
Dassault Mirage III	PV	01	65
Dassault Mirage IIIC	PV	7	c63
Dassault Mirage IIIC	PV	87	c63
Dassault Mirage IIIV	PV	01	c66
Dassault Mystere IVA	PV	299	c54
Dassault Mystere IVA	PV	289	c54
Dassault Mystere IVA	PV	1	54
Dassault Mystere IVA	PV	245	c54
Dassault Mystere XX	PV	01	c56
Dassault Super Mystere B.2	PV	11	c57
De Havilland D.H.9	PV	1258	18
De Havilland D.H.80A Puss Moth	RA	F-ANRZ	35
De Havilland D.H.89A Dragon Rapide	A	F-BHCD	34
De Havilland D.H.100 Vampire	PV	04	c50
Deperdussin B	PV		11
Deperdussin Monocoque	PV	F1	13
Dewoitine D.520	PV	408	39
Dewoitine D.520	PV	277	39
Dewoitine D.530	PV	06	37
Dewoitine D.VII	RA	16	23
Donnet-Leveque A Flying Boat	PV		12
Dornier Do 28B-1	PV	F-ZBBF	c64
Douglas A-26 Invader (B-26)	PV	34773	44
Douglas AD-4N Skyraider	PV	126979	c52
Douglas DC-3 (C-47 Dakota)	PV	92449	42
Douglas DC-7C	PV	LN-MOG	57
Dumolard Pou du Ciel	S	01	62
English Electric Canberra	PV	WJ763	c55
Fabre Hydravion (First seaplane)	PV		10
Farman (Henri) F.20	PV		12
Farman (Maurice)	PV	446	11
Farman F.60 Goliath (fuselage)	PVI	F-HMFU	19
Farman F.192	PV	F-BAOP	29
Farman F.455 Moustique	PV	01	36
Fauvel AV.36	PV	F-CRRB	c57
Fieseler Fi 156 Criquet (MS.500)	RA	D-EM+AW	44
Focke-Achgelis Fa 330 Rotor Kite	PV		42
Focke-Wulf Fw 190	PV	63	42
Focke-Wulf Fw 190A-8	PV	7298	43
Fokker D.VII (Albatros)	PV	6796/18	18
Fouga C.M.170 Magister	PV		c58 .
Fournier RF-2	PV	F-BJSY	c70
Gary GR-1 (autogyro)	PV	F-WYDD	
Gloster G.47 Meteor NF.11	RA	24	48
Gourdou-Leseurre B.7/192	PV	F-APOZ	37
Grassi (experimental glider)	RA		38
Guerchais-Roche SA.104	PV	F-CRLL	c45
Hanriot HD-14	RA		24
Heinkel He 111 (CASA 2111)	PV	BR21129	42
Heinkel He 162 Volksjaeger	PV	2	44
Hirsch HR-100	PV	F-WGVC	c54
Hurel Aviette	PV	F-WTXS	
Hurel-Dubois H.D.10	PV	F-BFAM	48
Hurel-Dubois H.D.34	PV	F-BICR	c57
Jodel D.9 Bebe	PV	F-PEPF	47
Jodel D.119	PV	F-PINS	c55
Junkers D.I (J 9)	PV		18
Junkers F 13	PV	609	24
Junkers Ju 52/3m	PV	216	32
Kellner-Bechereau E-60	PV	01	
L.V.G. C.VI	PV	904	18
Lavavasseur Antoinette	PV		09
Leduc 010 (Exp. manned ramjet)	PV	001	46
Leduc 022 (Exp. manned ramjet)	PV	001	53
Lilienthal Glider	PV		95
Liore-et-Oliver C.302 (Cierva)	PV	F-BDAD	36
Lockheed L749A Constellation	PV	F-ZVMV	c48
Lockheed P2V-7 Neptune	PV	148335	c55
Lockheed T-33A Shooting Star	PV	553097	c50
Lockheed T-33A Shooting Star	PV	535055	c50
Maerc-Sarl H-100	RA	F-WGVC	54
Martin B-26 Marauder	RA		42
Max Holste M.H.1521M Broussard	S	07	57
Messerschmitt Bf 109 (HA.1112)	PV	471.28	53
Mignet HM-8	PV		c30
Mignet HM-14 Pou du Ciel	PV		34
Mignet HM-280 Pou-Maquis	PV		44
Morane-Saulnier A1	PV	F-ABAO	21
Morane-Saulnier A1	RA	293	17
Morane-Saulnier G	PV		13
Morane-Saulnier MS.149	RA	F-AJFJ	29
Morane-Saulnier MS.230	PV	1048	29
Morane-Saulnier MS.315	S	F-BCBR	46
Morane-Saulnier MS.317	PV	328	c35
Morane-Saulnier MS.406	PV	15	38
Morane-Saulnier MS.472 Vanneau	PV	122	
Morane-Saulnier MS.880 Rallye	PV	F-BJSF	c60
Moynet M 360 Jupiter	PV	F-BLKE	c65
Nieuport 2N	PV		10
Nieuport-Delage 11	PV	N976	15
Nieuport-Delage 29C-1	PV	10	18
Nord N.702 Martinet (Siebel)	S	282	45
Nord N.1101 Noralpha	PV	135	c48
Nord N.1203 Norecrin	PV	F-BICY	47
Nord N.1500 Griffon	PV	2	57
Nord N.2501 Noratlas	PV	50	c60
Nord N.3400	RA	131	58
North American AT-6G Texan	PV	5114915	c45
North American F-86K Sabre	PV	552736	c55
North American F-100D Super Sabre	PV	552736	c57
North American P-51K Mustang	PV	63871	c45
Oehmichen (Helicopter)	PV	6	35
Oehmichen (Helicopter)	RA	7	37
Oehmichen (Helicopter)	RA	2	23
Oehmichen (Helicopter)	RA	3	27
Oehmichen (Helicopter)	RA	1	20
Packard-Le Pere C.2	PV	SC42133	18
Payen Pa-49	PV	F-WGVA	54
Perrin (helicopter)	PV		24
Pescara F.3 (helicopter)	PV	3	23
Pfalz D.XII	PV	2690/18	18
Piel CP.1310 Super Emeraude	PV	F-BMJJ	c62
Piper L-18B Super Cub	RA	18-1430	53
Polikarpov I-153 Chicka	PV		38
Potez 36	RA	F-ALQT	29
Potez 43/7	PV	F-APXO	c32
Potez 53	PV	3402	33
Potez 58	RA	F-ANYA	35
Potez 842	PV	F-BNAN	c64
R.E.P. D	RA		11
R.E.P. K	PV		13
Republic F-84F Thunderstreak	PV	F6-46	52
Republic P-47D Thunderbolt	PV	4420371	44
Royal Aircraft Factory B.E.2c	PV	9969	15
SAAB 29A (J-29A)	RA		54
SAAB 35A Draken (J-35A)	PV	35069	c62
SNECMA C.400P2 Atar Volant	PV		57
SPAD XIII C1	PV	15295	17
SPAD 54	RA	F-AHBE	22
SPAD-Herbemont 52	PV	3125	21

254

Aircraft Type	Stat.	Number	Yr.
SZD-24 Foka	PV	F-CCHX	
Santos-Dumont Demoiselle	PV		08
Schmitt (Paul)	PV		14
Schneider Grunau Baby II (glider)	PV	10849	32
Schneider Grunau S.G.38 (glider)	PV	173	26
Schreck FBA 17 HT4 (flying boat)	PV	F-AJOR	30
Short Sandringham ("Bermuda")	PV	F-OBIP	c46
Sikorsky S-55 (Chickasaw H-19D)	RA		55
Siren C.34 Edelweiss	PV	F-CCAY	
Sopwith 1 1/2-Strutter IA2	RA	556	17
Stampe S.V.4C	PV	F-BBQL	c45
Stampe S.V.4C	RA		45
Stampe S.V.4C	RA	38	45
Sud-Aviation SA-3210 Super Frelon	PV	01	c63
Sud-Aviation SE-210 Caravelle	PV	F-BJTR	c59
Sud-Ouest SO-535 Mistral	RA	002	51
Sud-Ouest SO-1110 Ariel II	PV	01	49
Sud-Ouest SO-1220 Djinn	PV	02	53
Sud-Ouest SO-3101 (helicopter)	RA	1	48
Sud-Ouest SO-4050 Vautour IIB	PV	640	c57
Sud-Ouest SO-4050 Vautour IIB	PV	634	c57
Sud-Ouest SO-4050 Vautour IIN	PV	330	c57
Sud-Ouest SO-6000 Triton (exp.)	PV	3	46
Sud-Ouest SO-9000 Trident (exp.)	PV	01	53
Supermarine Spitfire Mk.IX	PV	BS464	42
Supermarine Spitfire Mk.XVI	PV	TB597	c45
Sustentateur Ludion	PV		67
Vertol CH-21C Shawnee	RA	FR69	53
Voisin LA 5B2	PV		15
Voisin-Farman (Henri) 1bis	PV		07
Vuia	PV		06
Wright Brothers Baby	PV		10
Yakovlev Yak-3	PV		43
Zeppelin C.IV (JA)	RA		18
Zlin Z.326 Trener Master	PV	F-BORT	c59

290A/F   Ailes Ancienees—Toulouse Avenue Clement Ader, 31776 Colomiers. (A number of Ailes Ancienees which restore a/c in support of the Musee de l'Air exist across France.)

Aircraft Type	Stat.	Number	Yr.
Beech D.18S Expeditor	PV	753	c42
Dassault MD 312 Flamant	PV	227	c50
Dassault Mystere IVA	PV	1	c54
Dassault Mystere IVA	PV	44	c54
Dassault Super Mystere B.2	PV	48	c57
Fouga C.M.170 Magister	PV	103	c58
Gloster Meteor NF.11	PV	11-8	c50
Lockheed T-33A	PV	51-4230	c50
Max Holste M.H.1521M Broussard	PV	133M	c55
Merville S.M.31	PV		01
Morane-Saulnier MS.733 Alcyon	PV	F-BMMT	c56
Nord N.1101 Noralpha	PV	81	c48
Nord N.3400	PV	130	c60
North American AT-6 Texan	PV	132	c45
Republic F-84G Thunderjet	PV		c55
Sud-Ouest SO-4050 Vautour IIB	PV	640	c57

291/ F   Musee National des Techniques (National Technical Museum) 27 Rue Saint Martin, 75141, Paris.

Aircraft Type	Stat.	Number	Yr.
Ader Avion III "Chauve Souris"	C		97
Bleriot XI "La Manche"	PV		09

Aircraft Type	Stat.	Number	Yr.
Breguet Avion	PV	40	11
Esnault-Pelterie Monoplane	PV		07

EAST GERMANY (DM)

295/DM   Verkehrsmuseum (Transportation Museum) Augustusstrasse 1, Dresden 801.

Aircraft Type	Stat.	Number	Yr.
Aero Super 45	PV	DM-VMD	54
Grade Monoplane	PV		09
Lilienthal Glider (R)	PV		93
Segelflugzeug LG125 Sohaj 2 (Zlin)	RA	DM-2075	

295A/DM   Armeemuseum der Deutschen Demokratischen Republik (Army Museum of the German Democratic Republic) Dr. Kurt Fischer Platz 3, Dresden.

Aircraft Type	Stat.	Number	Yr.
Aero L-29 Delfin	PV	313	60
Antonov An-14	PV	996	60
Fieseler Fi 103	PV		41
Mikoyan-Gurevich MiG-17	PV	621	c60
Mikoyan-Gurevich MiG-17F	PV	300	c60
Mikoyan-Gurevich MiG-17PF	PV	850	c60
Mikoyan-Gurevich MiG-21F	PV	884	c65
Mikoyan-Gurevich MiG-21F	PV	268	c65
Mil Mi-4	PV	785	c60
Polikarpov Po-2	PV		c40
Yakovlev Yak-18	S		50

WEST GERMANY (D)

300/D   Deutsches Museum (National Technical Museum) Museumsinsel 1, 8000 Munich.

Aircraft Type	Stat.	Number	Yr.
Akaflieg Hannover Vampyr	PV		21
Akaflieg Munchen Mu 10 Milan	RA	D-1001	34
Akaflieg Munchen Mu 13E Bergfalke	RA	D-1653	51
Akaflieg Stuttgart Fs 24 Phoenix	PV	D-9093	57
Bachem Ba 349 Natter (BP20)	PV		45
Bleriot XI Monoplane	PV		09
D.F.S. Kranich II (glider)	RA	D-6171	c39
D.F.S. Meise Olympia (glider)	RA	D-1469	59
D.F.S. Meise Olympia (glider)	RA	D-6336	c59
Dornier Do 27B-1	PV	D-EHAV	59
Dornier Do 29 (S/VTOL)	S	YA+101	58
Dornier Do 31E (VTOL)	PV	D-9531	67
Dornier Do 32E Kiebitz helicopter	PV	D-HOPA	64
Douglas DC-3 (C-47 Dakota)	RA	26989	44
E.W.R.-Sud VJ 101C	PV	D-9518	65
Etrich Taube (Rumpler)	PV	19	10
Fauvel AV.36 (glider)	RA	D-8273	57
Fieseler Fi 156C Storch	PV	A-29	39
Finsterwalder Bergflex	RA		76
Focke-Achgelis Fa 330 Bachstelze	PV		42
Fokker D.VII	PVX	4404/18	18
Fokker Dr.I Triplane (R)	PV	425/17	c17
Grade Libelle	PV		09
Haase-Kensche-Schmet HKS-3	PV	D-6426	55
Hamburger Flugzeugbau HFB 320	PV	D-CLOU	64
Hatry-Opel RAK-1 Rocket Glider (R)	RA		

Aircraft Type	Stat.	Number	Yr.
Heinkel He 111H (CASA 2111)	SX	B21-177	49
Hirth-Huetter GOE-4 Goevier III	RA	OE-0223	53
Hirth-Huetter GOE-4 Goevier III	RA	D-6007	52
Horten Ho.IV (glider-wings only)	RAI	7856	42
Huber Alpengleiter	RA		72
Hunting-Percival P.66 Pembroke	PV2	G-AOJG	c56
Hutter Hu 17A (sailplane)	RA	D-8129	42
Junkers A.50 Junior	PV	D-2054	31
Junkers F 13	PVX	D-366	28
Junkers Ju 52/3m (French Amiot)	PVX	363	45
Klemm Kl 25F	PV	D-EMDU	35
Lilienthal Type 11 Glider	PV		95
Lilienthal Type 11 Glider (R)	RA		62
Lockheed F-104F Starfighter	RA	2903	54
Lockheed F-104G Starfighter	PV	21+53	c60
Lockheed T-33A Shooting Star	PV	9447	48
Messerschmitt Bf 108 Taifun (Nord)	PVX	D-IBFW	45
Messerschmitt Bf 109E-3	PVX	790	38
Messerschmitt M-17	PV	D-779	25
Messerschmitt Me 163B-1 Komet	PV	1203-70	44
Messerschmitt Me 262A-1 Schwalbe	PV	500071	44
North American AT-6A Texan	RA	F-BMJO	c45
North American F-86 Sabre VI	PV	JD+105	57
Pacific Kites Seagull (glider)	RA		74
Pelzner Glider (R)	RA		77
Puetzer Doppelraab	RA	D-1220	c50
Puetzer Motorraab	RA	D-EHOG	55
Republic RF-84F Thunderflash	RA	EB-231	c52
Rumpler C.IV	PV	301	17
SAAB 35A Draken (J-35A)	PV	35086	c62
Scheibe Mu 13E Bergfalke (glider)	RA	D-1085	52
Scheibe Spatz 55 (glider)	RA	D-1509	58
Scheibe Spatz 55M	RA	D-KIBA	61
Schleicher Ka 6BR Roensegler	PV	D-9099	58
Schmetz Condor IV (glider)	RA	D-8802	
Schneider Grunau Baby IIB (glider)	RA	D-1065	44
Schneider Grunau Baby IIB (glider)	RA	D-1283	57
Schneider Grunau Baby III (glider)	RA	D-1094	52
Schneider Grunau S.G.38 (glider)	RA		c40
Schneider Grunau S.G.38 (glider)	RA		30
Schneider Grunau S.G.38 (glider)	RA		56
Schneider Grunau S.G.38 (glider)	RA		38
Schulz F.S.3 Besenstiel Glider (R)	RA		
Sikorsky S-55 (Chickasaw H-19B)	PV	53-4458	49
Sikorsky S-58 (Choctaw H-34G)	RA	58-1157	65
V.F.W. Fokker VAK 191B (VTOL)	RA	D-9563	72
Wolfmueller Glider	RA		07
Wright Brothers Type A	PV		08

300A/D Air Classik Collection Berlin-Tegel Airport (1) Dusseldorf Airport (2) Frankfort Rhein-Main Airport (3) Monchengladbach Airport (4) Stuttgart Airport (5)

Aircraft Type	Stat.	Number	Yr.
Aero L-60 Brigadyr	PV2	OK-LGL	c58
Bristol 171 Sycamore Mk.52	PV2	78+09	c58
Bucker Bu 131B Jungmann	PV2	D-EBZE	c36
Bucker Bu 131B Jungmann	PV3	D-EFEI	c44
Bucker Bu 181B Bestmann	PV3	D-ECES	c44
Bucker Bu 181B Bestmann	PV2	D-EDIB	c44
D.F.S. 108-14 Schulgleiter (R)	RA		
De Havilland D.H.82A Tiger Moth	PV3	PG732	c36
De Havilland D.H.89A Dragon Rapide	PV3	G-YCYR	c35
De Havilland D.H.106 Comet 4C	PV2	G-BDIW	c62

Aircraft Type	Stat.	Number	Yr.
De Havilland D.H.112 Venom	PV3		c50
Dornier Do 27B	PV1	D-EDHS	c60
Dornier Do 27B	PV3	D-EFHO	c60
Douglas DC-3 (C-47)	PV3	N65371	c44
Douglas DC-3 (C-47)	PV5	D-CORA	c44
Fiat G.91R/3	PV3	32+43	c58
Fieseler Fi 156C Storch	RA3		c44
Focke-Wulf Fw 190 (R)	PV2		c43
Fokker Dr.1 (R)	PV3		c17
Gloster Javelin FAW.9	PV4	XH768	c53
Heinkel He 111 (CASA 2111)	PV3	B21-14	c42
Hutter Hu 17A (sailplane)	PV3		c42
Ikarus Windspiel 2	PV3		
Junkers Ju 52/3m (CASA 352L)	PV2	D-CIAK	c40
Junkers Ju 52/3m (CASA 352L)	PV5	D-CIAL	c40
Junkers Ju 52/3m (CASA 352L)	PV3	D-CIAS	c40
Junkers Ju 87 Stuka (R)	PV3	TG+KL	c40
Klemm Kl 35D	PV3	D-ELLY	c41
Klemm Kl 107B	RA	D-EFOW	c56
Lilienthal Biplane Glider (R)	PV3		c95
Lilienthal Monoplane Glider (R)	PV3		c95
Lockheed L-1049G Constellation	PV3	D-ADAM	c55
Lockheed T-33A Shooting Star	PV5	63659	c50
Messerschmitt Bf 108 Taifun (Nord)	PV3		c45
Messerschmitt Bf 109E (R)	PV2		c40
Messerschmitt Me 163B Komet	PV2		c44
Messerschmitt Me 262A	PV3		c44
Morane-Saulnier MS.317	RA	1004	c35
Morane-Saulnier MS.317	PV2	F-BFZP	c35
Morane-Saulnier MS.500 (Fi 156)	RA3	D-EMIL	c44
Nord N.1002 Pingouin (Bf 108)	PV3	D-EACS	c46
Nord N.1002 Pingouin (Bf 108)	PV2	D-EOAR	c46
North American AT-6A Texan	PV2	D-FOBY	c45
North American F-86 Sabre	PV2	JA+102	c50
Piaggio P.149D	PV2	D-EHMG	c55
Piaggio P.149D	RA	D-EABE	c55
Republic F-84F Thunderstreak	PV2	DD+348	c53
Republic F-84F Thunderstreak	PV3	DJ+134	c53
Scheibe Mu 13 Bergfalke II	RA	D-8090	c50
Schleicher Rhonbaby (R)	PV3		
Stampe S.V.4C	PV3	F-BDDY	c45
Vertol V-43C	PV5	83+17	c58
Vickers 498 Viking 1A	RA3	G-AGRW	c46
Vickers 614 Viking 2	PV2	D-BABY	c46

301/D Motoren und Turbinen Union Museum, Dachauerstrasse 665, 8000 Munich.

Aircraft Type	Stat.	Number	Yr.
Republic RF-84F Thunderflash	PV	52-7377	52

302/D Dornier Museum, Neues Schloss, 7758 Meersburg. (A/c at several locations.)

Aircraft Type	Stat.	Number	Yr.
Aerodyne	RA		c60
Dornier Do 19	PV	YA+101	c35
Dornier Do 24T-3	PV	HD5-3	c40
Dornier Do 27B	PV	D-ELUT	c60
Dornier Do 27B	PV	D-ENKN	c60
Dornier Do 27J	PV	D-EYLE	c60
Dornier Do 28A	PV	D-IPAT	c60
Dornier Do 31E-1	PV	E-1	c68
Dornier Do 32K Kiebitz helicopter	PV		c70
Dornier Libelle	RA	VQ-FAB	22
Fiat G.91R	PV	31+35	c58

303/D Hubschrauber Museum (Helicopter Museum) Postfach 1310, Sableplatz, 2062 Buckeburg.

Aircraft Type	Stat.	Number	Yr.
Air & Space U-18 Flymobil	PV	D-HOBB	62
Bell 47G-2 (OH-13A)	PV	0-85348	61
Bolkow Bo 46	PV	D-9514	63
Bolkow Bo 102 Helitrainer	PV	4502	59
Bolkow Bo 102 Helitrainer	S		59
Bolkow Bo 103	PV	D-9595	60
Bolkow Bo 105	PV	D-HAJY	65
Bolkow Flying Jeep (experimental)	PV		61
Bristol 171 Sycamore	PVI	78-20	58
Bristol 171 Sycamore	PV	78-33	58
Dornier Do 32-5 Kiebitz helicopter	PV	Exp	71
Dornier Do 132 (rotor test stand)	PV	Exp	76
Focke-Achgelis Fa 330 Bachstelze	PV	100406	42
Focke-Borgward FB 1 Kolibri	PVI	D-HDCE	60
Focke-Wulf Fw 61 (R) Helicopter	PV	D-EBVU	61
Georges G-1 Papillon	PV	Exp	71
Georges G-2	PV		74
Gosslich Pedalcopter	PV		58
Havertz HZ-5	PV	D-HAJU	63
Heimbacher 4	PV	Exp	51
Kaman HH-43B Huskie	PV	62-4547	58
Merckle M-133 (rotor test stand)	PV		64
Merckle SM-67	PV	D-9506	58
Mil Mi-1 helicopter	PV	CCCP712	c55
Mil SM-1-SZ Moskowitsch (Polish)	PV		58
SNCA SO-1221 Djinn	PV	7-FR8	58
Saunders Roe Skeeter A.O.P.12	PV	XN-348	58
Siemetzki Asro 4	C	V-1	64
Sikorsky S-55 (Westland Whirlwind)	PV		c55
Sikorsky S-58 (Choctaw H-34G)	PV	81+09	58
Sud-Aviation SE-3130 Alouette II	PV	18-71	61
V.F.W. H-2 (Compound)	PV	D-HIBY	68
V.F.W. H-2A (autogyro)	PV	Exp	68
V.F.W. H-3 Sprinter	PV	D-9543	70
V.F.W. H-3 Sprinter	S	D-9544	70
V.F.W. H-3A	RA	exp.	74
Vertol V-43B (H-21C)	PV	83+07	58
Wagner Rotocar 3	PV	Exp	62

305/D Luftwaffen Museum (Air Force Museum) Marseille-Kaserne Airfield (Uetersen Airfield) 2081 Appen.

Aircraft Type	Stat.	Number	Yr.
Bristol 171 Sycamore Mk.52	PV	7804	57
Bucker Bu 181B Bestmann	PV	NF+IR	42
Dornier DS 10 Fledermaus	PV	D-9534	
Dornier Do 27A-4	PV	5738	60
Fairey Gannet AS.MK.4	PV	UA+106	c57
Fiat G.91R/4	PV	BR+239	60
Fouga C.M.170 Magister	PV	AA+014	58
Hamburger Flugzeugbau HFB 320	PV	D-CARE	c64
Hawker Sea Fury FB.11	PV	D-CACY	c45
Hawker Sea Hawk FGA.6	PV	WV865	54
Heinkel He 111H-6 (CASA 2111)	PV	61AD	41
Hunting-Percival P.66 Pembroke	PV	5407	58
Lilienthal Type 13 Biplane Glider	PV		96
Lockheed F-104F Starfighter	PV	2906	59
Lockheed T-33A Shooting Star	PV	EB+399	51
Messerschmitt Bf 109F-3 (HA-1112)	PVX		c42
North American AT-6H Harvard IV	PV	D-FABU	53
North American AT-6H Harvard IV	PV	AA622	53

Aircraft Type	Stat.	Number	Yr.
North American F-86E Sabre VI(Can)	PV	JB+110	57
Republic F-84F Thunderstreak	PV	BF+106	53
Republic RF-84F Thunderflash	PV	EB+344	56
Sikorsky S-58 (Choctaw H-34G)	PV	8034	59
Vertol H-21B Shawnee	PV	8308	57

306/D Mercedes-Benz Museum Mercedesstrasse 137a Unterturkheim, 7000 Stuttgart.

	Stat.	Number	Yr.
Klemm L 20	PV	D-1433	c33

GREECE (SX)

318A/SX Polemico Moussio (Hellenic Military Museum) Vasilissis Sofias, Athens 139.

Aircraft Type	Stat.	Number	Yr.
Curtiss SB2C-5 Helldiver	PV	83321	c43
De Havilland D.H.82A Tiger Moth	PV	6776	c36
Farman Biplane (R)	PV		c19
Lockheed T-33A Shooting Star	PV	TR-771	c50
North American AT-6G Texan	PV	32803	c45
North American F-86D Sabre	PV	51-6171	51
Supermarine Spitfire IX	PV	MJ755	c44

HUNGARY (HA)

325/HA Kozlekedesi Museum (Museum of Transport) Varosligeti Koru 11, Budapest 1146.

Aircraft Type	Stat.	Number	Yr.
Aero-Letov L-60 Brigadyr	RA	HA-BRA	58
Alag A-08 Siraly	RA	HA-7017	58
Antonov An-2	PV	HA-MHI	c50
Benes-Mraz M-1C Sokol	RA	HA-REA	47
Beniczky E-31 Esztergom	PV	HA-4000	c50
Beniczky LM-30 Fergeteg	PV	HA-7013	c55
Beniczky M-30 Fergeteg	RA	HA-5147	55
D.F.S. Cinke/Meise	PV	HA-4154	
Douglas DC-3 (Lisunov LI-2)	RA	HA-LIQ	46
Fabian Levente II	RA	HA-LEB	41
Hansa-Brandenburg BI Seria-Loczy	RA	H-MAHE	26
Ilyushin Il-14T	RAC	-001750	c55
Janka Gyongyos 33	PV	C.05-01	33
Junkers F 13	PV	CH-59	21
Lampich-Thorotzkai L-2 Roma	PV	H-MAFD	25
Lloyd LS-1 (prototype)	PV	40.01	14
MEM RSZ-2 U-L-G	RA		78
Moravan Otrokovice A-326 Trener	RA	HA-TRO	58
Rubik F-22 Junious 18 "Laminar"	PV	HA-4141	c50
Rubik R-07B Vocsok	RA	HA-2254	40
Rubik R-08C Pilis	RA	HA-3136	42
Rubik R-08D Pilis	PV	HA-3319	c42
Rubik R-16 Lepke	RA	HA-1039	49
Rubik R-18C Kanya	RA	HA-RUF	49
Rubik R-22 Junius 18	PV	HA-4123	c50
Rubik R-22S Super Futar	PV	HA-4213	c55
Rubik R-25 Mokany	RA	HA-4300	59
Rubik Sportarutermel R-15 Koma	RA	HA-5096	50
Samu-Geonczy SG 2 Kek Madar	RA	I-004	48
Yakovlev Yak-18	PV	HA-FAA	c50
Zsebo-Bohn Z-03 Ifjusag	RA	HA-5211	52
Zselyi Aladar 2/1910 (R)	PV		10

257

326A/HA MEM Repuloges Szolgalat (Agricultural Ministry Collection) RSz2040 Budaors, Farkashegy (1) RSz7401 Kaposuijlak, Repuloter (2)

Aircraft Type	Stat.	Number	Yr.
Aero 45	RA	HA-RED	54
Aero Super 45	RA1	HA-OMD	c60
Alag A-08B Siraly II	RA	HA-7018	59
Antonov An-2M	RA1	HA-ANF	c55
Antonov An-2M	RA1	HA-MMG	c55
Beniczky E-31 Esztergom	RA1	HA-3421	c50
Beniczky E-31 Esztergom	RA1	HA-7021	c50
Beniczky-Vertes M-30S Super Ferg.	RA	HA-7013	56
D.F.S. 108-70 Meise	RA1	HA-4155	c47
Gerle 13	RAC1	HA-AAI	c30
LET L-200D Morava	RA2	HA-LDC	c62
Mikoyan-Gurevich MiG-15	RA2	1974	c54
Mikoyan-Gurevich MiG-19	RA2	1978	c60
P.Z.L.101A Gawron	RA1	HA-PZT	c60
P.Z.L.101A Gawron	RA1	HA-PXT	c60
P.Z.L.101A Gawron	RA2	HA-PZJ	c60
Polikarpov Po-2	RA	HA-PAO	c40
Rubik R-07B Vocsok	RAA1	HA-2336	c40
Rubik R-08D Pilis	RAA1	HA-3319	c42
Rubik R-11B Cimbora	RAA1	HA-5035	
Rubik R-15F Fem Koma	S	HA-5300	
Rubik R-16 Lepke	RA1	HA-1308	c49
Rubik R-18 Kanya	RA	HA-RUG	54
Rubik R-22 Futar	RA1		c50
Rubik R-22S Junius 18	RA1	HA-4112	c50
Rubik R-22S Junius 18	RA1	HA-4208	c50
Rubik R-22S Junius 18	RA1	HA-4141	c50
Rubik R-22S Super Futar C	RA1	HA-4212	c55
Rubik R-25 Mokany	RA1	HA-3333	c59
Rubik R-26 Gobe	RA1	HA-5302	
Yakovlev Yak-18	RA2	12	c50
Yakovlev Yak-18	RA1		c50
Zlin Z.226 Trener	RA2	HA-TRG	c55
Zlin Z.226 Trener	RA1	HA-TRM	c55
Zlin Z.526 Trener Master	RA1	HA-SAF	

IRELAND (EI)

349A/EI Irish Aviation Museum C/O Air Lingus, Dublin Airport, Dublin.

Aircraft Type	Stat.	Number	Yr.
Avro 652A Anson	RA	141	c42
De Havilland D.H.84 Dragon	PVX	EI-ABI	c39
De Havilland D.H.115 Vampire T.11	RA	191	c56
Miles M.14A Magister	RA	34	c40
Miles M.75 Aries	RA	G-AOGA	
Vickers 803 Viscount	PV	EI-AOH	c56

ITALY (I)

350/I Museo Storico di Bari (Bari Historical Museum) Largo Urbano 11, Bari.

Aircraft Type	Stat.	Number	Yr.
Lohner TE (flying boat)	RA	L127	17

352/I Museo del Genio (Museum of Military Transport) Piazzale Maresciallo Giardino, Rome.

Aircraft Type	Stat.	Number	Yr.
Bleriot XI Monoplane	RA	412	

353/I Museo Storico dell'Aeronautica Militaire (Military Aviation History Museum) Aeroporto di Vigna di Valle, 00062, Vigna di Valle.

Aircraft Type	Stat.	Number	Yr.
Aer Lualdi L.59	PV	MM576	59
Aerfer Ariete	PV	MM569	53
Aerfer Sagittario II	PV	MM561	53
Aliante S.I.A.I. 3V1 Eolo (glider)	PV	I-BIGI	
Ambrosini Supersette	PV	MM558	50
Ansaldo AC.2	PV	MM1208	25
Ansaldo S.V.A.5	PV	11721	18
Avia F.13	RA	I-ADOD	39
Beech C-45 Expeditor (D-18)	PV	MM61734	c42
Bell AB47G Sioux (Agusta)	PV	MM88113	c59
Bell AB47J Sioux (Agusta)	PV	MM80178	c59
Bell AB102 (Agusta)	PV	I-ECIN	59
Bleriot XI (R)	PV		c13
Bleriot XI-2 (2-seat) (R)	PVX	BL246	c13
C.V.V Canguro (Aero. Lombarda)	PV	MM10028	c50
Cant Z.506S Airone	PV	MM45425	40
Caproni Ca.33	PVX	4166	16
Caproni Ca.100	PV		28
Caproni-Campini CC.1	PV	MM487	40
Caproni-Reggiane Re.2002 Ariete	C	126	42
Caproni-Trento F.5 Sagitario	PV	I-RAIA	51
Crocco-Ricaldoni Idroplano	PV		
Curtiss A1 Triad (R)	PV		c11
D'Ascanio Elicottero D'A.T-3	PV		30
De Bernardi MdB.01 Aeroscooter	PV	I-REDI	58
De Havilland D.H.100 Vampire	C	MM105	c50
De Havilland D.H.113 Vampire	PV	MM6152	55
Douglas DC-3 (C-47 Dakota)	PV	MM61894	c44
Fairchild C-119J Flying Boxcar	RA		c53
Fairchild F-24 (UC-61K Forwarder)	RA	I-FAMA	37
Fiat C.29	PV	MM130	29
Fiat C.R.32	PV	MM4666	32
Fiat G.46-3B	RA	I-AEHF	48
Fiat G.46-4	RA	MM53292	48
Fiat G.46-4A	PV	MM53283	48
Fiat G.46-4A	RA	I-AELM	48
Fiat G.49-2	PV	I-FIAT	52
Fiat G.59-4A	SD	MM53265	c50
Fiat G.59-4B	RA	MM53772	c53
Fiat G.59-4B	PV	MM53776	53
Fiat G.5bis	PV	I-BFFI	35
Fiat G.80-3B	RA	MM53882	
Fiat G.82	pV	MM53886	58
Fiat G.82	RA	MM53885	c58
Fiat G.82	RA	MM53888	c58
Fiat G.91PAN	PV	MM6250	c64
Fiat G.212CR	PV	MM61804	40
Fiat G.222	PVC	RS-07	
Fiat-Aeritalia G.91Y Yankee	PV	MM580	c66
Fieseler Fi 156	PV		36
Glider (Type unknown)	RA	MM10042	
Grumman HU-16 Albatross	PV	MM50179	c58
Grumman S-2F Tracker	PV	41-6	c60
Hanriot HD-1	PV	515	16
IMAM Ro.43	PV	MM27050	40
Leonardo da Vinci (R) Flying Mach.	PV		
Macchi M.39	PV	MM76	26
Macchi M.67	RAC	MM105	29
Macchi M.416 Instructor	RA	I-AELS	c52
Macchi M.416 Instructor	RA	I-AELI	c52
Macchi M.416 Instructor	PV	I-ALEY	c52
Macchi M.416 Instructor	RA	I-AEPF	c52
Macchi MB 308 Macchino	PV	I-GORI	46

Aircraft Type	Stat.	Number	Yr.
Macchi MB 308 Macchino	RA	I-DONT	46
Macchi MB 323 Bipo	PV	MM554	51
Macchi MC 200 Saetta	PVX	MM7707	39
Macchi MC 202 Folgore	PV	91-3	42
Macchi MC 205V Veltro	X	MM9345	43
Macchi-Castoldi MC 72	PV	MM181	33
Nardi FN.305	RA		
North American AT-6J Harvard IV	PV	MM54097	c53
North American F-86 Sabre (CL13)	PV	MM19792	c55
North American F-86 Sabre (Fiat)	PV	128	c55
North American P-51D Mustang	PV	MM4323	44
Piaggio P.136 (amphibian)	PV	MM80005	50
Piaggio P.136 (amphibian)	RA	MM80078	c50
Piaggio P.136 (amphibian)	RA	MM80083	c50
Piaggio P.150	PV	MM555	52
Piaggio P.166M	PV	MM61874	c60
Piaggio-D'Ascanio PD.3 (R)	PV		
Portobello 1980 (homebuilt)	RA		80
Republic F-84F Thunderstreak	PV	MM5368-	c53
Republic P-47D Thunderbolt	RA	MM4653	43
Republic RF-84F Thunderflash	PV	MM5274-	c52
SAAB 29F Tunnan (J-29F)	PV	FV29543	c54
SAIMAN 202-M	RA	I-SARD	c40
SPAD VII	PV		17
SPAD VII	PV		17
Savoia-Marchetti S.M.56	PV	30	
Savia-Marchetti S.M.79 Sparviero	PVX	MM24327	40
Savoia-Marchetti S.M.82 Marsupiale	PVX	MM61850	40
Stinson L-5 Sentinel	PV	I-AEEU	c42
Supermarine Spitfire IX	RA	MM4084	c44
Weber A.VII Etiopia I	PV		c35
Wright Brothers 1909 (R)	PV		09

354/I   Museo Storico della Motorizzani Militaire (Motorized Army Historical Museum) Via dell'Esercito 86, Rome.

	Stat.	Number	Yr.
Bell 47J-3B Sioux (Augusta)	PV	MM80263	c60
Piper L-21B Super Cub	PV	I-EIJA	c54
Piper PA-18 Super Cub (L-18C)	PV	EI-00	c53

355/I   Museo Aeronautico Caproni di Taliedo (Caproni Aeronautical Museum) Vizzola Ticino (1) Venegono Superiore (2)

	Stat.	Number	Yr.
Ambrosini S.A.I.2	PV1	I-LANC	36
Ansaldo A-1 Balilla	RA1	16552	18
Ansaldo S.V.A.5	RA2	11777	18
Asiago Glider (Aerolombarda)	PV1	I-DASI	38
Asiago Glider (Aerolombarda)	PV1	I-ZUME	c38
Asiago Glider (Aerolombarda)	PV1	I-VERG	c38
Badini Prototype	PV1	proto.	43
Breda Ba 19	RA1	MM70019	32
Bristol-Coanda No.153 (Caproni)	RA1	153	13
Bucker Bu 131 Jungmann	PV1	I-CERM	c35
CAT 20 (glider)	PV1		39
Caproni Ca.1	RA2		10
Caproni Ca.6	PV1		10
Caproni Ca.9	PV1		11
Caproni Ca.18	PV1	231	13
Caproni Ca.20	RA2		14
Caproni Ca.22 Parasol	RA2		13
Caproni Ca.36	RA2	2378	17

Aircraft Type	Stat.	Number	Yr.
Caproni Ca.53 Triplane	PV1		17
Caproni Ca.60 (bow only)	RA1		21
Caproni Ca.100 (floatplane)	PV1	I-DISC	34
Caproni Ca.100 Capronicino	PV1	I-GTAB	34
Caproni Ca.100 Capronicino	PV1	I-BIZZ	37
Caproni Ca.113	PV1	I-MARY	38
Caproni Ca.163 Biplane	PV1	I-WEST	37
Caproni Ca.193	PV1	I-POLD	48
Caproni-Reggiane Re.2000 (partial)	PV1	MM8287	40
Caproni-Reggiane Re.2005	RA2	MM92352	43
De Bernardi MdB.02 Aeroscooter	PV1	I-SELI	61
Fairchild F-24C	PV1	I-GENI	34
Fokker D.VIII (fuselage)	RA2		20
Francis Lombardi F.L.3	PV1	I-AIAE	47
Gabardini 1918 (trainer)	RA2	I-AXIC	18
Gabardini 2 (seaplane)	RA2		13
Gabardini 2 (seaplane)	RA2		13
Macchi M.20 (fuselage)	PV1		23
Macchi MB 308 Macchino	PV1	I-ACSN	50
Mantelli AM-6	PV1		48
North American F-86K Sabre	PV1	538300	c55
Republic F-84G Thunderjet	PV1	27458	58
Republic RC-3 Seabee	PV1	I-SIBI	46
SAIMAN 202	PV1	I-BIOL	38
Savoia-Marchetti S.M.56	PV1	I-AEDA	30
Savoia-Marchetti S.M.80bis	PV1	I-ELIO	34
Savoia-Marchetti S.M.102	PV1	I-AEVO	47
Viberti Musca	PV1	I-DIAN	49
Vizzola II	PV1	I-RENI	38

356/I   Museo Nazionale della Scienza e della Tecnica (National Science and Technology Museum), Via San Vittore 21, 20123 Milano.

	Stat.	Number	Yr.
Aliante Caproni TM2 (glider)	PV	MM511	43
Aliante Zoegling (R)	S		30
Ambrosini Supersette	PV	I-PAIN	51
Bleriot XI (R)	PV		c10
Breda Ba 15	PV		29
Caproni-Campini CC.2 (fuselage)	PVI		40
Cierva C.30 (autogiro)	PV	I-CIER	36
De Havilland D.H.80A Puss Moth	PV	I-FOGL	30
De Havilland D.H.100 Vampire	PV	MM6112	50
Farman (Henri) 1909	PV	I-FARM	09
Frati-Pasotti F.9 Sparviero	PV	I-HAWK	
Junkers J 1 (fuselage)	PVI		18
Macchi MC 205V Veltro	PV	MM92166	43
Magni Vale 37	PV	I-TITI	37
Nardi FN.333 Amphibian (S.I.A.I.)	PV		c55
Nieuport-Macchi Ni.10 (XVIII)	PV	I-BORA	10
North American AT-6 Texan	PV	MM54114	50
North American F-86K Sabre	PV	M554812	c53
Republic F-84F Thunderstreak	PV	M536805	53
Ricci 6 Triplane (R)	PV		19
SAIMAN 202-M	PV	I-CUPI	c40
Savoia-Marchetti S.M.102	PV	I-GION	48

357/I   Museo Storico Italiano della Guerra (Italian War History Museum) Castello di Rovereto Via Castelbarço 7, Rovereto.

	Stat.	Number	Yr.
Nieuport-Macchi Ni.10 Biposto	PV	13469	16

357A/I Museo Vittoriale di Gardone Vittoriale degli Italiani 25083 Gardone Riviera.

Aircraft Type	Stat.	Number	Yr.
Ansaldo S.V.A.5	PV		18

357B/I Museo del Risorgimento di Bergamo Citta Bergamo.

Aircraft Type	Stat.	Number	Yr.
Ansaldo A-1 Balilla	PV	16553	18

357C/I Museo Baracca Castello di Lugo di Romagna, Romagna.

Aircraft Type	Stat.	Number	Yr.
SPAD VII	PV		17

MALTA (VPM)

360A/VP National War Museum, Drill Hall, Saint Elmo, Valletta.

Aircraft Type	Stat.	Number	Yr.
Gloster Sea Gladiator (Faith)	PVI	N5520	c40
Junkers Ju 87 Stuka	PVD	16970	c40
Messerschmitt Bf 109F	PVD		c40
Supermarine Spitfire VC	PVD		c40

NETHERLANDS (PH)

410/PH Aviodome, Schiphol Centrum, 1118A, Amsterdam.

Aircraft Type	Stat.	Number	Yr.
Auster J/1 Autocrat	PV	PH-NFH	46
Bensen B-6 (gyro-glider)	PV		54
Bleriot XI	PV	54	09
Cierva C.30A (autogyro)	PV	SE-AF1	c34
De Havilland D.H.82A Tiger Moth	PV	A-38	c36
De Havilland D.H.104 Dove	PVX	PH-MAD	55
Douglas DC-3 (C-47 Dakota)	PV	PH-PBA	c44
Fokker C.V-D	PVX	684	26
Fokker Dr.I Triplane (R)	PV		c17
Fokker F.VIIA	PVX	H-NACT	28
Fokker S.11 Instructor	RA	E-9	50
Fokker S.11 Instructor	PV	E-24	50
Fokker S.12	RA	PH-NDC	49
Fokker S.14 Mach-Trainer	PV	PH-XIV	51
Fokker Spinne (R)	PV		11
Gloster G.41 Meteor F. MK.8	PV	I-189	52
Grumman S-2H Tracker	PV	159	60
Hawker Hunter F.Mk 51	PVX	E-410	56
Hawker Sea Fury FB.51	PV	6-43	51
Hawker Sea Hawk Mk.50	PVX	118	c54
Lilienthal Glider (R)	PV		93
Mignet HM-14 Pou Du Ciel	PV	G-AEOF	36
Mignet HM-14 Pou du Ciel	PVX	G-AEOF	36
Ned. Helicopter Ind. H.3 Kolibri	PV	PH-NHI	57
North American AT-6 Harvard 11B	PVX	B-182	c44
Piper L-4J Grasshopper	PV	PH-NLA	45
R.R.G. Pander (Zogling glider) (R)	PVX	PH-1	29
Rienks (Gyroglider)	PV		56
SAAB 91D Safir	PV	PH-RLN	59
Schleicher Rhonlerche	S	PH-251	59
Schneider Grunau Baby (glider)	S	PH-170	47
Sikorsky S-55 (Chickasaw HO4S-3)	PV	076	53
Snellen V-20 (glider)	RA	PH-90	38

Aircraft Type	Stat.	Number	Yr.
Supermarine Spitfire Mk.IXC	PVX	MJ271	43
Vertol HUP-2 Retriever	PVX	130082	54
Wright Brothers Flyer 1903 (R)	PV		03

411A/PH Nationaal Automobiel Museum Steurweg 8, Raamsdonksveer.

Aircraft Type	Stat.	Number	Yr.
Koolhoven F.K.43	PV	PH-NAK	47

415/PH Militaire Luchtvaart Museum (Military Aviation Museum) Kamp von Zeist, 3769 ZK, Soesterberg.

Aircraft Type	Stat.	Number	Yr.
Auster A.O.P.3 Mk.II	PV	MZ-236	c40
Auster A.O.P.5 Mk.V	RA	PH-NET	c44
Avro 652A Anson	PVX	VM-352	c46
Beech AT-7 Kansas (D-18S)	PV	PH-UDT	c40
Consolidated PBY-5A Catalina	C	16-212	c43
De Havilland D.H.82A Tiger Moth	PV	A-10	35
De Havilland D.H.89A Dominie	PV	NF-869	c37
De Havilland DHC-2 Beaver	PV	S-9	c50
Douglas DC-3 (C-47A Skytrain)	PV	ZU-5	c44
Farman (Maurice) Shorthorn F.II(R)	S	2880	18
Fokker S.11 Instructor	PV	E-22	c50
Fokker S.14 Mach Trainer	PV	L-11	c52
Fokker S.14 Mach Trainer	PV	L-17	c52
Gloster G.41 Meteor F. Mk.4	PV	VZ-409	c50
Gloster G.41 Meteor F. Mk.7	PV	WH-233	c50
Grumman S-2A Tracker	PV	160	c55
Hawker Hunter F.Mk.6	S	N-258	c55
Hawker Hunter F.Mk.6	PV	M-226	c55
Hawker Hunter Mk.4	RA	N-122	c55
Hawker Hunter Mk.4	RA	N-144	c55
Hawker Hunter Mk.7	PV	N-305	c55
Hiller OH-23C Raven	PV	OH-12A	c60
Lockheed 12A Electra	PV	L2-38	c37
Lockheed SP-2H Neptune	PV	201	c60
Lockheed T-33A Shooting Star	PV	M-5	c50
North American AT-6 (Noorduyn)	PV	B-184	c44
North American AT-6 (Noorduyn)	RA	B-64	c44
North American AT-6 Harvard	RA	B-71	c44
North American AT-6 Harvard	RA	B-177	c44
North American B-25J Mitchell	PV	M-464	c44
North American F-86F Sabre	PV	FU-385	c53
North American F-86F Sabre	RA	53-1206	c53
North American F-86K Sabre	PVX	Q-305	54
North American P-51K Mustang	PV	H-307	c45
Piper L-18C Super Cub	RA	R-87	c53
Piper L-21A Super Cub	RA	R-0213	c53
Republic F-84F Thunderstreak	PV	P-230	c53
Republic F-84G Thunderjet	PV	MU-L	c55
Supermarine Spitfire Mk.XI		A-ZB	43

416A/PH Nederlands Nationaal Oorlogs en Verzetsmuseum (Netherlands National War and Resistance Museum), Museumpark 1, 58225AM Overloon.

Aircraft Type	Stat.	Number	Yr.
Fieseler Fi 103	PV		c41
North American AT-6 Texan	PV	FT-223	c42
North American B-25D Mitchell	PV	FR193	c44
Supermarine Spitfire PR.XI	PV	PL965	c42

NORWAY (LN)

440/LN   Norsk Teknisk Museum (Norwegian Technical Museum) Fyrstikkaleen 1, Etterstad, Oslo.

Aircraft Type	Stat.	Number	Yr.
Bleriot "Jul Hansen" (R)	S		10
Bleriot XI "Nordsjoen"	PV	218	14
De Havilland D.H.100 Vampire T.55	PV	Fv28456	c50
Farman (Maurice) Longhorn MF.7	RA	16	13
Grumman G-44 Widgeon	RA	LN-HAL	43
Lockheed TF-104G Starfighter	PV	469	c64
Loening C-2C "Leiv Eiriksson"	RA	LN-BAH	33
Miles M.65 Gemini 1A	RA	LN-TAH	c47
Rumpler Taube	PV	"START"	12
Sud-Aviation SE-210 Caravelle	RA	LN-KLH	59

440A/LN   Kongelige Norsk Luftforsvaret (Royal Norwegian Air Force Collection) Gardermoen Lufthavn. (A/c located at a number of sites.)

Avro 504K	RA	103	c18
Bell 204 (UH-1B)	RA	995	c62
Bell 47D-1	PV	BE-D	c49
D.F.S. 108-14 Schulgleiter S.G.38	RA	LN-GBM	c45
De Havilland D.H.82A Tiger Moth	PV	N6972	c36
De Havilland D.H.100 Vampire F.3	PV	P42408	c48
Douglas DC-3 (C-47A)	PV	93797	c44
Fairchild PT-19 Cornell	PV	103	c40
Fairchild PT-26 Cornell	PV	L-DM	c44
Farman F.46	PV		25
Fieseler Fi 103	RA		c40
Focke-Wulf Fw 190	RA	931862	c43
Fokker C.V-D	PV	349	c30
Gloster Gladiator II	PV	N5641	c38
Haerens Flyvemaskinfabrik FF9	RA		33
Heinkel He 111P-1	PV	5J+CN	c41
Henschel Hs 293	RA	21816	
Junkers Ju 52/3m	RA	CA+JY	c40
Junkers Ju 88	RAC		c40
Kjolseth P.K. X-1	PV	1	
Lockheed F-104G Starfighter	RA	870	c64
Lockheed F-104G Starfighter	RA	104	c64
Lockheed F-104G Starfighter	PV	801	c64
Lockheed T-33A Shooting Star	PV	117546	51
Lockheed T-33A Shooting Star	RA	51-6571	51
Noorduyn Norseman IV	PV	R-AV	c40
North American AT-6J Texan	RA	M-BS	c53
North American F-86F Sabre	RA	31082	c53
North American F-86F Sabre	RA	25202	c53
North American F-86F Sabre	RA	Several	c53
North American F-86F Sabre	RA	25069	c53
North American F-86K Sabre	RA	Several	c55
Northrop F-5A	PV	905	c65
Northrop F-5A	RA	Several	c65
Northrop N-3PB (seaplane fighter)	PV	20	40
Piper PA-18 Super Cub	PV	53-4845	c57
Republic F-84G Thunderjet	RA	Several	52
Republic F-84G Thunderjet	PV	52-2912	52
Republic RF-84F Thunderflash	Ra	Several	51
Republic RF-84F Thunderflash	PV	5117053	51
Royal Aircraft Factory B.E.2e	PV	131	c16
SAAB 91B Safir	RA	Several	c56
SAAB 91B Safir	PV	57-333	c56
Supermarine Spitfire L.F.IX	RA	MH350	c44
Supermarine Spitfire PR.XI	PV	PL979	c45

440B/LN   Forsvarsmuseet (National War Museum) Akershus, Oslo.

Aircraft Type	Stat.	Number	Yr.
De Havilland D.H.82 Tiger Moth	PV	151	c40
De Havilland D.H.100 Vampire FB.52	PV	VO-184	c53
Henschel Hs 293	PV	21816	
SAAB 91B Safir	PV	53-058	c53
Supermarine Spitfire L.F.X	PV	MH350	c44

POLAND (SP)

480/SP   Muzeum Wojska Polskiego (Polish Army Museum) Palac Kultury i Nauki, Warsaw.

Ilyushin Il-2 Stormovik	PV		40
Ilyushin Il-10	PV		44
Ilyushin Il-28	PV		49
LIM-1 (MiG-15)	PV		52
Mikoyan-Gurevich MiG-15	PV		54
Petlyakov Pe-2 Peszka	PV		40
Tupolev Tu-2	PV		42
Yakovlev Yak-9P	PV		47
Yakovlev Yak-23	PV		51

485/SP   Muzeum Lotnictwa i Astronautyki (National Air and Space Museum) Rakowice Airport, 30-969 Krakow 28.

A.E.G. E.II	RA		14
Aero 45-S	PV	SP-LXC	56
Aero 145	PV	SP-TNA	59
Aero 145	PV	SP-LXH	59
Aero L-60 Brigadyr	PV	SP-FXA	c58
Albatros B.IIA	RA	NG+UR	c16
Albatros C.I	RA	197/15	15
Albatros H.1 (Siemens-Sch. D.IV)	RA	10114	24
Albatros L.101	RA	D-EKY.Q	
Aviatik C.III	RA	1996	17
Bleriot XI "La Manche" (R)	PV		09
Bucker Bu 131 Jungmann	PV	SP-AFO	c35
C.S.S. 12 (cockpit only)	D	SP-BAR	c51
C.S.S. 13 (Polikarpov Po-2)	PV	SP-AXT	c51
C.S.S. 13 (Polikarpov Po-2)	PV	SP-API	c51
C.S.S. 13 (armed version)	PV	SP-ANB	c51
Cessna T-50 Bobcat (UC-78)	PV	SP-GLC	c42
Curtiss Hawk II(Udet '36 Olympics)	S	D-3165	c32
D.F.W. C.V	S	17077	17
Farman IV (Russian version) (R)	PV		c17
Fokker Spinne	RAD		11
Geest Mowe (Moewe)	S		
Grigorovitch M.15 (flying boat)	S		17
Heinkel He 5E (floatplane)	S	D-1	c25
I.L. BZ-1 Gil (prototype)	S	SP-GIL	
I.L. BZ-4 Zuk (prototype)	S		
I.L. JK-1 Trzmiel	PV	2	
I.L. TS-8 Bies	PV	0309	c56
I.L. TS-8 Bies (prototype)	S	P.1	55
I.L. TS-11 Iskra (prototype)	S	4	61
Ilyushin Il-10 (Avia built B-33)	PV	3061	c44
Ilyushin Il-28	S	S-3	c50

261

Aircraft Type	Stat.	Number	Yr.
Ilyushin Il-28R	S	72	c50
Jeannin Stahltaube	S	A118	
L.V.G. B.II	S	18	
L.W.D. Junak-1 (prototype)	S	SP-GLA	48
L.W.D. Junak-2	PV	SP-ADM	c52
L.W.D. Junak-3	PV	SP-BPL	c54
L.W.D. Szpak-2 (prototype)	S	SP-AAA	45
L.W.D. Szpak-3 (prototype)	S	SP-AAB	47
L.W.D. Szpak-4T	PV	SP-AAG	c48
L.W.D. Zak-3	PV	SP-AAX	c48
L.W.D. Zuch-1	S	SP-BAD	
L.W.D. Zuch-2	PV	SP-BAM	
L.W.D. Zuch-2	S	SP-BAO	
L.W.D. Zuraw (prototype)	S	SP-GLB	
LIM-1 (MiG-15, Polish A/F Colors)	PV	712	c54
Lavavasseur Antoinette	S		09
Messerschmitt Me 209V-1 (spd recd)	SI	D-INJR	c39
Mikoyan-Gurevich MiG-19PM	PV	905	c60
Mil Mi-1 (Polish WSK SM-1)	PV	SP-SAD	c55
Mil Mi-1 (Polish WSK SM-1)	PV	SP-SXD	c55
Mil SM-2 helicopter (Polish)	S	SP-SAP	c60
P.W.S. 26	PV	SP-AJB	
P.Z.L. M-4 Tarpan	PV	SP-PAK	64
P.Z.L. MD-12F (Photo-survey)	PV	SP-PBL	62
P.Z.L. P.11C	PV	562	c34
P.Z.L. S-4 (Kania 3)	PV	SP-PBB	58
Pegaz (powered glider)	PV	SP-590	
Piper J-3 Cub	PV	SP-AFB	c46
Piper J-3 Cub	S	SP-BAL	c46
Polikarpov Po-2	S	SP-ADE	44
Polikarpov Po-2	S	641-646	c40
R.W.D. 13	PV	SP-ARL	c35
R.W.D. 21 (ex-Rumanian A/F)	S	SP-AKG	
Roland D.VI (L.F.G.)	S	2225/18	18
Sopwith Camel F.1	S	B7280	18
Staaken R.IV (nacelle only)	SI	R-30/16	c16
Stinson L-5 Sentinel	S	98643	42
Supermarine Spitfire Mk.XV	PV	SM411	c43
Tupolev Tu-2	PV		c42
W.S.K. M-15 Belphegor	PV	1S00601	
Yakovlev Yak-11	PV	64236	c52
Yakovlev Yak-12	PV	SP-ASZ	c45
Yakovlev Yak-17	PV		c48
Yakovlev Yak-18	PV	SP-AOP	c50
Yakovlev Yak-18	S	SP-APR	c50
Yakovlev Yak-18	S	SP-BRI	c50
Yakovlev Yak-18	S	SP-AOU	c50
Yakovlev Yak-23	PV		c50
Zlin Z.26 Trener	S	SP-ARM	c48

486/SP Muzeum Techniki Nacelnej Organizacji Technicznej (Polytechnic and Science Museum) Palac Kultury i Nauki, Warsaw.

L.W.D. Junak 3	PV	9436	c54
Lilienthal Glider	PV		c95
Santos-Dumont Demoiselle (R)	PV		c08
Tanskiego (glider) (R)	PV		

486A/SP Muzeum Marynarki Wojennej (Naval Military Museum) Bulwar Szwedzki, Gdynia.

Ilyushin Il-28R	PV	41302	c50
Mikoyan-Gurevich MiG-17P	PV	926	

Aircraft Type	Stat.	Number	Yr.
Mil Mi-4A	PV	021	c56
Yakovlev Yak-9P	PV		

PORTUGAL (CS)

490/CS Museo do Ar (National Air Force Museum) Alverca do Ribatejo 2615, Alverca.

Amiot AAC-1 Toucan	RA	6311	46
Amiot AAC-1 Toucan	RA	6315	46
Auster D5/160 Husky	PV	3564	63
Auster D5/160 Husky	RAA	3548	63
Avro 631 Cadet	RA	501	34
Beech AT-11 Kansas	RA	2504	47
Beech C-45 Expeditor (D-18)	RA	2515	c42
Beech C-45H Expeditor	RA	2513	47
Beech C-45H Expeditor (parts)	RA	2517	c47
Caudron G.3 (R)	PV		c14
Cid Varela Hydro	RAD		34
D.F.S. Kranich (glider)	RA	CS-PAD	c43
D.F.S. Weihe (glider)	RA	CS-PAF	c50
De Havilland D.H.82 Tiger Moth	RAA	CS-AEF	34
De Havilland D.H.82 Tiger Moth	RA	CS-AEL	c36
De Havilland D.H.82A Tiger Moth	PV	111	38
De Havilland D.H.87B Hornet Moth	RA	CR-AAC	c38
De Havilland D.H.89A Dragon Rapide	RA	CS-ADI	39
De Havilland D.H.100 Vampire	RA	5801	50
Dornier Do 27A-1	RAA	3358	58
Dornier Do 27A-4	RA	3487	c60
Dornier Do 27A-4	RA	3489	51
Douglas A-26 Invader (B-26)(parts)	RAI	7104	c44
Douglas DC-3 (C-47A Dakota)	RA	6157	43
Douglas DC-4 (C-54 Skymaster)	RA	6606	41
Douglas DC-6B Liftmaster	RA	6706	c48
Fairey IIID "Santa Cruz" (R)	PV	17	22
Farman (Maurice) Longhorn (R)	PV	12	c15
Grumman G-44 Widgeon	PV	129	42
J.V. (Le Cerf Aero-Kite)	PV		13
Junkers Ju 52/3m	RA	6311	c40
Junkers Ju 52/3m	RA	6300	c40
Junkers Ju 52/3m	RA	6306	c40
Junkers Ju 52/3m	RA	6301	c40
Junkers Ju 52/3m	RA	6309	c40
Lockheed P2V-5 Neptune	RA	4711	51
Lockheed PV-2 Harpoon	RAC	620	c44
Lockheed T-33 Silver Star (Can)	RA	1951	48
Max Holste M.H.1521M (parts)	RAI	3303	c55
Max Holste M.H.1521M Broussard	RAA	3304	c55
Max Holste M.H.1521M Broussard	RA	3301	c55
Nord N.2501D Noratlas	RA	6420	59
Nord N.2501D Noratlas (parts)	RAI	6417	c60
Nord N.2502A Noratlas	RA	6403	c60
Nord N.2502F Noratlas	RA	6412	62
North American AT-6 Harvard II	RA	1546	c44
North American AT-6 Harvard III	RA	1662	42
North American AT-6J Harvard IV	RAA	1774	52
North American AT-6J Harvard IV	RAA	1769	52
North American AT-6J Harvard IV	RA	1737	c53
North American F-86F Sabre	RA	5360	53
North American F-86F Sabre	RA	5320	52
North American F-86F Sabre	RA	5347	52
North American F-86F Sabre	RA	5337	52
North American F-86F Sabre	RA	5333	52
North American F-86F Sabre	RA	5338	52
North American F-86F Sabre	RA	5361	53

Aircraft Type	Stat.	Number	Yr.
Oliveira, Rolando Nikus Miniplane	PV		74
Piper J-3 Cub	RA	CS-ABY	46
Piper L-18C Super Cub 95	RA	CS-ALQ	52
Piper L-21B Super Cub 135	PV	3212	54
Piper L-21B Super Cub 135	RAA	3218	54
Piper PA-12 Super Cruiser	RA	CS-ADW	46
R.R.G. (Zogling sailplane)	RA		36
Republic F-84G Thunderjet	RA	5187	51
Republic F-84G Thunderjet	RA	5216	51
Republic F-84G Thunderjet (parts)	RAI	5176	c55
Santos-Dumont XX Demoiselle (R)	PV		72
Schneider Grunau Baby IIB (glider)	PV	CS-PAE	41
Schneider Grunau Baby IIB (glider)	RA	CS-PAA	c40
Schneider Grunau S.G.38 (glider)	PV	PE-1	c40
Schneider Grunau S.G.38 (glider)	RA	PE-2	c40
Sikorsky S-55 (Chickasaw)	RA	57-5979	58
Sikorsky S-55 (Chickasaw)	SI	9101	51

493/CS Museo de Marinha (National Maritime Museum) Prado do Imperio 15, 1480 Lisbon.

Aircraft Type	Stat.	Number	Yr.
Fairey IIID "Santa Cruz"	PV	17	22
Grumman G-44 Widgeon	PV	128	40
Schreck FBA B	PV	2	c15

ROMANIA (YR)

495A/YR Muzeil Militar Central (Central Military Museum) Str. Izvor 137, Sectorul 5, Bucharest.

Aircraft Type	Stat.	Number	Yr.
Fleet 10G	PV	351	c38
I.A.R.813	PV	74	
Ilyushin Il-10	PV	49	c44
Lavochkin La-9	PV	66	c45
Mil Mi-4	PV	127	c55
Nardi FN-305	PV	87	
S.102 (Czech. MiG-15UTI)	PV	246	c50
Vliacu II (R)	PV		
Vuia 1 (R)	PV	1	c06
Yakovlev Yak-11	PV	47	c52
Yakovlev Yak-18	PV	38	c50
Yakovlev Yak-23	PV	52	c50

495B/YR Muzeil Tehnic 'Professor Inginer Dimitrie Leonica' (Professor Leonida Technical Museum) Str. Candiano Popescu 2, Sectoral 5, Bucharest.

Aircraft Type	Stat.	Number	Yr.
Bucker Bu 133C Jungmeister	PV	YR-AMH	c36
Cil Reghin RG 4 Pioneerter	PV		
I.A.R.813	PV	YR-IBB	
I.A.R.817	PV	YR-ASB	c56
Silimon IS 28	PV	YR-1002	
Silimon IS 29D	PV	YR-185	
Silimon IS 30	PV	YR-941	

SPAIN (EC)

520/EC Museo de Aeronautica y Astronautica Carretera de Extremadura km 10.500 Cuatra Vientos.

Aircraft Type	Stat.	Number	Yr.
AISA I-11B	PV	EC-BLD	56
AISA I-11B	PV	EC-AKL	55
AISA I-115	PV	E-9-119	56
Aerotecnica AC-12	PV	Z.2-11	59
Aerotecnica AC-12	PV	Z.2-7	59
Aerotecnica AC-14	PV	Z.4-6	58
Bell 47J-3B Sioux (Agusta)	PV	HD.11-1	58
Bleriot XI "Vilanova-Acedo" (R)	PV		11
Breguet 19TR "Jesus Del Grand"	PV	12-72	28
Bucker Bu 131B Jungmann	PV	E-3B198	44
Bucker Bu 133C Jungmeister	PV	E-1-14	38
CASA C-207C Azor	PV	T.7-17	62
Cessna L-19A Bird Dog (0-1A)	PV	L.12-2	51
Cierva C.19 MkIV autogyro-Avro	PV	EC-AIM	32
D.F.S. Kranich III (glider)	PV	EC-ODK	51
D.F.S. Weihe (glider) (AISA)	PV	EC-RAB	50
De Havilland D.H.60G Moth Major	PV	EC-AFQ	31
De Havilland D.H.89 Dragon Rapide	PV	G-ACYR	35
Dornier Do 24T-3 Hydroavion	PV	HD.5-2	40
Dornier Do 28A-1	PV	U.14-1	59
Douglas DC-3 (C-47B Dakota)	PV	T.3-36	45
Douglas DC-4 (C-54A Skymaster)	PV	T.4-10	42
Fiat C.R.32 Chirri (H.A.132L) (R)	PV	31-2	39
Grumman HU-16E Albatros	PV	AD-1B-8	58
Gurripato II (Glider)	PV		59
Heinkel He 111 (CASA 2111)	PV	T-8B-97	51
Heinkel He 111E-3	PV	B.2-82	38
Hispano Aviacion Ha.200 Supersaeta	PV	20-110	68
Hispano Aviacion Ha.200R Saeta	PV	XE.14-2	55
Hispano Suiza H.S.34	PV	EC-AFJ	42
Huarte-Mendicoa H.M.1-B	PV	E.4-161	52
Junkers Ju 52/3m (CASA 352)	PV	T.2B211	42
Junkers Ju 52/3m (CASA 352)	PV	T.2B254	42
Messerschmitt Bf 109 (HA.1112)	PV	C4J-10	52
Messerschmitt Bf 109 (HA.1112)	PV	C4K-158	54
Morane-Saulnier MS.733 Alcyon	PV	F-BMMS	56
North American AT-6 Texan	PV	C-6-155	57
North American F-86F Sabre	PV	C-5-71	48
North American F-86F Sabre	PV	C-5-58	48
North American F-86F Sabre	PV	C-5-223	48
Schneider Grunau Baby IIB (AISA)	PV	EC-MFG	42
Schneider Grunau S.G.38 (glider)	PV	EC-MFG	41
Sikorsky S-55 (Westland Whirlwind)	PV	ZD.1B22	55
Zwergreiher Lo-100 (glider)	A	EC-OCI	52

SWEDEN (SE)

541/SE Luftfartmuseet (National Aviation Museum) Stiftelsen Luft-och Rymdartmuseet, Museivagen 7, S115 27, Stockholm. (A/c in store at Arlanda and other.)

Aircraft Type	Stat.	Number	Yr.
Albatros NAB 9	RAD3		
Auster A.O.P.5	RA3	SE-BZR	c44
Auster Mk.V	RA	SE-CBT	c45
Avro 594 Avian	RA	SE-ADT	c28
Beda Flying Boat	RA3		c30
Beech F-50 Twin Bonanza	RA	LN-DBE	c54
Bell 47D-1	RA	SE-HAD	c49
Berger Bo	PVD1		
Bleriot XI (R)	RA3		c10
Bucker Bu 131B Jungmann	RA	SE-AGU	38
Cessna F-172G Skyhawk (Reims)	RAD1	SE-ESL	c64
Convair CV-440 (Cockpit)	RA	SE-BSU	c53
D.F.S. 108-14 Schulgleiter S.G.38	RA3	138	c45

Aircraft Type	Stat.	Number	Yr.
D.F.S. 108-70 Meise	S1	SE-SGF	c47
D.F.S. Kranich (glider)	RA	SE-SCC	43
D.F.S. Weihe	RA	SE-SNK	c43
D.F.S. Weihe	RA	SE-SND	c43
De Havilland D.H.60 Moth Major III	RA	SE-AGF	35
Douglas AD-4W Skyraider	RA1	SE-EBB	c52
Douglas DC-3 (C-47A)	RA	4224049	42
Fairchild F-24 R46A	RA	SE-BXE	c40
Fairey Firefly Mk.1	RA	DT989	44
Focke-Wulf Fw 44J Stieglitz	RA	SE-BWX	40
Goetaverken GV-38 (Rearwin)	RA	SE-AHG	38
Hutter Hu 17A (sailplane)	RA3	LN-GBD	c42
Junkers Ju 52/3m (cockpit)	RAI	SE-ADR	c40
Junkers W 34	PV	SE-BYA	30
Klemm Kl 34D	RAC3	SE-BGA	c41
Kockum Baby Falke	S1	SE-SGO	
Lockheed 18-56 Lodestar	RA	SE-BZE	43
MFH Junior (homebuilt)	RAC3	F-AHLE	
Malmo Flygindustri MFI-9B Junior	SD2	SE-EFG	c60
Malmo Flygindustri MFI-9B Trainer	SD1	SE-EFP	c60
Mignet HM-14 Pou du Ciel	RA		c36
Noorduyn Norseman IV (UC-64)	RAC3	SE-CPB	c42
North American AT-6 (Noorduyn)	RA	16128	c44
North American AT-6 (Noorduyn)	RA	16010	c44
Nyrop No.3 (Bleriot XXI)	PV1		c11
Persson (homebuilt)	S1		
Republic RC-3 Seabee	RA	SE-AXG	c46
Rieseler-Bendel RII/B (prototype)	RA	S-AAR	21
SAAB 10B Vipan	RA	SE-CPI	64
SAAB 35E Draken (J-35E)	PV1	35937	c65
Scheibe 138 Specht	RA3	D-6680	
Scheibe Mu 13 Bergfalke II	RA3	SE-SUA	c50
Schneider Grunau Baby IIB	RA	SE-SFA	c40
Schneider Grunau Baby IIB (glider)	RA	SE-SAZ	41
Schneider Grunau S.G.38 (glider)	RA	21	c40
Siebel Si.204D (Nord N.C.701)	RA	SE-KAL	c46
Siebel Si.204D (Nord N.C.701)	RA	SE-KAE	c46
Sud-Aviation SE-210 Caravelle III	S1	SE-DAF	c60
Svenskt Glider	RA		
Taylor J-2 Cub	RAC3	SE-AGL	c39
Thulin A	PV1		c15
Thulin B (sea version)	PV		15
Thulin G (seaplane biplane)	RA	15	18
Thulin N	PV1		c19
Thulin N Biplane	RA		19
Vertol V-44A (HKP-1)	PV1	01007	c60

542/SE Flygvapenmuseum (Swedish Air Force Museum) Box 13300, S580 13 Linkopping.

Aircraft Type	Stat.	Number	Yr.
Albatros 120 CFM/Sk-1	PV	04(464)	25
Bucker Bu 181B Bestmann/Sk-25	PV	D-EXWB	42
Bucker Bu 181B Bestmann/Sk-25	RA	D-EBIH	46
CFM 01 Tummelisa	PV	3656	28
Caproni-Reggiane Re.2000 Falco	PV	2340	42
Commonwealth CA-7 Wirraway	540	A20-233	c42
Consolidated PBY-5A Catalina	RA	47001	43
D.F.S. G.101 Schulgleiter S.G.38	RA	80	
D.F.S. Meise Olympia (glider)	RA	SE-SAE	c59
D.F.S. SE-102 Grunau Baby II	RA	SE-SAP	c47
D.F.S. SE-103 Kranich	RA	SE-SWN	
D.F.S. SE-104 Weihe/A.B.Flygind.	RA	8316	43
De Havilland D.H.60T Trainer Moth	PV	SE-BFI	31
De Havilland D.H.82A Tiger Moth	PV	515	36
De Havilland D.H.100 Vampire	PV	28001	46

Aircraft Type	Stat.	Number	Yr.
De Havilland D.H.100 Vampire	RA	28317	51
De Havilland D.H.100 Vampire	RA	28311	51
De Havilland D.H.112 Venom	RA	33015	53
De Havilland D.H.112 Venom	RA	33025	53
De Havilland D.H.115 Vampire	PV	28451	55
Douglas A-1 Skyraider	RA	WT947	52
Douglas DC-3 (TP79)	RA	79007	44
English Electric Canberra B	RA	52002	60
FFVS J22-1	RA	22185	44
FFVS J22-2	PV	22280	45
Fairey Firefly Mk.1	PV	PP392	c44
Fiat C.R.42 Falco/J11	PV	2543	41
Fieseler Fi 156 Storch	PV	3812	c42
Focke-Wulf Fw 44J Stieglitz	PV	SE-EGB	41
Fokker C.V-E	RA	386	34
GH Racer (homebuilt)	PV		37
Gloster G.41 Meteor T.7	RA	WF833	51
Gloster Gladiator	PV	278	38
Hawker Hart	PV	714	37
Hawker Hunter Mk.4/J.34	PV	34016	c55
Hawker Hunter Mk.50	RA	3406	56
Hughes 29-6A HKP5A	RA	05215	c65
Hunting-Percival P.66 Pembroke	RA	83008	55
Junkers Ju 86K-4	RA	155	38
Klemm Kl 35B SK15A	PV	SE-AIG	39
MFI-10B Vipan/FPL-54	RA	54382	63
MFI-15 Supporter (prototype)	PV	SE-XCB	69
MFI-9B Mili-Trainer	PV	801-42	66
Macchi-Nieuport M.7 Flying Boat	PV	945	19
Mignet HM-14 Pou du Ciel	PV		c36
Nieuport IV-G Monoplane	PV	M-1	12
Noorduyn Norseman VI (UC-64A)	RA	4335418	43
North American AT-6 Harvard II	PV	16109	47
North American P-51D Mustang	PV	4463992	44
Phoenix D.III J1	RA	947	19
Piper L-21B Super Cub 150	RA	SE-CKH	59
Raab-Katzenstein RK26	PV	536	34
SAAB 17A (B-17A)	RA	17239	42
SAAB 17B (S-17B)	RA	17005	42
SAAB 18B (B-18B)	RAC	18172	
SAAB 21A-3 (J-21A)	RA	21286	47
SAAB 21A-3 (J-21A)	RA	21311	48
SAAB 21A-3 (J-21A)	PV	21364	48
SAAB 22A (J-22A)	C	22185	44
SAAB 29A (J-29A)	RA	29171	52
SAAB 29B (J-29B)	PV	29398	53
SAAB 29C (S-29C)	RA	29970	66
SAAB 29F (J-29F)	RA	29575	c54
SAAB 29F (J-29F)	RA	29441	c54
SAAB 29F (J-29F)	RA	29670	55
SAAB 29F (J-29F)	RA	29507	c54
SAAB 32A Lansen (J-32A)	RA	32197	c56
SAAB 32A Lansen (J-32A)	RA	32233	c56
SAAB 32C Lansen (J-32C)	RA	32917	c59
SAAB 35 Draken (prototype J-35)	RA	35-5	c59
SAAB 35A Draken (J-35A)	RA	35221	62
SAAB 35A Draken (J-35A)	RA	35051	c62
SAAB 35B Draken (J-35B)	RA		c63
SAAB 35E Draken (J-35E)	RA	35906	c65
SAAB 37 Viggen (prototype AJ-37)	RA		67
SAAB 91A Safir	RA	SE-AYZ	46
SAAB 105 (prototype)	PV	SE-XBZ	
SAAB 210 Lill-Draken	PV		51
Seversky EP-106 (J.9)	PV	2134	40
Siebel Si.204D (Nord N.C.701)	RA	SE-KAE	c46
Sparman S1A P1	PV	814	37
Supermarine Spitfire Mk.XIX	RA	31051	45

Aircraft Type	Stat.	Number	Yr.
Soldenhoff S-5 (Tailless)	PV		35
Spalinger S-21 (Sailplane)	PV	HB-307	42
Spalinger S-21 (Sailplane)	S	HB-305	45
Stierlin (prototype helicopter)	PV		64
Sud-Aviation SA-316B Alouette	PV	HB-XDF	65

552/HB Museum der Schweizerischen Fliegertruppe (Swiss Air Force Museum) Abteilung der Militarflugplatz, CH-8600 Dubendorf.

Beech D-18S Expeditor (Twin Beech)	RA	HB-GAC	44
Bucker Bu 131B Jungmann	RA	A-43	36
Bucker Bu 131B Jungmann	PV	A-51	36
Bucker Bu 131B Jungmann	RA	A-32	36
Bucker Bu 131B Jungmann (@ Kloten)	PV	A-67	36
Bucker Bu 133C Jungmeister	RA	U-62	36
Bucker Bu 133C Jungmeister	RA	V-63	36
Bucker Bu 133C Jungmeister	PV	U-61	36
Bucker Bu 181B Bestmann	RA	25027	44
Comte AC-4 Gentleman	RA	HB-USI	30
Dassault Mirage IIIC	PV	J-2201	63
De Havilland D.H.100 Vampire Mk.6	RA		c50
De Havilland D.H.100 Vampire Mk.6	PV	J-1049	49
De Havilland D.H.100 Vampire T.11	PV	XD403	c50
De Havilland D.H.112 Venom Mk.1	A		53
De Havilland D.H.112 Venom Mk.1R	RA	J-1642	53
De Havilland D.H.112 Venom Mk.4	A		53
Dewoitine D.26	PV	U-288	31
E.F.W. C-3603-1	PV	C-534	42
E.F.W. N-20 Aiguillon	RA	Exp.	52
Fieseler Fi 156C-3 Storch	PV	A-100	44
Fokker C.V-E (E.K.W.)	PV	C-331	33
Fokker D.VII (R)	PV	640	c18
General Dynamics FFA P-16 Mk.II	PV	HB-VAD	55
Haefeli D.H.1 (semi-R)	PV		19
Haefeli D.H.5	PV	459	23
Hiller UH-12B	C	607	55
Junkers Ju 52/3m	A	A-703	39
Junkers Ju 52/3m	A	A-701	39
Junkers Ju 52/3m	PV	A702	39
Messerschmitt Bf 108B (@ Kloten)	PV	A-201	38
Messerschmitt Bf 108B Taifun	PV	A-209	38
Messerschmitt Bf 109E	PV		40
Morane-Saulnier MS.506	PV	J-276	41
Nieuport 28C-1 Bebe	PV	607	18
Nord N.1203 Norecrin	S	HB-HOI	48
North American AT-6 Harvard	S	U-332	44
North American AT-6 Harvard	PV	U-328	44
Pilatus P-2	S	U-157	48
Pilatus P-2	PV	U-134	48
Pilatus P-2/06	S	V-105	48
Rech Monoplane	S		12
Sud-Ouest SO-1221S Djinn	PV	38FR56	56

TURKEY (TC)

565/TC Turk Hava Kuvvetleri Hava Musesi (Turkish Air Force Museum) Hava Harp Okulu Komutanligi Hava Muzesi, Yesilyurt, Istanbul.

Curtiss CW-22 Falcon	PV		40
De Havilland D.H.89A Dragon Rapide	PV		c35

Aircraft Type	Stat.	Number	Yr.
Lockheed T-33A Shooting Star	PV		c50
M.K.E.K. 4 Ugar (Turkish Trainer)	S	TC-KUJ	
Miles M.14A Magister	S	TC-KAH	38
North American AT-6G Texan	PV		c45
North American F-86 Sabre	PV	19268	c50
North American F-86 Sabre	PV	19207	c52
P.Z.L. P.24	PV		36
Republic F-64G Thunderjet	PV	51-9953	51
Republic F-84F Thunderstreak	PV	52-8941	c53
Republic P-47 Thunderbolt	PV	TC-21	c44
Republic RF-84F Thunderflash	PV	51-1901	51
Republic RF-84G Thunderjet	PV	U-572	c52
Turk Hava Kirumu T.H.K.4	PV	TC-PCS	48
Turk Hava Kirumu T.H.K.7	RA	TC-PBP	45

SOVIET UNION (CCCP)

568A/CP Gagarin Academy/Red Banner Academy (Soviet Air Force Museum) 141170 Monino, Moscow.

Aero L-29 Delfin	PV		c60
Antonov An-2	PV		c50
Antonov An-8	PV	10	c50
Antonov An-10A	PV	11213	c57
Antonov An-12	PV	04	c59
Antonov An-15	PV		c60
Antonov An-24	PV		c60
Beriev Be-12 (flying boat)	PV	25	c61
Buryevestnik S-3	PV		c26
Ilyushin Il-2m3	PV	301060	c42
Ilyushin Il-10M	PV		c44
Ilyushin Il-12	PV	40	c45
Ilyushin Il-14P	PV	41860	c55
Ilyushin Il-28	PV	5305771	c50
Ilyushin Il-62	PV	86670	c65
Kamov Ka-18-62	PV	68627	c62
Lavochkin La-7	PV	27	c44
Lavochkin La-11	PV	20	c46
Lavochkin La-15	PV		c49
Lavochkin La-250	PV	04	
Lisunov Li-2 (DC-3)	PV	39	c44
Lisunov Li-2 (DC-3)	PV	84614	c44
Mikoyan-Gurevich MiG-3 (R)	PV		c39
Mikoyan-Gurevich MiG-9	PV	01	46
Mikoyan-Gurevich MiG-15UTI	PV	03	c50
Mikoyan-Gurevich MiG-15bis	PV	27	c54
Mikoyan-Gurevich MiG-17	PV		c60
Mikoyan-Gurevich MiG-19	PV		c60
Mikoyan-Gurevich MiG-21	PV	92	c65
Mikoyan-Gurevich MiG-23	PV	231	c70
Mikoyan-Gurevich MiG-25	PV		c70
Mikoyan-Gurevich Ye-166 (spd recd)	PV	E166	62
Mikoyan/Tupolev 144 (MiG-21 spl.)	PV		c70
Mil Mi-1 helicopter	PV		c55
Mil Mi-2	PV		c63
Mil Mi-4	PV	34	c55
Mil Mi-10 (heavy lift helicopter)	PV	8680604	c55
Mil V-12	PV	21142	
Myasishchev M-50	PV	12	c55
Petlyakov Pe-2FT	PV		c42
Polikarpov I-16	PV		c38
Polikarpov Po-2VS	PV		c40
Sikorsky S-58 (Westland Wessex)	PV	27491	c60
Sopwith Triplane	PV	N5486	c17
Sukhanov Diskoplan	PV		
Sukhoi Su-7B	PV	25	c56

Aircraft Type	Stat.	Number	Yr.
Sukhoi Su-9	PV		c57
Sukhoi Su-17	PV		c68
Tupolev ANT-2	PV		c23
Tupolev ANT-40	PV		c36
Tupolev Tu-2	PV		c42
Tupolev Tu-4	PV	2805103	c46
Tupolev Tu-16	PV	4201004	c55
Tupolev Tu-16	PV	1880302	c55
Tupolev Tu-20	PV		c60
Tupolev Tu-22	PV	505005	c61
Tupolev Tu-104	PV		c55
Tupolev Tu-114	PV	5611	c60
Tupolev Tu-144	PV	77106	c60
Vertol V-44	PV	N74506	c60
Voisin L	PV		c14
Yakovlev Yak-3	PV		c43
Yakovlev Yak-9	PV		c44
Yakovlev Yak-12R	PV	07	c52
Yakovlev Yak-17	PV	02	c48
Yakovlev Yak-18U	PV		c50
Yakovlev Yak-23	PV		c50
Yakovlev Yak-24U	PV	51	c58
Yakovlev Yak-25	PV	03	c55
Yakovlev Yak-26	PV		
Yakovlev Yak-27R	PV	14	
Yakovlev Yak-28	PV		c61
Yakovlev Yak-36	PV	36	
Yakovlev Yak-40	PV	87490	c67
Yakovlev Yak-50	PV		

568B/CP   Arctic Museum
Marat Street 24, Leningrad.

Aircraft Type	Stat.	Number	Yr.
Schavrov Sch-2	PV		c32

568C/CP   Central Museum of the Armed
Forces Kommuny Square, Moscow.

Aircraft Type	Stat.	Number	Yr.
Heinkel He 111	PVD		c42
Ilyushin Il-28	PV	10	c50
Lockheed U-2B	PVD	56-6693	56
Mikoyan-Gurevich MiG-15bis	PV	74	c54
Mikoyan-Gurevich MiG-17	PV	25	c60
Mikoyan-Gurevich MiG-21F	PV	01	c65
Mikoyan-Gurevich MiG-21MF	PV	70	c65
Mikoyan-Gurevich MiG-23S	PV	71	c70
Mil Mi-4	PV	64	c55
Mil Mi-24	PV	3202109	c55

568D/CP   Chkalovsk Museum, Chkalovsk.

Aircraft Type	Stat.	Number	Yr.
Polikarpov I-16	PV		c38
Polikarpov I-17	PV		c39
Tupolev ANT-25	PV	N025	c35

568E/CP   Zhukovsky Memorial Museum
17 Radio street, Moscow.

Aircraft Type	Stat.	Number	Yr.
Bell P-39 Aircobra	RA		c42
Curtiss P-40C	RA		c41
Hawker Hurricane	RA		c40
Heinkel He 100	RA		
Ilyushin Il-2m3	RA		c42
Lavochkin La-5	RA		c42

Aircraft Type	Stat.	Number	Yr.
Lilienthal Type 11 Glider (R)	PV		c95
Mikoyan-Gurevich MiG-3	RA		c39
Mikoyan-Gurevich MiG-21PF	RA		c65
North American P-51B Mustang	RA		c42
Petylakov Pe-2FT	RA		c42
Sukhoi Su-15VD	RA		c67
Yakovlev Yak-9	RA		c44
Yakovlev Yak-32	RA		c61

568F/CP   Yakovlev Museum
Tushino Airport, Moscow.

Aircraft Type	Stat.	Number	Yr.
Yakovlev AIR-1 (VVA-3)	RA	R-RAIR	
Yakovlev UT-1 (AIR-14)	RA		
Yakovlev UT-2	RA	3	
Yakovlev Yak-3	RA		c43
Yakovlev Yak-11	RA	25	c52
Yakovlev Yak-12A	RA	L5275	c55
Yakovlev Yak-15	RA	37	c46
Yakovlev Yak-18A	RA		c50
Yakovlev Yak-18T	RA	10	c50
Yakovlev Yak-30	RA	90	c60
Yakovlev Yak-32	RA	70	c61
Yakovlev Yak-50	RA		

568G/CP   Civil Aviation Museum
Central Training Center, Civil
Aviation Board, Ulyanovsk.

Aircraft Type	Stat.	Number	Yr.
Mil Mi-4	RA		c55
Tupolev ANT-4/G-1	RA	H317	c29
W.S.K. M-15 Belphegor	RA		

UNITED KINGDOM (G)

575/G   Aeroplane Collection
Warmingham Center, The Old Mill
Warmingham, Cheshire.

Aircraft Type	Stat.	Number	Yr.
Addyman Glider	S	BAPC-14	34
Addyman Ultra-light	D	BAPC-16	36
Auster J/1N	D	G-AJEB	c56
Chrislea Airguard	C	G-AFIN	38
Killick HDK.3 (helicopter)	C	BAPC-18	63
Mignet HM-14 Pou Du Ciel	RAD	BAPC-13	36
Murray (helicopter)	RA	BAPC-60	54
Slingsby T.7 Cadet	S	RA854	43
Woodhams Sprite	RA	BAPC-17	66

576/G   Airborne Forces Museum
Browning Barracks, Queen's Ave.
GU11 2DS, Aldershot.

Aircraft Type	Stat.	Number	Yr.
Airspeed A.S.58 Horsa II	PV		44
Douglas DC-3 (C-47 Dakota Mk.IV)	RAX	KP208	45
General Aircraft Hotspur MkII	PV		42

576A/G   Aircraft Radio Museum,
Coventry Airport, Bagington,
West Midlands.

Aircraft Type	Stat.	Number	Yr.
Percival P.40 Prentice T.1	RA	G-AOKO	c48
Percival P.40 Prentice T.1	RA	G-APJB	c48

Aircraft Type	Stat.	Number	Yr.
Percival P.50 Prince 6E	RA	G-AMLZ	c50
Percival P.84 Jet Provost T.4	RAI	XR654	

579/G British Rotorcraft Museum Weston-super-Mare Airport, Avon.

Aircraft Type	Stat.	Number	Yr.
Bristol 171 Sycamore Mk.14	PV	G-HAPR	56
Bristol 192 Belvedere Mk.I	PV	G-BRMB	60
Campbell Cougar	PV	G-BAPS	73
Fairey Rotodyne	PV	XE521	57
Fairey Ultralight	PV	G-AOUJ	56
Hafner Revoplane R.II	RA		31
Saunders Roe Skeeter A.O.P.12	PV	G-HELI	56
Sikorsky S-51 (Westland Dragonfly)	PV	G-BRMA	52
Sikorsky S-55 (Westland Whirlwind)	S	G-ANJV	54
Sikorsky S-55 (Westland Whirlwind)	PV	G-ANFH	54
Sikorsky S-55 (Westland Whirlwind)	S	G-ATKV	58
Sikorsky S-55 (Westland Whirlwind)	PV	XG-596	57
Thruxton HDW.I Gadfly	RA	G-AVKE	67
Watkinson CG4 Cyclogyroplane	RA		
Westland P.531 Scout(Saunders-Roe)	C	XP165	60
Westland P.531 Wasp	C	XS463	63
Westland WG.33	S		79

580/G Birmingham Museum of Science and Technology, Newhall Street, B3 1RZ, Birmingham.

Aircraft Type	Stat.	Number	Yr.
Hawker Hurricane Mk.IV	PV	KX829	43
Supermarine Spitfire L.F.IX	PV	ML427	44

580A/G Brooklands Museum of Aviation The Clubhouse, Brooklands Road, Weybridge, Surrey.

Aircraft Type	Stat.	Number	Yr.
Bleriot XI (R)	RA	G-LOTI	c10
British Aircraft Company Drone	RA	G-AEKV	
CLA.7 Swift	RA	G-ACTF	
Curtiss Model D	RA		c10
Mignet HM-14 Pou du Ciel	RA	G-ADRY	
Slingsby T.15 Gull 3	RA	BGA643	
Vickers Wellington	RAD	N2980	c38

581/G Cornwall Aero Park, Culdrose Manor, Clodgey Lane, Helston, TR13 0GA, Cornwall.

Aircraft Type	Stat.	Number	Yr.
Blackburn B-103 Buccaneer	PV	XN967	61
Blackburn Monoplane (R)	PV		12
Blackburn Monoplane (R)	PV		11
Bristol 171 Sycamore H.R.14	PV	XJ917	58
De Havilland D.H.110 Sea Vixen	PV	XN647	59
Douglas A-1 Skyraider	PV	WV106	51
Fairey Gannet ECM.6	PV	XG831	56
Fairey Gannet ECM.6	PV	WN464	56
Hawker Sea Hawk FB.5	PV	WM983	57
Hawker Sea Hawk FGA.6	PV	XE368	57
Hunting-Percival P.57 Sea Prince	PV	WF122	50
Royal Aircraft Factory S.E.5a (R)	PV		18
Santos-Dumont Demoiselle (R)	PV		c08
Sikorsky S-51 (Westland Dragonfly)	C	VZ962	50
Sikorsky S-51 (Westland Widgeon)	PV	G-APTW	60
Sikorsky S-55 (Westland Whirlwind)	PV	XN258	59

Aircraft Type	Stat.	Number	Yr.
Sikorsky S-55 (Westland Whirlwind)	PV	XA870	54
Sikorsky S-55 (Westland Whirlwind)	PV	XP350	59
Supermarine Scimitar F.1	PV	XD332	60
Whitaker MW26 Excaliber	PV	G-BDDX	77

582/G Dan-Air Collection, Lasham Airfield, nr. Alton, Hampshire.

Aircraft Type	Stat.	Number	Yr.
Airspeed A.S.57 Ambassador	RA	G-ALZO	c51
Avro 685 York	RA	G-ANTK	46
De Havilland D.H.106 Comet Mk.4C	RA	G-BDIX	c62
Douglas DC-3 (C-47 Dakota)	RA	G-AMPP	c44

586/G East Anglian Aviation Society Allenbrooke Barracks, Bassington, Cambridgeshire.

Aircraft Type	Stat.	Number	Yr.
De Havilland D.H.89A Dragon Rapide	C	G-AJHO	44
Miles M.14A Magister	C	G-AKPF	38

588/G Bomber Country Aviation Museum Leisure Park, Sourth Promenade, Cleethorpes, South Humberside.

Aircraft Type	Stat.	Number	Yr.
Bristol Baby (R)	PV	G-EASO	c18
Dassault Mystere IVA	PV	101	c54
De Havilland D.H.115 Vampire T.11	PV	XD375	54
De Havilland D.H.115 Vampire T.11	PV	XD445	54
English Electric Canberra	PV	WH946	51
Hawker Hunter GA.11	PV	WT741	c54
Mignet HM-14 Pou du Ciel	PV	G-AFFI	c36
Mignet HM-14 Pou du Ciel	PV	G-AEJZ	c36
Sikorsky S-51 (Westland Dragonfly)	PV	WP503	53
Stewart Ornithopter	PV		

589/G Lashenden Air Warfare Museum Headcorn Airport, nr. Ashford, TN27 9HX, Kent.

Aircraft Type	Stat.	Number	Yr.
Dassault Mystere IVA	PV	84	c54
De Havilland D.H.115 Vampire T.11	PV	WZ589	53
Fieseler Fi 103R	PV		42
Sikorsky S-55 (Westland Whirlwind)	PV	XN380	c59
North American F-100F Super Sabre	PV	56-3938	56

590/G Fleet Air Arm Museum RNAS Yeovilton, Ilchester, Somerset.

Aircraft Type	Stat.	Number	Yr.
Aermacchi M.B.339B	PV	ARGA110	c63
B.A.C. Concorde	PV	G-BSST	69
B.A.C. Concorde 002	PV	B-BSST	c70
Beech T-34C Turbo-Mentor	RA	ARG411	c60
Bell UH-1 Iroquois	PV	AE422	c62
Bensen B-8M (gyrocopter)	PV	G-AZAZ	c60
Blackburn B-24 Skua (parts)	PV	L2940	37
Blackburn B-103 Buccaneer S.Mk.1	PV	XK488	58
Blackburn B-103 Buccaneer S.Mk.1	PV	XN957	63
Chukar Pilotless Target Drone	RA		
De Havilland D.H.82 Tiger Moth	PV	G-AOXG	40
De Havilland D.H.82 Tiger Moth	A	T.8190	40
De Havilland D.H.100 Sea Vampire	PV	LZ551/G	43
De Havilland D.H.100 Sea Vampire	PV	XA129	54
De Havilland D.H.110 Sea Vixen	PV	XS590	66
De Havilland D.H.110 Sea Vixen	PV	XJ481	58

Aircraft Type	Stat.	Number	Yr.
De Havilland D.H.112 Sea Venom	PV	WW138	55
Douglas A-1 Skyraider	PV	WT121	51
FMA IA-58B Pucara	PV	ARGA522	c75
Fairey Albacore	C	N4172	c42
Fairey Barracuda	RA	DP872	c43
Fairey Delta FD-2 (B.A.C.221)	PV	WG774	56
Fairey Firefly AS Mk.5	RA	WB271	48
Fairey Firefly FR.4	PV	VH127	47
Fairey Flycatcher (R)(winter only)	PVA	S1287	c25
Fairey Fulmar II	PV	N1854	39
Fairey Gannet 3	PV	XL503	60
Fairey Gannet AS.6	PV	XA454	57
Fairey Swordfish Mk.2	PV	W5984	43
Fairey Swordfish Mk.2	RA	LS326	35
Fairey Swordfish Mk.2	PV	AS618	c41
Fokker Dr.1 Triplane (R)	PVX		c17
Gloster G.41 Meteor T.7	S	WS103	c53
Gloster Sea Gladiator	PV	N5903	38
Grumman F4F Wildcat (Martlet I)	PV	AL246	40
Grumman F6F-5 Hellcat II	PV	KE209	42
Grumman TBF-3 Avenger (TBM)	PV	XB446	45
Handley Page H.P.115	PV	XP841	61
Handley Page H.P.115	PV	XP841	61
Hawker Sea Fury FB.11	RA	TF956	45
Hawker Sea Fury FB.11	RA	VR930	45
Hawker Sea Fury FB.11	PV	WJ231	45
Hawker Sea Fury T.20	RA	WG655	48
Hawker Sea Hawk FGA.6	PV	WV856	54
Hiller HPE-2	PV	XB480	53
Humber Monoplane (R)	PV	BAPC9	09
Hunting-Percival P.57 Sea Prince	RA	WP313	51
North American AT-6 Harvard III	RA	EX402	38
North American AT-6 Harvard III	PV	FX976	38
Saunders Roe P.531 Wasp Scout	PV	XN332	58
Saunders Roe P.531 Wasp Scout	S	XN344	58
Shelduck Piloless Target Drone	PV		
Short S.27 (R)	RA	BAPC149	
Sikorsky S-51 (Westland Dragonfly)	PV	WN493	53
Sikorsky S-55 (Westland Whirlwind)	PV	ZA864	53
Sikorsky S-55 (Westland Whirlwind)	S	XG574	53
Sikorsky S-55 (Westland Whirlwind)	RA	XJ402	c57
Sikorsky S-58 (Westland Wessex)	PV	XP142	c60
Sopwith Baby Seaplane	PV	N2078	15
Sopwith Camel (R)	PV		17
Supermarine Attacker I	PV	WA473	51
Supermarine Scimitar F.1	PV	XD317	59
Supermarine Scimitar F.1	S	XD220	59
Supermarine Seafire F.XVII	PV	SX137	45
Supermarine Walrus	PV	L2301	39
Vought F4U Corsair IV	PV	KD431	44
Westland Wyvern	PV	VR137	47
Yokosuka Ohka (Kamikazi)	PV	MXY-17	45

591/G Loughborough and Leicestershire Aircraft Museum, East Midlands Airport, Castle Donington, Leicestershire.

De Havilland DHC-1 Chipmunk T.10	RA	WZ873	53
Saunders Roe Skeeter A.O.P.12	RA	XL811	59

593/G Manchester Air and Space Museum Liverpool Road, Castlefield, M3 4FP, Manchester.

Avro 594 Avian 111A	PV	G-EBZM	28

Aircraft Type	Stat.	Number	Yr.
Bensen B-7 (gyrocopter)	PV	G-APUD	59

594/G Nene Valley Aviation Society Gibson Aerodrome, Peterborough, Northamptonshire.

Avro 707A	PV	WZ736	52
Avro 716 Shackleton	RA	WR960	54
Avro 716 Shackleton II	PV	WR960	54
Bristol 171 Sycamore H.R.14	PV	XL824	c58
English Electric Lightning P.1A	PV	WG763	55
Hawker Hunter I	PV	WT619	54
Kugisho OHKA 11 (Kamikazi)	PV		44
Miles M.14A Magister	PV	T9707	40
Scottish Aviation Pioneer CC-1	PV	XL703	56
Supermarine Spitfire Mk.VB	PV	BL614	41

595/G Imperial War Museum Lambeth Road, SE1 6HZ, London.

Avro 683 Lancaster (nose section)	PV	DV372	c42
De Havilland D.H.98 Mosquito	PV	TV959	c44
Fieseler Fi 156 Criquet (MS.500)	PV	F-BCDG	42
Focke-Wulf Fw 190A-8	PV	733682	c43
Fokker Dr.1 Triplane (R)	RA	N78001	c17
Gloster G.41 Meteor NF.14	PV	WS760	c53
Handley Page H.P.57 Halifax (fuse)	PVI	PN323	45
Hawker Typhoon (cockpit)	PVI		44
Heinkel He 162A-2 Volksjaeger	PV	120235	45
Mitsubishi A6M-5 Zero (cockpit)	PVI	BI-05	c43
Sopwith Camel	PV	N6812	18
Supermarine Spitfire Mk.1	PV	R6915	c40

595A/G Imperial War Museum Duxford Airfield, CB2 4QR, Cambridgeshire. (Incl. Duxford Aviation Society and the Russavia collection.)

Airspeed A.S.40 Oxford	PV	V3388	40
Auster A.O.P.9	PV	XP281	61
Auster J/1N Autocrat	PV	G-AGTO	c56
Avro 652A Anson	PV	TX183	c46
Avro 652A Anson I	PV	N4877	38
Avro 698 Vulcan B.2	PV	XJ824	c61
Avro 716 Shackleton Mk.3	PV	XF708	57
Avro Canada CF-100 Canuck 4B	PV	18393	55
B.A.C. Concorde 101	PV	G-AXDN	c70
B.A.C. TSR-2	PV	XR222	64
Beagle B.121 Pup	RA	G-AVDF	67
Beagle B.206X (prototype)	RA	G-ARRM	61
Beech D-17S Traveler (Staggerwing)	PV	N18V	c40
Beech D-18 Expeditor (Twin Beech)	PV	G-BKGL	c44
Bleriot XI Monoplane	PV	BAPC132	10
Boeing B-17G Flying Fortress	C	4483735	44
Boeing B-17G Flying Fortress	PV	4485784	44
Boeing B-29A Super Fortress	RA	4461748	44
Boeing B-52D Stratofortress	PV	56-0689	c56
Bristol 149 Bolingbroke (RCAF)	RA	10038	c44
Bristol 149 Bolingbroke IV (RCAF)	PV	9893	c44
Bristol 171 Sycamore Mk.3	PV	G-ALSX	51
Bristol 175 Britannia 312	PV	G-AOVT	59
Bristol F.2B Fighter	PV	E2581	18
British Aircraft Company Drone	PV	G-AEDB	c35
Cierva C.30 (autogyro)	PV	G-ACUU	34

Aircraft Type	Stat.	Number	Yr.
Curtiss P-40E Warhawk	PVA	N94466	c44
Curtiss P-40N	PVA	NL1009N	c45
Dassault Mystere IV	PV	57	c54
De Havilland D.H.82 Tiger Moth	PV	G-MOTH	c36
De Havilland D.H.89A Dragon Rapide	RA	G-AGJG	c35
De Havilland D.H.89A Dragon Rapide	PVA	NF875	c39
De Havilland D.H.98 Mosquito TT.35	PV	TA719	45
De Havilland D.H.100 Vampire FB5	Pv	VZ304	c50
De Havilland D.H.104 Dove 6	PV	G-ALFU	48
De Havilland D.H.106 Comet 4	PV	G-APDB	c60
De Havilland D.H.106 Comet C2R	PV	XK695	54
De Havilland D.H.110 Sea Vixen	PV	XS576	c59
De Havilland D.H.110 Venom FB.50	PVA	G-BLIF	c59
De Havilland D.H.112 Sea Venom	PV	XG613	c54
De Havilland D.H.115 Sea Vampire	RA	XG743	54
De Havilland D.H.115 Vampire T.11	RA	WZ515	c55
De Havilland D.H.115 Vampire T.11	PV	WZ590	52
De Havilland DHC-1 Chipmunk	PVA	WZ868	c52
Douglas DC-3 (C-47 Dakota III)	PV	G-DAKS	c44
Douglas DC-3 (C-47A Skytrain)	PV	G-BHUB	c44
English Electric Canberra B.2	PV	WH725	51
English Electric Lightning P.1	PV	XM135	60
FMA IA-58A Pucara	PVC	A-549	c75
Fairey Firefly	PV	Z2033	44
Fairey Gannet AS.6	PV	XG797	57
Fairey Swordfish Mk.3	PV	NF370	c42
Focke-Achgelis Fa 330 Bachstelze	PV	100143	c44
Gloster G.41 Meteor NF.11	PV	WD686	52
Gloster G.41K Meteor Mk.8	PV	WK991	c50
Gloster Javelin FAW.9	PV	XH897	58
Grumman F8F-2 Bearcat	PVA	N700H	c46
Grumman TBF Avenger (TBM)	PV	CF-KCG	c44
Handley Page H.P.67 Hastings IA	PV	TG528	47
Handley Page H.P.68 Hermes 4	PVI	G-ALDG	c48
Handley Page H.P.80 Victor	PV	XH648	59
Hawker Hunter F.2	PV	WN904	54
Hawker Sea Hawk FB.5	PV	WM969	c57
Hawker Sea Hurricane 1B	PV	Z7015	c44
Hawker Siddeley D.H.121 Trident 2E	PV	G-AVFB	c68
Hawker Siddely D.H.121 Trident 2E	PV	G-AVFB	c68
Hawker Tempest Mk.II	PV	LA607	c45
Hunting-Percival P.86 Jet Provost	PV	XN637	c60
Junkers Ju 52/3m	PVA	G-BFHG	c44
Junkers Ju 52/3m (French Amiot)	PVX	PAF6316	37
Lockheed T-33 Shooting Star	RA	51-4286	c50
Lockheed T-33A Shooting Star	PVA	G-TJET	c50
Max Holste M.H.1521M Broussard	PVA	G-BJGW	c55
Messerschmitt Me 163B Komet	PV	191660	c44
Miles M.14A Magister	PV	G-AFBS	37
Miles M.65 Gemini	PV	G-AKKH	c47
North American AT-6 Harvard IIB	PVA	G-BGPB	c44
North American B-25J Mitchell	PVC	4431171	c44
North American B-25J Mitchell	PV	4430861	c44
North American F-100 Super Sabre	PV	54-2165	54
North American P-51 Mustang	PV	G-HAEC	45
North American P-51D Mustang	PVA	63221	43
North American P-51D Mustang	PVX	4472258	44
Northrop SD-1 Drone	RA		
Percival P.31 Proctor Mk.III	PV	G-ALCK	40
Percival P.31 Proctor Mk.III	PV	G-ANPP	c42
Percival Q.6	RA	G-AFFD	37
Republic P-47D Thunderbolt	PVA	223719	c44
Royal Aircraft Factory B.E.2c	PV	2699	c15
Royal Aircraft Factory R.E.8	PV	F3556	c17
SAAB 35A Draken (J-35A)	PV	35075	c62
SPAD VII	PVX	S4523	18
SPAD VII	PV	S248	18

Aircraft Type	Stat.	Number	Yr.
Saunders Roe S.R.A.1 (flying boat)	PV	TG263	46
Short 184 (seaplane)	RA	8359	15
Short Sherpa (fuselage)	RAI	G-36-1	53
Short Sunderland V	PVC	ML796	45
Sikorsky S-55 (Westland Whirlwind)	RA	XG577	56
Sikorsky S-55 (Westland Whirlwind)	PV	XK936	59
Stearman PT-17	RA	CF-EQS	c42
Stearman PT-17 Kaydet	RA	CF-EQS	c42
Supermarine Spitfire Mk.IX	PVA	MH434	c42
Supermarine Spitfire Mk.V	PVA	AR501	c40
Supermarine Spitfire Mk.XVI	PVA	ML417	c43
Vickers 668 Varsity	PVA	WJ945	51
Vickers 668 Varsity T.1	PV	WF425	c51
Vickers 701 Viscount	PV	G-ALWF	c53
Vickers 1151 Super VC-10	PV	G-ASGC	c65
Vought F4U-7 Corsair	PVA	33722	c44
Westland Lysander	PVC	V9300	c42
Westland Wessex HAS.1	PV	XS863	c58
Yakovlev Yak-11 (Let C-11)	PV	G-KYAK	c52

596/G   Leicestershire Museum of Technology, Corporation Road, Leicester, Leicestershire.

	Stat.	Number	Yr.
Auster A.O.P.9 B.5	RA	XP280	61
Auster Mk.V (Prototype)	A	G-AGOH	45
Taylorcraft B (Auster V)	RAC	G-AFTN	39

598/G   Lincolnshire Aviation Museum Tattershall, Lincoln, Lincolnshire.

	Stat.	Number	Yr.
De Havilland D.H.104 Dove 1B	PV	G-AHRI	46
De Havilland D.H.115 Vampire	PV	XD447	54
De Havilland D.H.115 Vampire	PV	WZ549	53
Focke-Achgelis Fa 330 Bachstelze	PV	100502	44
Hunting-Percival P.56 Provost	PV	WW421	54
Mignet HM-14 Pou Du Ciel	PV	BAPC43	37
Percival P.34 Proctor Mk.IV	PV	NP294	44
Sikorsky S-51 (Westland Dragonfly)	PV	WH991	53
Slingsby T.8 Tutor	C	BGA794	57
Stewart Ornithopter	RA	BAPC-61	
Ward P.45 Gnome	PV	G-AXEI	66

599/G   Merseyside Aviation Society 5 Barndale Road, L18 1EN, Liverpool.

	Stat.	Number	Yr.
De Havilland D.H.115 Vampire Mk.II	RA	WZ553	53
Focke-Achgelis Fa 330A1 Bachstelze	RA	100549	44

600/G   Midland Air Museum, Coventry Airport, Coventry, Warwickshire.

		Stat.	Number	Yr.
Avro	652A Anson	C	WM325	47
Avro 698 Vulcan	B.2	PV	XL360	c62
Bleriot	(R)	PV	BAPC-9	c10
Boulton Paul	P.111A	PV	VT935	50
Crossley Tom	Thumb	RA	BAPC32	37
De Havilland D.H.83	Fox Moth	RA	G-ACCB	32
De Havilland D.H.100 Vampire F.1		PVC	VF301	c46
De Havilland D.H.104 Dove Mk.2		PV	G-ALCU	47
De Havilland D.H.115 Vampire T.11		PV	XE872	54
De Havilland DHC-2 Beaver		PV	082062	c50
English Electric Canberra P.R.3		PV	WF922	c55
Fairey Gannet T.2		PV	XA508	55
Fairey Helicopter (ultra-light)		PV	G-APJJ	58

270

Aircraft Type	Stat.	Number	Yr.
Flettner Fl 282 Kolibri	RA	28368	44
Folland Fo.141 Gnat F.1	PVC	XK741	56
Gloster G.41 Meteor F. Mk.4	PV	EE531	c50
Gloster Javelin FAW.5	PV	XA699	57
Hawker Hunter F.Mk.51	PV	E425	55
Hawker Hurricane (R)	PV	H3426	c40
Hawker Sea Hawk P.1040	PV	WF299	c54
Luton L.A.4 Minor (wings)	RAI	G-BAPC	44
Messerschmitt Bf 109 (HA-1112)	PV	BAPC67	c40
Mignet HM-14 Pou Du Ciel	RA	G-AEGV	36
Miles M.38 Messenger I	RA	VP-KJL	42
North American F-100D Super Sabre	PV	54-2174	c54
Parnall Pixie III	RAD	G-EBJG	24
Percival P.40 Prentice T.1	PV	G-AOKZ	c48
Rollason Turbulent (Druine D.31)	PV	BAPC126	c60
SAAB 35F Draken (J-35F)	PV	29640	c63
Schneider Grunau Baby IIA (glider)	C	VT921	44
Sikorsky S-55 (Westland Whirlwind)	PV	XK907	57
Sikorsky S-55 (Westland Whirlwind)	PV	XA862	52
Slingsby T.7 Cadet	C	BGA804	c43
Wheeler Slymph	PV	G-ABOI	31

601/G Mosquito Aircraft Museum, Salisbury Hall, London Colney, AL2 1BU, Hertfordshire.

Aircraft Type	Stat.	Number	Yr.
Airspeed A.S.58 Horsa (fuselage)	PVC	HHM317	43
Airspeed A.S.58 Horsa II	SD	TL615	44
Cierva C.24 (autogiro)	PV	G-ABLM	34
De Havilland D.H.82A Tiger Moth	PV	G-ANRX	39
De Havilland D.H.82A Tiger Moth	PV	DE363	40
De Havilland D.H.87B Hornet Moth	PV	G-ADOT	35
De Havilland D.H.98 Mosquito B.35	PV	TA634	45
De Havilland D.H.98 Mosquito FB.VI	PVI	TA122	45
De Havilland D.H.98 Mosquito(prot)	PV	W4050	40
De Havilland D.H.100 Vampire F.B.6	PV	J-1008	48
De Havilland D.H.103 Sea Hornet	PVI	VX250	50
De Havilland D.H.104 Dove 6	PV	04379	53
De Havilland D.H.110 Sea Vixen	PV	XJ565	60
De Havilland D.H.112 Sea Venom	PV	XG730	57
De Havilland D.H.112 Venom NF.3	PV	WX853	55
De Havilland D.H.115 Vampire T.11	PVC	WX476	53
De Havilland D.H.115 Vampire T.11	PV	XD452	53
De Havilland D.H.121 Trident	PVI	G-AVLH	70
De Havilland D.H.125 Dominie	PV	G-ARYC	63
De Havilland DHC-1 Chipmunk	PV	WP790	52
Royal Aircraft Factory B.E.2c	PVC	A1325	18

602/G Museum of Army Flying, Middle Wallop, Stockbridge, SO20 8DY, Hants.

Aircraft Type	Stat.	Number	Yr.
Airspeed A.S.58 Horsa II	PV	TL659	43
Auster A.O.P.6 K	C	G-ARYD	c46
Auster A.O.P.9 B.5	PV	WZ724	57
Auster A.O.P.9 B.5	PVX	WZ721	57
Auster A.O.P.9 B.5	RA	XR244	c57
Auster Mk.V (Model J)	RA	G-AKOW	45
Bell 47G-3B Sioux (5 in storage)	S/RA	several	64
Bell 47G-3B Sioux (Agusta)	A	XT131	64
Bristol 171 Sycamore H.R.14	RA	XG502	53
Cody Military Flyer (R)	RA		09
De Havilland DHC-2 Beaver (Canada)	S	XP821	c50

Aircraft Type	Stat.	Number	Yr.
Hafner Revoplane	RA	R2	30
Hafner Rotochute 1	RA	P5	42
M.L. Aviation Delta 1	RA	XK776	53
Saunders Roe P.531/2 Scout(proto.)	S	XR436	62
Saunders Roe Skeeter A.O.P.12	A	XL814	57
Saunders Roe Skeeter A.O.P.12	PV	XL813	57
Saunders Roe Skeeter A.O.P.12	PV	XL738	57
Short Mats "B"	S	ZA209	78
Sikorsky S-55 (Westland Whirlwind)	RA	XK988	63
Sikorsky S-55 (Westland Whirlwind)	RA	XN382	c59
Sikorsky S-55 (Westland Whirlwind)	RA	XL853	c59
Skyleader Mats "A"	S		45
Sud-Aviation SE-341 Gazelle(proto)	RA	XW876	71
Taylorcraft D/1 Plus (Auster I)	RAA	G-AHXE	40

603/G National Aeronautical Collection Science Museum, Exhibition Road, South Kensington SW7 2DD, London (1) Wroughton, nr. Swindon, Wilts. (2)

Aircraft Type	Stat.	Number	Yr.
Avro 504K	PV1	D7560	18
Bensen B-7	RA2		c59
Birdman Grasshopper	RA2		76
Bleriot (J.A.P. Harding)	PV1		10
Boeing 247D	RA2	N18E	c35
Chargus Midas E	RA2	BAPC172	77
Cierva C.30A (autogyro)	PV1	G-ACWP	34
Clarke Biplane Glider	RA2	BAPC100	10
Cody Military Biplane	PV1	304	12
De Havilland D.H.60G Moth (Jason)	PV1	G-AAAH	30
De Havilland D.H.106 Comet 4B	RA2	G-APYD	60
Douglas DC-3	RA2	N16071	36
Fieseler Fi 103	RA2	442795	c41
Focke-Achgelis Fa 330 Rotor Kite	PV1	100509	43
Fokker D.VII	S2	236/18	18
Fokker E.III	PV1	210/16	16
Folland Fo.144 Gnat T.1	PV1	XP505	c55
Gloster E.28/39 (1st Whittle Jet)	PV1	W4041G	41
Handley Page H.P.39 Gugnunc	RA2	G-AACN	29
Hawker Hurricane Mk.I	PV1	L1592	38
Hawker Siddeley D.H.121 Trident 1E	RA2	G-AVYE	67
Hinkler 1bis	D2	G-AAIS	29
Huntair Pathfinder II	RA2	G-MMCB	
Lavavasseur Antionette VII	PV1		09
Lilienthal Glider	PV1		95
Lilienthal Glider (R)	RA2		96
Lockheed 10A	RA2	G-LIOA	c39
Lockheed L749A Constellation	RA2	N7777G	c54
Messerschmitt Me 163B-1 Komet	PV1	191316	c44
Mignet HM-14 Pou Du Ciel	RA2	G-AEHM	36
Piaggio P.166	RA2	G-APWY	c60
Pilcher (Percy) Hawk Glider (R)	PV1		96
Roe Triplane No.1	PV1		09
Royal Aircraft Factory S.E.5a	PV1	F939	18
Saunders Roe Skeeter A.O.P.12	PV1	XN344	60
Short S.C.1 (VTOL)	RA2	XG900	57
Sikorsky S-55 (Westland Whirlwind)	RA2	XD163	54
Supermarine S.6B (Schneider Cup)	PV1	S.1595	31
Supermarine Spitfire Mk.1A	PV1	P9444	40
Vickers F.B.27 Vimy (Alcock-Brown)	PV1		19
Wallis WA.120	RA2	G-AYVO	c65
Westland-Hill Pterodactyl 1	PV1	J8067	25
Wright Brothers Flyer (R)	PV1		03

Newark Air Museum,
Winthorpe Airfield, Newark,
Nottinghamshire.

Aircraft Type	Stat.	Number	Yr.
Avro 652A Anson 19	PV	G-AVVO	48
Avro 696 Shackleton Mk.3/3	PV	WR977	56
Avro 698 Vulcan B.2	PV	XM594	62
Bell 47G-3 Sioux AH.1	PV	XT200	60
Bristol 171 Sycamore H.R.14	PV	G-AMWO	56
Bristol 171 Sycamore Mk.3	PV	WT933	52
De Havilland D.H.114 Heron 1B	PV	G-ANYB	55
De Havilland D.H.115 Vampire T.11	PV	XD593	54
Fairey Gannet 17	PV	XP226	60
General Aircraft ST-12 Monospar	PV	VH-UTH	35
Gloster G.41G Meteor F.MF.4	PV	VT229	48
Gloster G.41L Meteor F.R.9	PV	VZ608	51
Gloster G.47 Meteor NF.12	PV	WS692	53
Gloster Javelin FAW.8	PV	XH992	59
Handley Page H.P.67 Hastings T.5	PV	TG517	48
Hunting-Percival P.56 Provost T.1	PV	WV606	55
Lee-Richards Annular Biplane	PVD	BAPC-20	64
Miles M.14A Magister	PV	G-AKAT	40
Percival P.40 Prentice	PV	G-APIY	48
SAAB 91B Safir	PV	56321	56
Saunders Roe Skeeter A.O.P.12	PV	XL764	58
Sikorsky S-55 (Westland Whirlwind)	PV	XM685	57
Supermarine Swift F.R.5	PV	WK277	55
Vickers 668 Varsity T.1	PV	WF369	51

Norfolk and Suffolk Aviation
Museum The Buck, Flixton,
Bungay, Suffolk.

Avro 652A Anson 19	PVC	VL349	46
Bensen (gyro-glider)	PV		76
Dassault Mystere IVA	PV	79	c54
De Havilland D.H.110 Sea Vixen	PV	XJ482	58
De Havilland D.H.115 Vampire	PV	XK624	56
Gloster G.41K Meteor F.Mk.8	PVC	WF643	51
Gloster Javelin FAW.9	PV	XH892	58
Hunting-Percival P.56 Provost	PV	OV605	54
Hunting-Percival P.56 Provost T.1	PV	WV605	54
Hunting-Percival P.57 Sea Prince	PV	WF128	52
North American F-100D Super Sabre	PV	542196	c57
North American T-28 Trojan	D	49-1639	c53
North American T-28C Trojan	D	146289	56
Sikorsky S-55 (Westland Whirlwind)	PV	XN304	59
Sikorsky S-55 (Westland Whirlwind)	PV	XR485	c59
Vickers 659 Valetta	PV	VX580	50

North East Aircraft Museum
Sunderland Airport, Sunderland,
Tyne and Wear, SR5 3HZ.

Avro 652A Anson 19	PVC	G-AWRS	46
Avro 698 Vulcan	PV	XL319	60
Boulton Paul P.108 Sea Balliol T.2	PVC	WN516	50
Bristol 164 Brigand TT.1	PVC	RH746	45
Bristol 171 Sycamore Mk.14	PV	XG518	53
Bristol 171 Sycamore Mk.3	PV	G-ALST	51
De Havilland D.H.112 Sea Venom	PV	XG680	54
De Havilland D.H.115 Vampire Mk.II	PV	WZ518	53
Fairey Firefly Mk.6	PVC	VT409	48
Gloster G.41 Meteor Mk.8	PV	WL181	54
Gloster G.41 Meteor T.7	D	WL405	54
Hawker Hunter F.Mk.51	PV	E-419	c55

Aircraft Type	Stat.	Number	Yr.
Hunting-Percival P.86 Jet Provost	RA	XP627	c60
North American F-86D Sabre Jet	PV	51-6151	51
North American F-100D Super Sabre	PV	54-2157	54
Republic F-84F Thunderstreak	PV	52-6541	52
Sikorsky S-51 (Westland Dragonfly)	PV	WG724	52
Supermarine Swift F.4	RAD	WK198	53
Vickers 659 Valetta	PV	VX577	50

RAF Cosford Aerospace Museum
Wolverhampton, WV7 3EX,
West Midlands.

Armstrong Whitworth 660 Argosy	PV	XP411	c60
Avro 652A Anson	PV	TX214	c46
Avro 685 York C.1	PVC	MW100	46
Avro 694 Lincoln	PV	RF398	44
Avro 696 Shackleton Mk.3/3	RA	WR974	c55
Avro 698 Vulcan B.1	PV	XA900	c61
Avro 698 Vulcan B.2	PV	XM598	c61
Avro 707C	PV	WZ744	52
B.A.C. TSR-2	PV	XR220	64
Boeing 707-436	PV	G-APFJ	c60
Boulton Paul P.108 Sea Balliol	PV	WL732	c54
Bristol 171 Sycamore H.R.14	PV	XJ918	c58
Bristol 175 Brittania 312	PV	G-AOVF	c59
Bristol 188	PV	XF926	62
Britten-Norman BN-IF	PV	G-ALZE	c60
Consolidated B-24 Liberator	PV	KN751	44
Consolidated PBY-6A Catalina	PV	L-866	43
De Havilland D.H.98 Mosquito TT.35	PV	TA639	45
De Havilland D.H.104 Devon C.2	PV	VP952	c53
De Havilland D.H.106 Comet 1A	PV	G-APAS	53
De Havilland D.H.112 Venom Mk.4	PV	J1704	56
De Havilland D.H.115 Vampire F.B.6	PV	J1172	50
De Havilland D.H.121 Trident	PV	G-ARPH	c70
De Havilland DHC-1 Chipmunk	PV	WP912	46
Douglas DC-3 (C-47 Dakota)	PV	KN645	43
Douglas DC-3 (C-47B Dakota)	PV	KG374	c44
English Electric Canberra B.8	PV	WF346	54
English Electric Lightning P.1A	PV	WG760	c55
FMA IA-58 Pucara	PV	A-528	c75
Fairey Delta FD-2 (B.A.C.221)	PV	WG777	54
Fairey Gyrodyne	PV	XJ389	49
Fieseler Fi 103V-1	PV	FZG76	c40
Focke-Achgelis Fa 330 Rotor Kite	PV	8469M	42
Folland Fo.1 Gnat Mk.1F	PV	XK740	55
Folland Fo.144 Gnat T.1	PV	XR977	c55
Folland Fo.144 Gnat T.1	PV	XR571	55
Gloster G.41A Meteor F.9/40 proto.	PV	DG202/G	43
Gloster G.41F Meteor Nf.14	PV	WS838	54
Gloster G.41K Meteor Mk.8	PV	WK935	54
Gloster Javelin FAW.1	PV	XA564	55
Handley Page H.P.67 Hastings	PV	TG511	48
Handley Page H.P.80 Victor B Mk.1	PV	XH923	58
Hawker Fury (R)	PV	K7271	c34
Hawker Hunter F.1	PV	WT555	53
Hawker Hunter F.3	PV	WB188	c55
Hawker P.1052	PV	VX272	48
Hunting H.126	PV	XN714	63
Hunting-Percival P.56 Provost T.1	PV	WV562	c55
Junkers Ju 52/3m (CASA 352)	PV	T2B-272	51
Kawasaki Ki-100 "Tony"	PV	8476M	45
Lockheed SP-2H Neptune	PV	204	c60
Lockheed T-33A	PV	51-7473	51
Messerschmitt Me 163B Komet	PV	191614	44
Messerschmitt Me 262A-1 Schwalbe	PV	VK893	44

Aircraft Type	Stat.	Number	Yr.
Messerschmitt Me 410A-1 Hornisse	PV	420430	43
Pitts S-2A Special	PV	G-BADW	77
Saunders Roe S.R.53	PV	XD145	57
Scottish Aviation Twin Pioneer	PV	XL993	58
Short S.B.5	PV	WG768	52
Short S.C.5/10 Belfast C.Mk.I	PV	XR371	65
Sikorsky S-51 (Westland Dragonfly)	PV	WP495	53
Sikorsky S-55 (Westland Whirlwind)	PV	XP299	c59
Stampe-Renard S.V.4B	PV	G-AWIW	c45
Supermarine 510	PV	VV106	51
Supermarine Spitfire Mk.XIV	PV	MT847	c42
Vickers 659 Valetta	PV	VX573	46
Vickers 668 Varsity T.MkI	PV	WF408	52
Vickers 701 Viscount	PV	G-AMOG	53
Vickers 1101 VC-10	PV	G-ARUM	c62
Yokosuka Ohka (Kamikaze)	PV	MXY-7	c45

609/G RAF St. Athan Historic Aircraft Collection, RAF St. Athan, Barry, Glamorgan, CF6 9WA, Wales.

Auster A.O.P.9	PV	XR243	c55
Auster Mk.7 Antarctic	RA	WE600	50
Avro 504K	PV	G-EBKN	18
Avro 698 Vulcan B.2	PV	XM602	c62
Bristol Scout (R)	PV	A1742	c18
De Havilland D.H.100 Vampire F.B.9	PV	WL505	c55
English Electric Canberra B.2	RA	WD935	c55
Fairey Battle	RA	L5343	c39
Fieseler Fi 103V-1	PV		c40
Fieseler Fi 156 Storch	RA	475081	c42
Focke-Wulf Fw 190A-8	RA	584219	c43
Gloster G.41 Meteor NF.14	PV	WS843	c50
Gloster G.41 Meteor T.7	RA	WA634	c50
Gloster G.41F Meteor Mk.4	S	EE549	45
Gloster G.41K Meteor F.M.8	PV	WL168	c50
Hawker Hunter F.3	PV	WB188	c55
Heinkel He 162B Volksjaeger	RA	120227	45
Hunting-Percival P.56 Provost T.1	PV	WV499	c55
Hunting-Percival P.86 Jet Provost	RA	XD674	c60
Kawasaki Ki-100b	PV	8476M	c44
Messerschmitt Me 163B Komet	RA	191904	45
Messerschmitt Me 262A	PV	112372	c45
Messerschmitt Me 410A-1 Hornisse	PV	420430	c44
Mignet HM-14 Pou Du Ciel	PV	G-AEEH	c36
Mitsubishi Ki-46 "Dinah"	C	5439	c45
Percival P.31 Proctor Mk.III	PV	Z7197	c42
Royal Aircraft Factory B.E.2c (R)	PV	6232	c16
Saunders Roe Skeeter A.O.P.12	RA	XN341	c54
Sopwith Camel (R)	PV	D4319	c18
Supermarine Spitfire L.F. Mk.XVI	PV	RW386	c45
Supermarine Spitfire Mk.IX	PV	MK356	c42
Supermarine Spitfire Mk.IX	PV	Mk732	c42
Supermarine Swift	PV	WK281	c56
Watkins Monoplane	RA		

609A/G RAF Manston Spitfire Memorial RAF Manston, Ramsgate, CR12 5BS, Kent.

English Electric Canberra P.R.3	PV	WE168	c55
Gloster Javelin FAW.9	PV	XH764	
Supermarine Spitfire L.F.XVI	PV	TB752	c44

610/G Royal Air Force Museum, Aerodrome Road, Hendon, NW9 5LL, London.

Aircraft Type	Stat.	Number	Yr.
Avro 504K	PV	E449	c18
B.A.C. VC-10	RA	G-ARVM	c60
Beagle B.206 Basset	RA	XS770	c64
Blackburn B-101 Beverly	PV	XH124	57
Bleriot XI Monoplane	PV	164	c13
Bristol 149 Blenheim (Bolingbroke)	PVX	10001	c44
Bristol 156 Beaufighter T.10	PV	RD253	c42
Bristol 192 Belvedere	PV	XG474	c61
Caudron G.3	PV	3066	c14
Cayley (Sir George) c1800 (R)	PV		
Cierva C.30A (autogyro-Avro)	PV	K4232	c34
Clarke Biplane Glider	RAC		10
Cody Kite Biplane	PV		08
Curtiss JN-4 Jenny	RA		c15
De Havilland D.H.82A Tiger Moth	PV	T6296	c36
De Havilland D.H.100 Vampire MkIII	PV	VT812	c50
Dornier Do 24T Wal	PV	HD5-1	38
English Electric Lightning P.1B	PV	XA847	c55
Gloster G.41K Meteor Mk.8	PV	WH301	c50
Gloster Gladiator	PV	N5628	c37
Hanriot HD-1	PV	75	17
Hawker Cygnet	PV	G-EBMB	c20
Hawker Hart Trainer IIA	PV	K4972	c37
Hawker Hind (Afghan)	PV	K4672	37
Hawker Hunter F.5	PV	WP185	c55
Hawker P.1127	PV	XP831	
Hawker Sea Fury FB.11	PV	VX653	c45
Hawker Tempest Mk.V	PV	NV778	c44
Hawker Typhoon Mk.1B	PV	MN235	c43
Lockheed 16 Hudson	C	A16-199	c41
Royal Aircraft Factory S.E.5a	PV	F938	18
Sikorsky VS-316 Hoverfly I	PV	KK995	45
Sopwith 1 1/2-Strutter	PV	A8226	c17
Sopwith Camel	PV	F6314	18
Sopwith Pup (R)	PV	N5182	c16
Sopwith Triplane	PV	N5912	17
Supermarine Spitfire F. Mk.24	PV	PK724	c46
Supermarine Spitfire Mk.1	PV	K9942	c40
Supermarine Stranraer	PV	CF-8X0	40

610A/G Battle of Britain Museum, Aerodrome Road, Hendon, NW9 5LL, London.

Boulton Paul P.82 Defiant	PV	N1671	40
Fiat C.R.42 Falco	PV	BT474	c40
Gloster Gladiator II	PV	K8042	c37
Hawker Hurricane Mk.1	PV	P2617	40
Heinkel He 111H	PV	701152	c42
Junkers Ju 87D Stuka	PV	W8+A	c40
Junkers Ju 88R-1	PV	D5+EV	c44
Messerschmitt Bf 109E-4	PV	4101	40
Messerschmitt Bf 110	PV	740301	40
Short Sunderland V	PV	ML824	c45
Supermarine Spitfire Mk.1	PV	X4590	c40
Supermarine Walrus (Seagull V)	PV	A2-4	c41
Westland Lysander III	PV	R9125	40

610B/G RAF Bomber Command Museum, Aerodrome Road Hendon, NW9 5LL, London.

Avro 683 Lancaster	PV	R5868	c42

273

Aircraft Type	Stat.	Number	Yr.
Avro 698 Vulcan B.2	PV	XL318	61
Boeing B-17G Flying Fortress	PV	4483868	44
De Havilland D.H.9A (Airco)	PV	F1010	18
De Havilland D.H.98 Mosquito T.III	PV	TW117	c44
English Electric Canberra P.R.3	PV	WE139	c55
Handley Page H.P.57 Halifax II	PVD	W1048	c41
Hawker Hart	PV	J9941	c37
North American B-25J Mitchell	PVX	34037	44
Sopwith Tabloid (R)	PV	168	c14
Vickers F.B.27A Vimy (R)	PV	F8614	18
Vickers Valiant	PV	XD818	c57
Vickers Wellington	PV	MF628	38

610C/G RAF Museum Reserve Collection RAF Cardington, Cardington, Bedfordshire. (A/c stored at Cardington or Henlow or loaned to other museums.)

Aircraft Type	Stat.	Number	Yr.
Airspeed A.S.40 Oxford	RA	MP425	c40
Airspeed A.S.58 Horsa	RAI	8596M	c42
Airspeed A.S.65 Consul	RA	G-AJLR	c47
Avro 504K	RA	G-ABAA	c18
Bleriot XXVII(Gordon Bennett Race)	PV	433	14
Bristol 156 Beaufighter (cockpit)	PV	c42	
Bristol 171 Sycamore H.R.12	RA	WV783	52
Bristol 173 (twinrotor helicopter)	RA	G-ALBN	51
Bristol F.2B Fighter (fuselage)	C	c18	
De Havilland D.H.89 Dominie	RA	G-AHED	c37
De Havilland D.H.106 Comet II	RA	XK699	56
De Havilland D.H.112 Venom Mk.3	RA	WX905	c54
De Havilland D.H.115 Vampire	RA	XE920	c55
Elliott Newbury Eton (glider)	PV	WP270	
Fairchild F-24 Argus	RA	G-AIZE	c40
Fairchild PT-19 Cornell	S		c40
Fairey Swordfish	RA	HS503	c41
Farman Biplane F.141	PV	F-HMFI	19
Fokker D.VII	PV	8417/18	18
Hafner Rotochute	RA	P-5	c42
Hawker Siddeley Kestrel (VTOL)	RA	XS695	c69
Hunting-Percival P.56 Provost T.1	RA	XF545	c55
Lockheed Ventura	RA	AJ468	c41
Messerschmitt Bf 109G-2	RA	RN228	c44
Miles M.2H Hawk Major	RA	G-ADMW	c38
Miles M.38 Messenger 4A	RA	G-ALAH	44
Morane-Saulnier BB (MS.816) (fuse)	PVI	A301	
Royal Aircraft Factory B.E.2a	PV	2699	c13
Sikorsky S-51 (Westland Dragonfly)	S	VX595	c52
Slingsby T.7 Cadet	RA		c43
Sopwith Dolphin (parts)	RAI	D5329	18
Supermarine Southampton I	RACI	N9899	
Supermarine Spitfire Mk.22	PV	PK624	c45
Supermarine Spitfire Mk.VB	RA	A8871	c41
Supermarine Spitfire Mk.XIX	PV	PS915	c45
Supermarine Spitfire Mk.XXI	RA	LA255	c45
Vickers F.B.5 Gun Bus	PV	2345	c15
Westland Wallace II	RAD	K6038	c33
Wright Flyer (R)	RA	BAPC-28	03

610D/G Battle of Britain Memorial Flight RAF Coningsby, LN4 4SY, Lincolnshire.

Aircraft Type	Stat.	Number	Yr.
Avro 683 Lancaster	RAA	PA474	c42
Hawker Hurricane Mk.II	RAA	PZ865	c41

Aircraft Type	Stat.	Number	Yr.
Hawker Hurricane Mk.IIC	RAA	LF363	44
Supermarine Spitfire Mk.II	RAA	P7350	40
Supermarine Spitfire Mk.VB	RAA	A8910	41
Supermarine Spitfire Mk.XIX	RAA	PM631	45
Supermarine Spitfire Mk.XIX	RAA	PS853	45

612/G Solway Aviation Society, Carlisle Airport, Carlisle, Cumbria.

Aircraft Type	Stat.	Number	Yr.
Gloster G.47 Meteor NF.14	PV	WS832	c53

612A/G City of Norwich Aviation Museum, Norwich Airport, Old Norwich Road Horsham, Norwich, Norfolk.

Aircraft Type	Stat.	Number	Yr.
Avro 652A Anson 19	PV	TX228	c46
Avro 698 Vulcan B.2	PV	XM612	c62
Dassault Mystere IVA	PV	121	c54
De Havilland D.H.110 Sea Vixen	PV	XP919	c59
De Havilland D.H.115 Vampire T.11	PV	XD375	c56
Handley Page H.P.R.7 Dart Herald	PV	G-ASKK	c60
Westland Whirlwind WS.55	PV	XP355	c60

613/G South Yorkshire Aviation Society, Home Farm, Firbeck, Nottinghamshire.

Aircraft Type	Stat.	Number	Yr.
Cessna F-150 (Reims)	C		68
Cessna T-210L Turbo Centurian	D	G-BAGE	72
English Electric Canberra B.8	PV	XM279	59
Royal Aircraft Factory S.E.5a (R)	PV	BAPC176	18
Socata TB.10 Tobago	PV	G-BGTB	79

615/G City of Bristol Museum, Queen's Road, Clifton, BS8 1RL, Bristol.

Aircraft Type	Stat.	Number	Yr.
Bristol 171 Sycamore	PV	XL829	59
Bristol Boxkite (R)	PV	BM7281	10

617/G Pennine Aviation Museum, Moorlands Park, Bacup, Lancastershire.

Aircraft Type	Stat.	Number	Yr.
Avro 652A Anson T.21	C	VV901	49
Boulton Paul P.108 Sea Balliol T.2	S	WN534	54
De Havilland D.H.115 Vampire T.11	C	XK627	56
English Electric Canberra B.2	C	WF911	52
Waco CG-4A Hadrian (Troop Glider)	D		c42

618/G Southampton Hall of Aviation (R. J. Mitchell Memorial Museum) Albert Road South, SO1 0GB, Southampton.

Aircraft Type	Stat.	Number	Yr.
Britten-Norman BN-1	PV	G-ALZE	
Short Sandringham	PV	JM715	43
Supermarine S.6A (Schneider Cup)	PV	N248	29
Supermarine Spitfire F. Mk.24	PV	PK683	46

618A/G Second World War Aircraft Preservation Society, Lasham Airport, nr. Alton, Hants.

Aircraft Type	Stat.	Number	Yr.
Auster A.O.P.9	PV	XK418	c55

Aircraft Type	Stat.	Number	Yr.
De Havilland D.H.115 Vampire T.11	PV	XE856	c56
De Havilland DHA.3 Drover	PVX	VH-FDT	c48
Gloster Meteor F.8	PV	WH291	c50
Gloster Meteor NF.13	PV	FX-FNA	c50
Hawker Hunter F.51	PV	E-423	c56
Hawker Sea Hawk FGA.6	PV	WV798	c54
Percival P.40 Prentice T.1	C	G-APIP	c48
Percival P.57 Sea Prince T.1	PV	WF137	c53
Westland Wessex WS.58	PV	XM833	c58
Westland Whirlwind HAR.10	PV	XP360	c60
Westland Whirlwind HAR.9	PV	XN309	c60

620/G Shuttleworth Collection Old Warden Aerodrome, nr. Biggleswade, SG18 9ER, Bedfordshire.

Aircraft Type	Stat.	Number	Yr.
A.N.E.C. II Monoplane	S	G-EBJO	23
Auster A.O.P.9	A	XR241	55
Avro 504K	A	E3404	18
Avro 621 Tutor	A	K3215	31
BAT Bantom	D	G-EACN	19
Blackburn B Monoplane	A	G-AANI	12
Blake Bluetit	S		25
Bleriot XI Monoplane	A	14	09
Bristol Boxkite (R)	A	G-ASPP	10
Bristol F.2B Fighter	A	D8096	18
British Aircraft Company Swallow	PV	G-AFCL	37
Cierva C.30A (autogyro)	D	G-AHMJ	34
De Havilland D.H.51	A	G-EBIR	24
De Havilland D.H.53 Humming Bird	A	G-EBHX	23
De Havilland D.H.60G Moth	A	G-ABAG	30
De Havilland D.H.60X Hermes Moth	A	G-EBWD	25
De Havilland D.H.80A Puss Moth	PV	G-AEOA	31
De Havilland D.H.82A Tiger Moth	A	G-ANKT	40
De Havilland D.H.87B Hornet Moth	A	G-ADND	38
De Havilland D.H.88 Comet (Racer)	C	G-ACSS	34
De Havilland D.H.89A Dragon Rapide	PV	G-AHGD	34
De Havilland D.H.94 Moth Minor	PV	G-AFNG	38
De Havilland DHC-1 Chipmunk	C	G-AOTD	50
Deperdussin Monoplane	A	G-AANH	10
Desoutter I	D	G-AAPZ	31
English Electric Wren	A	G-EBNV	23
Gloster Gladiator	PVA	G-AMRK	37
Granger Archaeopteryx	PV	G-ABXL	30
Hawker Hind	A	G-AENP	37
Hawker Hurricane Mk.I	C	Z7515	40
Hawker Tomtit	A	G-AFTA	30
Hunting-Percival P.56 Provost T.1	A	G-AWRY	50
Hunting-Percival P.86 Jet Provost	RA	G-AOBV	54
L.V.G. C.IV	A	7198/18	18
Mignet HM-14 Pou Du Ciel	PV	G-AEBB	35
Miles M.14A Magister	A	G-AJRS	39
Parnall Elf II	A	G-AAIN	29
Roe Triplane IV (R)	A	G-ARSG	c10
Royal Aircraft Factory S.E.5a	A	F904	17
Sopwith Pup	A	N5180	16
Southampton Univ. Sumpac	PV		60
Southern Martlet	D	G-AAYX	31
Supermarine Spitfire Mk. V	A	AR501	42

621/G Torbay Aircraft Museum, Higher Blagdon, TQ3 3YG, Devon.

Aircraft Type	Stat.	Number	Yr.
Bristol 171 Sycamore	PV	XG544	56
De Havilland D.H.82A Tiger Moth	C	G-ANSM	c36

Aircraft Type	Stat.	Number	Yr.
De Havilland D.H.100 Vampire	PV	XE995	55
De Havilland D.H.104 Dove	PV	G-ALFT	c55
De Havilland D.H.112 Sea Venom	PV	XG629	c55
De Havilland DHC-1 Chipmunk	PV	WB758	50
Focke-Achgelis Fa 330 Bachstelze	PV	6000120	43
Fokker Dr.I Triplane (R)	PV		c17
Gloster G.41 Meteor	PV	WF877	51
Hawker Hurricane	PV		c40
Hawker Sea Hawk FB.3	PV	WM961	c54
Hunting-Percival P.56 Provost T.1	PV	WV679	54
Messerschmitt Bf 109 (R)	PV	KM¹51	c40
Miles M.38 Messenger	PV	G-AKEZ	c44
Percival P.34 Proctor Mk.IV	PV	G-ANYP	c40
Saunders Roe Skeeter A.O.P.12	PV	XN351	54
Sikorsky S-51 (Westland Dragonfly)	PV	WN499	c53
Sikorsky S-55 (Westland Whirlwind)	PV	XN299	59
Supermarine Spitfire (R)	PV		c40

622/G Warbirds of Great Britain, Blackbushe Airport, Camberley, Surrey.

Aircraft Type	Stat.	Number	Yr.
Avro 694 Lincoln B.2	RA	G-291	44
Consolidated B-24 Liberator	RA	44052	44
De Havilland D.H.98 Mosquito	RA	G-MOSI	c44
De Havilland D.H.106 Comet 4C	RA	G-BDIT	62
De Havilland D.H.115 Vampire T.11	RA	XD599	54
De Havilland DHA.3 Drover	RA	VH-FDT	c48
De Havilland DHC-2 Beaver	RA	G-APXX	c50
Gloster G.43 Meteor TT.20	RA	WM167	57
Grumman TBF-3 Avenger (TBM)	RA	Bu85650	44
Hawker Hunter T.7	RA	ET-271	c55
Junkers Ju 52/3m (CASA 352)	RA	G-BFHD	c40
Junkers Ju 52/3m (CASA 352)	RA	G-BECL	c40
Junkers Ju 52/3m (CASA 352)	RA	G-BFHF	c40
Junkers Ju 52/3m (CASA 352)	RA	G-BFHG	c40
Messerschmitt Bf 109K	RA	FE-124	c44
North American AT-6 Texan	RA	FT323	c45
North American P-51 Mustang	RA	G-PSID	c44
Percival P.56 Provost	RA	WV686	c54
Pilatus P-2	RA	U-125	48
Republic P-47D Thunderbolt	RA	49205	45
Stearman PT-17 Kaydet	RA	G-AWLO	c42
Supermarine Spitfire FR.XIV	RA	G-SPIT	c42
Supermarine Spitfire FR.XIV	RA	NH799	c42
Supermarine Spitfire L.F.IX	RA	N238V	44
Supermarine Spitfire L.F.XIV	RA	RW386	c42
Westland Lysander IIIA	RA	V9281	c43

623/G Wessex Aviation Society, Stapehill Road, Stapehill, BH21 7ND, Wimborne.

Aircraft Type	Stat.	Number	Yr.
A.F.E.E. Rotachute 10.42 (R)	C	B415	
Bell 47 Sioux AH.1	C	XT242	66
De Havilland D.H.82 Tiger Moth	C	G-ADWO	36
De Havilland D.H.112 Sea Venom	RA	WM571	54
Gloster G.41 Meteor Mk.8	PV	WA984	50
Wight Quadroplane (R)	C	WAS-2	

639/G Ulster Folk and Transport Museum, Cultra Manor, Holywood, BT18 0EU, County Down, Northern Ireland.

Aircraft Type	Stat.	Number	Yr.
De Havilland D.H.82 Tiger Moth	S	G-AOUR	c36

Aircraft Type	Stat.	Number	Yr.
Ferguson Mk.V Monoplane (R)	PV		
Miles M.38 Messenger	RA	G-AJOC	47
Short S.16 Scion I	RA	G-ACUX	34
Short S.C.1 (VTOL)	PV	XG905	56
Supermarine Spitfire Mk.XVI	PV	TE184	45

640/G Royal Scottish Museum, Chambers Street, EH1 1JF, Edinburgh, Scotland (1) Museum of Flight, East Fortune Airfield, North Berwick, EH39 5LF, East Lothian (2)

Aircraft Type	Stat.	Number	Yr.
Avro 652A Anson	C2	VM360	47
Beech E-18S Expeditor (Twin Beech)	PV2	G-ASUG	55
Bristol 149 Bolingbroke IV (RCAF)	PV2	9940	42
British Aircraft Company Swallow 2	PV2	G-AEVZ	37
Chargus 18/50 (hang glider)	PV2		75
De Havilland D.H.80A Puss Moth	RA2	VH-UQB	30
De Havilland D.H.82A Tiger Moth	RA2	G-AOEL	40
De Havilland D.H.84 Dragon I	RA2	VH-SNB	42
De Havilland D.H.89A Dragon Rapide	PV2	G-ADAH	35
De Havilland D.H.104 Dove	PV2	G-ANOV	54
De Havilland D.H.106 Comet 4C	PV2	G-BDIX	62
De Havilland D.H.112 Sea Venom	PV2	WW145	54
De Havilland D.H.115 Sea Vampire	PV2	XA109	53
English Electric Lightning P.1B	S2	XN776	63
Fieseler Fi 156 Criquet (MS.505)	PVA	G-BIRW	45
General Aircraft G.A.L.42 Cygnet 2	PV2	G-AGBN	41
Gloster G.47 Meteor NF.14	PV2	WM261	53
Hardy-Roger M.P.A. Dragonfly II	S2	G-BDFU	81
Hawker Sea Hawk Mk.2	PV2	WF259	54
Hunting-Percival P.56 Provost T.1	RA2	WV493	53
Messerschmitt Me 163B Komet	PV2	191659	44
Mignet HM-14 Pou Du Ciel	PV2	BAPC-12	36
Pilcher (Percy) Hawk Glider	PV1	BAPC49	96
Piper PA-24 "Myth Too"	C2	G-ATOY	66
SAAB 91C Safir	PV2	91311	54
Saunders Roe Skeeter A.O.P.12	PV2	XL762	58
Scottish Aviation Twin Pioneer III	RA2	G-BBVF	59
Slingsby T.8 Tutor	RA2	TS291	38
Slingsby T.12 Gull (glider)	PV2	BGA902	38
Slingsby T.21A Sedbergh	RA2	556	49
Spartan Cruiser III (fuselage)	PVI	G-ACYK	35
Supermarine Spitfire L.F. Mk.XVI	PV2	TE462	45
Weir W-2 Autogyro	PV2	W2	34

640A/G Aircraft Preservation Society of Scotland, Museum of Flight, East Fortune Airfield, North Berwick, East Lothian, Scotland.

Aircraft Type	Stat.	Number	Yr.
Auster A.O.P.5	PVX	TJ472	c44
Avro 698 Vulcan B.2	PV	XM597	c62
Beagle Bulldog	PV	G-AXEH	
Bensen B-8M	PV	7	c60
Brantly B.2B	PV	G-AXSR	c55
Miles M.17 Monarch	RAC	G-AFJU	c38

641/G Glasgow Museum of Transport 25 Albert Dr., G41 2PE, Glasgow, Scotland.

Aircraft Type	Stat.	Number	Yr.
Kay 331 Gyroplane	PV	G-ACVA	35
Pilcher (Percy) Hawk Glider (R)	PV		96

642/G Strathallen Aircraft Collection, Strathallen Airfield, Auchterarder, PH3 1LA, Perthshire, Scotland.

Aircraft Type	Stat.	Number	Yr.
Avro 652A Anson 19	S	G-AYWA	46
Avro 683 Lancaster Mk.X	PV	G-BCOH	45
Avro 696 Shackleton T.4	PV	VP293	51
Bristol 149 Bolingbroke IV	S	10201	42
British Aircraft Company Swallow 2	PVA	G-ADPS	35
De Havilland D.H.82A Tiger Moth	C	G-ANTS	39
De Havilland D.H.106 Comet II	PV	XK655	56
De Havilland D.H.115 Vampire II	PV	XD547	54
De Havilland D.H.115 Vampire II	PVX	XD403	54
Fairey Battle I	C	R3950	39
Fairey Swordfish Mk.2	PVC	W5856	42
Fokker S.11 Instructor	PVA	G-BEPV	48
Hawker Hurricane Mk.IIB (RCAF)	PVX	5588	42
Hawker Sea Hawk FGA.6	PV	XE340	54
Miles M.14A Magister	PV	G-AHUJ	39
Rolls Royce Flying Bedstead	PV	XJ314	54
Sikorsky S-55 (Westland Whirlwind)	PV	XG594	54
Westland Lysander III	AX	V9441	42

643/G Dumfries and Galloway Aviation Museum, Tinwald Downs, Dumfries, Scotland.

Aircraft Type	Stat.	Number	Yr.
De Havilland D.H.100 Vampire T.II	PV	XD425	54
Gloster G.41 Meteor T.7	PV	WL375	54

644/G Scottish Aircraft Collection Trust, Perth Aerodrome, Tayside, Scotland.

Aircraft Type	Stat.	Number	Yr.
De Havilland D.H.87B Hornet Moth	RA	G-ADMT	c38
Miles M.18	RA	G-AHKY	40
Percival P.40 Prentice	RA	G-AOLU	c48
Reid and Sigrist RS.4 Desford	RA	VZ728	45
Westland Wessex I	PV	XS881	58

645/G Wales Aircraft Museum, Cardiff Airport, South Glamorgan, Wales.

Aircraft Type	Stat.	Number	Yr.
Auster A.O.P.9	PV	WZ662	54
Avro 698 Vulcan	PV	XM569	62
Avro 706 Ashton (fuselage)	PV	WB491	50
Blackburn B-103 Buccaneer S.Mk.1	PV	XN928	c61
Dassault Mystere IVA	PV	59	c54
De Havilland D.H.110 Sea Vixen	PV	XN650	59
De Havilland D.H.112 Sea Venom	PV	XG737	55
De Havilland D.H.112 Venom Mk.3	PVI	WX788	54
De Havilland D.H.115 Vampire T.11	PV	WZ425	52
English Electric Canberra	PV	WH798	51
Fairey Gannet AS.4	PV	XA459	57
Fairey Gannet Mk.1	D		c55
Fairey Gannet T.5	PV	XG883	57
Gloster G.41 Meteor T.7	PV	WL332	52
Gloster G.43 Meteor TT.20	PV	WM292	57
Hawker Hunter F.Mk.51	PVX	XF383	c55
Hawker Sea Hawk Mk.4	PV	WV826	51
Hunting-Percival P.66 Pembroke	PV	WV753	57
North American F-100D Super Sabre	PV	54-2160	54
Percival P.44 Proctor Mk.V	PV	G-AHTE	46
Sikorsky S-55 (Westland Whirlwind)	PV	XG592	57
Vickers 668 Varsity Mk.1	PV	WJ944	53

Aircraft Type	Stat.	Number	Yr.
Vickers 732 Viscount (fuselage)	PVI	G-ANRS	55
Vickers 802 Viscount	PV	G-AOJC	56

YUGOSLAVIA (YU)

990/YU Muzej Jugoslovenskog Vazduh-
plovsta (Yugoslav National Aviation Museum) Aerodrom Surcin
Beograd, 1100d, Belgrade.

Aircraft Type	Stat.	Number	Yr.
Aero 2-D	RA	YU-CVB	47
Aero 3/2 (prototype)	RA	Proto.	54
Antonov An-2M	RA	YU-ABY	c55
Bucker Bu 133 Jungmeister	RA	9102	c36
Caproni Ca.51 (Cvjetkovic)	RA	YU-CMK	52
Cavka Sostaris (glider)	RA	YU-2127	39
Cijab Orao IIC (glider)	'S	YU-4021	51
D.F.S. 108 Kranich (glider)	S	YU-5014	49
D.F.S. 108 Meuse	S	YU-4106	
De Havilland D.H.82A Tiger Moth	RA	YU-CHX	c36
De Havilland D.H.104 Dove	RA	72201	53
De Havilland DHC-2 Beaver (Canada)	S	211536	c50
Douglas DC-3	RA	YU-ABB	c44
Douglas DC-3 (C-47 Skytrain)	S	71214	c44
Fiat G.50bis	RA	3505	c40
Fizir FN	RA	9009	30
Focke-Wulf Fw 190	RA	930838	43
Folland Fo.141 Gnat MK.IF	RA	11601	c56
Hawker Hurricane MK.IV	RA	9539	c43
Ikarus 214P	RA	YU-ABP	59
Ikarus 451 Pionir	RA		50
Ikarus 451M Zolja (prototype)	RA		50
Ikarus 451MMT Strsljen	RA	21002	54
Ikarus S-451MM Matica	RA	20001	57
Ikarus S-49A	RA	2319	49
Ilindenka (Glider)	S	YU-4109	56
Ilyushin Il-2 Stormovik	RA	4154	c40
Ilyushin Il-14R	RA	71301	c55
Kosava (Ikarus glider)		YU-5052	53
Koser-Horvat Jadran (glider)	S	YU-5001	49
Letov 22 (glider)	S	YU-5086	
Libis KB-6 Matajur	S	YU-CDF	52
Lisunov Li-3	RA	7011	
Lockheed T-33A Shooting Star	RA	52-9958	c50
Messerschmitt Bf 109G	RA		c43
Messerschmitt Bf 109G	RA	9663	c43
North American F-86D Sabre	RA		c51
North American F-86F Sabre	RA		c53
Petlyakov Pe-2	RA	6054	c41
Polikarpov Po-2	RA	YU-CNT	28
Polikarpov Po-2	RA	YU-CNS	c40
Republic F-84G Thunderjet	S	52-2936	52

Aircraft Type	Stat.	Number	Yr.
Republic P-47D Thunderbolt	RA	13024	c44
Republic P-47D Thunderbolt	S		c44
Republic RF-84G Thunderjet	S	52-2939	52
Saric 1 1910 (R)	RA		c10
Saric 2	RAC	01	c11
Schneider Grunau Baby (glider)	RA	YU-2259	51
Schneider Grunau Baby II (glider)	RA	YU-2113	c40
Short S.A.6 Sealand Mk.1	RA	0662	c52
Sikorsky S-51 (Westland Dragonfly)	RA		c53
Soko 522	S	134	
Soko 522	S	204	
Sostaric Macka (glider)	S	YU-5047	
Sostaric Roda (glider)	S	YU-5210	49
Sostaric Vrabac (glider)	S		38
Stearman PT-17 Kaydet (Boeing)	RA	YU-BAD	c42
Student (prototype)	RA	YU-CKK	52
Sud-Aviation SE-210 Caravelle	RA	YU-AHB	c59
Supermarine Spitfire Mk.V	RA	9489	c40
UTVA 213	S	1421	48
Vajic V-55 (prototype)	S	YU-CDM	59
Weihe (Glider)	S	YU-4073	c51
Weihe (Glider)		YU-4048	51
Yakovlev Yak-3	S	2252	c43
Yakovlev Yak-9P	S	2826	c47

991/YU Tehnicki Muzej Slovenide
(Slovakian Technical Museum)
Tarmova 33, 6100 Ljubljana. (A/c
stored at Brnik Airport, Bistra.)

Aircraft Type	Stat.	Number	Yr.
Bartlett M-8	S		
Kunaver (prototype autogyro)	PV		
North American F-86D Sabre	PV	147	c51
North American F-86D Sabre	PV	146	c51
Republic F-84G Thunderjet	PV		c55
Soko 522	PV		

992/YU Tehnicki Muzej Zagreb
(Technical Museum of Zagreb)
Savska Cesta 18, 41000, Zagreb.

Aircraft Type	Stat.	Number	Yr.
Aero 3/1 (UTVA prototype)	PV	40001	c52
Bucker Bu 131 Jungmann	RA	YU-CLY	c35
Fizir FNH	S	YU-CGO	c32
Focke-Wulf Fw 44 Stieglitz (DAR-9)	PV	YU-CDG	c40
Ikarus Cham C-3 Trojka	PV	YU-CGT	
Republic P-47D Thunderbolt	PV	13109	42
Sostaric Jastreb (glider)	PV	YU-3015	
Sostaric Roda (glider)	PV	YU-5153	
Vajic V-55	S	YU-CXE	c60
Yakovlev UT-2	RA	YU-CGL	

A forgotten sound, the rising whine of a hand-cranked inertia starter would cough this Bücker Bestmann into life. Musée de l'Aéronautique de Nancy.

It is not an Aeronca; it is an Adam RA.14 Loisirs at the Musée Aéronautique de Champagne.

Table B-2: Aircraft Locations

A.E.G. E.II: 485/SP.
A.F.E.E. Rotachute 10.42 (R): 623/G.
A.N.E.C. II Monoplane: 620/G.
AISA I-11B: 520/EC.
AISA I-115: 520/EC.
Abraham 2 Iris: 285/F.
Adam RA.14 Loisirs: 286A/F.
Adaridy: 276/OH.
Addyman Glider: 575/G.
Addyman Ultra-light: 575/G.
Ader Avion III: 290/F, 291/F.
Aer Lualdi L.59: 353/I.
Aerfer Ariete: 353/I.
Aerfer Sagittario II: 353/I.
Aermacchi M.B.339B: 590/G.
Aero 2-D: 990/YU.
Aero 3: 990/YU, 992/YU.
Aero 45: 235/OK, 246A/OY, 295/DM, 326A/HA, 485/SP.
Aero 145: 235/OK, 286D/F, 485/SP.
Aero A 10: 235/OK.
Aero A 11: 275/OH.
Aero A 32: 275/OH.
Aero L-29 Delfin: 235/OK, 295A/DM, 568A/CP.
Aero L-39 Albatros: 235/OK.
Aero L-60 Brigadyr: 235/OK, 300A/D, 485/SP, 543A/SE.
Aero L-200 Moravia: 235/OK.
Aero XL-160: 235/OK.
Aero-Letov L-60 Brigadyr: 325/HA.
Aerodyne: 302/D.
Aeronca 7EC: 543A/SE.
Aerospatiale Concorde: 290/F.
Aerotechnik Uh. Haradiste A-70: 235A/OK.
Aerotecnica AC-12: 520/EC.
Aerotecnica AC-14: 520/EC.
Agusta-Bell 47G: 285/F, 286B/F, 290/F.
Air & Space U-18 Flymobil: 303/D.
Airspeed A.S.40 Oxford: 165/OO, 595A/G, 610C/G.
Airspeed A.S.57 Ambassador: 582/G.
Airspeed A.S.58 Horsa: 576/G, 601/G, 602/G, 610C/G.
Airspeed A.S.65 Consul: 610C/G.
Akaflieg Hannover Vampyr: 300/D.
Akaflieg Munchen Mu 10 Milan: 300/D.
Akaflieg Munchen Mu 13E Bergfalke: 300/D.
Akaflieg Stuttgart Fs 24 Phoenix: 300/D.
Alag A-08 Siraly: 325/HA, 326A/HA.
Albatros 120 CFM/Sk-1: 542/SE.
Albatros B.1: 160A/OE.
Albatros B.IIA: 485/SP.
Albatros C.I: 485/SP.
Albatros C.III: 285/F.
Albatros H.1 (Siemens-Sch. D.IV): 485/SP.
Albatros L.101: 485/SP.
Albatros NAB 9: 541/SE.
Aliante Caproni TM2 (glider): 356/I.
Aliante S.I.A.I. 3V1 Eolo (glider): 353/I.
Aliante Zoegling (R): 356/I.
Ambrosini S.A.I.2: 355/I.
Ambrosini Supersette: 353/I, 356/I.
Amiot AAC-1 Toucan: 490/CS.
Anatra DS Anasal: 237/OK.
Ansaldo A-1 Balilla: 355/I, 357B/I.
Ansaldo AC.2: 353/I.
Ansaldo S.V.A.5: 353/I, 355/I, 357A/I.
Antonov An-2: 285/F, 325/HA, 326A/HA, 568A/CP, 990/YU.

Antonov An-8: 568A/CP.
Antonov An-10A: 568A/CP.
Antonov An-12: 568A/CP.
Antonov An-14: 295A/DM.
Antonov An-15: 568A/CP.
Antonov An-24: 568A/CP.
Arado Ar 196A-3: 180A/LZ.
Armstrong Whitworth 660 Argosy: 608/G.
Arsenal Air 100: 285/F, 290/F.
Arsenal Air 102: 285/F.
Asiago Glider (Aerolombarda): 355/I.
Auster A.O.P.3: 415/PH.
Auster A.O.P.5: 415/PH, 541/SE, 640A/G.
Auster A.O.P.6: 602/G.
Auster A.O.P.9: 595A/G, 596/G, 602/G, 609/G, 618A/G, 620/G, 645/G.
Auster D5/160 Husky: 490/CS.
Auster J/1 Autocrat: 246A/OY, 285/F, 410/PH, 575/G, 595A/G.
Auster Mk.V: 165/OO, 541/SE, 545/SE, 596/G, 602/G.
Auster Mk.VI: 165/OO.
Auster Mk.7 Antarctic: 609/G.
Avia 40P (glider): 290/F.
Avia B 534: 235/OK.
Avia BH-9: 237/OK.
Avia BH-10: 237/OK.
Avia BH-11C: 235/OK.
Avia CS-129: 235/OK.
Avia F.13: 353/I.
Avia XV A (glider): 290/F.
Aviatik C.I: 165/OO.
Aviatik C.III: 485/SP.
Aviatik D.I(Austro-Hungarian Berg): 160/OE.
Avro 504K: 277/OH, 440A/LN, 603/G, 609/G, 610C/G, 620/G.
Avro 504N: 248/OY.
Avro 594 Avian: 541/SE, 593/G.
Avro 621 Tutor: 620/G.
Avro 631 Cadet: 490/CS.
Avro 652A Anson: 349A/EI, 415/PH, 595A/G, 600/G, 604/G, 605/G, 606/G, 608/G, 612A/G, 617/G, 640/G, 642/G.
Avro 683 Lancaster: 595/G, 610B/G, 610D/G, 642/G.
Avro 685 York: 582/G, 608/G.
Avro 694 Lincoln: 608/G, 622/G.
Avro 696 Shackleton: 604/G, 608/G, 642/G.
Avro 698 Vulcan: 595A/G, 600/G, 604/G, 606/G, 608/G, 609/G, 610B/G, 612A/G, 640A/G, 645/G.
Avro 706 Ashton (fuselage): 645/G.
Avro 707: 594/G, 608/G.
Avro 716 Shackleton: 594/G, 595A/G.
Avro Canada CF-100 Canuck: 165/OO, 595A/G.
B.A.C. Concorde: 590/G, 595A/G.
B.A.C. TSR-2: 595A/G, 608/G.
B.A.C. VC-10: 610/G.
B.D.M. 01 (helicopter): 290/F.
BAT Bantam: 620/G.
Bachem Ba 349 Natter (BP20): 300/D.
Badini Prototype: 355/I.
Bartlett M-8: 991/YU.
Bataille Triplane: 165/OO.
Beagle B.121 Pup: 595A/G.
Beagle B.206: 595A/G, 610/G.
Beagle Bulldog: 640A/G.
Beda Flying Boat: 541/SE.
Beech AT-7 Kansas (D-18S): 415/PH.

Beech AT-11 Kansas: 490/CS.
Beech UC-45: 286A/F, 353/I, 490/CS.
Beech D-17S Traveler (Staggerwing): 595A/G.
Beech D-18S Expeditor: 285/F, 290/F, 290A/F, 552/HB, 595A/G.
Beech E-18S Expeditor: 285/F, 640/G.
Beech F-50 Twin Bonanza: 541/SE.
Beech T-34C Turbo-Mentor: 590/G.
Bell 47: 160/OE, 276/OH, 285/F, 303/D, 354/I, 440A/LN, 520/EC, 541/SE, 550/HB, 602/G, 604/G, 623/G.
Bell 204 (UH-1B): 440A/LN.
Bell AB47G Sioux (Agusta): 353/I.
Bell AB102 (Agusta): 353/I.
Bell P-39 Aircobra: 277/OH, 568E/CP.
Bell UH-1 Iroquois: 590/G.
Benes-Mraz L-40 Meta-Sokol: 235/OK.
Benes-Mraz M-1C Sokol: 235/OK, 237/OK, 325/HA.
Beniczky E-31 Esztergom: 325/HA, 326A/HA.
Beniczky M-30 Fergeteg: 325/HA.
Beniczky-Vertes M-30S Super Ferg.: 326A/HA.
Bensen (gyro-glider): 605/G.
Bensen B-6 (gyro-glider): 410/PH.
Bensen B-7 (gyrocopter): 593/G, 603/G.
Bensen B-8W (gyrocopter): 237/OK, 590/G, 640A/G.
Berg und Storm Monoplane: 248/OY.
Berg-Krupka (glider): 160/OE.
Berger Bo: 541/SE.
Beriev Be-12 (flying boat): 568A/CP.
Bernard 191 ''Oiseau Canari'': 290/F.
Biot Planeur (glider): 290/F.
Birdman Grasshopper: 603/G.
Bison PG-2 (Mauboussin M.123 mod.): 286C/F.
Blackburn B Monoplane: 620/G.
Blackburn B-24 Skua (parts): 590/G.
Blackburn B-101 Beverly: 610/G.
Blackburn B-103 Buccaneer: 581/G, 590/G, 645/G.
Blackburn Monoplane: 581/G.
Blackburn T.5D Ripon ?275/OH.
Blake Bluetit: 620/G.
Bleriot ''Jul Hansen'': 440/LN.
Bleriot (J.A.P. Harding): 603/G.
Bleriot IX (fuselage): 290/F.
Bleriot XI: 237/OK, 285/F, 286D/F, 290/F, 291/F, 300/D, 352/I, 353/I, 356/I, 410/PH, 440/LN, 485/SP, 520/EC, 541/SE, 550/HB, 580A/G, 595A/G, 600/G, 610/G, 620/G.
Bleriot XI-2 (2-seat): 165/OO, 290/F, 353/I.
Bleriot XXVII(Gordon Bennett Race): 610C/G.
Boeing 247D: 603/G.
Boeing 707: 165/OO, 290/F, 608/G.
Boeing B-17G Flying Fortress: 290/F, 595A/G, 610B/G.
Boeing B-29A Super Fortress: 595A/G.
Boeing B-52D Stratofortress: 595A/G.
Bohemia B-5: 237/OK.
Bolkow Bo 46: 303/D.
Bolkow Bo 102 Helitrainer: 303/D.
Bolkow Bo 103: 303/D.
Bolkow Bo 105: 303/D.
Bolkow Flying Jeep: 303/D.
Boulton Paul P.82 Defiant: 610A/G.
Boulton Paul P.108 Sea Balliol: 606/G, 608/G, 617/G.
Boulton Paul P.111A: 600/G.
Brantly B.2B: 640A/G.
Breda Ba 15: 356/I.
Breda Ba 19: 355/I.
Breguet 19TR ''Jesus Del Grand'': 520/EC.
Breguet 14: 275/OH, 285/F, 290/F.
Breguet 19 Grand-Raid: 290/F.
Breguet 901: 290/F.

Breguet 904: 285/F, 286A/F, 286B/F, 286C/F, 286D/F.
Breguet 905S: 165/OO.
Breguet 941S: 290/F.
Breguet 1050 Alize: 290/F.
Breguet Avion: 291/F.
Breguet III (gyroplane): 290/F.
Breguet/B.A.C. Jaguar: 290/F.
Brewster B239 Buffalo (VL Humu): 277/OH.
Bristol 105A Bulldog IVA: 278/OH.
Bristol 142M Blenheim: 277/OH.
Bristol 149 Blenheim (Bolingbroke): 610/G.
Bristol 149 Bolingbroke IV: 165/OO, 595A/G, 640/G, 642/G.
Bristol 156 Beaufighter: 610/G, 610C/G.
Bristol 164 Brigand TT.1: 606/G.
Bristol 171 Sycamore: 300A/D, 303/D, 305/D, 579/G, 581/G, 594/G, 595A/G, 602/G, 604/G, 606/G, 608/G, 610C/G, 615/G, 621/G.
Bristol 173 (twinrotor helicopter): 610C/G.
Bristol 175 Brittania 312: 595A/G, 608/G.
Bristol 188: 608/G.
Bristol 192 Belvedere: 579/G, 610/G.
Bristol Baby: 588/G.
Bristol Boxkite: 615/G, 620/G.
Bristol F.2B Fighter: 595A/G, 610C/G, 620/G.
Bristol Scout: 609/G.
Bristol-Coanda No.153 (Caproni): 355/I.
British Aircraft Company Drone: 580A/G, 595A/G.
British Aircraft Company Swallow: 620/G, 640/G, 642/G.
Britten-Norman BN-IF: 608/G.
Brochet MB 50 Pipistrelle: 286A/F.
Brochet MB 72: 285/F.
Brochet MB 850: 290/F.
Bucker Bu 131 Jungmann: 235/OK, 237/OK, 285/F, 355/I, 485/SP, 992/YU.
Bucker Bu 131B Jungmann: 300A/D, 520/EC, 541/SE, 550/HB, 552/HB.
Bucker Bu 133 Jungmeister: 285/F, 495B/YR, 520/EC, 550/HB, 552/HB, 990/YU.
Bucker Bu 181 Bestmann: 165/OO, 235/OK, 237/OK, 285/F, 286B/F, 290/F, 300A/D, 305/D, 542/SE, 552/HB.
Buryevestnik S-3: 568A/CP.
C.S.S. 12 (cockpit only): 485/SP.
C.S.S. 13 (Polikarpov Po-2): 485/SP.
C.V.V Canguro (Aeronaut. Lombarda): 353/I.
CAP.10: 285/F.
CAP.20LS: 285/F.
CASA C-207C Azor: 520/EC.
CAT 20 (glider): 355/I.
CFM 01 Tummelisa: 542/SE.
CLA.7 Swift: 580A/G.
Campbell Cougar: 579/G.
Cant Z.506S Airone: 353/I.
Caproni Ca.1: 355/I.
Caproni Ca.6: 355/I.
Caproni Ca.9: 355/I.
Caproni Ca.18: 355/I.
Caproni Ca.20: 355/I.
Caproni Ca.22 Parasol: 355/I.
Caproni Ca.33: 353/I.
Caproni Ca.36: 355/I.
Caproni Ca.51 (Cvjetkovic): 990/YU.
Caproni Ca.53 Triplane: 355/I.
Caproni Ca.60 (bow only): 355/I.
Caproni Ca.100: 353/I, 355/I.
Caproni Ca.113: 355/I.
Caproni Ca.163 Biplane: 355/I.

Caproni Ca.193: 355/I.
Caproni-Campini CC.1: 353/I.
Caproni-Campini CC.2 (fuselage): 356/I.
Caproni-Reggiane Re.2000: 355/I, 542/SE.
Caproni-Reggiane Re.2002 Ariete: 353/I.
Caproni-Reggiane Re.2005(fuselage): 355/I.
Caproni-Trento F.5 Sagitario: 353/I.
Castel C.25S: 286A/F, 286B/F, 286C/F.
Castel C.242: 290/F.
Castel C.301S: 290/F.
Castel C.310P: 286A/F.
Castel-Mauboussin C.M. 813: 290/F.
Caudron C.59: 275/OH.
Caudron C.60: 275/OH, 290/F.
Caudron C.69: 285/F.
Caudron C.109: 290/F.
Caudron C.270 Luciole: 285/F.
Caudron C.275 Luciole: 285/F.
Caudron C.277 Luciole: 290/F.
Caudron C.282 Phalene: 285/F, 286A/F, 290/F.
Caudron C.600 Aiglon: 286D/F.
Caudron C.601 Aiglon: 285/F.
Caudron C.635 Simoun: 290/F.
Caudron C.714R: 290/F.
Caudron C.800: 165/OO, 285/F, 286A/F, 290/F.
Caudron C.801: 286D/F.
Caudron G.3: 165/OO, 278/OH, 290/F, 490/CS, 610/G.
Caudron G.4: 290/F.
Caudron-Regnier C.366: 290/F.
Caudron-Renault C.714: 275/OH.
Cavka Sostaris (glider): 990/YU.
Cayley (Sir George) (R): 610/G.
Centre Aviation GA-620 Gaucho: 286A/F.
Cessna 310B: 165/OO.
Cessna F-150 (Reims): 613/G.
Cessna F-172H Skyhawk (Reims): 277/OH, 541/SE.
Cessna L-19A Bird Dog: 286B/F, 520/EC.
Cessna T-210L Turbo Centurian: 613/G.
Cessna T-50 Bobcat (UC-78): 485/SP.
Chandellon (helicopter): 165/OO.
Chanute Glider: 286A/F, 290/F, 550/HB.
Chapeau EC.19 Planeur (glider): 286A/F.
Chargus 18/50 (hang glider): 640/G.
Chargus Midas E: 603/G.
Chrislea Airguard: 575/G.
Chukar Pilotless Target Drone: 590/G.
Cid Varela Hydro: 490/CS.
Cierva C.19 MkIV autogyro-Avro 620: 520/EC.
Cierva C.24 (autogiro): 601/G.
Cierva C.30 (autogiro): 356/I, 547/SE.
Cierva C.30A (autogyro): 410/PH, 595A/G, 603/G, 610/G, 620/G.
Cierva CB.11 (autogyro): 290/F.
Cijab Orao IIC (glider): 990/YU.
Cil Reghin RG 4 Pioneerter: 495B/YR.
Clarke Biplane Glider: 603/G, 610/G.
Cody Kite Biplane: 610/G.
Cody Military Biplane: 603/G.
Cody Military Flyer (R): 602/G.
Commonwealth CA-7 Wirraway II(AT6): 542/SE.
Comte AC-4 Gentleman: 550/HB, 552/HB.
Consolidated B-24 Liberator: 608/G, 622/G.
Consolidated PBY-5A Catalina: 248A/OY, 415/PH, 542/SE.
Consolidated PBY-6A Catalina: 248A/OY, 608/G.
Convair CV-340/440 Metropolitan: 276/OH, 541/SE.
Convair CV-990A Coronado II: 550/HB.
Crocco-Ricaldoni Idroplano: 353/I.
Crosses Mini Criquet (Pou du Ciel): 290/F.

Crossley Tom Thumb: 600/G.
Curtiss A1 Triad (R): 353/I.
Curtiss CW-22 Falcon: 565/TC.
Curtiss Hawk II(Udet '36 Olympics): 485/SP.
Curtiss JN-4 Jenny: 610/G.
Curtiss Model D: 580A/G.
Curtiss P-40: 568E/CP, 595A/G.
Curtiss SB2C-5 Helldiver: 318A/SX.
Curtiss Wright CW-1 Junior: 286D/F.
D'Ascanio Elicottero D'A.T-3: 353/I.
D.F.S. 108-14 Schulgleiter S.G.38: 276/OH, 286A/F, 286B/F, 300A/D, 440A/LN, 541/SE.
D.F.S. 108-70 Meise: 326A/HA, 541/SE, 990/YU.
D.F.S. 108-70 Olympia: 276/OH, 277/OH.
D.F.S. Cinke/Meise: 325/HA.
D.F.S. G.101 Schulgleiter S.G.38: 542/SE.
D.F.S. Habicht: 290/F.
D.F.S. Kranich (glider): 490/CS, 541/SE, 543/SE, 990/YU.
D.F.S. Kranich II: 290/F, 300/D.
D.F.S. Kranich III: 520/EC.
D.F.S. Meise Olympia (glider): 277/OH, 300/D, 542/SE, 546/SE.
D.F.S. SE-102 Grunau Baby II: 542/SE.
D.F.S. SE-103 Kranich: 542/SE.
D.F.S. SE-104 Weihe: 542/SE.
D.F.S. Weihe: 237/OK, 245/OY, 277/OH, 490/CS, 520/EC, 541/SE.
D.F.W. C.V: 485/SP.
Dassault MD 311 Flamant: 285/F.
Dassault MD 312 Flamant: 286A/F, 286B/F, 290/F, 290A/F.
Dassault MD 315R Flamant: 290/F.
Dassault MD 450 Ouragan IV: 165/OO, 290/F.
Dassault Mirage G.8: 290/F.
Dassault Mirage III: 290/F, 552/HB.
Dassault Mystere IV: 286A/F, 286B/F, 290A/F, 588/G, 589/G, 595A/G, 605/G, 612A/G, 645/G.
Dassault Mystere XX: 290/F.
Dassault Super Mystere B.2: 290/F, 290A/F.
De Bernardi MdB.01 Aeroscooter: 353/I.
De Bernardi MdB.02 Aeroscooter: 355/I.
De Havilland D.H.9: 290/F, 610B/G.
De Havilland D.H.51: 620/G.
De Havilland D.H.53 Humming Bird: 620/G.
De Havilland D.H.60 Moth: 277/OH, 279/OH, 520/EC, 541/SE, 542/SE, 545/SE, 546/SE, 603/G, 620/G.
De Havilland D.H.80A Puss Moth: 290/F, 356/I, 620/G, 640/G.
De Havilland D.H.82 Tiger Moth: 165/OO, 246A, 247/OY, 285/F, 286C/F, 286D/F, 300A/D, 318A/SX, 410/PH, 415/PH, 440A/LN, 440B/LN, 490/CS, 542/SE, 543/SE, 546/SE, 590/G, 595A/G, 601/G, 610/G, 620/G, 621/G, 623/G, 639/G, 640/G, 642/G, 990/YU.
De Havilland D.H.83 Fox Moth: 600/G.
De Havilland D.H.84 Dragon: 349A/EI, 640/G.
De Havilland D.H.87B Hornet Moth: 246A/OY, 490/CS, 601/G, 620/G, 644/G.
De Havilland D.H.88 Comet (Racer): 620/G.
De Havilland D.H.89 Dragon Rapide/Dominie: 165/OO, 245/OY, 285/F, 290/F, 300A/D, 415/PH, 490/CS, 520/EC, 565/TC, 586/G, 595A/G, 610C/G, 620/G, 640/G.
De Havilland D.H.94 Moth Minor: 285/F, 620/G.
De Havilland D.H.98 Mosquito NF.30: 165/OO, 595/G, 595A/G, 601/G, 608/G, 610B/G, 622/G.
De Havilland D.H.100 Vampire: 277/OH, 278/OH, 286D/F, 290/F, 353/I, 356/I, 440/LN, 440A/LN, 440B/LN, 490/CS, 542/SE, 550/HB, 552/HB, 590/G,

281

595A/G, 600/G, 601/G, 609/G, 610/G, 621/G, 643/G.
De Havilland D.H.103 Sea Hornet: 601/G.
De Havilland D.H.104 Dove: 160/OE, 245/OY, 410/PH, 595A/G, 598/G, 600/G, 601/G, 608/G, 621/G, 640/G, 990/YU.
De Havilland D.H.106 Comet: 300A/D, 582/G, 595A/G, 603/G, 608/G, 610C/G, 622/G, 640/G, 642/G.
De Havilland D.H.110 Sea Vixen: 581/G, 590/G, 595A/G, 601/G, 605/G, 612A/G, 645/G.
De Havilland D.H.112 Venom: 300A/D, 542/SE, 550/HB, 552/HB, 590/G, 595A/G, 601/G, 606/G, 608/G, 610C/G, 621/G, 623/G, 640/G, 645/G.
De Havilland D.H.113 Vampire: 353/I.
De Havilland D.H.114 Heron 1B: 604/G.
De Havilland D.H.115 Vampire: 165/OO, 276/OH, 277/OH, 349A/EI, 542/SE, 546/SE, 588/G, 589/G, 595A/G, 598/G, 599/G, 600/G, 601/G, 604/G, 605/G, 606/G, 608/G, 610C/G, 612A/G, 617/G, 618A/G, 622/G, 640/G, 642/G, 645/G.
De Havilland D.H.121 Trident: 601/G, 608/G.
De Havilland D.H.125 Dominie: 601/G.
De Havilland DHA.3 Drover: 618A/G, 622/G.
De Havilland DHC-1 Chipmunk: 165/OO, 248A/OY, 285/F, 591/G, 595A/G, 601/G, 608/G, 620/G, 621/G.
De Havilland DHC-2 Beaver: 415/PH, 600/G, 602/G, 622/G, 990/YU.
De Havilland DHC-3 Otter: 165/OO.
Deperdussin B: 290/F.
Deperdussin Monocoque: 285/F, 290/F.
Deperdussin Monoplane: 620/G.
Desoutter I: 620/G.
Dewoitine D.26: 285/F, 552/HB.
Dewoitine D.27: 550/HB.
Dewoitine D.520: 285/F, 290/F.
Dewoitine D.530: 290/F.
Dewoitine D.VII: 290/F.
Donnet-Leveque "Maagen 3": 246/OY.
Donnet-Leveque A Flying Boat: 290/F.
Donnet-Leveque II "Maagen 2": 246/OY.
Donnet-Leveque L.II Flying Boat: 547/SE.
Dornier DS 10 Fledermaus: 305/D.
Dornier Do 19: 302/D.
Dornier Do 24T: 302/D, 520/EC, 610/G.
Dornier Do 27: 165/OO, 300/D, 300A/D, 302/D, 305/D, 490/CS.
Dornier Do 28B-1: 290/F, 302/D, 520/EC.
Dornier Do 29 (S/VTOL): 300/D.
Dornier Do 31E (VTOL): 300/D, 302/D.
Dornier Do 32E Kiebitz helicopter: 300/D, 302/D, 303/D.
Dornier Do 132 (rotor test stand): 303/D.
Dornier Libelle: 302/D.
Douglas A-1 Skyraider: 542/SE, 546/SE, 581/G, 590/G.
Douglas A-26 Invader (B-26): 165/OO, 290/F, 490/CS.
Douglas AD-4N Skyraider: 285/F, 290/F, 541/SE.
Douglas DC-2: 277/OH.
Douglas DC-3 (C-47): 165/OO, 248A/OY, 276/OH, 277/OH, 285/F, 290/F, 300/D, 300A/D, 353/I, 410/PH, 415/PH, 440A/LN, 490/CS, 520/EC, 541/SE, 542/SE, 550/HB, 576/G, 582/G, 595A/G, 603/G, 608/G, 990/YU.
Douglas DC-3 (Lisunov Li-2D): 235/OK, 325/HA.
Douglas DC-4 (C-54 Skymaster): 490/CS, 520/EC.
Douglas DC-6B Liftmaster: 490/CS.
Douglas DC-7C: 247/OY, 290/F.
Drezair Hang-Glider: 286A/F.
Druine D.31 Turbulent: 246A/OY, 286A/F, 286D/F.
Dufaux IV (biplane): 550/HB.
Dumolard Pou du Ciel: 290/F.

E.F.W. C-3603-1: 550/HB, 552/HB.
E.F.W. N-20 Aiguillon: 552/HB.
E.F.W. N-20 Arbalette: 550/HB.
E.K.W. C-35: 550/HB.
E.W.R.-Sud VJ 101C (tilt-eng.VTOL): 300/D.
Eklund TE-1: 276/OH.
Ellehammer 1906: 245/OY.
Ellehammer Biplane: 246/OY.
Ellehammer Helicopter: 246/OY.
Ellehammer Monoplane: 246/OY.
Elliott Newbury Eton (glider): 610C/G.
Elsnic El-2M Sedy Vic: 235/OK.
English Electric Canberra: 290/F, 542/SE, 546/SE, 588/G, 595A/G, 600/G, 608/G, 609/G, 609A/G, 610B/G, 613/G, 617/G, 645/G.
English Electric Lightning P.1: 594/G, 595A/G, 608/G, 610/G, 640/G.
English Electric Wren: 620/G.
Erco 415-D Ercoupe: 546/SE.
Esnault-Pelterie Monoplane: 291/F.
Etrich Limusine: 237/OK.
Etrich Taube: 160/OE, 300/D.
FFVS J22: 542/SE, 546/SE.
FMA IA-58 Pucara: 590/G, 595A/G, 608/G.
Fabian Levente II: 325/HA.
Fabre Hydravion (First seaplane): 290/F.
Fairchild C-119 Flying Boxcar: 165/OO, 353/I.
Fairchild F-24: 165/OO, 245/OY, 285/F, 286B/F, 353/I, 355/I, 541/SE, 610C/G.
Fairchild PT-19 Cornell: 440A/LN, 610C/G.
Fairchild PT-26 Cornell: 245/OY, 440A/LN.
Fairey Albacore: 590/G.
Fairey Barracuda: 590/G.
Fairey Battle: 609/G, 642/G.
Fairey Delta FD-2 (B.A.C.221): 590/G, 608/G.
Fairey Firefly: 541/SE, 542/SE, 590/G, 595A/G, 606/G.
Fairey Flycatcher: 590/G.
Fairey Fulmar II: 590/G.
Fairey Gannet: 305/D, 581/G, 590/G, 595A/G, 600/G, 604/G, 645/G.
Fairey Gyrodyne: 608/G.
Fairey Helicopter (ultra-light): 600/G.
Fairey IIID: 490/CS, 493/CS.
Fairey Rotodyne: 579/G.
Fairey Swordfish: 590/G, 595A/G, 610C/G, 642/G.
Fairey Ultralight: 579/G.
Farman (Henri) 1909: 356/I.
Farman (Henri) F.20: 290/F.
Farman (Maurice): 290/F.
Farman (Maurice) Longhorn: 440/LN, 490/CS.
Farman (Maurice) Shorthorn: 415/PH.
Farman Biplane: 318A/SX, 610C/G.
Farman F.46: 440A/LN.
Farman F.60 Goliath: 290/F.
Farman F.192: 290/F.
Farman F.400: 285/F.
Farman F.455 Moustique: 290/F.
Farman IV (Russian version) (R): 485/SP.
Farman Shorthorn: 165/OO.
Farman Svendsen Glenten: 246/OY.
Farman-Voisin (Dabert II): 165/OO.
Farner WF-7 (Sailplane): 550/HB.
Fauvel AV.36: 285/F, 286A/F, 290/F, 300/D.
Fauvel AV.45: 286C/F.
Ferguson Mk.V: 639/G.
Fiat C.29: 353/I.
Fiat C.R.32: 353/I, 520/EC.
Fiat C.R.42 Falco: 542/SE, 610A/G.
Fiat G.5bis: 353/I.

Fiat G.46: 353/I.
Fiat G.49-2: 353/I.
Fiat G.50bis: 990/YU.
Fiat G.59: 353/I.
Fiat G.80: 353/I.
Fiat G.82: 353/I.
Fiat G.91: 165/OO, 300A/D, 302/D, 305/D, 353/I.
Fiat G.212CR: 353/I.
Fiat G.222: 353/I.
Fiat-Aeritalia G.91Y Yankee: 353/I.
Fibera KK-1 (UTI): 276/OH.
Fieseler Fi 103: 295A/DM, 416A/PH, 440A/LN, 589/G, 603/G, 608/G, 609/G.
Fieseler Fi 156 Storch: 160/OE, 165/OO, 235/OK, 237/OK, 276/OH, 290/F, 300/D, 300A/D, 353/I, 542/SE, 550/HB, 552/HB, 595/G, 609/G, 640/G.
Finsterwalder Bergflex: 300/D.
Fizir FN: 990/YU.
Fizir FNH: 992/YU.
Fleet 10G: 495A/YR.
Flettner Fl 282 Kolibri: 600/G.
Fleury Vedette: 286A/F.
Focke-Achgelis Fa 330 Bachstelze: 245/OY, 290/F, 300/D, 303/D, 595A/G, 598/G, 599/G, 603/G, 608/G, 621/G.
Focke-Borgward FB 1 Kolibri: 303/D.
Focke-Wulf Fw 44J Stieglitz: 278/OH, 541/SE, 542/SE, 543/SE, 546/SE, 992/YU.
Focke-Wulf Fw 50: 165/OO.
Focke-Wulf Fw 61 helicopter: 303/D.
Focke-Wulf Fw 190: 290/F, 300A/D, 440A/LN, 595/G, 609/G, 990/YU.
Fokker C.V-D: 410/PH, 440A/LN, 542/SE, 550/HB, 552/HB.
Fokker C.X: 277/OH.
Fokker D.VII: 290/F, 300/D, 552/HB, 603/G, 610C/G.
Fokker D.VIII: 355/I.
Fokker D.XXI: 277/OH.
Fokker Dr.I Triplane (R): 285/F, 300/D, 300A/D, 410/PH, 590/G, 595/G, 621/G.
Fokker E.III: 603/G.
Fokker F.VIIA: 410/PH, 550/HB.
Fokker S.11 Instructor: 410/PH, 415/PH, 642/G.
Fokker S.12: 410/PH.
Fokker S.14 Mach Trainer: 410/PH, 415/PH.
Fokker Spinne: 410/PH, 485/SP.
Folland Fo.141 Gnat: 275/OH, 276/OH, 277/OH, 278/OH, 600/G, 608/G, 990/YU.
Folland Fo.144 Gnat T.1: 603/G, 608/G.
Fouga C.M.8/15: 285/F.
Fouga C.M.170 Magister: 165/OO, 286A/F, 286B/F, 290/F, 290A/F, 305/D.
Fouga C.M.173: 286B/F.
Fournier RF-2: 290/F.
Francis Lombardi F.L.3: 355/I.
Frati-Pasotti F.9 Sparviero: 356/I.
GH Racer: 542/SE.
Gabardini 1918: 355/I.
Gabardini 2 (seaplane): 355/I.
Gardan GY-201 Minicab (Bearn): 286A/F.
Gary GR-1 (autogyro): 290/F.
Geest Mowe (Moewe): 485/SP.
General Aircraft G.A.L.42 Cygnet 2: 640/G.
General Aircraft Hotspur MkII: 576/G.
General Aircraft ST-12 Monospar: 604/G.
General Aircraft ST-25 Monospar: 245/OY.
General Dynamics FFA P-16 Mk.II: 552/HB.
Georges G-1 Papillon: 303/D.
Georges G-2: 303/D.

Gerle 13: 326A/HA.
Glider (Type unknown): 353/I.
Gloster E.28/39 (1st Whittle Jet): 603/G.
Gloster Meteor:: 248A/OY, 290A/F, 618A/G.
Gloster G.41 Meteor: 165/OO, 286A/F, 410/PH, 415/PH, 542/SE, 546/SE, 590/G, 595/G, 595A/G, 600/G, 606/G, 609/G, 621/G, 623/G, 643/G, 645/G.
Gloster G.41A Meteor: 608/G.
Gloster G.41F Meteor: 608/G, 609/G.
Gloster G.41G Meteor: 604/G.
Gloster G.41K Meteor: 595A/G, 605/G, 608/G, 609/G, 610/G.
Gloster G.41L Meteor: 604/G.
Gloster G.43 Meteor: 248/OY, 622/G, 645/G.
Gloster G.47 Meteor: 165/OO, 290/F, 604/G, 612/G, 640/G.
Gloster Gauntlet: 278/OH.
Gloster Gladiator: 440A/LN, 542/SE, 610/G, 610A/G, 620/G.
Gloster Javelin: 300A/D, 595A/G, 600/G, 604/G, 605/G, 608/G, 609A/G.
Gloster Sea Gladiator: 360A/VP, 590/G.
Goetaverken GV-38 (Rearwin): 541/SE.
Gosslich Pedalcopter: 303/D.
Gourdou-Leseurre B.3: 277/OH.
Gourdou-Leseurre B.7/192: 290/F.
Grade Libelle: 300/D.
Grade Monoplane: 295/DM.
Granger Archaeopteryx: 620/G.
Grankvist: 546/SE.
Grassi: 290/F.
Great Lakes 2T: 285/F.
Grigorovitch M.15: 485/SP.
Grumman F4F Wildcat (Martlet I): 590/G.
Grumman F6F-5 Hellcat II: 590/G.
Grumman F8F-2 Bearcat: 595A/G.
Grumman G-44 Widgeon: 440/LN, 490/CS, 493/CS.
Grumman HU-16 Albatros: 353/I, 520/EC.
Grumman S-2 Tracker: 353/I, 410/PH, 415/PH.
Grumman TBF Avenger (TBM): 590/G, 595A/G, 622/G.
Guerchais-Roche SA.103 Emouchet: 286A/F, 286B/F, 286D/F.
Guerchais-Roche SA.104 Emouchet: 286A/F, 290/F.
Gumpert G-2: 160/OE, 246A/OY.
Gurripato II: 520/EC.
Haase-Kensche-Schmet HKS-3: 300/D.
Haefeli D.H.1: 552/HB.
Haefeli D.H.5: 552/HB.
Haerens Flyvemaskinfabrik FF9 Kaie: 440A/LN.
Hafner Revoplane R.II: 579/G, 602/G.
Hafner Rotochute 1: 602/G, 610C/G.
Halberstadt C.V: 165/OO.
Hamburger Flugzeugbau HFB 320: 300/D, 305/D.
Handley Page H.P.39 Gugnunc: 603/G.
Handley Page H.P.57 Halifax: 595/G, 610B/G.
Handley Page H.P.67 Hastings: 595A/G, 604/G, 608/G.
Handley Page H.P.68 Hermes: 595A/G.
Handley Page H.P.80 Victor: 595A/G, 608/G.
Handley Page H.P.115: 590/G.
Handley Page H.P.R.7 Dart Herald: 612A/G.
Hanriot HD-1: 165/OO, 353/I, 550/HB, 610/G.
Hanriot HD-14: 290/F.
Hansa-Brandenburg BI Seria-Loczy: 325/HA.
Hardy-Roger M.P.A. Dragonfly II: 640/G.
Hatry-Opel RAK-1 Rocket Glider: 300/D.
Havertz HZ-5: 303/D.
Hawker Cygnet: 610/G.
Hawker Dankok F.B.II: 248/OY.
Hawker Fury: 608/G.

Hawker Hart: 542/SE, 610B/G.
Hawker Hart: 610/G.
Hawker Hind: 610/G, 620/G.
Hawker Hunter: 165/OO, 248A/OY, 410/PH, 415/PH, 542/SE, 546/SE, 588/G, 594/G, 595A/G, 600/G, 606/G, 608/G, 609/G, 610/G, 618A/G, 622/G, 645/G.
Hawker Hurricane: 165/OO, 277/OH, 568E/CP, 580/G, 600/G, 603/G, 610A/G, 610D/G, 620/G, 621/G, 642/G, 990/YU.
Hawker P.1052: 608/G.
Hawker P.1127: 610/G.
Hawker Sea Fury: 305/D, 410/PH, 590/G, 610/G.
Hawker Sea Hawk: 305/D, 410/PH, 581/G, 590/G, 595A/G, 600/G, 618A/G, 621/G, 640/G, 642/G, 645/G.
Hawker Sea Hurricane 1B: 595A/G.
Hawker Siddeley D.H.121 Trident: 595A/G, 603/G.
Hawker Siddeley Kestrel: 610C/G.
Hawker Tempest: 595A/G, 610/G.
Hawker Tomtit: 620/G.
Hawker Typhoon: 595/G, 610/G.
Heimbacher 4: 303/D.
Heinkel He 5E: 485/SP.
Heinkel He 35: 546/SE.
Heinkel He 100: 568E/CP.
Heinkel He 111: 290/F, 300/D, 300A/D, 305/D, 440A/LN, 520/EC, 568C/CP, 610A/G.
Heinkel He 162 Volksjaeger: 290/F, 595/G, 609/G.
Heinonen HK-1 Keltiainen: 276/OH.
Henschel Hs 293: 440A/LN, 440B/LN.
Hiller HPE-2: 590/G.
Hiller OH-23C Raven: 415/PH.
Hiller UH-12B: 552/HB.
Hinkler 1bis: 603/G.
Hirsch HR-100: 290/F.
Hirth-Huetter GOE-4 Goevier III: 300/D, 300/D.
Hispano Aviacion Ha.200 Supersaeta: 520/EC.
Hispano Suiza H.S.34: 520/EC.
Hogslund-Olsen 2G: 245/OY.
Hollaender A.H.1: 245/OY.
Hollschmidt 222: 246A/OY.
Horten Ho.IV: 300/D.
Huarte-Mendicoa H.M.1-B: 520/EC.
Huber Alpengleiter: 300/D.
Hug Spyr III: 550/HB.
Hughes 29-6A HKP5A: 542/SE.
Humber Monoplane: 590/G.
Huntair Pathfinder II: 603/G.
Hunting H.126: 608/G.
Hunting-Percival P.56 Provost: 598/G, 604/G, 605/G, 608/G, 609/G, 610C/G, 620/G, 621/G, 640/G.
Hunting-Percival P.57 Sea Prince: 581/G, 590/G, 605/G.
Hunting-Percival P.66 Pembroke: 165/OO, 245/OY, 277/OH, 300/D, 305/D, 542/SE, 546/SE, 645/G.
Hunting-Percival P.86 Jet Provost: 595A/G, 606/G, 609/G, 620/G.
Hurel Aviette: 290/F.
Hurel-Dubois H.D.10: 290/F.
Hurel-Dubois H.D.34: 290/F.
Hutter Hu 17B: 160/OE, 245/OY, 247/OY, 300/D, 300A/D, 541/SE.
I.A.R.813: 495A/YR, 495B/YR.
I.A.R.817: 495B/YR.
I.L. BZ-1 Gil (prototype): 485/SP.
I.L. BZ-4 Zuk (prototype): 485/SP.
I.L. JK-1 Trzmiel: 485/SP.
I.L. TS-8 Bies: 485/SP, 485/SP.
I.L. TS-11 Iskra (prototype): 485/SP.
I.V.L. A.22 Hansa: 276/OH.

I.V.L. C.24: 278/OH.
I.V.L. D.26 Haukka: 275/OH.
I.V.L. D.27 Haukka II: 278/OH.
I.V.L. K.1 Kurki: 275/OH.
Ikarus 214P: 990/YU.
Ikarus 451 Pionir: 990/YU.
Ikarus 451M Zolja (prototype): 990/YU.
Ikarus 451MMT Strsljen: 990/YU.
Ikarus Cham C-3 Trojka: 992/YU.
Ikarus S-451MM Matica: 990/YU.
Ikarus S-49A: 990/YU.
Ikarus Windspiel 2: 300A/D.
Ilindenka: 990/YU.
Ilyushin Il-2: 180B/LZ, 235/OK, 480/SP, 568A/CP, 568E/CP, 990/YU.
Ilyushin Il-10: 235/OK, 480/SP, 485/SP, 495A/YR, 568A/CP.
Ilyushin Il-12: 568A/CP.
Ilyushin Il-14: 325/HA, 568A/CP, 990/YU.
Ilyushin Il-28: 235/OK, 277/OH, 480/SP, 485/SP, 486A/SP, 568A/CP, 568C/CP.
Ilyushin Il-62: 568A/CP.
IMAM Ro.43: 353/I.
J.V. (Le Cerf Aero-Kite): 490/CS.
Janecek Delta-C Glider: 237/OK.
Janka Gyongyos 33: 325/HA.
Jeannin Stahltaube: 485/SP.
Jodel D.9 Bebe: 165/OO, 290/F.
Jodel D.112: 286A/F.
Jodel D.119: 290/F.
Jodel D.120: 285/F.
Johansen CAJO-1: 246A/OY.
Jonathan Livingston BD-2: 165/OO.
Junkers A.50 Junior: 276/OH, 300/D.
Junkers D.I (J 9): 290/F.
Junkers F 13: 290/F, 300/D, 325/HA, 547/SE.
Junkers J 1: 356/I.
Junkers Ju 52/3m: 290/F, 300/D, 300A/D, 440A/LN, 490/CS, 520/EC, 541/SE, 552/HB, 595A/G, 608/G, 622/G.
Junkers Ju 86K-4: 542/SE.
Junkers Ju 87 Stuka: 300A/D, 360A/VP, 610A/G.
Junkers Ju 88: 440A/LN, 610A/G.
Junkers W 34: 541/SE.
Jurca MJ.2A Tempete: 246A/OY.
Jurca MJ.5 Sirocco: 286C/F.
KSM Kromeriz KD-67: 235A/OK.
Kaman HH-43B Huskie: 303/D.
Kamov Ka-18-62: 568A/CP.
Kamov Ka-26: 546/SE.
Karhumaeki Karhu 48 Nalle: 278/OH.
Karhumaeki Karhu 48 Tavi: 276/OH.
Kassel 12: 165/OO, 275/OH.
Kawasaki Ki-100 ''Tony'': 608/G, 609/G.
Kay 331 Gyroplane: 641/G.
Kellner-Bechereau E-60: 290/F.
Kermer Wien: 160/OE.
Killick HDK.3: 575/G.
Kjolseth P.K. X-1: 440A/LN.
Klemm Kl 25F: 300/D.
Klemm Kl 34D: 541/SE.
Klemm Kl 35D: 245/OY, 300A/D, 542/SE, 545/SE, 546/SE.
Klemm Kl 107B: 300A/D.
Klemm L 20: 306/D.
Knoller C.II: 237/OK.
Kockum Baby Falke: 541/SE.
Kokkola Ko-04 Super Upstart: 276/OH.
Koolhoven F.K.43: 411A/PH.

Kosava (Ikarus glider): 990/YU.
Koser-Horvat Jadran: 990/YU.
Kreit KL-1: 165/OO.
Kugisho OHKA 11 (Kamikazi): 594/G.
Kunaver (prototype): 991/YU.
Kunkadlo (Simunek VBS-1): 237/OK.
L.V.G. B.II: 485/SP.
L.V.G. C.IV: 620/G.
L.V.G. C.VI: 165/OO, 290/F.
L.W.D. Junak-1: 485/SP.
L.W.D. Junak-2: 485/SP.
L.W.D. Junak-3: 485/SP, 486/SP.
L.W.D. Szpak-2: 485/SP.
L.W.D. Szpak-3: 485/SP.
L.W.D. Szpak-4: 485/SP.
L.W.D. Zak-3: 485/SP.
L.W.D. Zuch-1: 485/SP.
L.W.D. Zuch-2: 485/SP.
L.W.D. Zuraw: 485/SP.
L.W.F. V Scout: 237/OK.
LET L-13 Blanik: 235/OK.
LET L-200D Morava: 235/OK, 326A/HA.
LIM-1 (MiG-15): 480/SP, 485/SP.
Lachassagne AL.07: 286A/F.
Lampich-Thorotzkai L-2 Roma: 325/HA.
Latecoere 17P: 285/F.
Lavavasseur Antoinette: 290/F, 485/SP, 603/G.
Lavochkin La-5: 568E/CP.
Lavochkin La-7: 235/OK, 568A/CP.
Lavochkin La-9: 495A/YR.
Lavochkin La-11: 568A/CP.
Lavochkin La-15: 568A/CP.
Lavochkin La-250: 568A/CP.
Leduc 010: 290/F.
Leduc 022: 290/F.
Leduc RL.19: 286A/F.
Lee-Richards Annular Biplane: 604/G.
Lemaire RL-1: 286A/F.
Leonardo da Vinci Flying Mach.: 353/I.
Leopoldoff L.3 (Colibri): 285/F.
Leopoldoff L.6 (Colibri): 285/F.
Leopoldoff L.55 (Colibri): 285/F.
Letov 22: 990/YU.
Letov LF-107 Lunak: 235/OK, 235A/OK.
Letov LF-109 Pionyr: 235/OK.
Letov S-20: 235/OK.
Letov S-218: 235/OK.
Libis KB-6 Matajur: 990/YU.
Lilienthal Biplane: 300A/D.
Lilienthal Glider: 160/OE, 290/F, 295/DM, 410/PH, 486/SP, 603/G.
Lilienthal Monoplane: 300A/D.
Lilienthal Type 11: 300/D, 568E/CP.
Lilienthal Type 13: 305/D.
Liore-et-Oliver C.302 (Cierva): 290/F.
Lisunov Li-2 (DC-3): 568A/CP.
Lisunov Li-3: 990/YU.
Lloyd LS-1: 325/HA.
Lockheed 9-C Orion: 550/HB.
Lockheed 10A: 603/G.
Lockheed 12A Electra: 415/PH.
Lockheed 16 Hudson: 610/G.
Lockheed 18 Lodestar: 276/OH, 541/SE.
Lockheed F-104G Starfighter: 165/OO, 248A/OY, 300/D, 305/D, 440A/LN.
Lockheed L-749A Constellation: 290/F, 603/G.
Lockheed L-1049G Constellation: 300A/D.
Lockheed P2V Neptune: 286A/F, 290/F, 490/CS.
Lockheed PV-2 Harpoon: 490/CS.

Lockheed SP-2H Neptune: 286B/F, 415/PH, 608/G.
Lockheed T-33 Shooting Star: 165/OO, 246A/OY, 248A/OY, 286A/F, 286B/F, 290/F, 290A/F, 300/D, 300A/D, 305/D, 318A/SX, 415/PH, 440A/LN, 490/CS, 565/TC, 595A/G, 608/G, 990/YU.
Lockheed TF-104G Starfighter: 440/LN.
Lockheed U-2B: 568C/CP.
Lockheed Ventura: 610C/G.
Loening C-2C: 440/LN.
Lohner TE: 350/I.
Lund HL-1: 245/OY.
Luton L.A.4 Minor: 600/G.
L.W.L. WWS-1 Salamandra: 276/OH.
M.K.E.K. 4 Ugar: 565/TC.
M.L. Aviation Delta 1: 602/G.
MEM RSZ-2 U-L-G: 325/HA.
MFH Junior: 541/SE.
Malmo Flygindustri MFI-9B Junior: 541/SE, 543A/SE.
MFI-9B Mili-Trainer: 542/SE.
MFI-10B Vipan/FPL-54: 542/SE.
MFI-15 Supporter: 542/SE.
Macchi M.20: 355/I.
Macchi M.39: 353/I.
Macchi M.67: 353/I.
Macchi M.416 Instructor: 353/I.
Macchi MB 308 Macchino: 353/I, 355/I.
Macchi MB 323 Bipo: 353/I.
Macchi MC 200 Saetta: 353/I.
Macchi MC 202 Folgore: 353/I.
Macchi MC 205V Veltro: 353/I, 356/I.
Macchi-Castoldi MC 72: 353/I.
Macchi-Nieuport M.7: 542/SE.
Maerc-Sarl H-100: 290/F.
Magni Vale 37: 356/I.
Mantelli AM-6: 355/I.
Martin B-26 Marauder: 290/F.
Martinsyde F.4 Buzzard: 277/OH.
Mauboussin M.120: 285/F.
Mauboussin M.127 Corsaire: 285/F.
Mauboussin M.130 Corsaire: 285/F.
Max Holste M.H.52: 286C/F.
Max Holste M.H.1521M Broussard: 285/F, 286A/F, 286B/F, 290/F, 290A/F, 490/CS, 595A/G.
Merckle M-133: 303/D.
Merckle SM-67: 303/D.
Merville S.M.31: 290A/F.
Messerschmitt Bf 108 Taifun: 300/D, 300A/D, 550/HB, 552/HB.
Messerschmitt Bf 109: 235/OK, 290/F, 520/EC, 600/G, 621/G.
Messerschmitt Bf 109E: 300/D, 300A/D, 552/HB, 610A/G.
Messerschmitt Bf 109F: 277/OH, 305/D, 360A/VP.
Messerschmitt Bf 109G: 277/OH, 610C/G, 990/YU.
Messerschmitt Bf 109K: 622/G.
Messerschmitt Bf 110: 610A/G.
Messerschmitt M-17: 300/D.
Messerschmitt Me 163 Komet: 235/OK, 300/D, 300A/D, 595A/G, 603/G, 608/G, 609/G, 640/G.
Messerschmitt Me 209V-1: 485/SP.
Messerschmitt Me 262A: 235/OK, 300/D, 300A/D, 608/G, 609/G.
Messerschmitt Me 262B: 235/OK.
Messerschmitt Me 410A-1 Hornisse: 608/G, 609/G.
Michel Hangleiter: 550/HB.
Mignet HM-8: 285/F, 290/F.
Mignet HM-14 Pou du Ciel: 235/OK, 237/OK, 246A/OY, 277/OH, 279/OH, 290/F, 410/PH, 541/SE, 542/SE, 543A/SE, 575/G, 580A/G, 588/G, 598/G, 600/G,

285

603/G, 609/G, 620/G, 640/G.
Mignet HM-280 Pou-Maquis: 290/F.
Mignet HM-290 Pou du Ciel: 165/OO.
Mignet HM-360 Pou du Ciel: 286A/F.
Mignet/Donat/Guignard Pou du Ciel: 550/HB.
Mignet/Roland PY HM-14 Pou du Ciel: 550/HB.
Mikoyan-Gurevich MiG-3: 568A/CP, 568E/CP.
Mikoyan-Gurevich MiG-9: 568A/CP.
Mikoyan-Gurevich MiG-15: 235/OK, 275/OH, 277/OH, 278/OH, 326A/HA, 480/SP.
Mikoyan-Gurevich MiG-15UTI: 568A/CP.
Mikoyan-Gurevich MiG-15bis: 568A/CP, 568C/CP.
Mikoyan-Gurevich MiG-17: 235/OK, 295A/DM, 486A/SP, 568A/CP, 568C/CP.
Mikoyan-Gurevich MiG-19: 235/OK, 235A/OK, 326A/HA, 485/SP, 568A/CP.
Mikoyan-Gurevich MiG-21: 235/OK, 295A/DM, 568A/CP, 568C/CP, 568E/CP.
Mikoyan-Gurevich MiG-23: 568A/CP, 568C/CP.
Mikoyan-Gurevich MiG-25: 568A/CP.
Mikoyan-Gurevich Ye-166: 568A/CP.
Mikoyan/Tupolev 144 (MiG-21 spl.): 568A/CP.
Mil Mi-1 : 235/OK, 277/OH, 278/OH, 279/OH, 303/D, 485/SP, 568A/CP.
Mil Mi-2: 568A/CP.
Mil Mi-4: 277/OH, 295A/DM, 486A/SP, 495A/YR, 568A/CP, 568C/CP, 568G/CP.
Mil Mi-10: 568A/CP.
Mil Mi-24: 568C/CP.
Mil SM-1-SZ Moskowitsch: 303/D.
Mil SM-2 : 485/SP.
Mil V-12: 568A/CP.
Miles M.2H Hawk Major: 610C/G.
Miles M.14 Magister: 165/OO, 285/F, 349A/EI, 565/TC, 586/G, 594/G, 595A/G, 604/G, 620/G, 642/G.
Miles M.17 Monarch: 640A/G.
Miles M.18: 644/G.
Miles M.28 Mercury 6: 246A/OY.
Miles M.38 Messenger: 165/OO, 546/SE, 600/G, 610C/G, 621/G, 639/G.
Miles M.65 Gemini: 245/OY, 440/LN, 595A/G.
Miles M.75 Aries: 349A/EI.
Miroue Dodier Pou du Ciel: 286A/F.
Mitsubishi A6M-5 Zero: 595/G.
Mitsubishi Ki-46 Dinah: 609/G.
Moelhede Petersen XMP-2: 245/OY.
Morane-Saulnier A1: 285/F, 286D/F, 290/F.
Morane-Saulnier BB (MS.816): 610C/G.
Morane-Saulnier G: 290/F.
Morane-Saulnier MS.50C: 277/OH.
Morane-Saulnier MS.130E: 285/F.
Morane-Saulnier MS.138: 285/F.
Morane-Saulnier MS.149: 290/F.
Morane-Saulnier MS.181: 285/F.
Morane-Saulnier MS.185: 285/F.
Morane-Saulnier MS.230: 165/OO, 285/F, 290/F.
Morane-Saulnier MS.315: 165/OO, 285/F, 290/F.
Morane-Saulnier MS.317: 285/F, 286C/F, 290/F, 300A/D.
Morane-Saulnier MS.341: 285/F.
Morane-Saulnier MS.406: 290/F.
Morane-Saulnier MS.472 Vanneau: 290/F.
Morane-Saulnier MS.500 (Fi 156): 300A/D.
Morane-Saulnier MS.504: 286D/F.
Morane-Saulnier MS.505: 285/F, 286B/F, 286C/F.
Morane-Saulnier MS.506: 552/HB.
Morane-Saulnier MS.733 Alcyon: 285/F, 286B/F, 286C/F, 286D/F, 290A/F, 520/EC.
Morane-Saulnier MS.880 Rallye: 290/F.

Moravan Otrokovice A-326 Trener: 325/HA.
Moynet M 360 Jupiter: 290/F.
Mrkev Or Racek: 237/OK.
Murray: 575/G.
Musger Mg 19A Steinadler: 160/OE.
Musger Mg 23SL: 160/OE.
Myasishchev M-50: 568A/CP.
Nardi FN.305: 353/I, 495A/YR.
Nardi FN.333: 356/I.
Navion Rangemaster G: 285/F.
Ned. Helicopter Ind. H.3 Kolibri: 410/PH.
Nieuport 2N: 290/F.
Nieuport 11: 285/F.
Nieuport 17C1: 165/OO.
Nieuport 28C-1 Bebe: 552/HB.
Nieuport IV-G Monoplane: 542/SE.
Nieuport-Delage 11: 290/F.
Nieuport-Delage 29C-1: 290/F.
Nieuport-Macchi Ni.10: 356/I, 357/I.
Noorduyn Norseman (UC-64A): 285/F, 440A/LN, 541/SE, 542/SE.
Nord N.702 (Siebel Si 204): 285/F, 286D/F, 290/F.
Nord N.856A: 285/F, 286A/F, 286B/F, 286C/F.
Nord N.1002 Pingouin (Bf 108): 165/OO, 285/F, 300A/D.
Nord N.1101 Noralpha: 285/F, 286D/F, 290/F, 290A/F.
Nord N.1203 Norecrin: 285/F, 286B/F, 290/F, 552/HB.
Nord N.1300: 286C/F.
Nord N.1500 Griffon: 290/F.
Nord N.2000: 285/F, 286A/F.
Nord N.2501 Noratlas: 286A/F, 286D/F, 290/F, 490/CS.
Nord N.2502A Noratlas: 490/CS.
Nord N.3202: 285/F, 286B/F, 286C/F, 286D/F.
Nord N.3400: 286B/F, 286D/F, 290/F, 290A/F.
North American AT-6 Texan/Harvard: 160A/OE, 165/OO, 246A/OY, 247/OY, 248A/OY, 285/F, 286D/F, 290/F, 290A/F, 300/D, 300A/D, 305/D, 318A/SX, 353/I, 356/I, 410/PH, 415/PH, 416A/PH, 440A/LN, 490/CS, 520/EC, 541/SE, 542/SE, 546/SE, 552/HB, 565/TC, 590/G, 595A/G, 622/G.
North American B-25 Mitchell: 415/PH, 416A/PH, 595A/G, 610B/G.
North American F-86 Sabre: 300/D, 300A/D, 353/I, 565/TC.
North American F-86D Sabre: 248A/OY, 318A/SX, 606/G, 990/YU, 991/YU.
North American F-86E Sabre: 305/D.
North American F-86F Sabre: 165/OO, 415/PH, 440A/LN, 490/CS, 520/EC, 990/YU.
North American F-86K Sabre: 290/F, 355/I, 356/I, 415/PH, 440A/LN.
North American F-100D Super Sabre: 290/F, 589/g, 595A/G, 600/G, 605/G, 606/G, 645/G.
North American P-51 Mustang: 595A/G, 622/G.
North American P-51B Mustang: 568E/CP.
North American P-51D Mustang: 353/I, 542/SE, 550/HB, 595A/G.
North American P-51K Mustang: 290/F, 415/PH.
North American T-28 Trojan: 285/F, 605/G.
North American TF-100F Super Sabre: 248A/OY.
Northrop F-5A: 440A/LN.
Northrop N-3PB: 440A/LN.
Northrop SD-1 Drone: 595A/G.
Nyrop No.3: 541/SE, 547/SE.
Oehmichen: 290/F.
Oliveira, Rolando Nikus Miniplane: 490/CS.
Omnipol L.13 Blanik: 235/OK.
Opel RAK-1 (R): 285/F.
Osterreich Aero Club Austria: 160/OE.

P.W.S. 26: 485/SP.
P.Z.L. M-4 Tarpan: 485/SP.
P.Z.L. MD-12F: 485/SP.
P.Z.L. P.11C: 485/SP.
P.Z.L. P.24: 565/TC.
P.Z.L. S-4 (Kania 3): 485/SP.
P.Z.L.101A Gawron: 326A/HA.
PIK 3A Kantti: 276/OH.
PIK 3B: 277/OH.
PIK 5B: 276/OH, 277/OH.
PIK 5C: 277/OH.
PIK 10 Paukkulauta: 276/OH.
PIK 11 Tumppu: 276/OH.
Paatalo "Tiira": 277/OH.
Pacific Kites Seagull: 300/D.
Packard-Le Pere C.2: 290/F.
Parnall Elf II: 620/G.
Parnall Pixie III: 600/G.
Payen Pa-49: 290/F.
Pegaz: 485/SP.
Pelzner Glider (R): 300/D.
Percival P.1 Gull: 165/OO.
Percival P.31 Proctor: 245/OY, 595A/G, 609/G.
Percival P.34 Proctor: 165/OO, 543/SE, 598/G, 621/G.
Percival P.40 Prentice: 165/OO, 576A/G, 600/G, 604/G, 618A/G, 644/G.
Percival P.44 Proctor: 165/OO, 543A/SE, 645/G.
Percival P.50 Prince: 576A/G.
Percival P.56 Provost: 622/G.
Percival P.57 Sea Prince: 618A/G.
Percival P.84 Jet Provost: 576A/G.
Percival Q.6: 595A/G.
Perrin: 290/F.
Persson: 541/SE.
Pescara F.3: 290/F.
Petlyakov Pe-2 Peszka: 480/SP, 568A/CP, 990/YU.
Petylakov Pe-2FT: 568E/CP.
Pfalz D.XII: 290/F.
Phoenix D.III J1: 542/SE.
Piaggio P.136: 353/I.
Piaggio P.149D: 300A/D.
Piaggio P.150: 353/I.
Piaggio P.166: 353/I, 603/G.
Piaggio-D'Ascanio PD.3 (R): 353/I.
Piel CP.80: 286A/F.
Piel CP.1310 Super Emeraude: 285/F, 290/F.
Pilatus P-2: 285/F, 552/HB, 622/G.
Pilcher (Percy) Hawk Glider: 603/G, 640/G, 641/G.
Piper J-3 Cub: 165/OO, 246A/OY, 285/F, 286D/F, 485/SP, 490/CS.
Piper L-4B Grasshopper: 235/OK, 237/OK, 410/PH.
Piper L-18B Super Cub: 290/F.
Piper L-18C Super Cub: 165/OO, 415/PH, 490/CS.
Piper L-21A Super Cub: 415/PH.
Piper L-21B Super Cub: 354/I, 490/CS, 542/SE.
Piper PA-12 Super Cruiser: 490/CS.
Piper PA-18 Super Cub: 354/I, 440A/LN, 550/HB.
Piper PA-24: 640/G.
Pischof Autoplan: 160/OE.
Pitts S-1S: 285/F.
Pitts S-2A: 285/F, 608/G.
Polikarpov I-16: 276/OH, 568A/CP, 568D/CP.
Polikarpov I-17: 568D/CP.
Polikarpov I-153 Chicka: 290/F.
Polikarpov Po-2: 235/OK, 277/OH, 285/F, 295A/DM, 326A/HA, 485/SP, 568A/CP, 990/YU, 990/YU.
Polyteknisk Flyvegr. Polyt II: 245/OY.
Portobello 1980: 353/I.
Potez 36: 290/F.

Potez 43/7: 290/F.
Potez 53: 290/F.
Potez 58: 290/F.
Potez 60: 286D/F.
Potez 600: 286C/F.
Potez 842: 290/F.
Poullin PJ.5B: 285/F.
Praga E-114M Air Baby: 235/OK.
Puetzer Doppelraab: 300/D.
Puetzer Motorraab: 300/D,
R.E.P. D: 290/F.
R.E.P. K: 290/F.
R.R.G. (Zogling sailplane): 490/CS, 550/HB.
R.R.G. Pander (Zogling glider): 410/PH.
R.W.D. 13: 485/SP.
R.W.D. 21: 485/SP.
Raab Doppelraab IV: 246A/OY.
Raab-Katzenstein RK26 Tigerschwalb: 542/SE.
Rearwin 9000 Sportster: 246A/OY, 546/SE.
Rech Monoplane: 552/HB.
Reid and Sigrist RS.4 Desford: 644/G.
Republic F-84F Thunderstreak: 165/OO, 290/F, 300A/D, 305/D, 353/I, 356/I, 415/PH, 565/TC, 606/G.
Republic F-84G Thunderjet: 165/OO, 246A/OY, 247/OY, 248A/OY, 290A/F, 355/I, 415/PH, 440A/LN, 490/CS, 565/TC, 990/YU, 991/YU.
Republic P-47 Thunderbolt: 285/F, 290/F, 353/I, 565/TC, 595A/G, 622/G, 990/YU, 992/YU.
Republic RC-3 Seabee: 355/I, 541/SE.
Republic RF-84F Thunderflash: 165/OO, 248A/OY, 300/D, 301/D, 305/D, 353/I, 440A/LN, 565/TC.
Republic RF-84G Thunderjet: 565/TC, 990/YU.
Rhonschwalbe KA 2: 165/OO.
Ricci 6 Triplane (R): 356/I.
Rienks (Gyroglider): 410/PH.
Rieseler-Bendel RII/B (prototype): 541/SE.
Roe Triplane IV (R): 620/G.
Roe Triplane No.1: 603/G.
Roland D.VI (L.F.G.): 485/SP.
Rollason Turbulent (Druine D.31): 600/G.
Rolls Royce Flying Bedstead: 642/G.
Royal Aircraft Factory B.E.2a: 610C/G.
Royal Aircraft Factory B.E.2c: 290/F, 595A/G, 601/G, 609/G.
Royal Aircraft Factory B.E.2e: 440A/LN.
Royal Aircraft Factory R.E.8: 165/OO, 595A/G.
Royal Aircraft Factory S.E.5a: 285/F, 581/G, 603/G, 610/G, 613/G, 620/G.
Rubik F-22 Junious 18 "Laminar": 325/HA.
Rubik R-07B Vocsok: 325/HA, 326A/HA.
Rubik R-08C Pilis: 325/HA.
Rubik R-08D Pilis: 325/HA, 326A/HA.
Rubik R-11B Cimbora: 326A/HA.
Rubik R-15F Fem Koma: 326A/HA.
Rubik R-16 Lepke: 325/HA, 326A/HA.
Rubik R-18C Kanya: 325/HA, 326A/HA.
Rubik R-22 Futar: 326A/HA.
Rubik R-22 Junius 18: 325/HA, 326A/HA.
Rubik R-22S Super Futar: 325/HA, 326A/HA.
Rubik R-25 Mokany: 325/HA, 326A/HA.
Rubik R-26 Gobe: 326A/HA.
Rubik Sportarutermel R-15 Koma: 325/HA.
Rumpler 6B: 278/OH.
Rumpler C.IV: 300/D.
Rumpler C.V: 165/OO.
Rumpler Taube: 440/LN.
Ryan Navion B: 285/F.
S.102 (Czech. MiG-15UTI): 495A/YR.
S.A.I. KZ G1: 246A/OY.

S.A.I. KZ II-K Koupe: 246A/OY.
S.A.I. KZ II-S Sport: 245/OY.
S.A.I. KZ II-T: 246A/OY.
S.A.I. KZ III: 165/OO, 245/OY, 246A/OY.
S.A.I. KZ IV: 245/OY, 246A/OY.
S.A.I. KZ VII: 246A/OY, 248A/OY.
S.F.A.N. II (Br. A/C Co. Drone): 285/F.
S.F.C.A. Bovin Taupine: 285/F.
S.I.P.A. S.121: 285/F.
S.I.P.A. S.903: 285/F, 286A/F.
S.R.C.M. 153 Joigny: 285/F.
SAAB 10B Vipan: 541/SE.
SAAB 17A (B-17A): 245/OY, 542/SE.
SAAB 17B (S-17B): 542/SE.
SAAB 18B (S-18B): 542/SE.
SAAB 21A-3 (J-21A): 542/SE.
SAAB 22A (J-22A): 542/SE.
SAAB 29A (J-29A): 290/F, 542/SE, 546/SE.
SAAB 29B (J-29B): 542/SE.
SAAB 29C (S-29C): 542/SE.
SAAB 29F Tunnan (J-29F): 160A/OE, 245/OY, 353/I,
   542/SE, 543/SE, 543A/SE.
SAAB 32A Lansen (J-32A): 542/SE.
SAAB 32B Lansen (J-32B): 546/SE.
SAAB 32C Lansen (J-32C): 542/SE.
SAAB 35 Draken (J-35): 542/SE.
SAAB 35A Draken (J-35A): 165/OO, 290/F, 300/D,
   542/SE, 545/SE, 546/SE, 595A/G.
SAAB 35B Draken (J-35B): 542/SE.
SAAB 35E Draken (J-35E): 541/SE, 542/SE.
SAAB 35F Draken (J-35F): 600/G.
SAAB 37 Viggen (prototype AJ-37): 542/SE.
SAAB 91A Safir: 542/SE.
SAAB 91B Safir: 440A/LN, 440B/LN, 604/G.
SAAB 91C Safir: 640/G.
SAAB 91D Safir: 276/OH, 278/OH, 410/PH.
SAAB 105 (prototype): 542/SE.
SAAB 210 Lill-Draken: 542/SE.
SABCA Junior: 165/OO.
SABCA Poncelet Vivette: 165/OO.
SAIMAN 202-M: 353/I, 355/I, 356/I.
SIL Harakka II: 276/OH.
SNCA SO-1221 Djinn: 303/D.
SNECMA C.400P2 Atar Volant: 290/F.
SPAD VII: 235/OK, 353/I, 357C/I, 595A/G.
SPAD XIII C1: 165/OO, 285/F, 290/F.
SPAD 54: 290/F.
SPAD-Herbemont 52: 290/F.
SZD 10bis Czapla (glider): 277/OH.
SZD-24 Foka: 290/F.
Salmson 2A2: 285/F.
Salmson D.6: 285/F.
Salmson D.7: 285/F.
Samu-Geonczy SG 2 Kek Madar: 325/HA.
Santos-Dumont Demoiselle: 286D/F, 290/F, 486/SP,
   581/G.
Santos-Dumont XX Demoiselle: 490/CS.
Saric 1: 990/YU.
Saric 2: 990/YU.
Saunders Roe A.19 Cloud: 235/OK.
Saunders Roe P.531 Scout: 590/G, 602/G.
Saunders Roe S.R.53 (jet + rocket): 608/G.
Saunders Roe S.R.A.1: 595A/G.
Saunders Roe Skeeter A.O.P.12: 303/D, 579/G, 591/G,
   602/G, 603/G, 604/G, 609/G, 621/G, 640/G.
Savoia-Marchetti S.M.56: 353/I, 355/I.
Savoia-Marchetti S.M.79 Sparviero: 353/I.
Savoia-Marchetti S.M.80bis: 355/I.
Savoia-Marchetti S.M.82 Marsupiale: 353/I.

Savoia-Marchetti S.M.102: 355/I, 356/I.
Schavrov Sch-2: 568B/CP.
Scheibe 138 Specht: 541/SE.
Scheibe Mu 13 Bergfalke II: 246A/OY, 300/D, 300A/D,
   541/SE.
Scheibe Spatz 55: 300/D.
Scheibe Spatz B: 246A/OY.
Schempp-Hirth GOE 4 Goevier: 165/OO.
Schleicher ASK-16: 286A/F.
Schleicher Ka 6BR Roensegler: 300/D.
Schleicher Rhonbaby: 300A/D.
Schleicher Rhonlerche: 410/PH.
Schmetz Condor IV (glider): 300/D.
Schmitt (Paul): 290/F.
Schneider Grunau 9: 276/OH.
Schneider Grunau Baby: 410/PH, 990/YU.
Schneider Grunau Baby II: 165/OO, 245/OY, 276/OH,
   290/F, 543/SE, 546/SE, 990/YU.
Schneider Grunau Baby IIA: 277/OH, 600/G.
Schneider Grunau Baby IIB: 160/OE,245/OY,246/OY,
   300/D, 490/CS, 520/EC, 541/SE
Schneider Grunau Baby III: 165/OO, 300/D.
Schneider Grunau Baby LH-22 Falken: 545/SE.
Schneider Grunau S.G.38: 165/OO, 245/OY, 290/F,
   300/D, 490/CS, 520/EC, 541/SE, 543/SE, 546/SE,
   547/SE.
Schreck FBA 17 HT4 (flying boat): 290/F.
Schreck FBA B: 493/CS.
Schreck FBA IV: 165/OO.
Schulz F.S.3 Besenstiel Glider: 300/D.
Scintex ML 250 Rubis: 285/F.
Scottish Aviation Pioneer CC-1: 594/G.
Scottish Aviation Twin Pioneer: 550/HB, 608/G,
   640/G.
Segelflugzeug LG125 Sohaj 2 (Zlin): 295/DM.
Seversky EP-106 (J.9): 542/SE.
Shelduck Piloless Target Drone: 590/G.
Short 184: 595A/G.
Short Mats "B": 602/G.
Short S.16 Scion I: 639/G.
Short S.27: 590/G.
Short S.A.6 Sealand Mk.1: 990/YU.
Short S.B.5: 608/G.
Short S.C.1 (VTOL): 603/G, 639/G.
Short S.C.5/10 Belfast C.Mk.I: 608/G.
Short Sandringham ("Bermuda"): 290/F.
Short Sherpa: 595A/G.
Short Sunderland: 595A/G, 610A/G.
Siebel Si.204D (Nord N.C.701): 541/SE, 542/SE.
Siemetzki Asro 4: 303/D.
Sikorsky S-51 (Westland Dragonfly): 579/G, 581/G,
   588/G, 590/G, 598/G, 606/G, 608/G, 610C/G, 621/G,
   990/YU.
Sikorsky S-51 (Westland Widgeon): 581/G.
Sikorsky (Chickasaw): 165/OO, 286B/F, 290/F, 300/D,
   410/PH, 490/CS.
Sikorsky S-55 (Westland Whirlwind): 303/D, 520/EC,
   579/G, 581/G, 589/G, 590/G, 595A/G, 600/G, 602/G,
   603/G, 604/G, 605/G, 608/G, 621/G, 642/G, 645/G.
Sikorsky S-55C: 248A/OY.
Sikorsky S-58 (Choctaw): 300/D, 303/D, 305/D.
Sikorsky S-58 (Westland Wessex): 568A/CP, 590/G.
Sikorsky VS-316 Hoverfly I: 610/G.
Silimon IS 28: 495B/YR.
Silimon IS 29D: 495B/YR.
Silimon IS 30: 237/OK, 495B/YR.
Siren C.30 Edelweiss: 286A/F.
Siren C.34: 286A/F, 290/F.
Skyleader Mats "A": 602/G.

288

Slechta Praha: 237/OK.
Slingsby T.7 Cadet: 575/G, 600/G, 610C/G.
Slingsby T.8 Tutor: 598/G, 640/G.
Slingsby T.12 Gull: 640/G.
Slingsby T.15 Gull 3: 580A/G.
Slingsby T.21A Sedbergh: 640/G.
Smrcek VSM-40 Demant: 235/OK.
Snellen V-20: 410/PH.
Socata TB.10 Tobago: 613/G.
Soko 522: 990/YU, 991/YU.
Soldenhoff S-5: 550/HB.
Sopwith 1 1/2-Strutter: 165/OO, 290/F, 610/G.
Sopwith Baby Seaplane: 590/G.
Sopwith Camel: 165/OO, 485/SP, 590/G, 595/G, 609/G, 610/G.
Sopwith Dolphin: 610C/G.
Sopwith Pup: 610/G, 620/G.
Sopwith Tabloid: 610B/G.
Sopwith Triplane: 568A/CP, 610/G.
Sostaric Jastreb: 992/YU.
Sostaric Macka: 990/YU.
Sostaric Roda: 990/YU, 992/YU.
Sostaric Vrabac: 990/YU.
Southampton Univ. Sumpac: 620/G.
Southern Martlet: 620/G.
Spalinger S-21: 550/HB.
Sparman S1A P1: 542/SE.
Spartan Cruiser III: 640/G.
Staaken R.IV: 485/SP.
Stamer-Lippisch A.12 Zogling: 543/SE.
Stampe S.V.4A: 285/F, 286C/F, 286D/F.
Stampe S.V.4C: 285/F, 286C/F, 300A/D.
Stampe-Renard S.R.7 Monitor: 165/OO.
Stampe-Renard S.V.4B: 165/OO, 608/G.
Stampe-Renard S.V.4C: 165/OO.
Stampe-Renard S.V.4D: 165/OO.
Stampe-Vertongen S.V.4 (Divoy-): 165/OO.
Stearman A75N1: 285/F.
Stearman PT-17: 595A/G, 622/G, 990/YU.
Stewart Ornithopter: 588/G, 598/G.
Stierlin: 550/HB.
Stinson 108 Voyager: 285/F.
Stinson L-5 Sentinel: 353/I, 485/SP.
Stinson SR-10C Reliant: 285/F.
Student (prototype): 990/YU.
Sud-Aviation SA-316B Alouette: 550/HB.
Sud-Aviation SA-3210 Super Frelon: 290/F.
Sud-Aviation SE-210 Caravelle: 165/OO, 245/OY, 290/F, 440/LN, 541/SE, 990/YU.
Sud-Aviation SE-341 Gazelle: 602/G.
Sud-Aviation SE-3130 Alouette II: 303/D.
Sud-Est SE-3160 Alouette: 248A/OY.
Sud-Ouest SO-535 Mistral: 290/F.
Sud-Ouest SO-1110 Ariel II: 290/F.
Sud-Ouest SO-1220 Djinn: 290/F.
Sud-Ouest SO-1221 Djinn: 286B/F, 552/HB.
Sud-Ouest SO-3101: 290/F.
Sud-Ouest SO-4050 Vautour IIB: 290/F, 290A/F.
Sud-Ouest SO-6000 Triton: 290/F.
Sud-Ouest SO-9000 Trident: 290/F.
Sukhanov Diskoplan: 568A/CP.
Sukhoi Su-7B: 568A/CP.
Sukhoi.Su-9: 568A/CP.
Sukhoi Su-15VD: 568E/CP.
Sukhoi Su-17: 568A/CP.
Supermarine 510: 608/G.
Supermarine Attacker I: 590/G.
Supermarine S.6A: 618/G.
Supermarine S.6B: 603/G.

Supermarine Scimitar: 581/G, 590/G.
Supermarine Seafire F.XVII: 590/G.
Supermarine Southampton I: 610C/G.
Supermarine Spitfire: 621/G.
Supermarine Spitfire Mk.I: 595/G, 610/G, 610A/G.
Supermarine Spitfire Mk.IA: 603/G.
Supermarine Spitfire Mk.II: 610D/G.
Supermarine Spitfire Mk.V: 360A/VP, 594/G, 595A/G, 610C/G, 610D/G, 620/G, 990/YU.
Supermarine Spitfire Mk.IX: 165/OO, 235/OK, 247/OY, 248/OY, 290/F, 318A/SX, 353/I, 410/PH, 440A/LN, 580/G, 595A/G, 609/G, 622/G.
Supermarine Spitfire Mk.X: 440B/LN.
Supermarine Spitfire Mk.XI: 415/PH, 416A/PH, 440A/LN.
Supermarine Spitfire Mk.XIV: 165/OO, 608/G, 622/G.
Supermarine Spitfire Mk.XV: 485/SP.
Supermarine Spitfire Mk.XVI: 290/F, 595A/G, 609/G, 609A/G, 639/G, 640/G.
Supermarine Spitfire Mk.XIX: 542/SE, 610C/G, 610D/G.
Supermarine Spitfire Mk.XXI: 610C/G.
Supermarine Spitfire Mk.22: 610C/G.
Supermarine Spitfire Mk.24: 610/G, 618G.
Supermarine Stranraer: 610/G.
Supermarine Swift: 604/G, 606/G, 609/G.
Supermarine Walrus: 590/G, 610A/G.
Sustentateur Ludion: 290/F.
Svenskt Glider: 541/SE.
Tanskiego: 486/SP.
Taylor E-2 Cub: 235/OK.
Taylor J-2 Cub: 285/F, 541/SE.
Taylorcraft B (Auster V): 596/G.
Taylorcraft D (Auster I): 246A/OY, 602/G.
Taylorcraft J/1 (Auster V): 546/SE.
Thruxton HDW.I Gadfly: 579/G.
Thulin A: 541/SE, 547/SE.
Thulin B: 541/SE, 545/SE.
Thulin D: 277/OH.
Thulin G: 541/SE, 542/SE.
Thulin N: 541/SE.
Thulin NA: 544/SE.
Tipsy B (Fairey): 546/SE.
Tipsy S.2 (Fairey): 165/OO, 546/SE.
Tupolev ANT-2: 568A/CP.
Tupolev ANT-4/G-1: 568G/CP.
Tupolev ANT-25: 568D/CP.
Tupolev ANT-40: 568A/CP.
Tupolev Tu-2: 180B/LZ, 480/SP, 485/SP, 568A/CP.
Tupolev Tu-4: 568A/CP.
Tupolev Tu-16: 568A/CP.
Tupolev Tu-20: 568A/CP.
Tupolev Tu-22: 568A/CP.
Tupolev Tu-104: 568A/CP.
Tupolev Tu-114: 568A/CP.
Tupolev Tu-144: 568A/CP.
Turk Hava Kirumu T.H.K.4: 565/TC.
Turk Hava Kirumu T.H.K.7: 565/TC.
UTVA 213: 990/YU.
V.F.W. Fokker VAK 191B (VTOL): 300/D.
V.F.W. H-2: 303/D.
V.F.W. H-3 Sprinter: 303/D.
VAAZ Brno XA-66 Aeron: 235A/OK.
VL E30 Kotka 2: 275/OH.
VL Myrsky II: 277/OH.
VL Pyorremyrsky: 277/OH.
VL Pyry 1: 279/OH.
VL Pyry 2: 276/OH, 277/OH.
VL Saaski II: 276/OH, 278/OH.

VL Tuisku: 276/OH.
VL Viima I: 278/OH.
VL Viima II: 277/OH.
VOSLM BAK-01: 235/OK.
VT-116 (glider): 235/OK.
VZLU HC-2 Heli-Baby: 235/OK.
VZLU L-8 Praha TOM-8: 235A/OK.
VZLU L-208 Praha TOM-208: 235A/OK.
VZLU TOM-8: 235/OK.
Vajic V-55: 990/YU, 992/YU.
Valmet Vihuri II: 277/OH.
Vega VSB-62: 235/OK.
Vertol CH-21C Shawnee: 290/F.
Vertol H-21B Shawnee: 305/D.
Vertol HUP-2 Retriever: 410/PH.
Vertol V-43C: 300A/D, 303/D.
Vertol V-44A (HKP-1): 541/SE, 542/SE, 543A/SE, 568A/CP.
Viberti Musca: 355/I.
Vickers 498 Viking 1A: 300A/D.
Vickers 614 Viking 2: 300A/D.
Vickers 659 Valetta: 605/G, 606/G, 608/G.
Vickers 668 Varsity: 542/SE, 595A/G, 604/G, 608/G, 645/G.
Vickers 701 Viscount: 595A/G, 608/G.
Vickers 732 Viscount: 645/G.
Vickers 802 Viscount: 645/G.
Vickers 803 Viscount: 349A/EI.
Vickers 1101 VC-10: 608/G.
Vickers 1151 Super VC-10: 595A/G.
Vickers F.B.27 Vimy: 603/G, 610B/G.
Vickers F.B.5 Gun Bus: 610C/G.
Vickers Valiant: 610B/G.
Vickers Wellington: 580A/G, 610B/G.
Vizzola II: 355/I.
Vliacu: 495A/YR
Voisin L: 568A/CP.
Voisin LA 5B Canon: 165/OO, 290/F.
Voisin-Farman (Henri) 1bis: 290/F.
Vought F4U Corsair: 590/G, 595A/G.
Vuia: 290/F, 495A/YR.
W.S.K. M-15 Belphegor: 485/SP, 568G/CP.
Waco CG-4A Hadrian: 617/G.
Wagner Rotocar 3: 303/D.
Wallis WA.120: 603/G.
Ward P.45 Gnome: 598/G.
Watkins Monoplane: 609/G.
Watkinson CG4 Cyclogyroplane: 579/G.
Weber A.VII Etiopia I: 353/I.
Weihe: 990/YU, 990/YU.
Weir W-2 Autogyro: 640/G.
Westland Lysander: 165/OO, 595A/G, 610A/G, 622/G, 642/G.
Westland P.531 Scout(Saunders-Roe): 579/G.
Westland WG.33: 579/G.
Westland Wallace II: 610C/G.
Westland Wessex HAS.1: 595A/G, 618A/G, 644/G.
Westland Whirlwind WS.55: 612A/G, 618A/G.
Westland Wyvern: 590/G.
Westland-Hill Pterodactyl 1: 603/G.
Wheeler Slymph: 600/G.
Whitaker MW26 Excaliber: 581/G.

Wight Quadroplane: 623/G.
Williams Motorfly: 286A/F.
Wolfmueller Glider: 300/D.
Woodhams Sprite: 575/G.
Wright Brothers 1909 (R): 353/I.
Wright Brothers Baby: 290/F.
Wright Brothers Flyer: 410/PH, 603/G, 610C/G.
Wright Brothers Type A: 300/D.
Yakovlev AIR-1 (VVA-3): 568F/CP.
Yakovlev UT-1 (AIR-14): 568F/CP.
Yakovlev UT-2: 568F/CP, 992/YU.
Yakovlev Yak-3: 290/F, 568A/CP, 568F/CP, 990/YU.
Yakovlev Yak-9: 180B/LZ, 480/SP, 486A/SP, 568A/CP, 568E/CP, 990/YU.
Yakovlev Yak-11: 160A/OE, 235/OK, 285/F, 485/SP, 495A/YR, 568F/CP, 595A/G.
Yakovlev Yak-12: 235/OK, 485/SP, 568A/CP, 568F/CP.
Yakovlev Yak-15: 568F/CP.
Yakovlev Yak-17: 235/OK, 485/SP, 568A/CP.
Yakovlev Yak-18: 160A/OE, 295A/DM, 325/HA, 326A/HA, 485/SP, 495A/YR, 568A/CP, 568F/CP.
Yakovlev Yak-23: 180B/LZ, 235/OK, 480/SP, 485/SP, 495A/YR, 568A/CP.
Yakovlev Yak-24: 568A/CP.
Yakovlev Yak-25: 568A/CP.
Yakovlev Yak-26: 568A/CP.
Yakovlev Yak-27: 568A/CP.
Yakovlev Yak-28: 568A/CP.
Yakovlev Yak-30: 568F/CP.
Yakovlev Yak-32: 568E/CP, 568F/CP.
Yakovlev Yak-36: 568A/CP.
Yakovlev Yak-40: 568A/CP.
Yakovlev Yak-50: 568A/CP, 568F/CP.
Yokosuka Ohka (Kamikazi): 590/G, 608/G.
Zeppelin C.IV (JA): 290/F.
Zeppelin L-30: 165/OO.
Zlin L.425 Sohaj 3: 235/OK.
Zlin VT.425 Sohaj 3: 235/OK.
Zlin Z.13: 235/OK.
Zlin Z.22 Junak: 235/OK.
Zlin Z.23 Honja: 235/OK.
Zlin Z.24 Krajanek: 235/OK, 237/OK.
Zlin Z.25 Sohaj: 237/OK.
Zlin Z.26: 235/OK, 485/SP.
Zlin Z.35 Helibaby (HC-102): 235A/OK.
Zlin Z.37 Cmelak: 276/OH.
Zlin Z.124: 235/OK.
Zlin Z.125 Sohaj: 235/OK, 237/OK.
Zlin Z.126: 235/OK.
Zlin Z.130 Kmotr: 235/OK, 237/OK.
Zlin Z.135 Heli-Trainer: 235/OK.
Zlin Z.225 Medak (prototype): 237/OK.
Zlin Z.226 Bohatyr: 235A/OK, 326A/HA.
Zlin Z.326 Trener Master: 285/F, 286D/F, 290/F.
Zlin Z.381 (Bucker Bu 181D): 235/OK.
Zlin Z.526 Trener Master: 326A/HA.
Zlin Z.XII: 235/OK, 285/F.
Zsebo-Bohn Z-03 Ifjusag: 325/HA.
Zselyi Aladar 2: 325/HA.
Zwergreiher Lo-100: 520/EC,

A lineup of experimental and prototype English Electric and other jet fighters at RAF Cosford.

A Boeing B-17G Flying Fortress, with late afternoon thunderstorms growing in the background, commands part of the ramp at the Musée de l'Air, Le Bourget, Paris.

Selected Bibliography

AIR MUSEUM AND COLLECTION ORIENTED

Bock, Claus, and Sepp Moser. *Flugzeuge im Verkehrshaus.* Orell Füssli, Zurich. 1984.

Boyne, Walter J. *The Aircraft Treasures of Silver Hill.* Rawson Associates, New York. 1982

Bryan, C.D.B. *The National Air and Space Museum.* Harry N. Abrams, Inc., New York. 1979.

Bunyan, I.T., J.D.Storer, and Christine L. Thompson. *East Fortune: Museum of Flight and History of the Airfield.* Crown Copyright, Edinburgh. 1983.

Garber, Paul E. *The National Aeronautical Collections.* Smithsonian Institution, Washington. 1956.

Guidebooks. Individual guidebooks of various types are available for, and from, most of the major museums.

Hunt, Leslie. *Veteran and Vintage Aircraft.* Charles Scribner's Sons, New York. 1974.

March, Peter R. *Preserved Aircraft.* Ian Allan Ltd., Shepperton. 1980.

Ogden, Bob. *Aircraft Museums Directory; European Edition.* Battle of Britain Prints International Ltd., London. 1978.

Ogden, Bob. *British Aviation Museums.* Key Publishing Ltd., London. 1983.

Ogden, Bob. *European Aviation Museums and Collections.* Key Publishing Ltd., Stamford, 1985.

Ogden, Bob. *Great Aircraft Collections of the World.* Gallery Books, W.H. Smith Publishers Inc.,New York. 1986.

Ogilvy, David. *The Shuttleworth Collection.* Airlife Publishing Ltd., Shrewsbury. 1982.

Pesce, Giuseppe. *Vigna di Valle: Da Cantiere Sperimentale a Museo Aeronautico.* Edizioni Dell'Ateneo & Bizzarri, Rome. 1979.

Riley, Gordon. *British Aircraft Museums Directory.* Aston Publications, Bourne End. 1986.

Riley, Gordon. *Vintage Aircraft Directory.* Aston Publications, Bourne End. 1985.

Riley, Gordon. *Vintage Aircraft of the World.* Ian Allan Ltd., Shepperton. 1983.

Zwakhals, Wim. *Dutch Wrecks and Relics.* Airnieuws Nederland, Rotterdam. 1984.

GENERAL INTEREST

Angelucci, Enzo. *The Rand McNally Encyclopedia of Military Aircraft, 1914-1980.* The Military Press, New York. 1981.

Angelucci, Enzo. *World Encyclopedia of Civil Aircraft.* Crown Publishers, Inc., New York. 1982.

Babington-Smith, Constance. *Testing Time.* Harper and Brothers, New York. 1961

Barker, Ralph. *The Schneider Trophy Races.* Chatto and Windus Ltd., London. 1971.

Boughton, Terence. *The Story of the British Light Aeroplane.* John Murray, London. 1963.

Boyne, Walter J. *The Leading Edge.* Stewart, Tabori & Chang, Inc., New York. 1986.

Clarke, D.H. *What Were They Like To Fly.* Ian Allen Ltd., Shepperton. 1964.

Collier, Richard. *Eagle Day; The Battle of Britain.* E.P. Dutton and Co., Inc., New York. 1966.

Crouch, Tom D. *A Dream of Wings.* W. W. Norton & Co., New York. 1981.

Cynk, Jerzy B. *History of the Polish Air Force 1918-1968.* Osprey Publishing Co. Ltd., Reading. 1972.

Editura Stiintifica Si Enciclopedica. *Istoria Aviatiei Ramâne.* Bucharest, 1984.

Emde, Heiner, and Carlo Demand. *Conquerors of the Air.* Bonanza Books, New York. 1968.

Gibbs-Smith, Charles H. *The Invention of the Aeroplane (1799-1909).* Faber and Faber, London. 1965.

Gibbs-Smith, Charles H. *The Rebirth of European Aviation.* Science Museum, London. 1974.

Grenfell, Russell. *The Bismarck Episode.* Faber and Faber Ltd., London. 1948.

Jackson, A.J. *British Civil Aircraft; 1919-1959.* Putnam and Co., Ltd., London. 1959.

Lewis, Cecil. *Farewell To Wings.* Temple Press Books, London. 1964.

Loening, Grover C. *Military Aeroplanes.* W.S. Best, Boston. 1918.

McDonough, Kenneth. *Atlantic Wings, 1919-1939.* Model Aeronautical Press Ltd. Hemel Hempstead. 1966.

Mondey, David, ed. *Complete Illustrated Encyclopedia of the World's Aircraft.* Chartwell Books Inc., Secaucus. 1987.

Parkinson, Roger. *Summer, 1940; The Battle of Britain.* David McKay Company, Inc., New York. 1977.

Penrose, Harald. *British Aviation, The Pioneer Years 1903-1914.* Putnam and Company Ltd., London. 1967.

Pesce, Giuseppe. *The Italian Airships.* Mucchi Editore, Modena. 1983.

Popham, Hugh. *Into Wind; A History of British Naval Flying.* Hamish Hamilton Ltd., London. 1969.

Postma, Thijs. *Vermetele Vliegende Hollanders.* Unieboek bv., Bussum. 1975.

Roseberry, C.R. *The Challenging Skies.* Doubleday and Company, Inc., Garden City. 1966.

Schliephake, Hanfried. *The Birth of the Luftwaffe.* Ian Allen Ltd., Shepperton. 1971.

Scott, C.W.A. *Scott's Book.* Hodder & Stoughton ltd., London. 1934.

Stolp, Gertrude Nobile. *Bibliografia di Umberto Nobile.* Biblioteconomia E Bibliografia, Firenze. 1984.

Stroud, John. *European Transport Aircraft Since 1910.* Putnam and Company Ltd., London. 1966.

Taylor, John W.R. ed. *Combat Aircraft of the World.* G.P.Putnam's Sons, New York. 1969.

Taylor, John W.R. *History of Aerial Warfare.* Hamlyn Publishing Group Limited, London. 1974.

Taylor, John W.R., and Kenneth Munson. History of Aviation. Crown Publishers, New York. 1972.

Taylor, John W.R., ed. *Jane's All the World's Aircraft.* Jane's Publishing Co. Ltd., London. 1909-1968 editions.

Thomas, G. Holt. *Aerial Transport.* Hodder and Stoughton, Ltd., London. 1920.

Thompson, Jonathan W. *Italian Civil and Military Aircraft, 1930-1945.* Aero Publishers, Inc., Los Angeles. 1963.

Villard, Henry Serrano. *Contact!, The Story of the Early Birds.* Thomas Y. Crowell Company, New York. 1968.

Wheeler, Allen. *Building Aeroplanes for 'Those Magnificent Men'.* Wood Westworth and Co., Ltd., St. Helens. 1965.

Index

About the authors:

Lou Divone is an aeronautical engineer with a notable career as a senior technical manager at several university laboratories, aircraft companies, and government agencies. He is the author of numerous technical papers and chapters in engineering handbooks. But he is also a pilot with land, sea, and instrument ratings and his first love is antique airplanes.

Judy Divone has been a docent at the Smithsonian's National Air and Space Museum since its opening at the 1976 Bicentennial. By profession an artist and writer, she is the author of several books on antiques. She is also an avid old-airplane buff and a frequent attendee at antique airplane fly-ins.

...and *Old Charlie* is a classic 1954 Cessna 180 tail-dragger the authors have owned (or been owned by) for well over two decades and in which they have traveled coast-to-coast and border-to-border. *Old Charlie* is also a familiar face at antique airplane fly-ins.